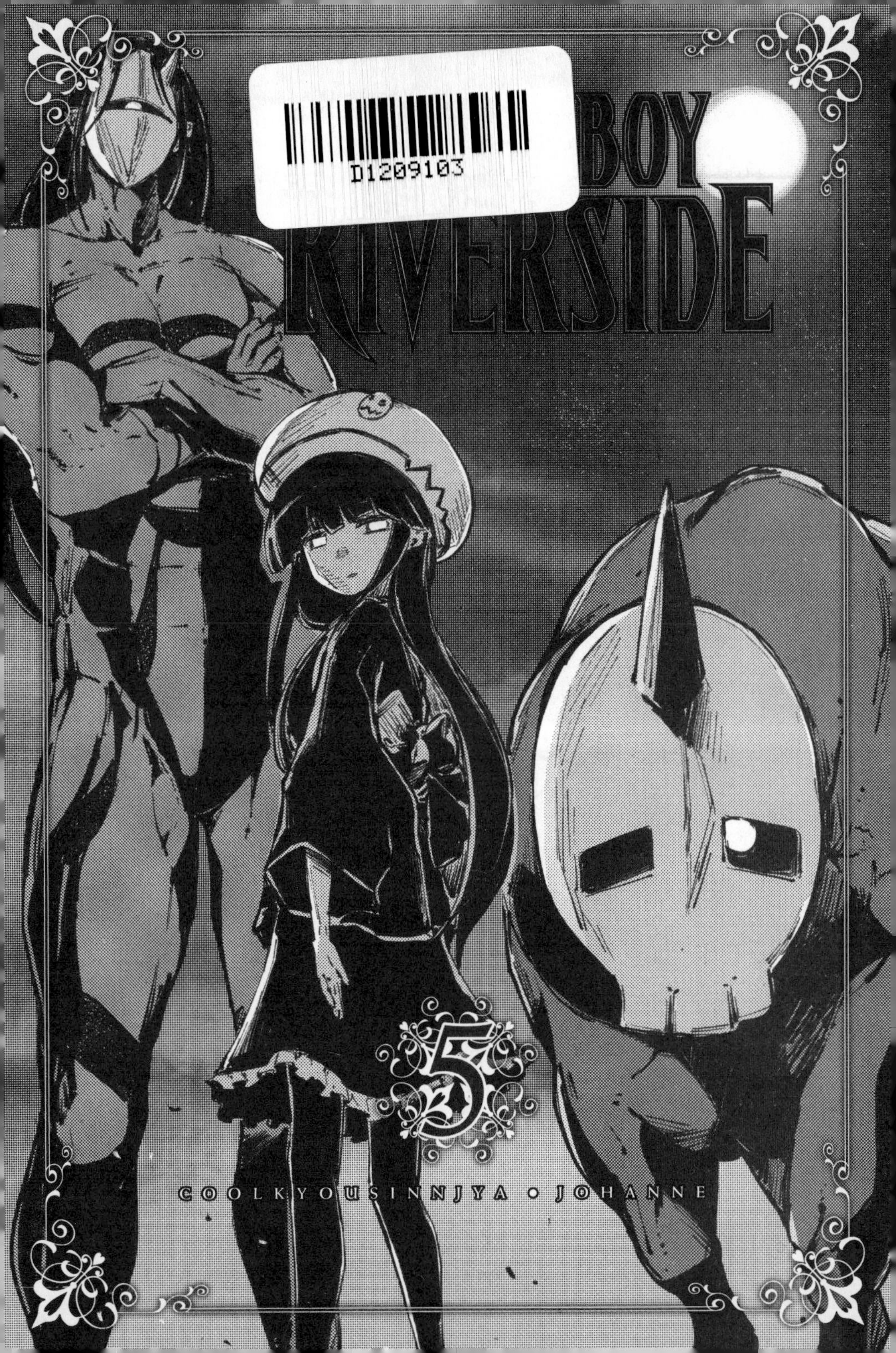
BOY
RIVERSIDE
5
COOLKYOUSINNJYA • JOHANNE

CONTENTS

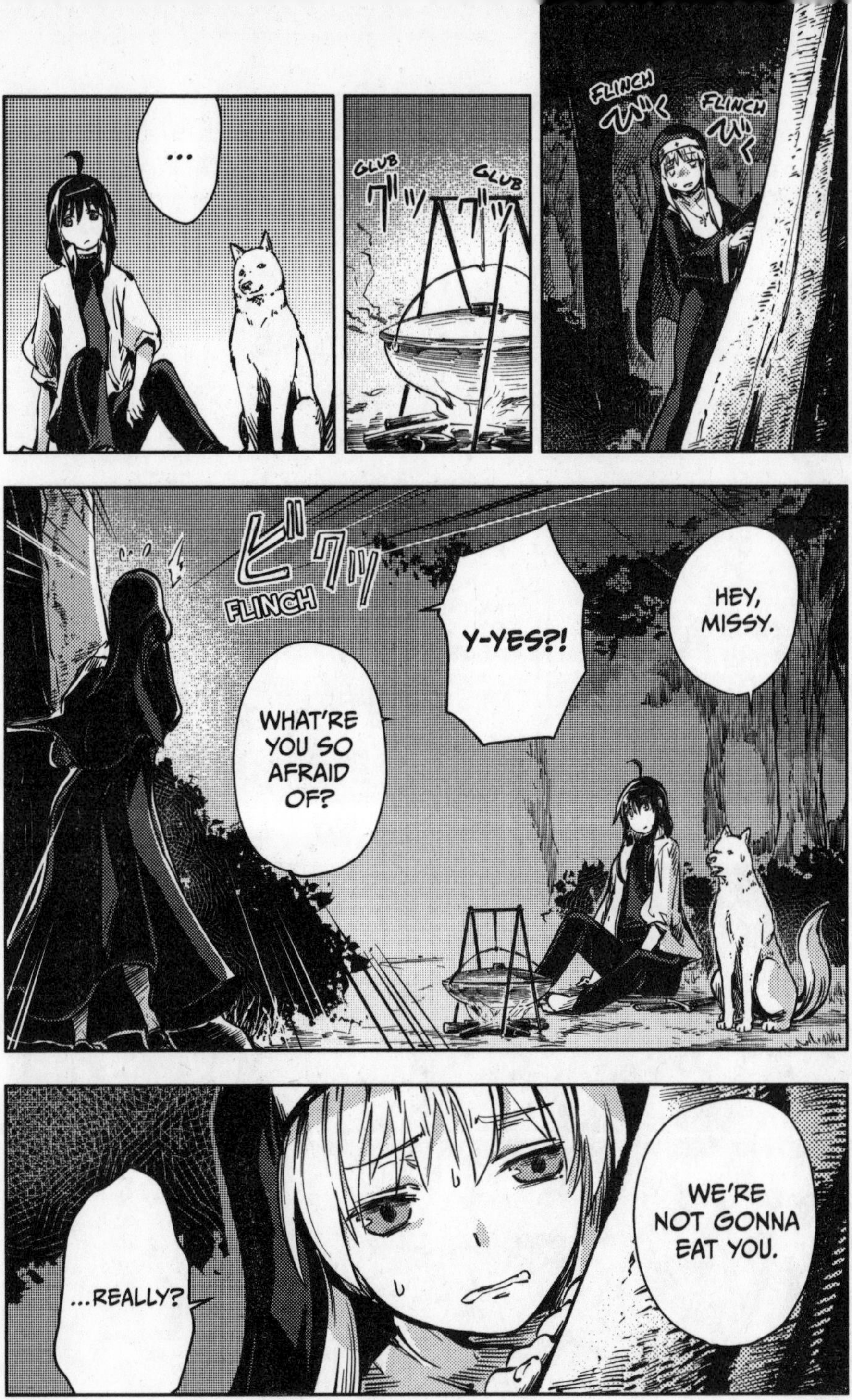
FLINCH
びく
FLINCH
びく
GLUB
グツ
GLUB
グツ
...
HEY, MISSY.
Y-YES?!
ビクッ
FLINCH
WHAT'RE YOU SO AFRAID OF?
WE'RE NOT GONNA EAT YOU.
...REALLY?

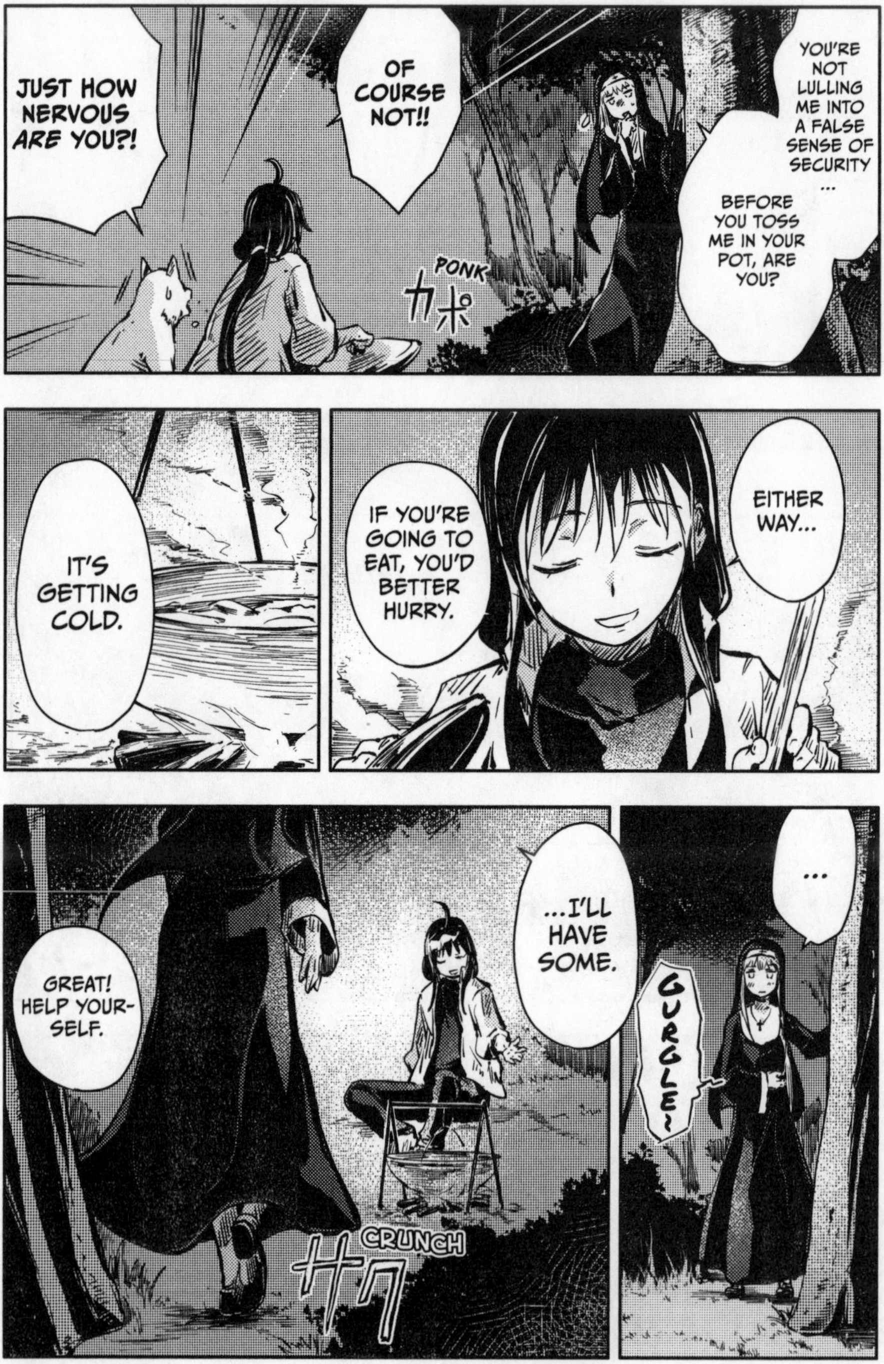
YOU'RE NOT LULLING ME INTO A FALSE SENSE OF SECURITY ...
BEFORE YOU TOSS ME IN YOUR POT, ARE YOU?
PONK
カポ
OF COURSE NOT!!
JUST HOW NERVOUS ARE YOU?!
EITHER WAY...
IF YOU'RE GOING TO EAT, YOU'D BETTER HURRY.
IT'S GETTING COLD.
...
GURGLE~
...I'LL HAVE SOME.
GREAT! HELP YOUR-SELF.
CRUNCH
サク

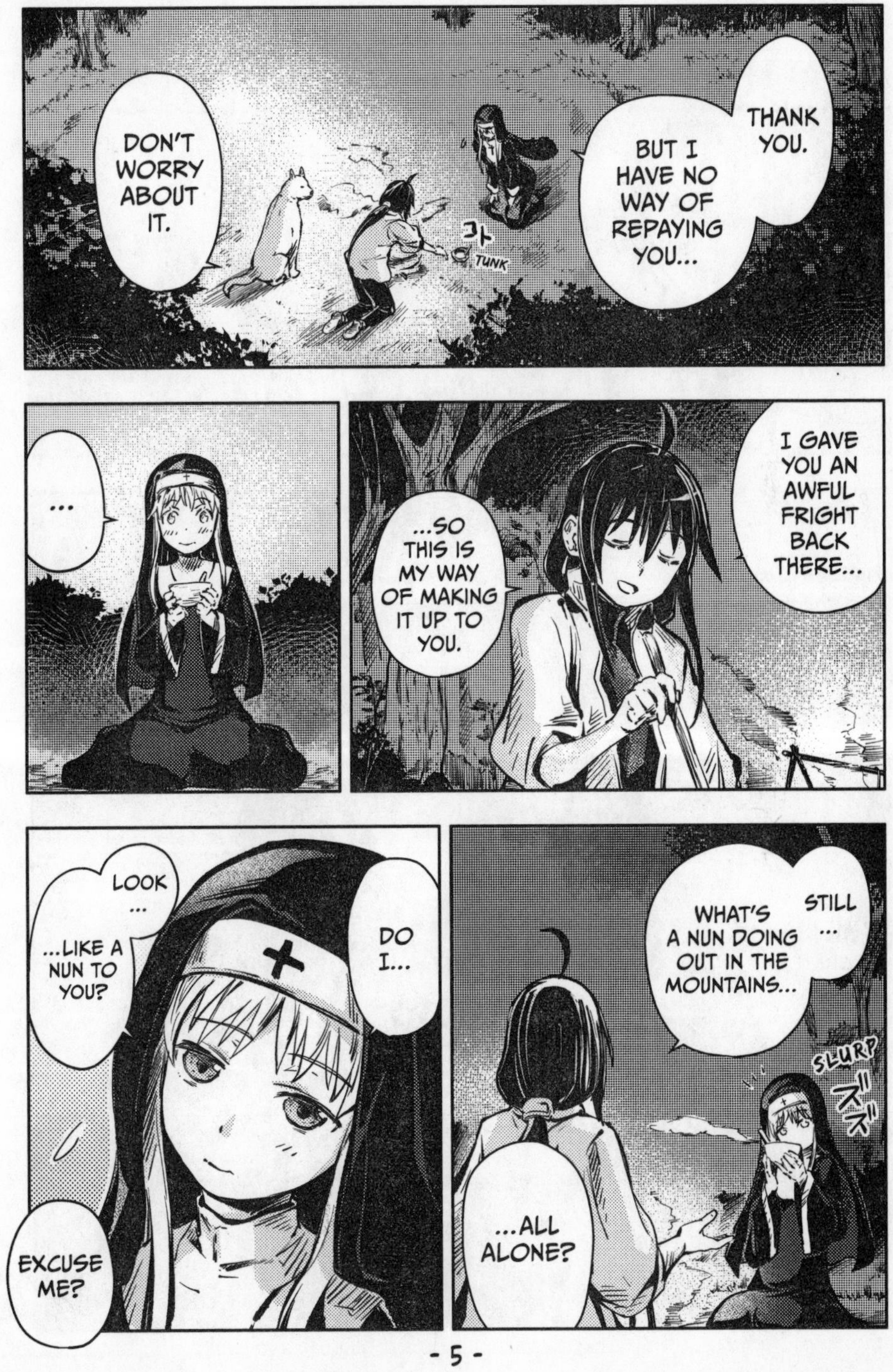
THANK YOU.
BUT I HAVE NO WAY OF REPAYING YOU...
DON'T WORRY ABOUT IT.
コト
TUNK
I GAVE YOU AN AWFUL FRIGHT BACK THERE...
...SO THIS IS MY WAY OF MAKING IT UP TO YOU.
...
STILL ...
WHAT'S A NUN DOING OUT IN THE MOUNTAINS...
SLURP
ズズ
...ALL ALONE?
DO I...
LOOK ...
...LIKE A NUN TO YOU?
EXCUSE ME?

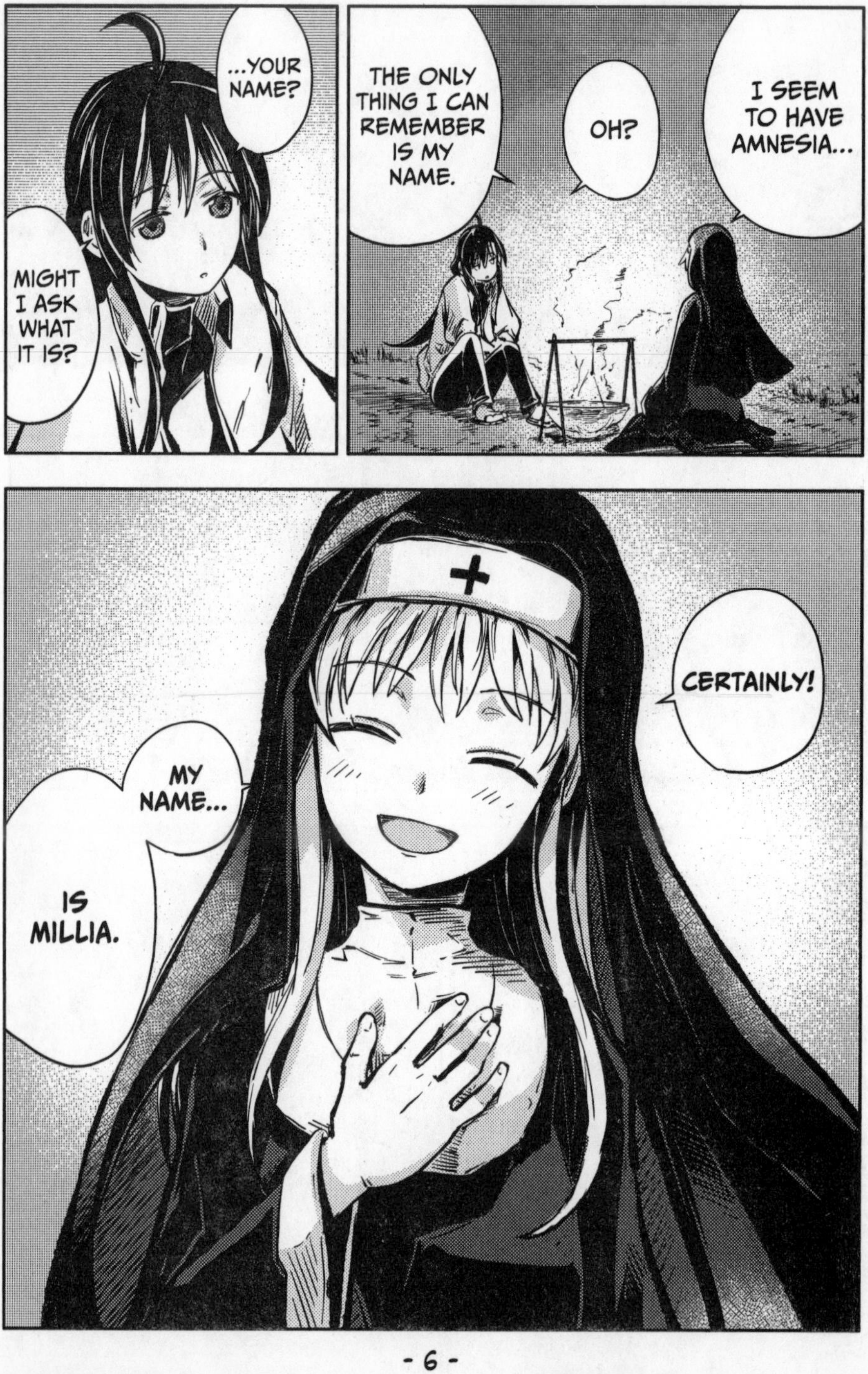
I SEEM TO HAVE AMNESIA...
OH?
THE ONLY THING I CAN REMEMBER IS MY NAME.
...YOUR NAME?
MIGHT I ASK WHAT IT IS?
CERTAINLY!
MY NAME...
IS MILLIA.

CHAPTER 16: THE OGRES AND MOMOTARO

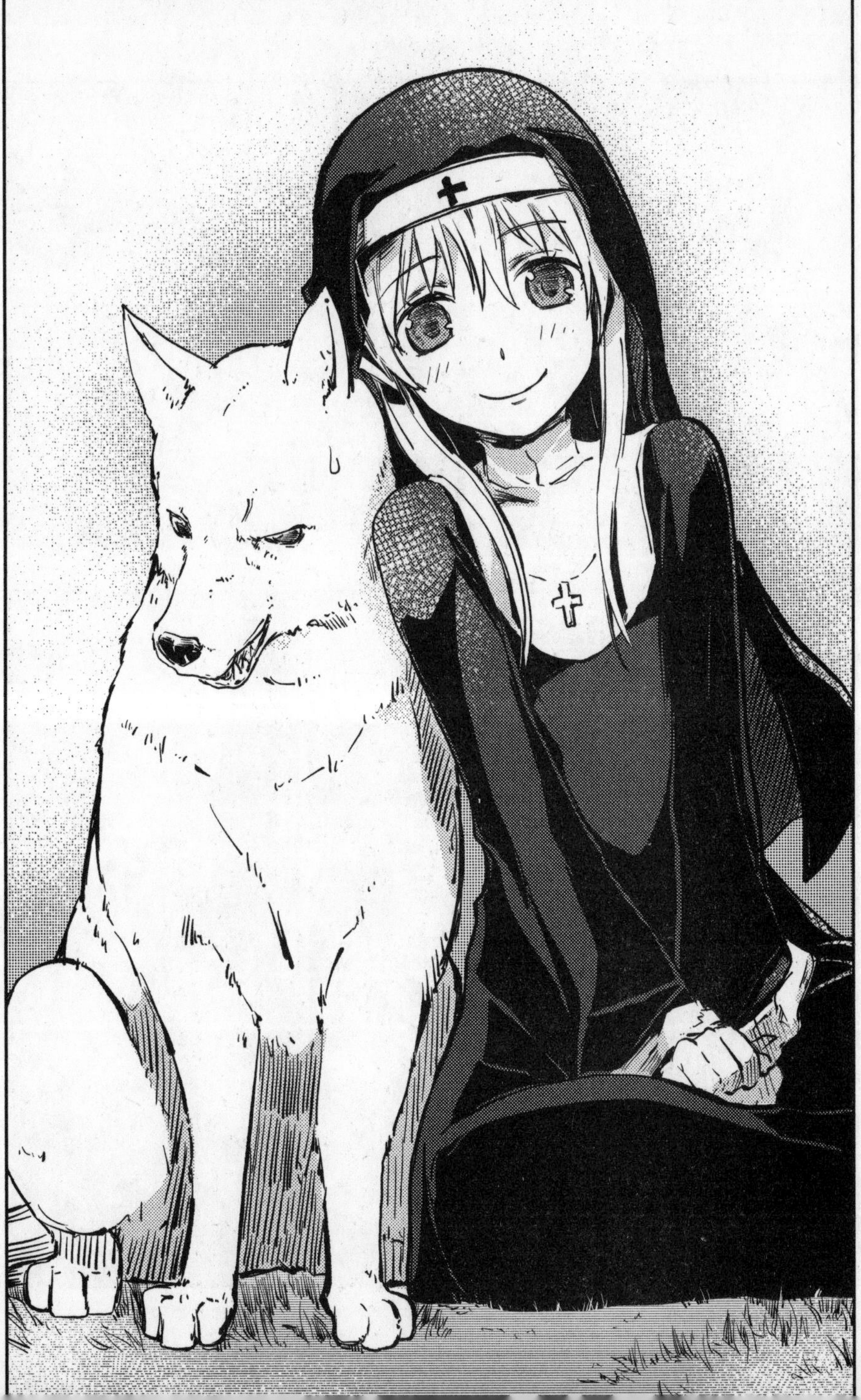

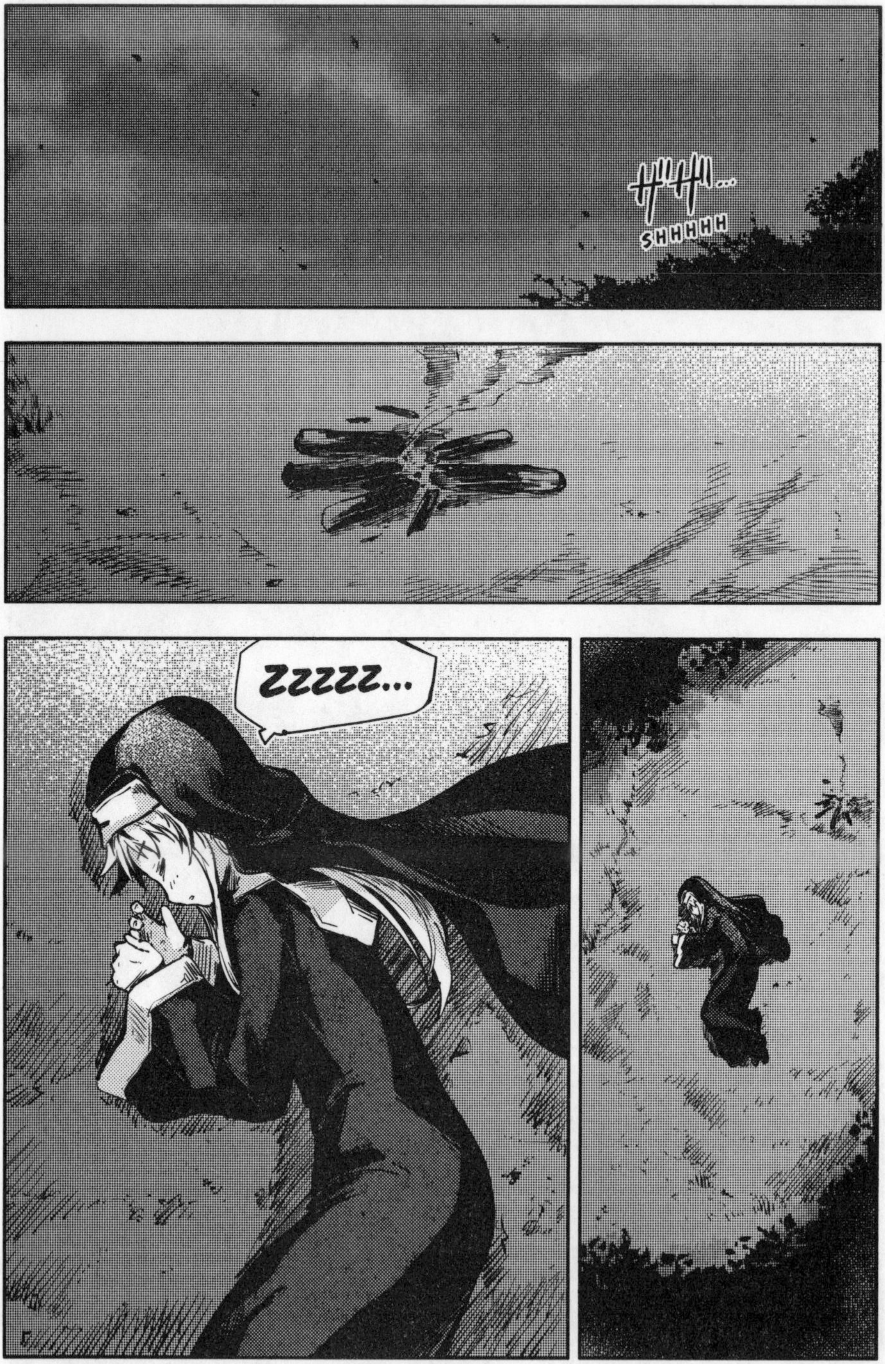
SHHHHH
ZZZZZ...

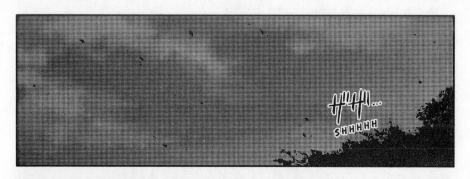

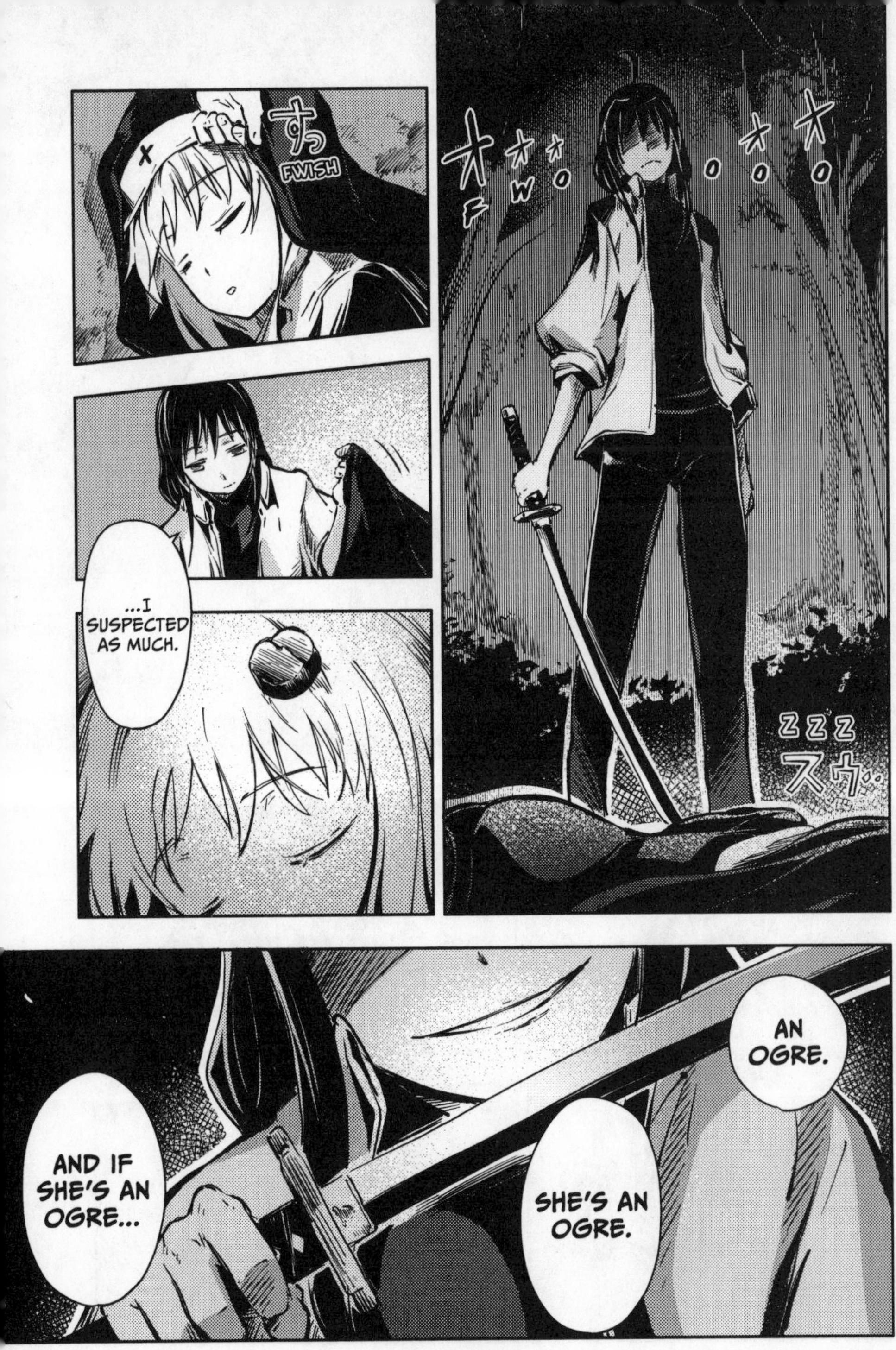
FWOOOO
ZZZ
スウ
すっ
FWISH
...I SUSPECTED AS MUCH.
AN OGRE.
SHE'S AN OGRE.
AND IF SHE'S AN OGRE...

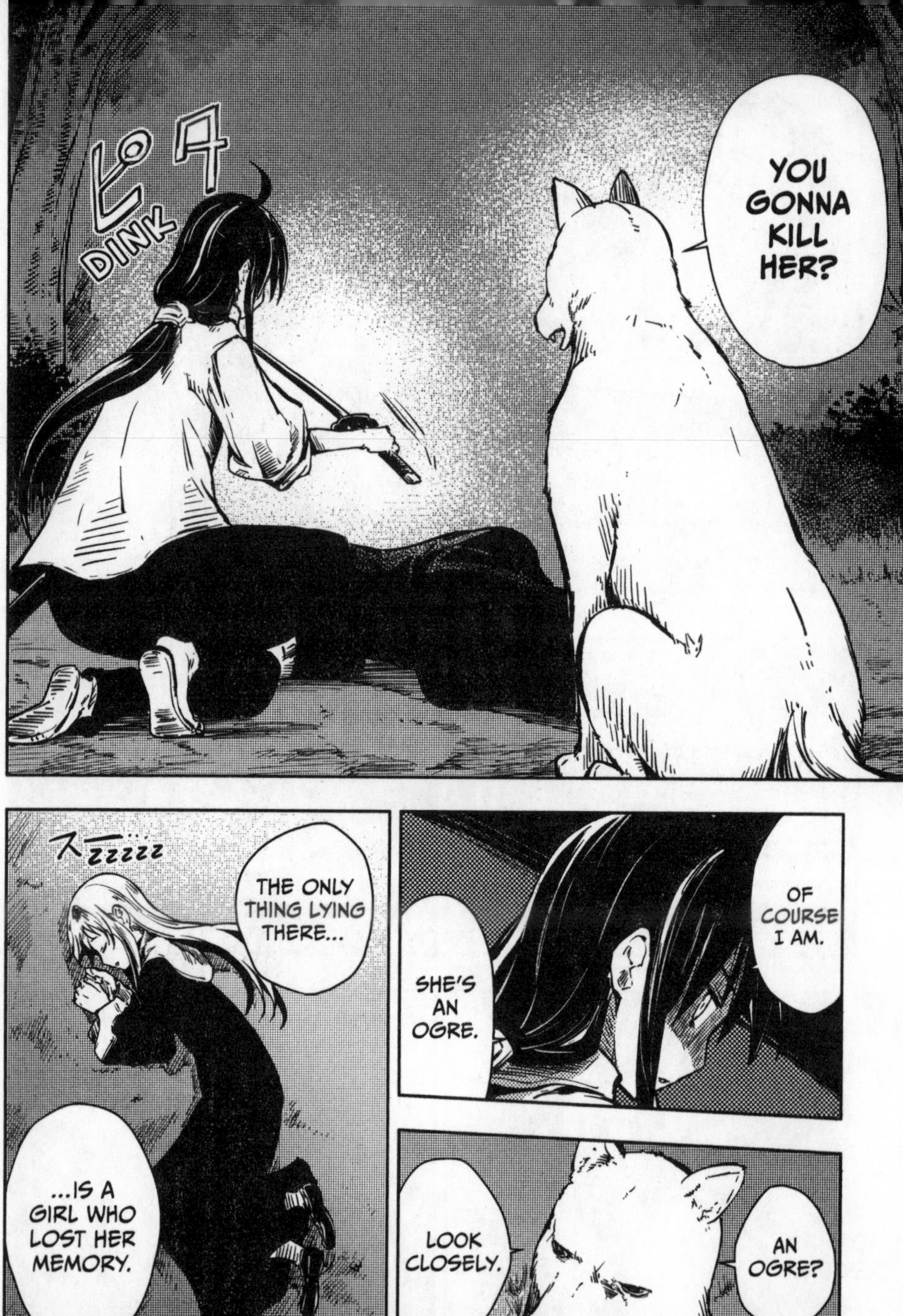
YOU GONNA KILL HER?
ピタ
DINK
OF COURSE I AM.
SHE'S AN OGRE.
AN OGRE?
LOOK CLOSELY.
スー…
zzzzz
THE ONLY THING LYING THERE...
...IS A GIRL WHO LOST HER MEMORY.

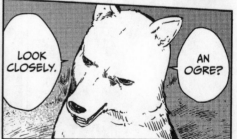

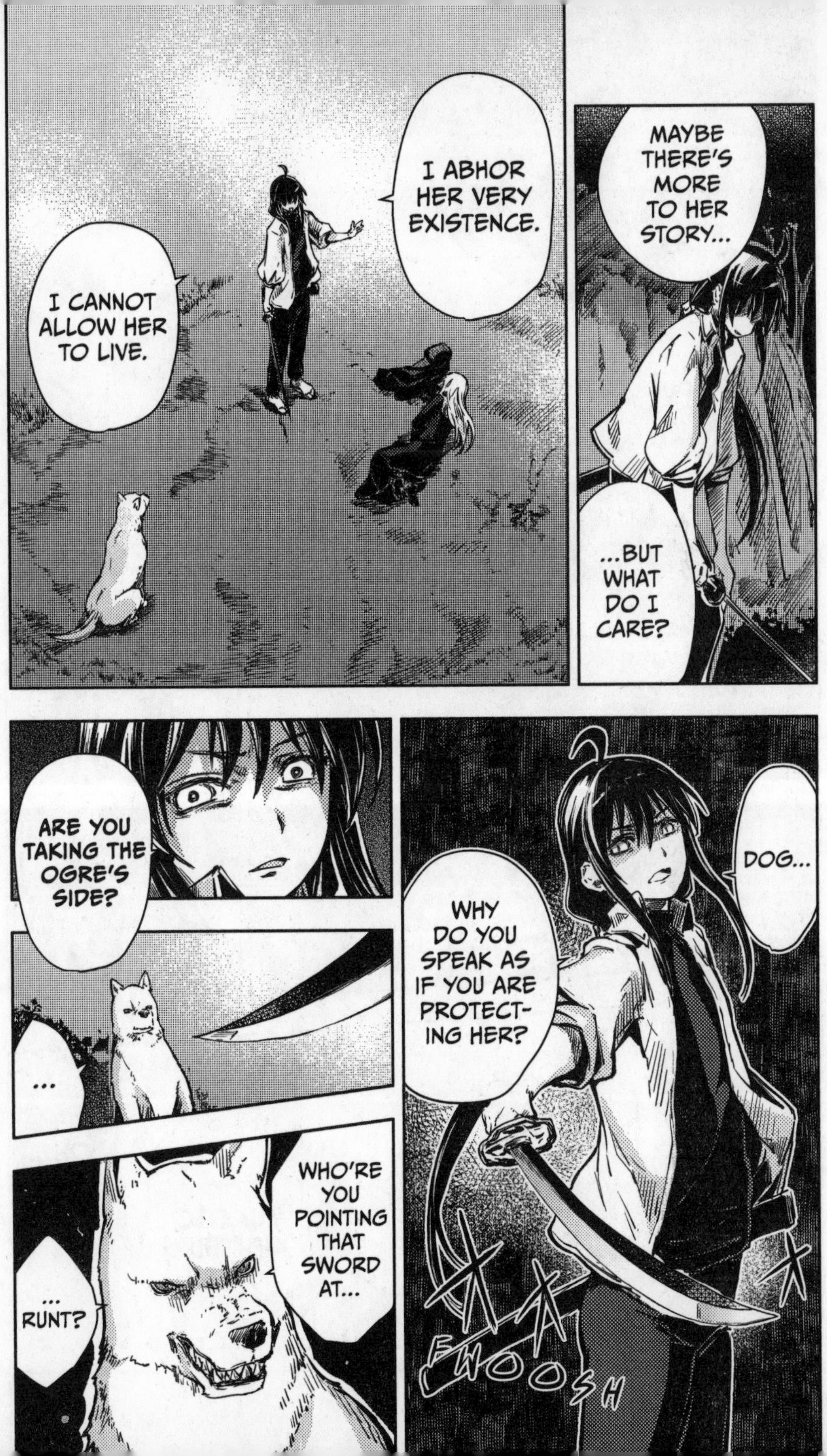
MAYBE THERE'S MORE TO HER STORY...
...BUT WHAT DO I CARE?
I ABHOR HER VERY EXISTENCE.
I CANNOT ALLOW HER TO LIVE.
DOG...
WHY DO YOU SPEAK AS IF YOU ARE PROTECT- ING HER?
FWOOSH
ARE YOU TAKING THE OGRE'S SIDE?
...
WHO'RE YOU POINTING THAT SWORD AT...
...RUNT?

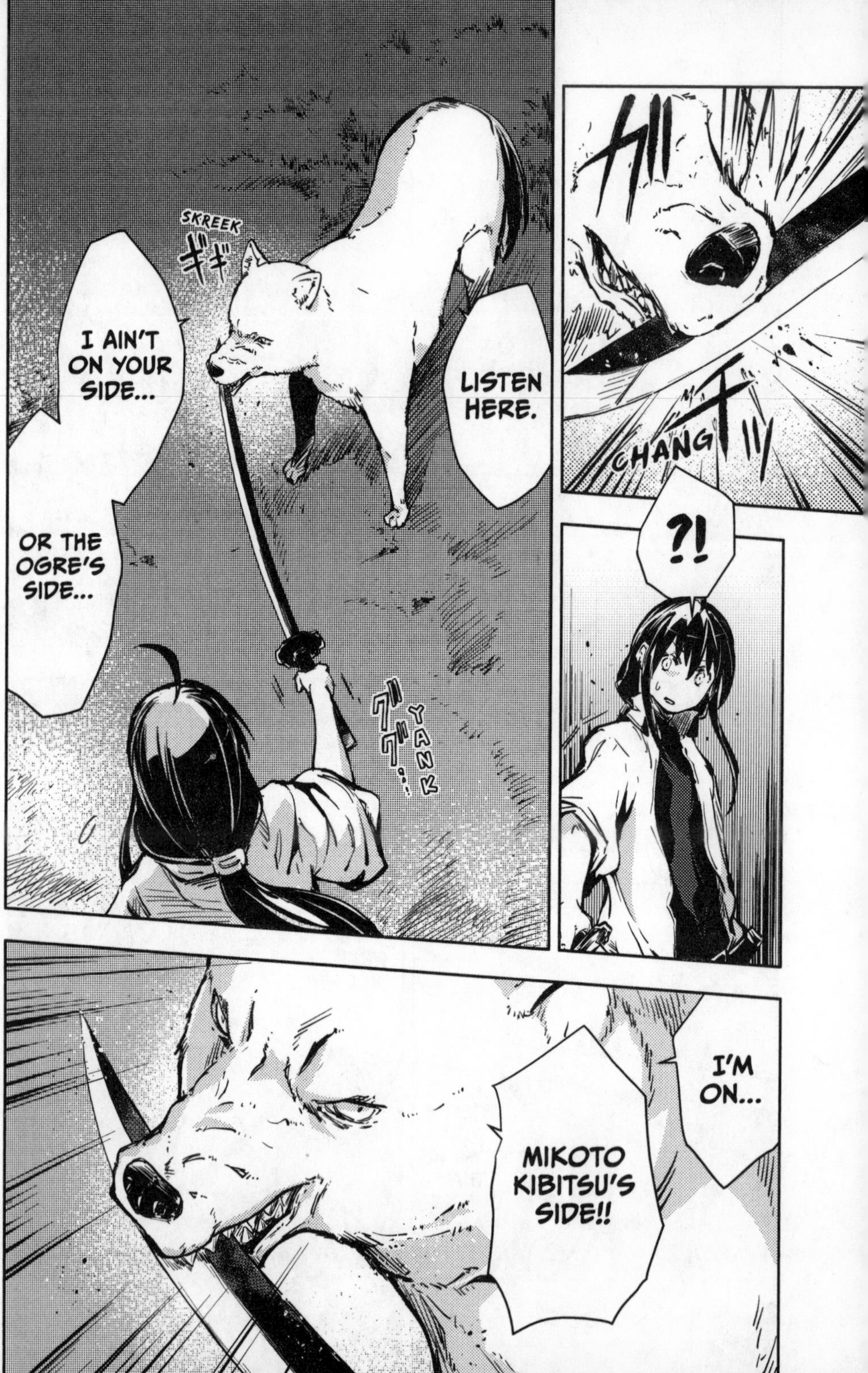
CHANG
?!
SKREEK
LISTEN HERE.
I AIN'T ON YOUR SIDE...
OR THE OGRE'S SIDE...
YANK
I'M ON...
MIKOTO KIBITSU'S SIDE!!

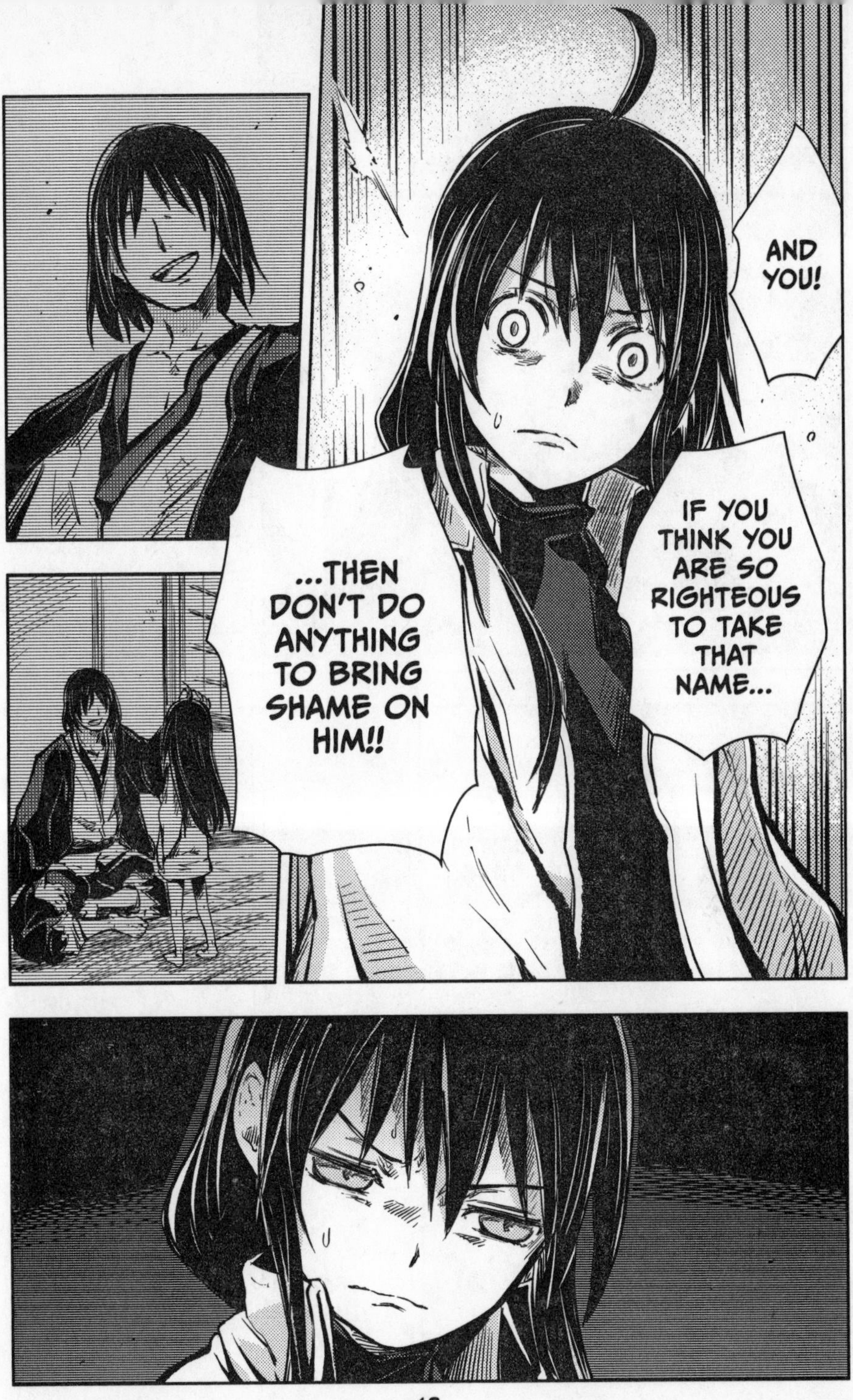
AND YOU!
IF YOU THINK YOU ARE SO RIGHTEOUS TO TAKE THAT NAME...
...THEN DON'T DO ANYTHING TO BRING SHAME ON HIM!!

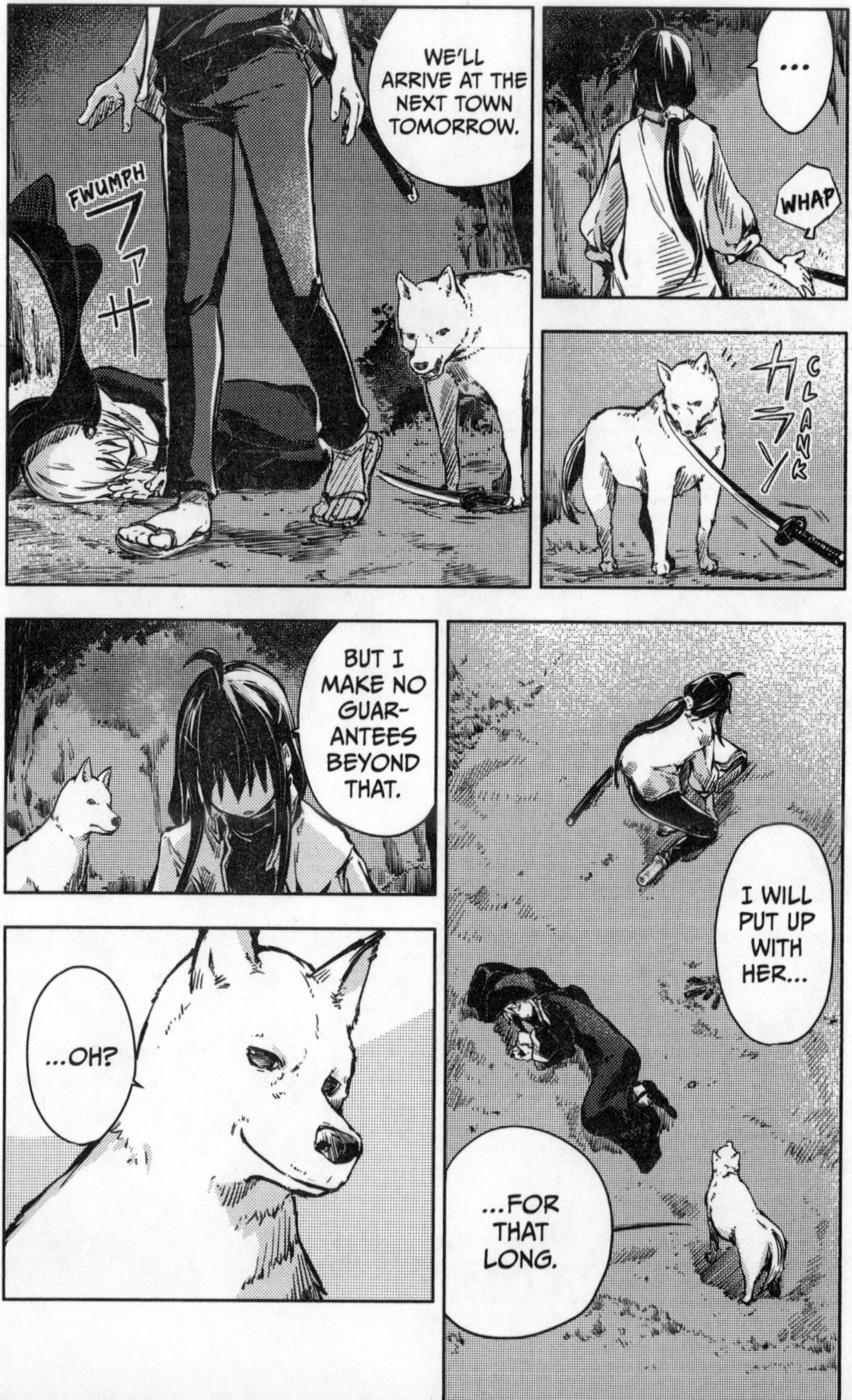
...
WHAP
CLANK
カランッ
WE'LL ARRIVE AT THE NEXT TOWN TOMORROW.
FWUMPH
ファサ
I WILL PUT UP WITH HER...
...FOR THAT LONG.
BUT I MAKE NO GUAR-ANTEES BEYOND THAT.
...OH?

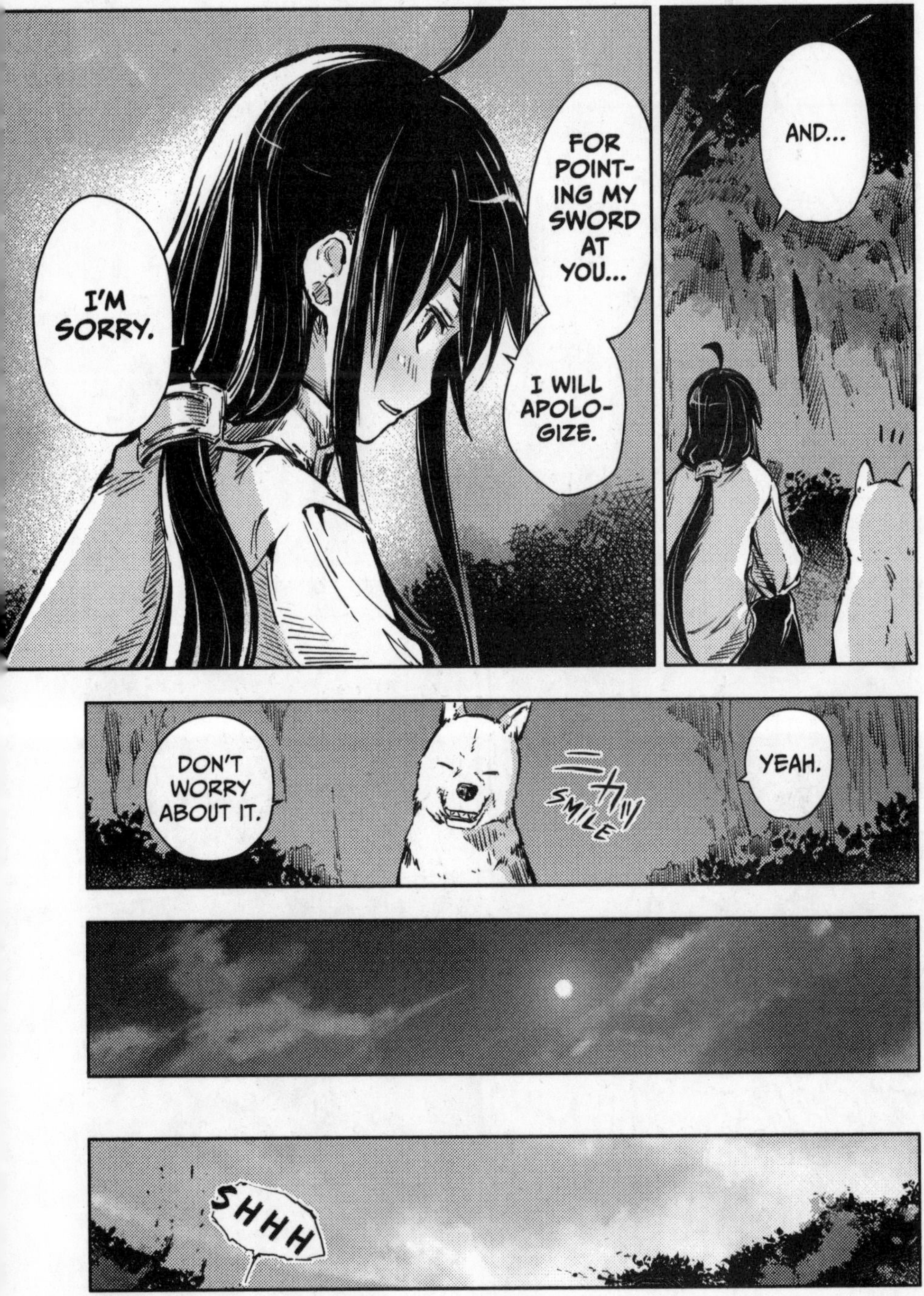

AND...
FOR POINTING-ING MY SWORD AT YOU...
I WILL APOLO-GIZE.
I'M SORRY.
YEAH.
SMILE
DON'T WORRY ABOUT IT.
SHHH

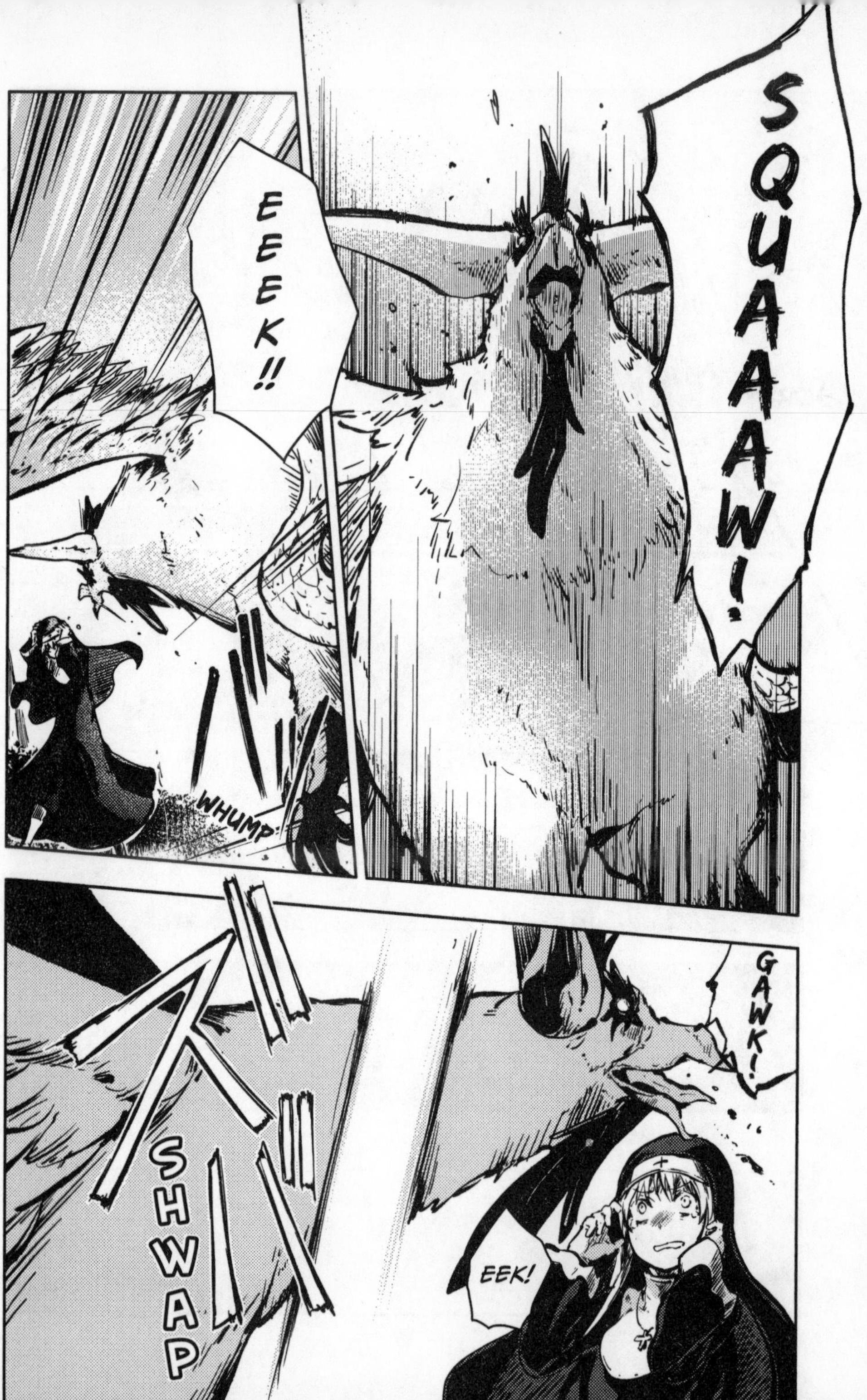
SQUAAAW!
EEEK!!
WHUMP
GAWK!
EEK!
SHWAP

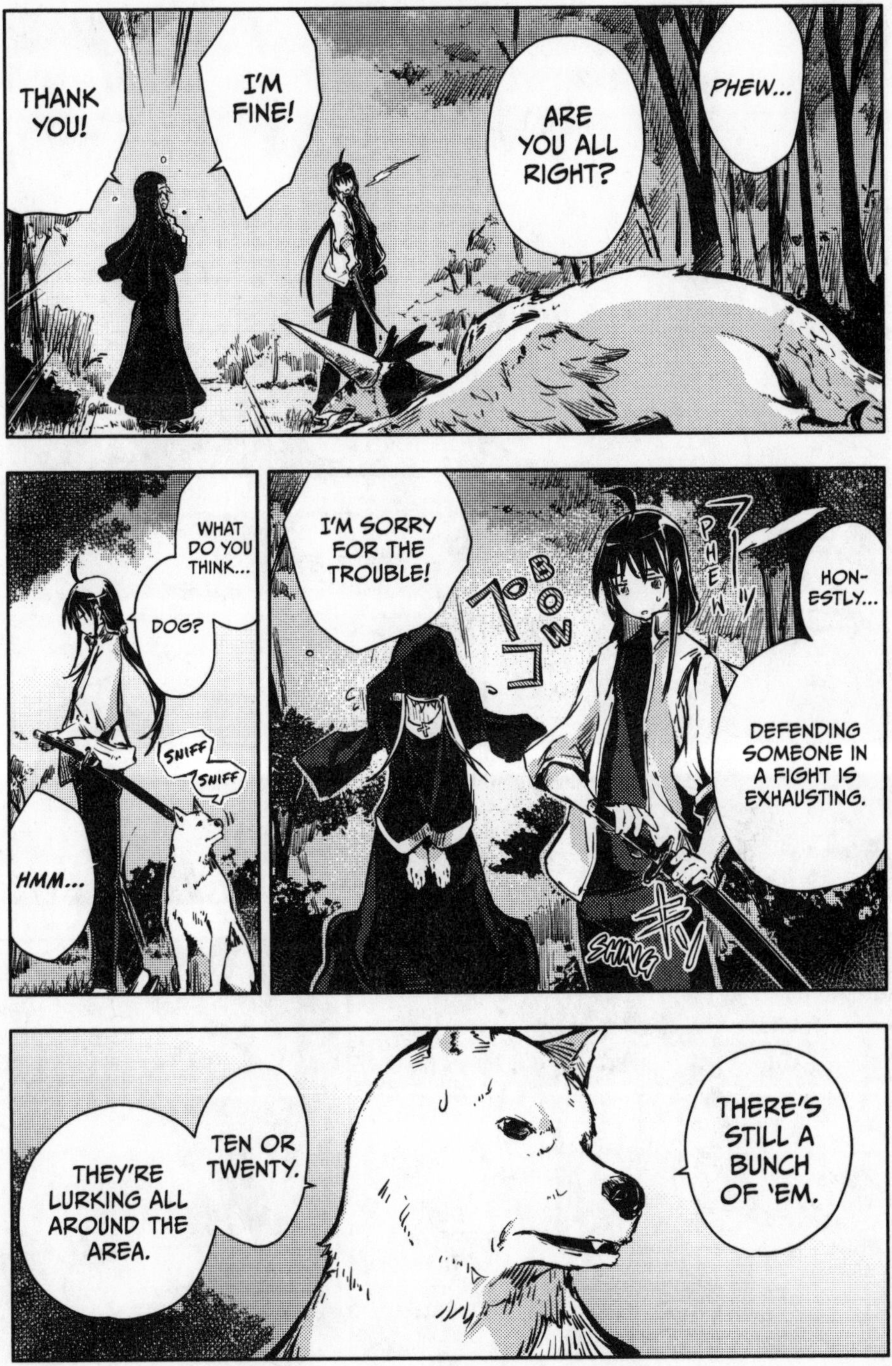
PHEW...
ARE YOU ALL RIGHT?
I'M FINE!
THANK YOU!
PHEW
HON-ESTLY...
DEFENDING SOMEONE IN A FIGHT IS EXHAUSTING.
SHING
BOW
I'M SORRY FOR THE TROUBLE!
WHAT DO YOU THINK...
DOG?
SNIFF
SNIFF
HMM...
THERE'S STILL A BUNCH OF 'EM.
TEN OR TWENTY.
THEY'RE LURKING ALL AROUND THE AREA.

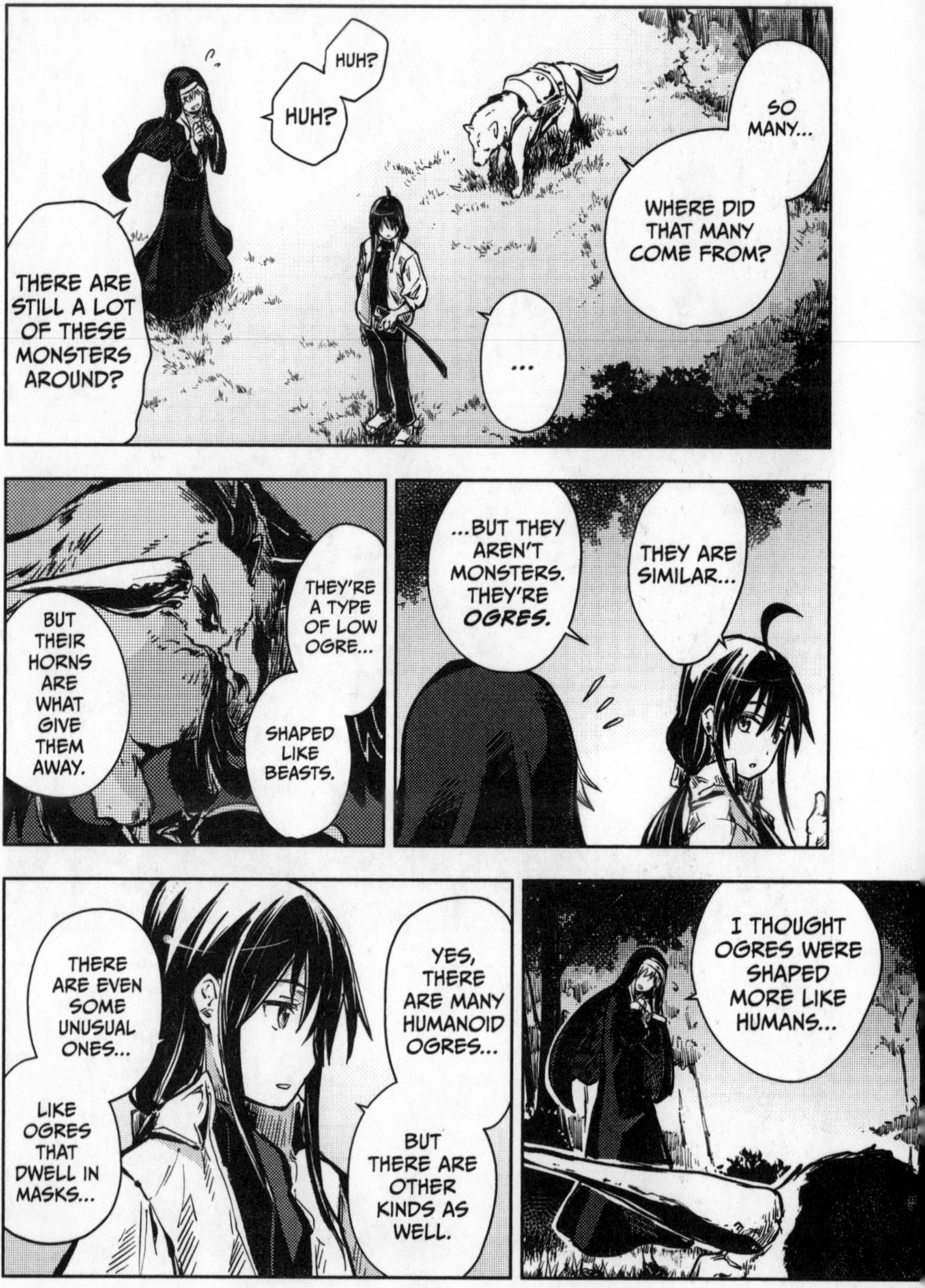
SO MANY... WHERE DID THAT MANY COME FROM?
HUH?
HUH?
...
THERE ARE STILL A LOT OF THESE MONSTERS AROUND?
THEY ARE SIMILAR...
...BUT THEY AREN'T MONSTERS. THEY'RE OGRES.
THEY'RE A TYPE OF LOW OGRE...
SHAPED LIKE BEASTS.
BUT THEIR HORNS ARE WHAT GIVE THEM AWAY.
I THOUGHT OGRES WERE SHAPED MORE LIKE HUMANS...
YES, THERE ARE MANY HUMANOID OGRES...
BUT THERE ARE OTHER KINDS AS WELL.
THERE ARE EVEN SOME UNUSUAL ONES...
LIKE OGRES THAT DWELL IN MASKS...

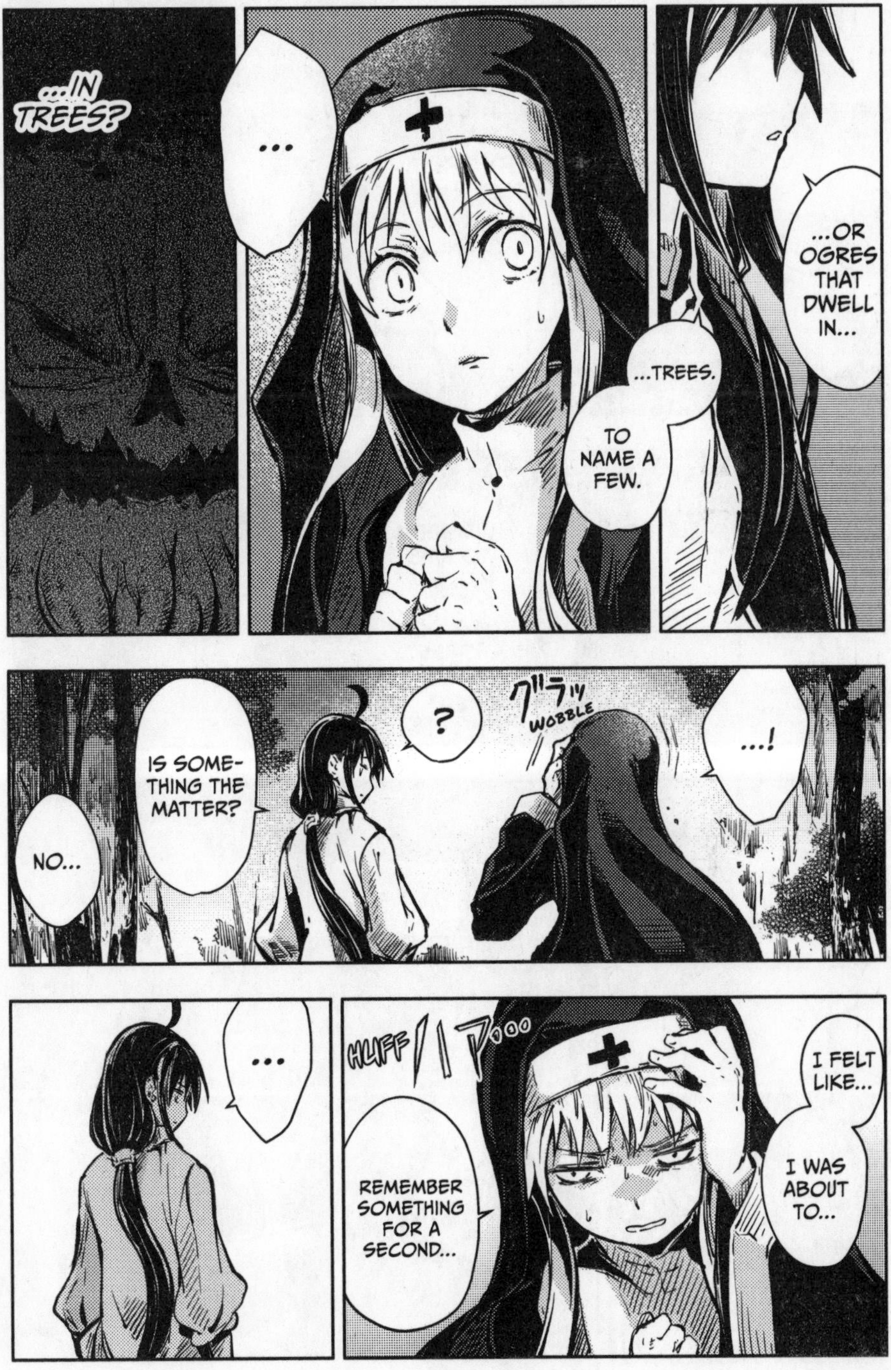

...OR OGRES THAT DWELL IN...
...TREES.
TO NAME A FEW.
...
...IN TREES?
...!
グラッ
WOBBLE
?
IS SOME-THING THE MATTER?
NO...
I FELT LIKE...
I WAS ABOUT TO...
HUFF
ハァ
REMEMBER SOMETHING FOR A SECOND...
...

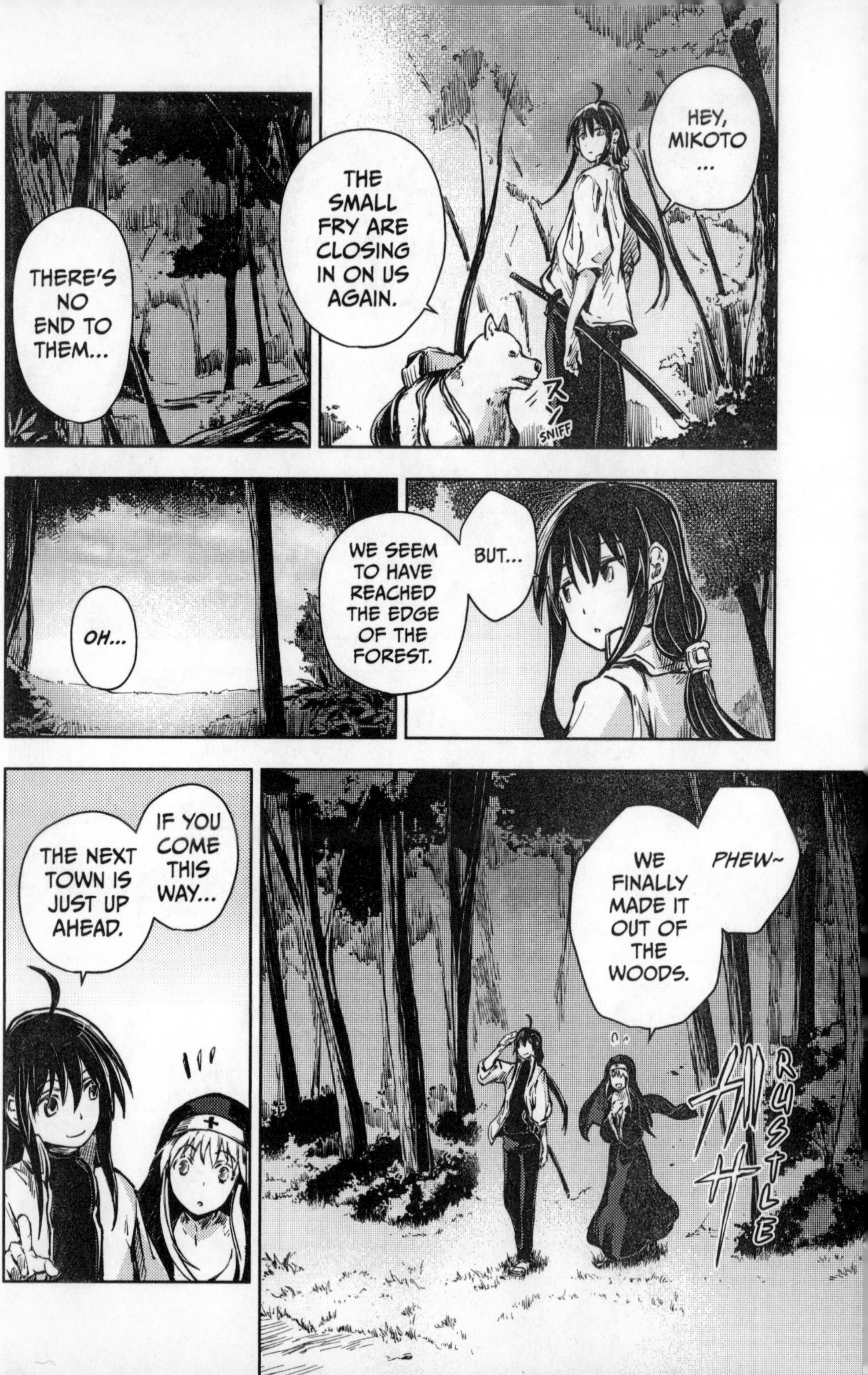
HEY, MIKOTO ...
THE SMALL FRY ARE CLOSING IN ON US AGAIN.
SNIFF
THERE'S NO END TO THEM...
BUT...
WE SEEM TO HAVE REACHED THE EDGE OF THE FOREST.
OH...
RUSTLE
PHEW~
WE FINALLY MADE IT OUT OF THE WOODS.
IF YOU COME THIS WAY...
THE NEXT TOWN IS JUST UP AHEAD.

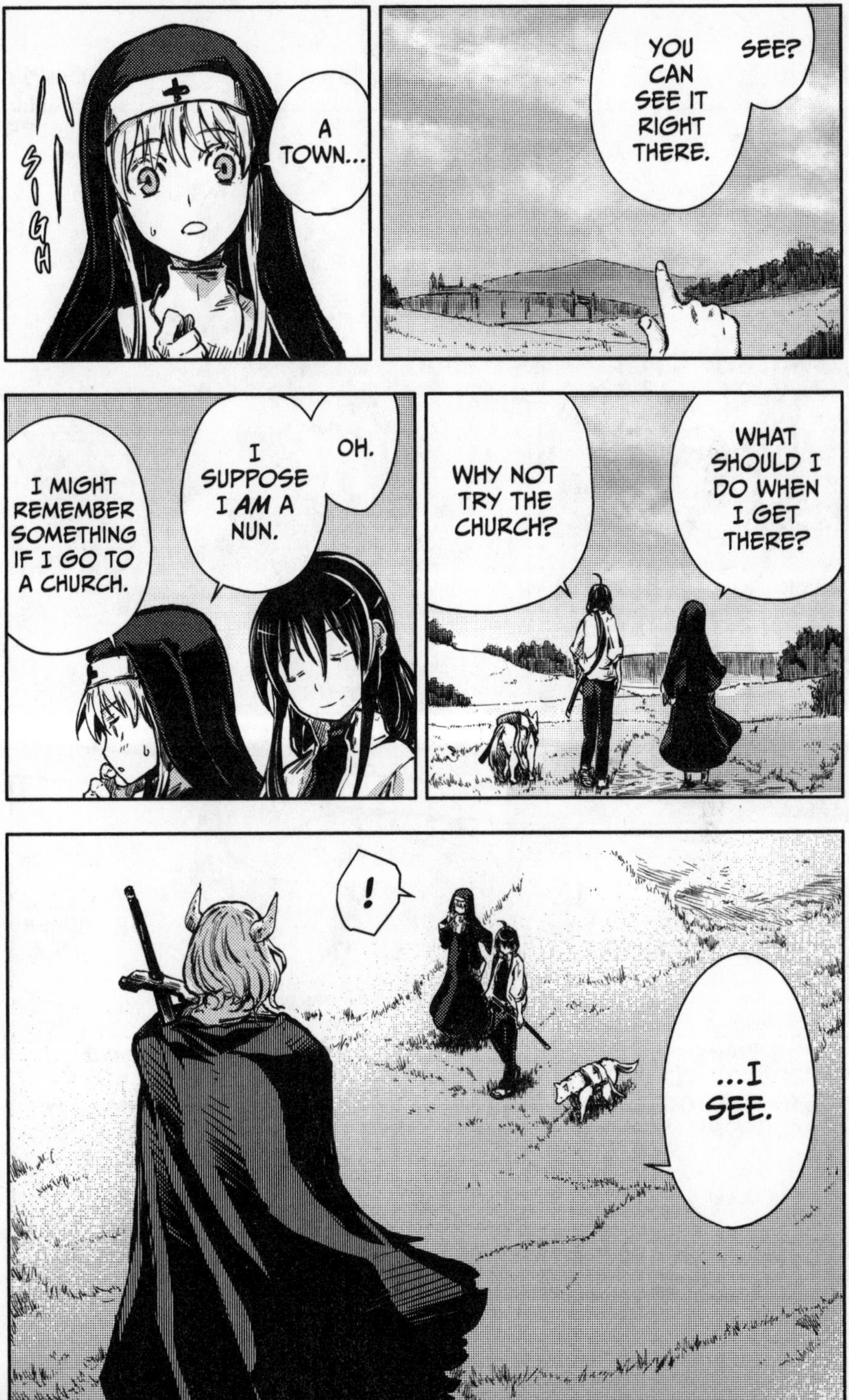
SEE?
YOU CAN SEE IT RIGHT THERE.
A TOWN...
SIGH
WHAT SHOULD I DO WHEN I GET THERE?
WHY NOT TRY THE CHURCH?
OH.
I SUPPOSE I *AM* A NUN.
I MIGHT REMEMBER SOMETHING IF I GO TO A CHURCH.
...I SEE.
!

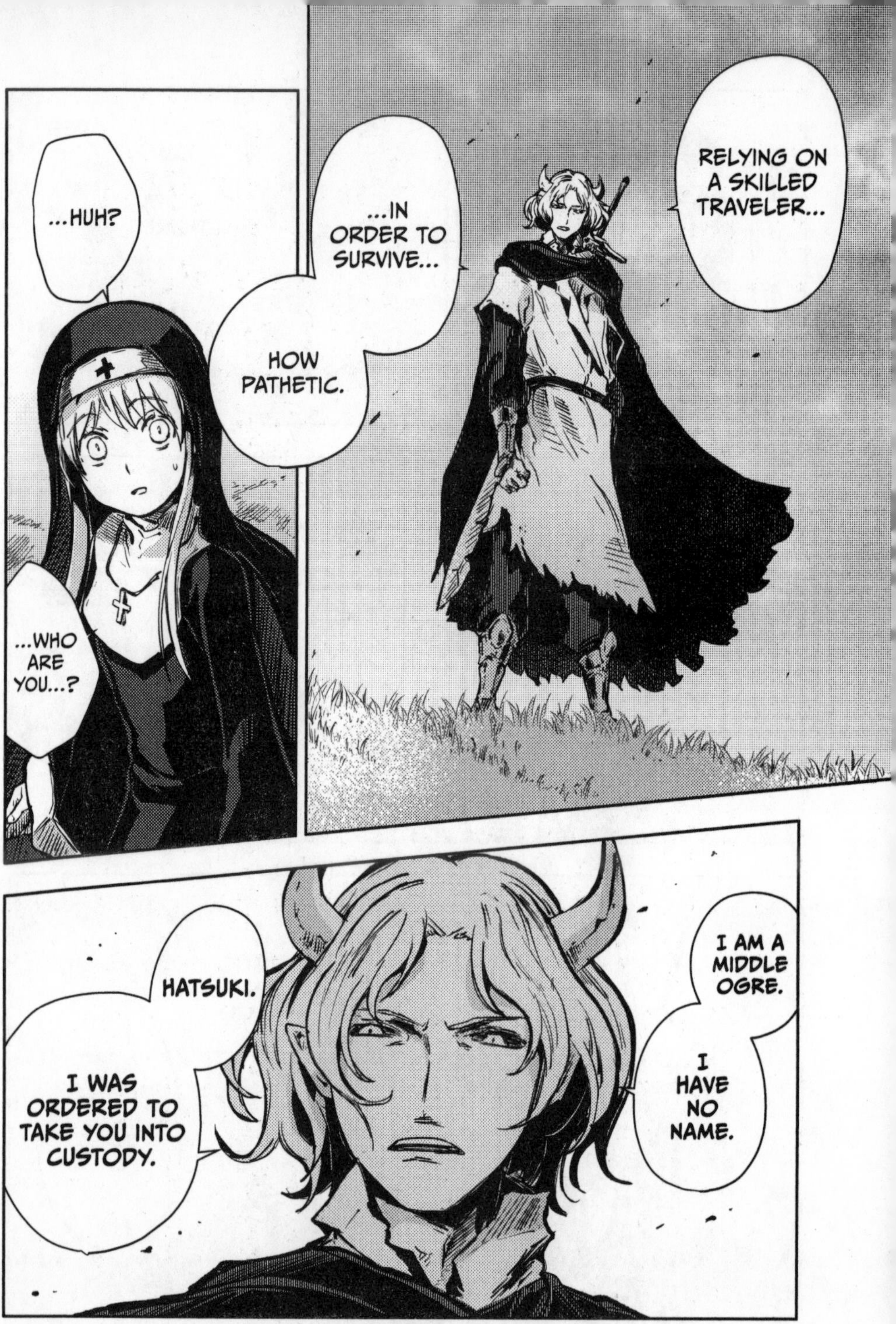

RELYING ON A SKILLED TRAVELER...
...IN ORDER TO SURVIVE...
HOW PATHETIC.
...HUH?
...WHO ARE YOU...?
I AM A MIDDLE OGRE.
I HAVE NO NAME.
HATSUKI.
I WAS ORDERED TO TAKE YOU INTO CUSTODY.

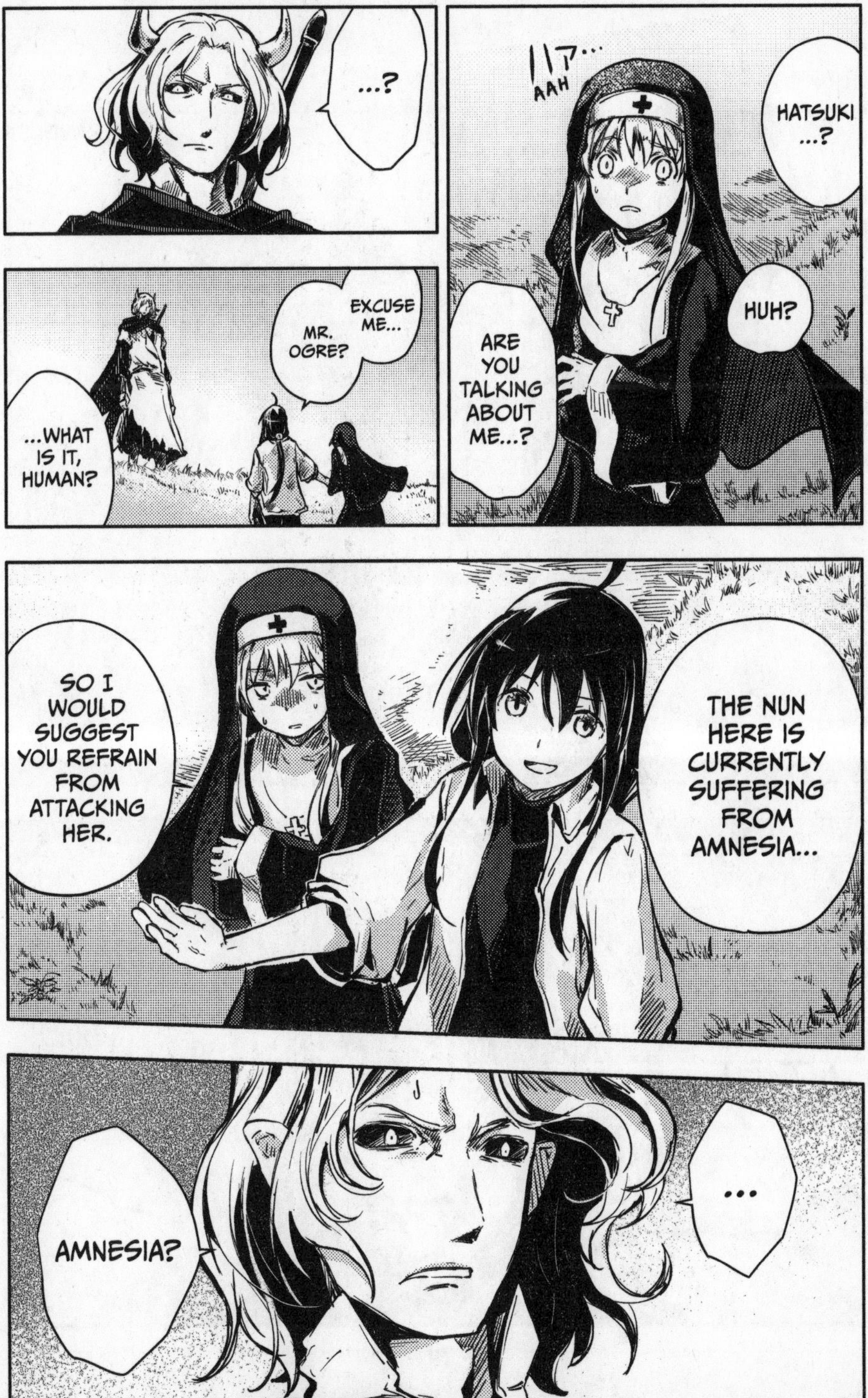
ハア…
AAH
HATSUKI ...?
HUH?
ARE YOU TALKING ABOUT ME...?
...?
EXCUSE ME... MR. OGRE?
...WHAT IS IT, HUMAN?
THE NUN HERE IS CURRENTLY SUFFERING FROM AMNESIA...
SO I WOULD SUGGEST YOU REFRAIN FROM ATTACKING HER.
...
AMNESIA?

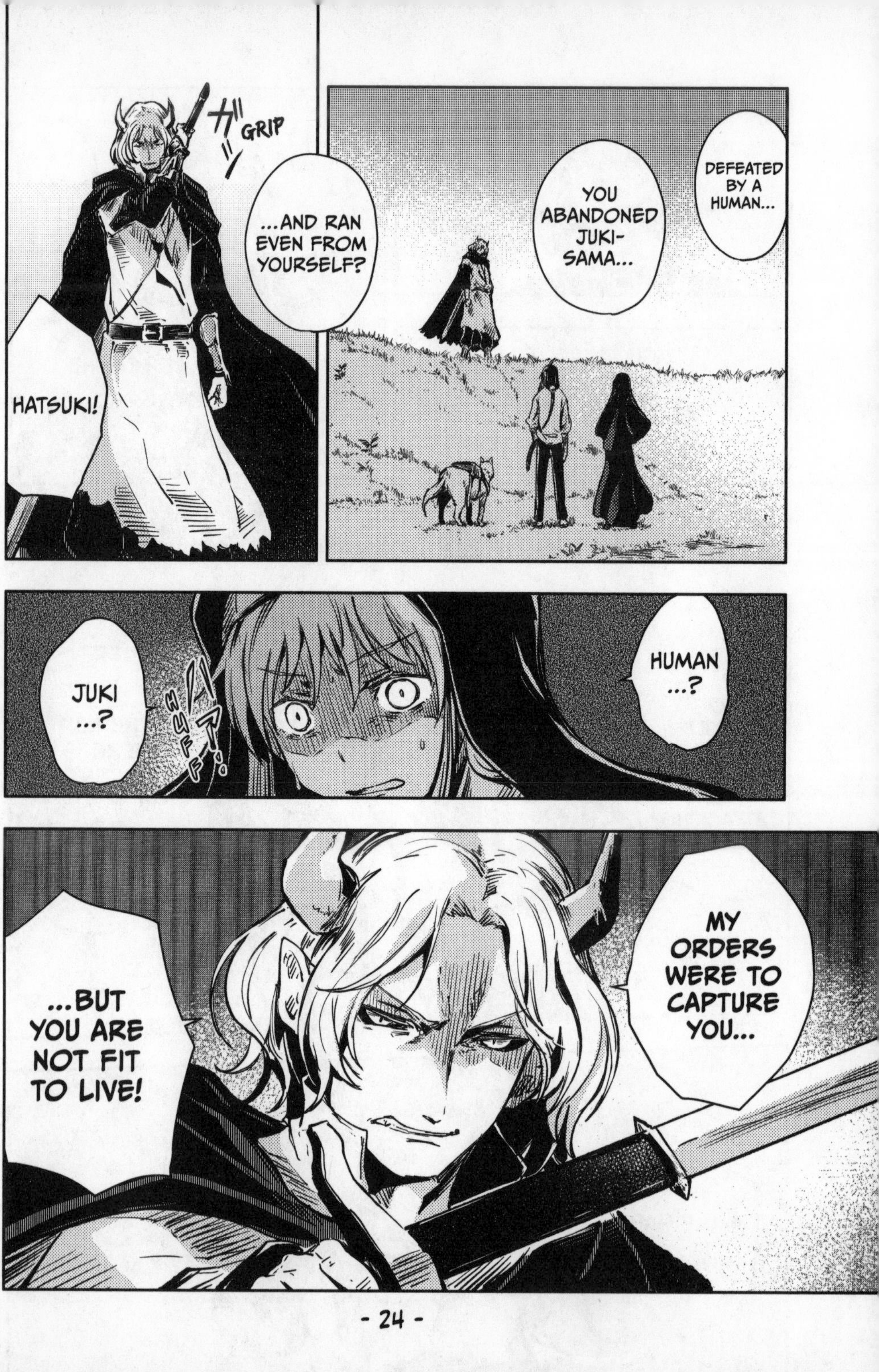
DEFEATED BY A HUMAN...
YOU ABANDONED JUKI-SAMA...
...AND RAN EVEN FROM YOURSELF?
GRIP
HATSUKI!
HUMAN ...?
JUKI ...?
HUFF
MY ORDERS WERE TO CAPTURE YOU...
...BUT YOU ARE NOT FIT TO LIVE!

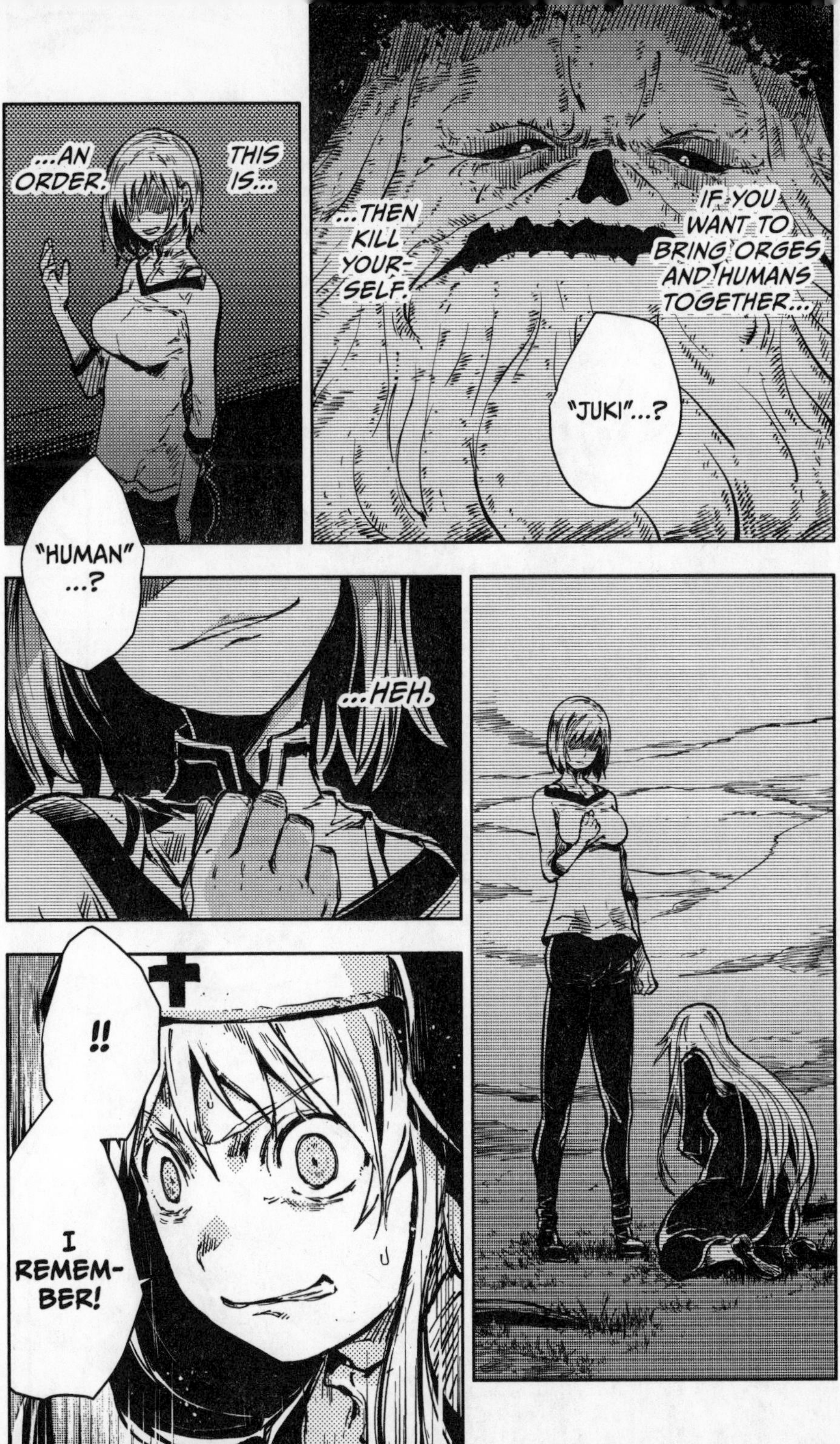
IF YOU WANT TO BRING ORGES AND HUMANS TOGETHER...
...THEN KILL YOURSELF.
"JUKI"...?
THIS IS...
...AN ORDER.
"HUMAN" ...?
...HEH.
!!
I REMEMBER!

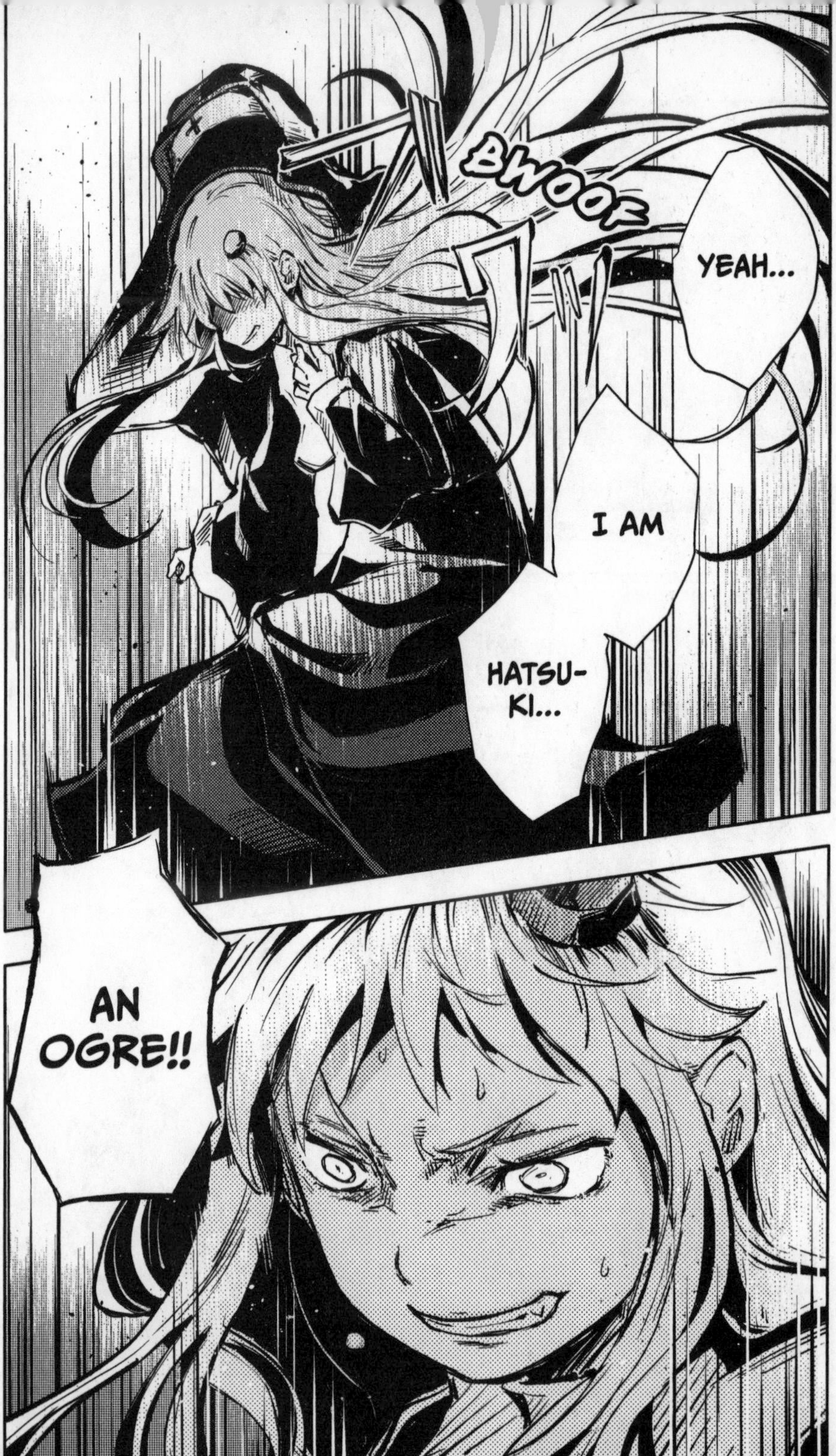
BWOOF
YEAH...
I AM
HATSU-KI...
AN OGRE!!

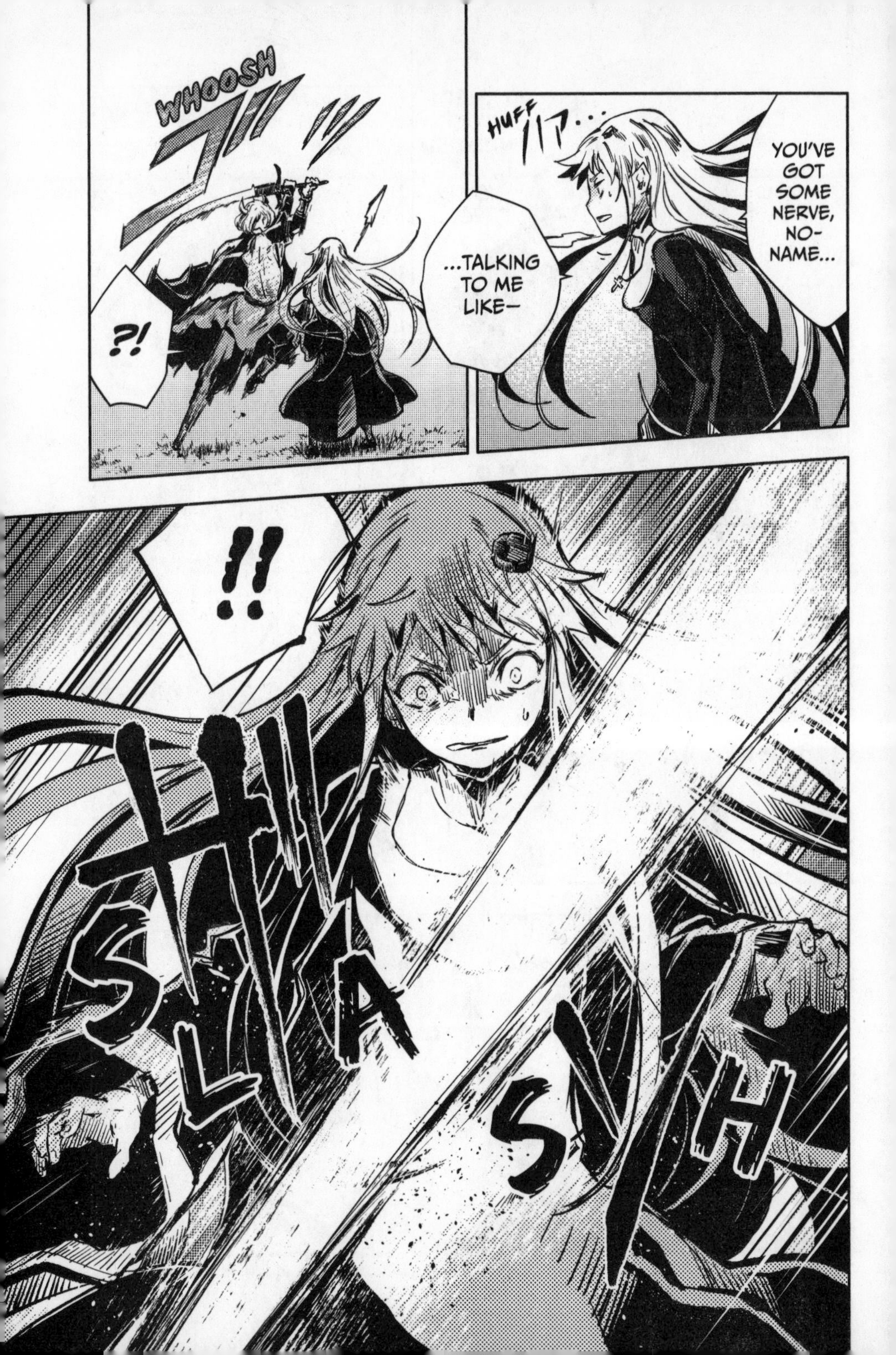
HUFF ハア…
YOU'VE GOT SOME NERVE, NO-NAME...
...TALKING TO ME LIKE—
WHOOSH
?!
!!
SLASH

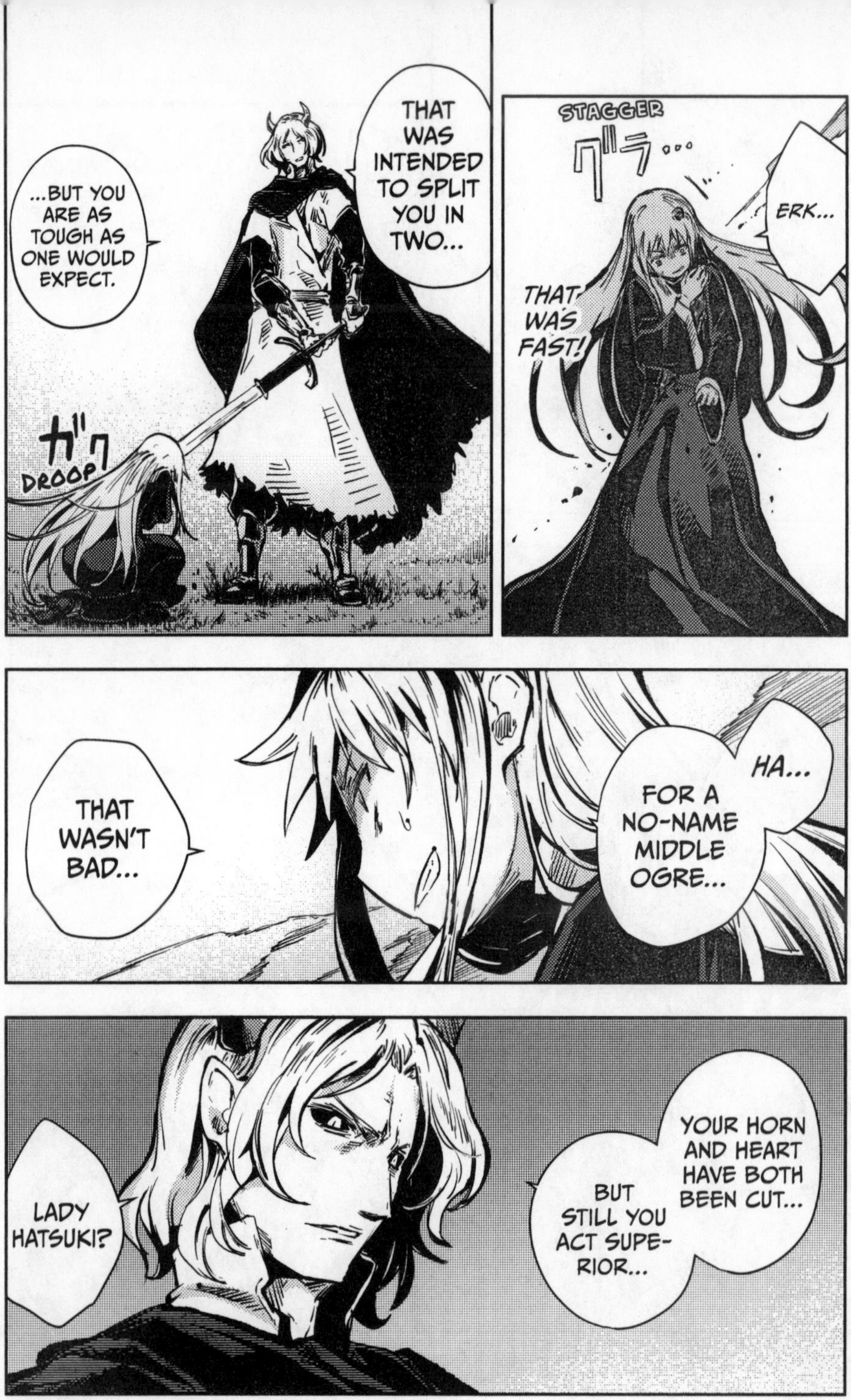
STAGGER
グラ...
ERK...
THAT WAS FAST!
THAT WAS INTENDED TO SPLIT YOU IN TWO...
...BUT YOU ARE AS TOUGH AS ONE WOULD EXPECT.
ガク
DROOP
HA...
FOR A NO-NAME MIDDLE OGRE...
THAT WASN'T BAD...
YOUR HORN AND HEART HAVE BOTH BEEN CUT...
BUT STILL YOU ACT SUPERIOR...
LADY HATSUKI?

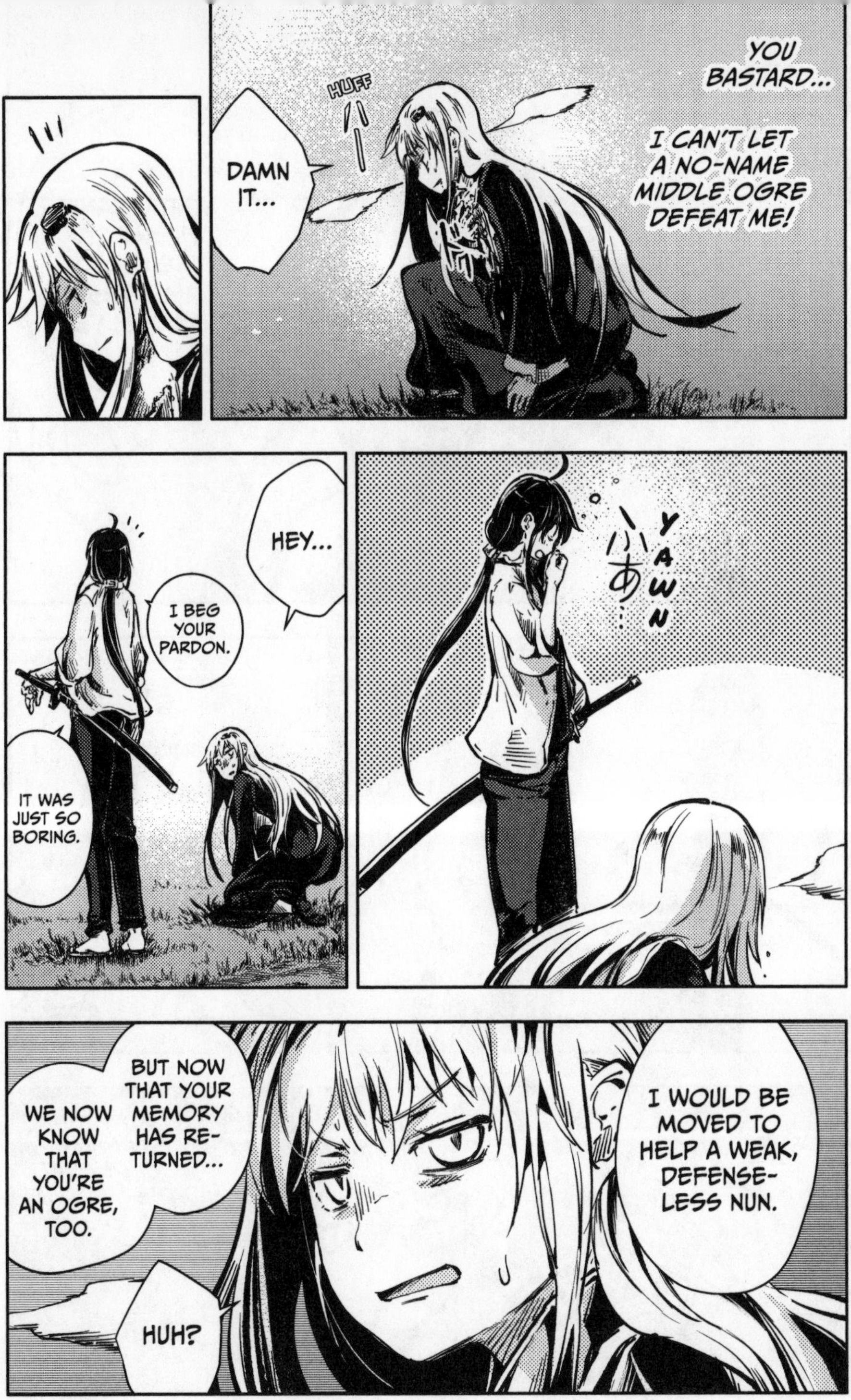
YOU BASTARD...
I CAN'T LET A NO-NAME MIDDLE OGRE DEFEAT ME!
HUFF
ハー
DAMN IT...
YAWN
ふぁあ…
HEY...
I BEG YOUR PARDON.
IT WAS JUST SO BORING.
I WOULD BE MOVED TO HELP A WEAK, DEFENSE-LESS NUN.
HUH?
BUT NOW THAT YOUR MEMORY HAS RE-TURNED...
WE NOW KNOW THAT YOU'RE AN OGRE, TOO.

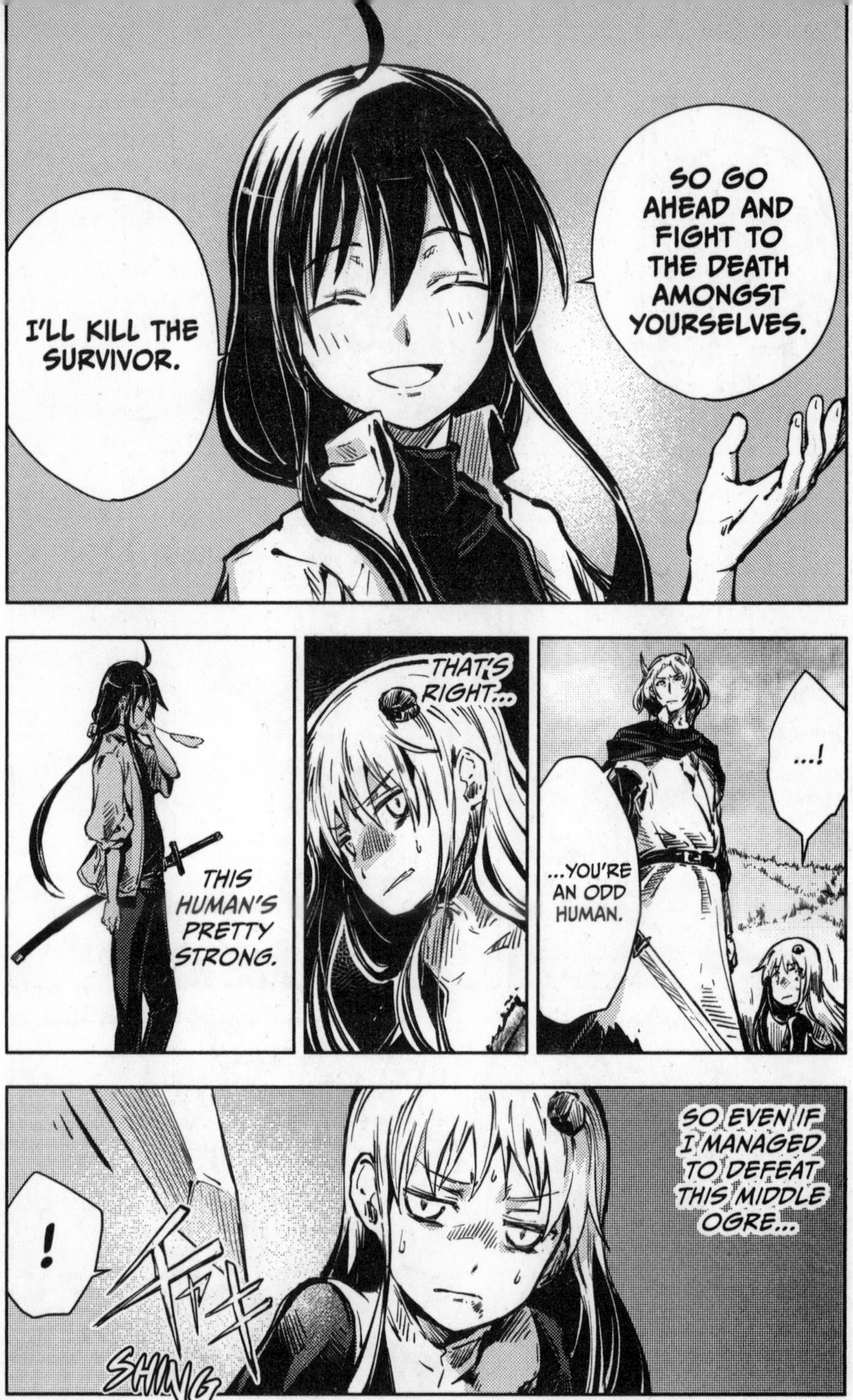
SO GO AHEAD AND FIGHT TO THE DEATH AMONGST YOURSELVES.
I'LL KILL THE SURVIVOR.
...!
...YOU'RE AN ODD HUMAN.
THAT'S RIGHT...
THIS HUMAN'S PRETTY STRONG.
SO EVEN IF I MANAGED TO DEFEAT THIS MIDDLE OGRE...
!
SHING

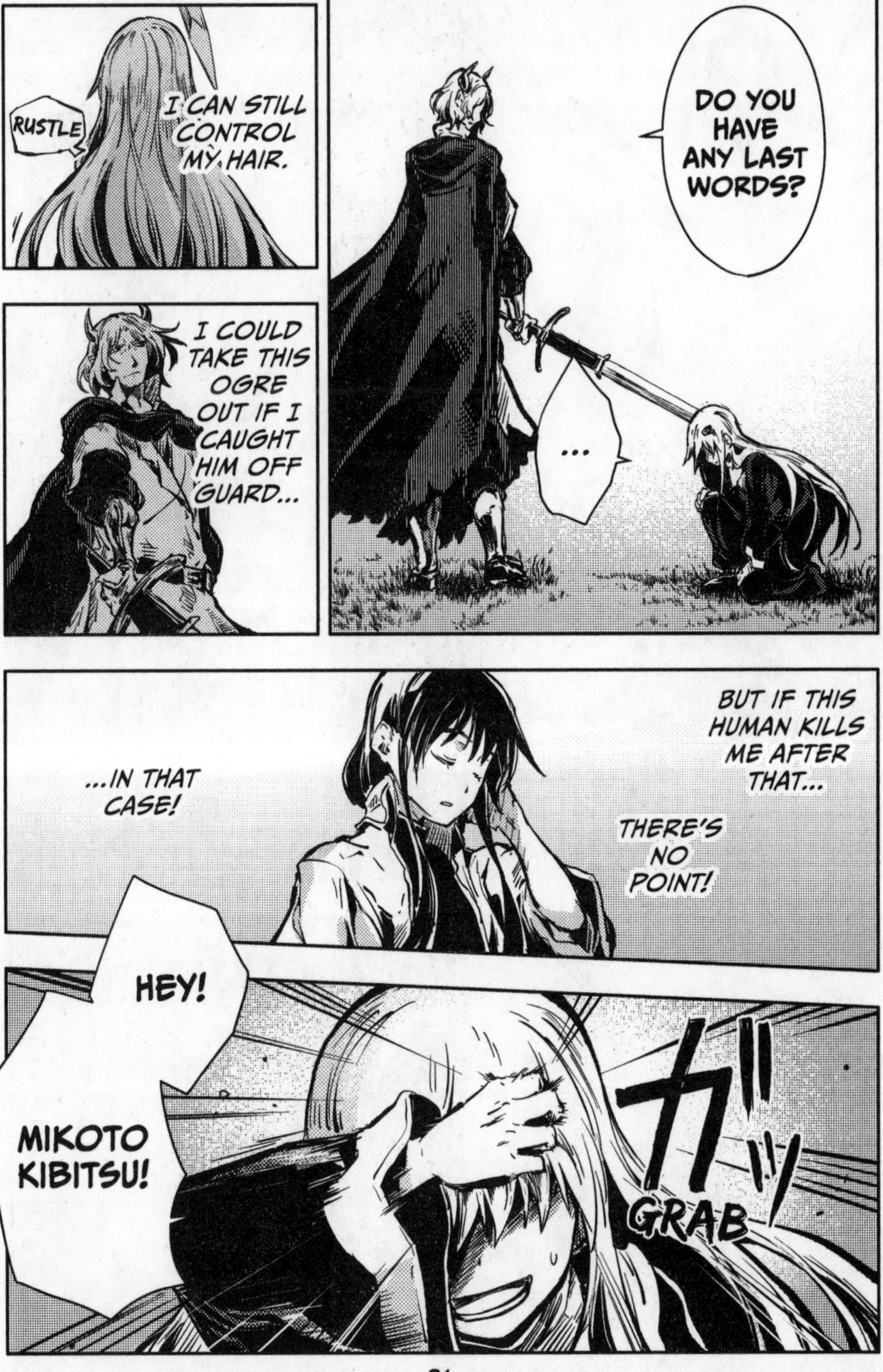
DO YOU HAVE ANY LAST WORDS?
...
RUSTLE
I CAN STILL CONTROL MY HAIR.
I COULD TAKE THIS OGRE OUT IF I CAUGHT HIM OFF GUARD...
BUT IF THIS HUMAN KILLS ME AFTER THAT...
THERE'S NO POINT!
...IN THAT CASE!
HEY!
MIKOTO KIBITSU!
ガッ
GRAB

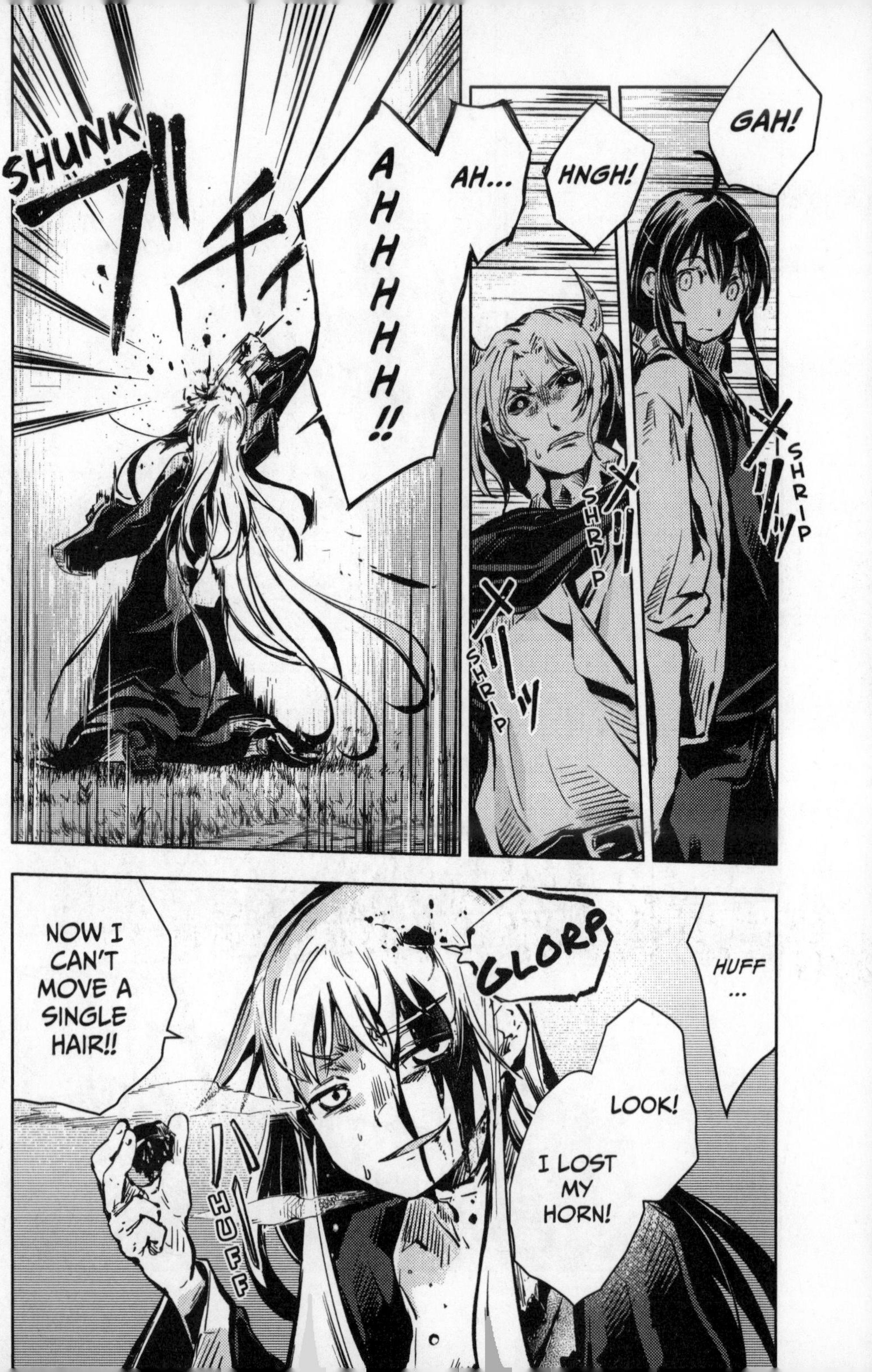
GAH!
HNGH!
SHRIP
SHRIP
SHRIP
AH...
AHHHHHH!!
SHUNK
HUFF ...
GLORP
NOW I CAN'T MOVE A SINGLE HAIR!!
LOOK!
I LOST MY HORN!
HUFF HUFF

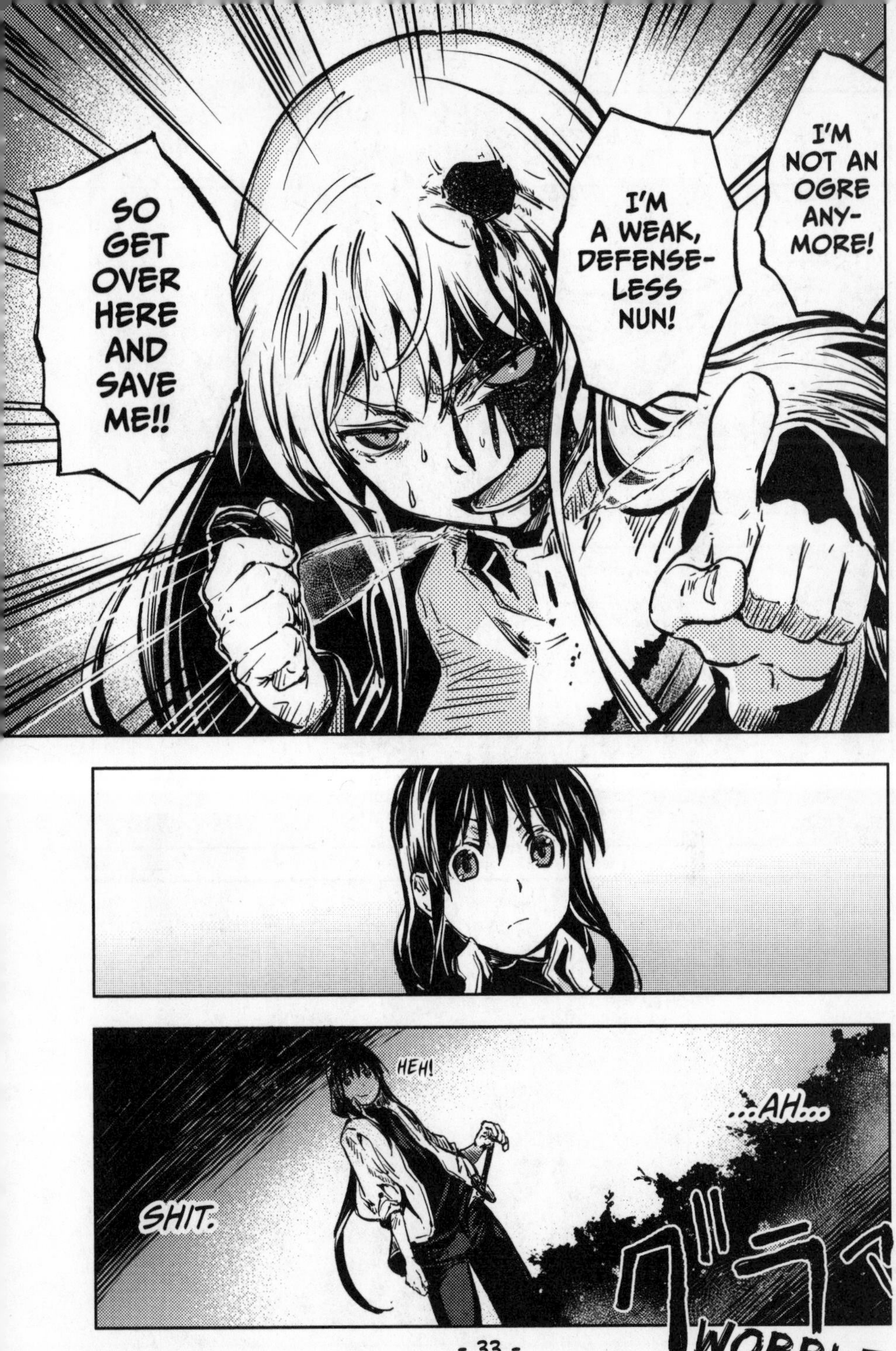
I'M NOT AN OGRE ANY-MORE!
I'M A WEAK, DEFENSE-LESS NUN!
SO GET OVER HERE AND SAVE ME!!
...AH...
HEH!
SHIT.
WOBBLE

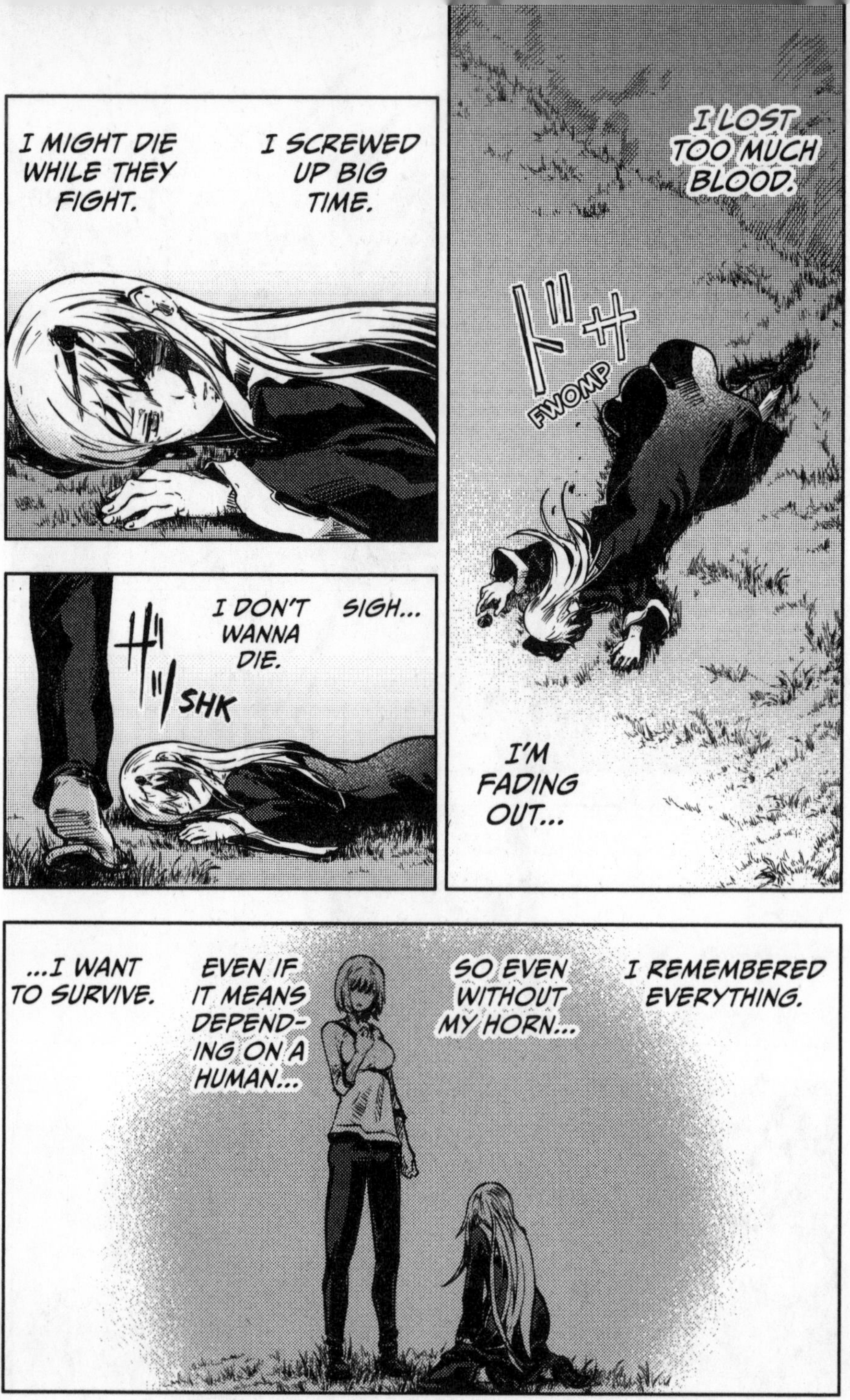
I LOST TOO MUCH BLOOD.
ドサ
FWOMP
I'M FADING OUT...
I SCREWED UP BIG TIME.
I MIGHT DIE WHILE THEY FIGHT.
SIGH...
I DON'T WANNA DIE.
ザッ
SHK
I REMEMBERED EVERYTHING.
SO EVEN WITHOUT MY HORN...
EVEN IF IT MEANS DEPEND-ING ON A HUMAN...
...I WANT TO SURVIVE.

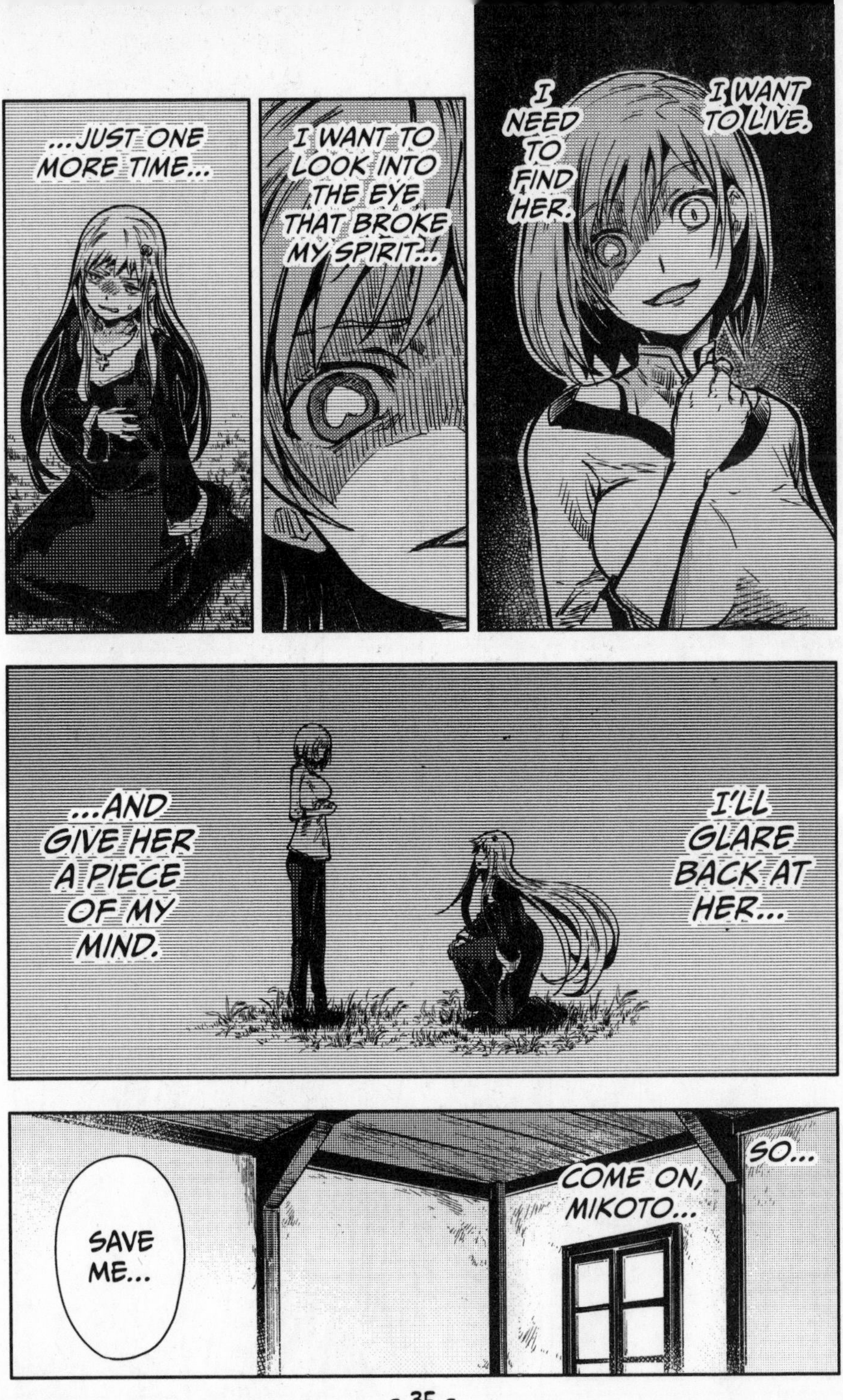
I WANT TO LIVE.
I NEED TO FIND HER.
I WANT TO LOOK INTO THE EYE THAT BROKE MY SPIRIT...
...JUST ONE MORE TIME...
I'LL GLARE BACK AT HER...
...AND GIVE HER A PIECE OF MY MIND.
SO...
COME ON, MIKOTO...
SAVE ME...

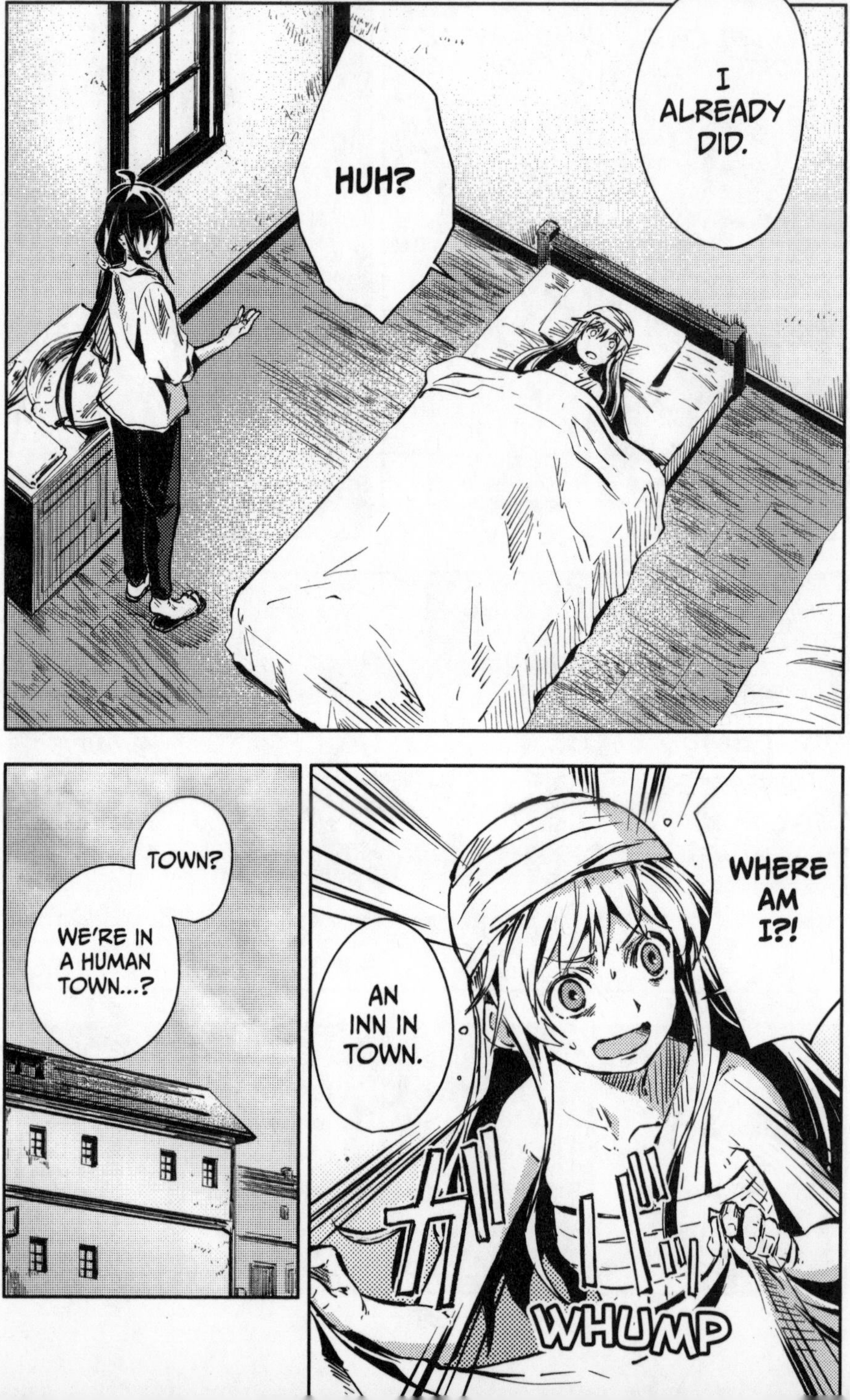
I ALREADY DID.
HUH?
WHERE AM I?!
AN INN IN TOWN.
WHUMP
TOWN?
WE'RE IN A HUMAN TOWN...?

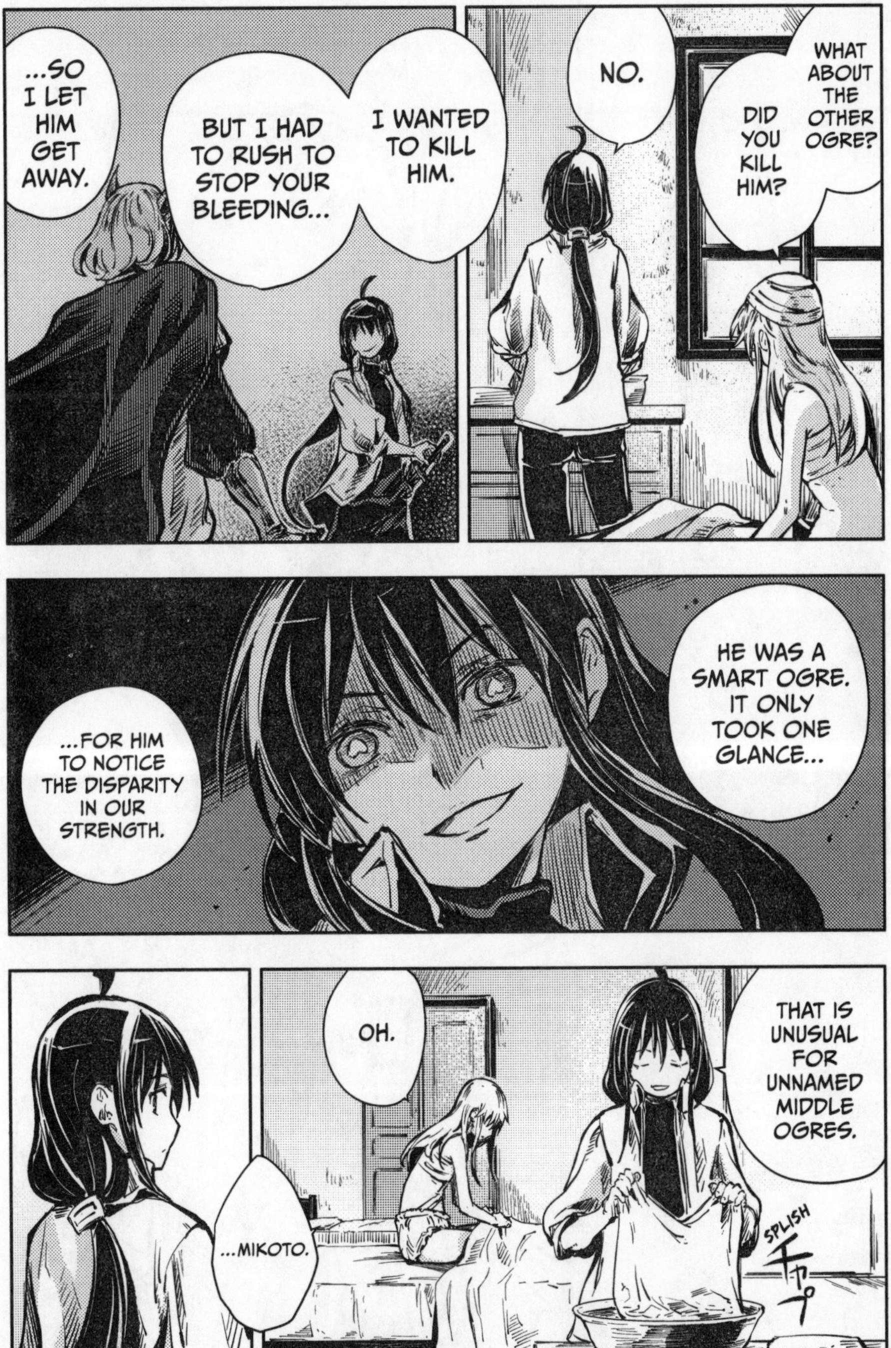
WHAT ABOUT THE OTHER OGRE?
DID YOU KILL HIM?
NO.
I WANTED TO KILL HIM.
BUT I HAD TO RUSH TO STOP YOUR BLEEDING...
...SO I LET HIM GET AWAY.
HE WAS A SMART OGRE. IT ONLY TOOK ONE GLANCE...
...FOR HIM TO NOTICE THE DISPARITY IN OUR STRENGTH.
THAT IS UNUSUAL FOR UNNAMED MIDDLE OGRES.
SPLISH
OH.
...MIKOTO.

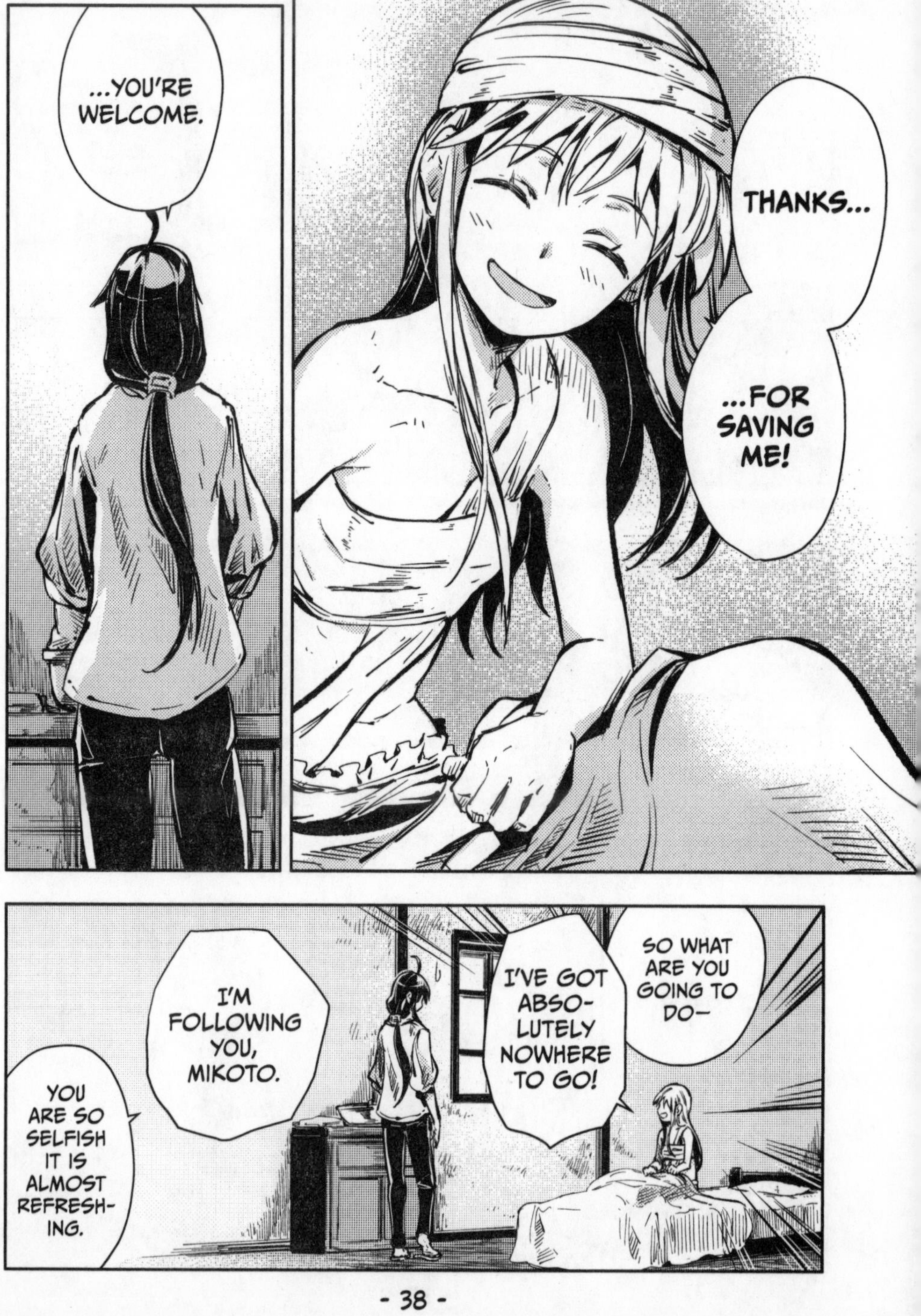
THANKS...
...FOR SAVING ME!
...YOU'RE WELCOME.
SO WHAT ARE YOU GOING TO DO—
I'VE GOT ABSO-LUTELY NOWHERE TO GO!
I'M FOLLOWING YOU, MIKOTO.
YOU ARE SO SELFISH IT IS ALMOST REFRESH-ING.

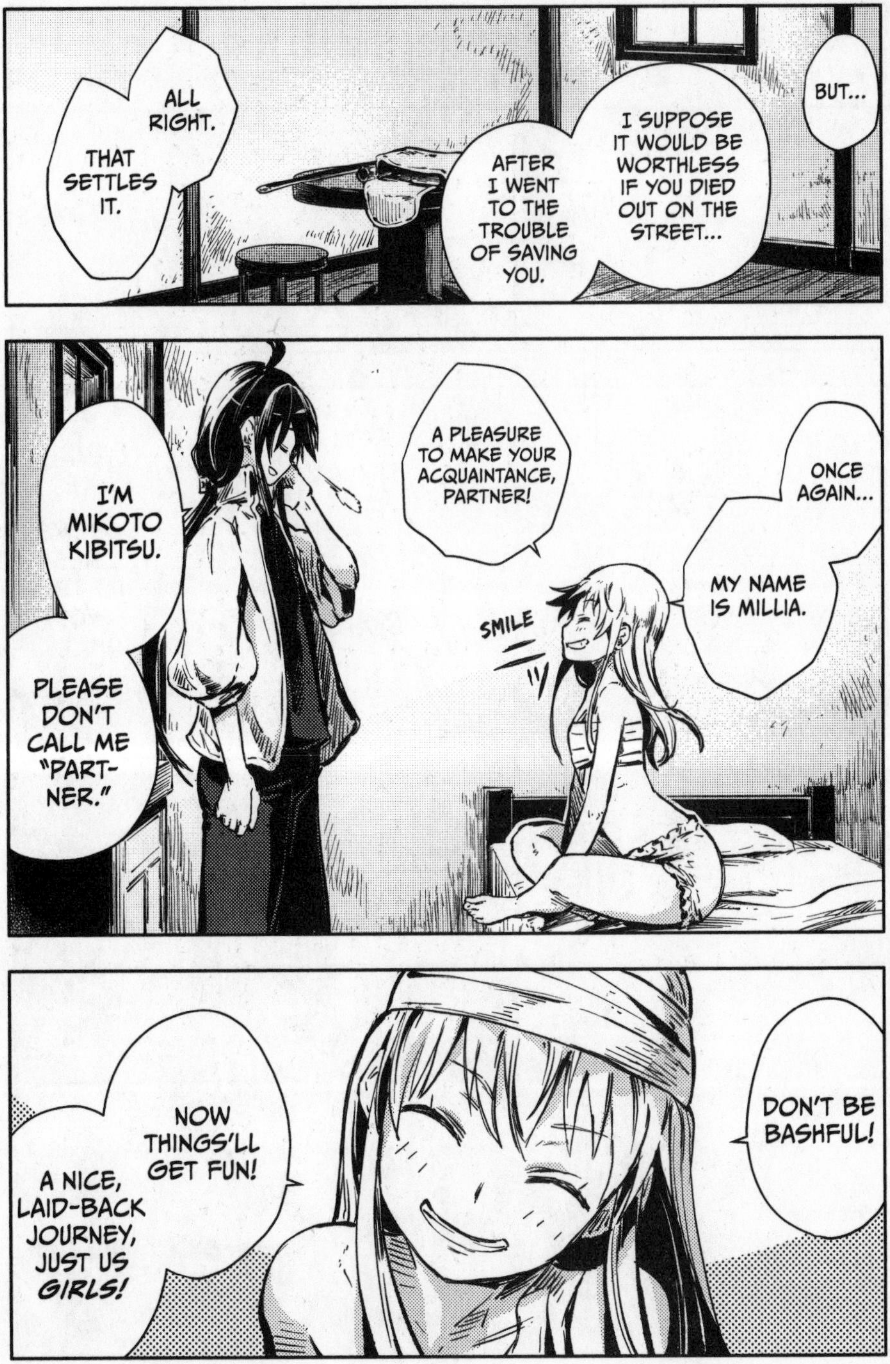
BUT...
I SUPPOSE IT WOULD BE WORTHLESS IF YOU DIED OUT ON THE STREET...
AFTER I WENT TO THE TROUBLE OF SAVING YOU.
ALL RIGHT.
THAT SETTLES IT.
ONCE AGAIN...
MY NAME IS MILLIA.
SMILE
A PLEASURE TO MAKE YOUR ACQUAINTANCE, PARTNER!
I'M MIKOTO KIBITSU.
PLEASE DON'T CALL ME "PARTNER."
DON'T BE BASHFUL!
NOW THINGS'LL GET FUN!
A NICE, LAID-BACK JOURNEY, JUST US *GIRLS!*

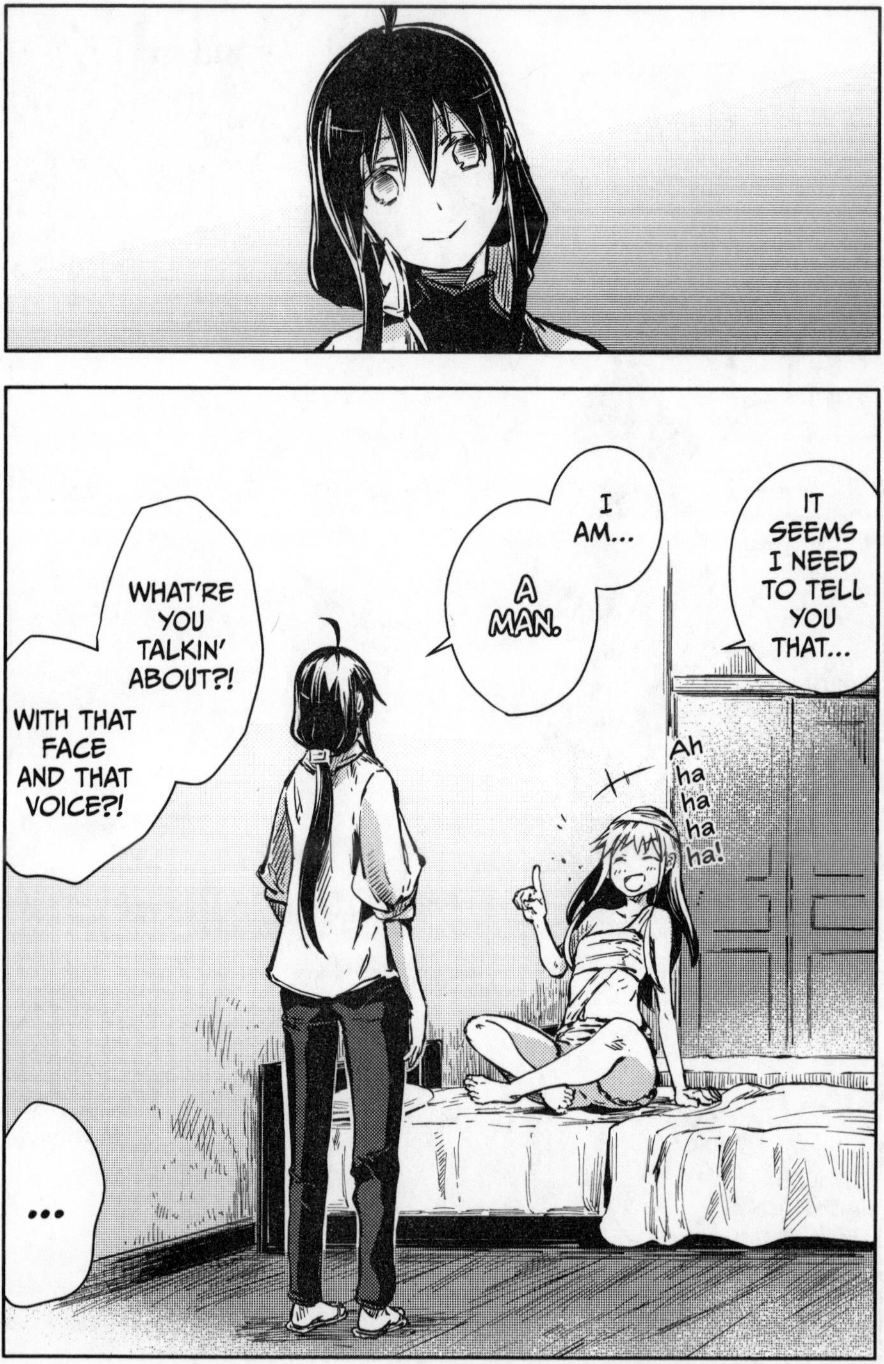
IT SEEMS I NEED TO TELL YOU THAT...
I AM...
A MAN.
Ah ha ha ha ha!
WHAT'RE YOU TALKIN' ABOUT?!
WITH THAT FACE AND THAT VOICE?!
...

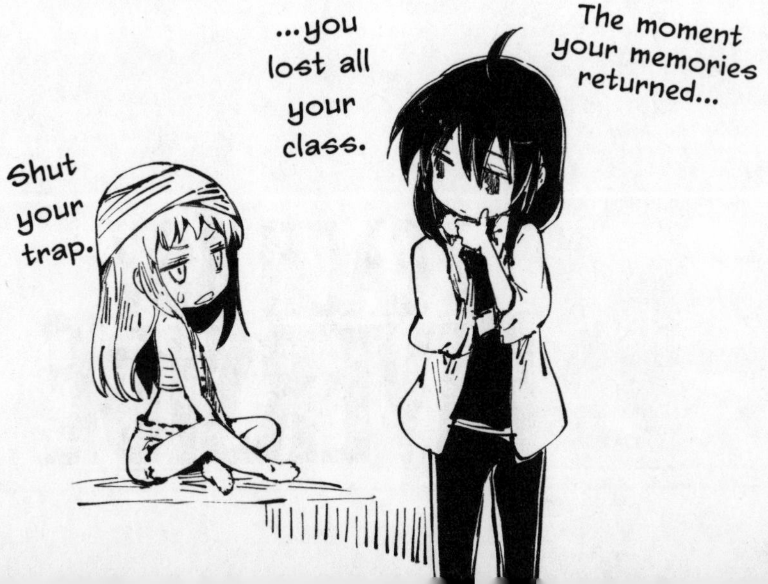
The moment your memories returned...
...you lost all your class.
Shut your trap.

PEACH BOY
RIVERSIDE

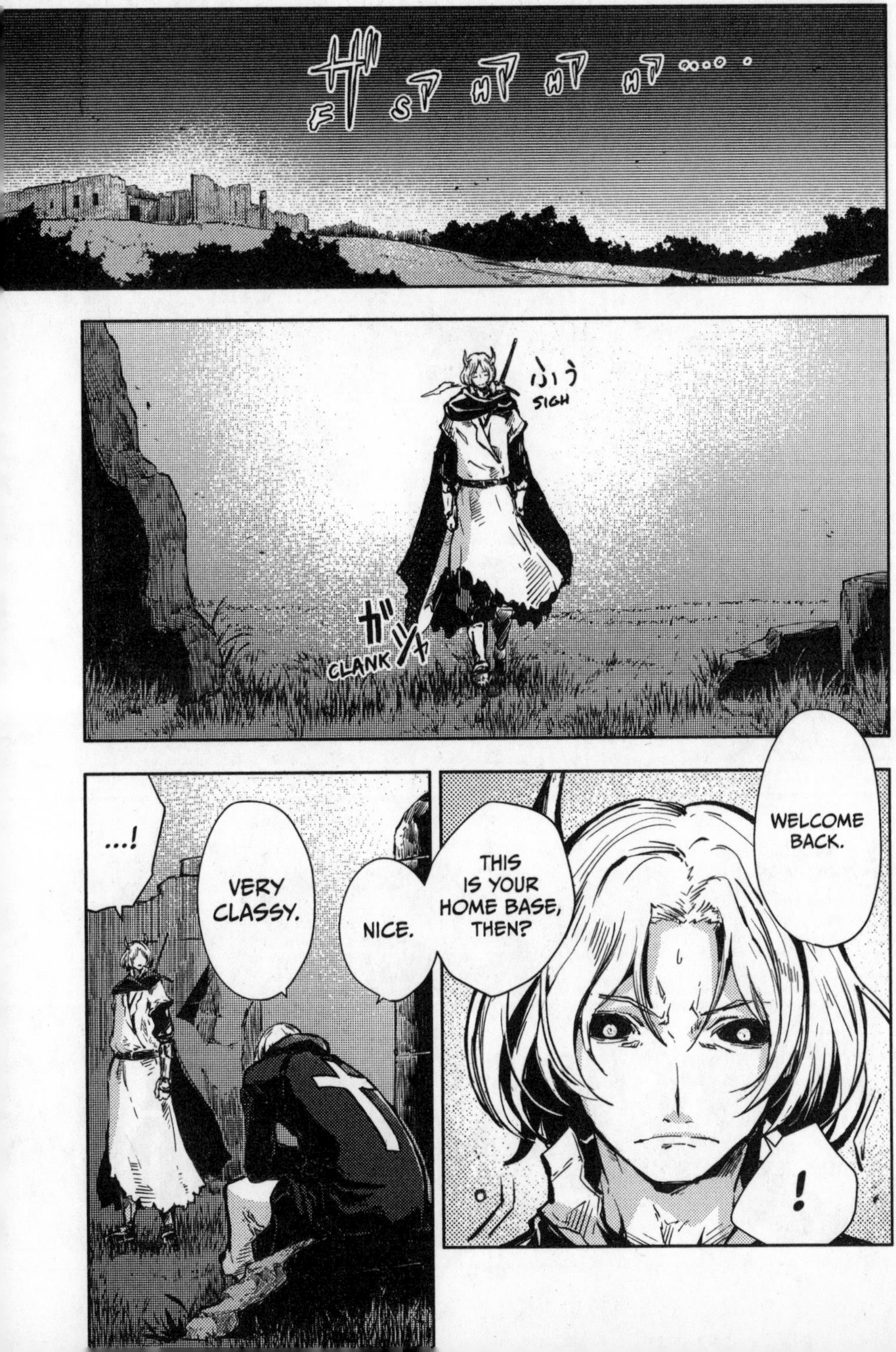
ザァァァァ……
FSHHH
ふぅ
SIGH
ガシャ
CLANK
WELCOME BACK.
!
THIS IS YOUR HOME BASE, THEN?
NICE.
VERY CLASSY.
...!

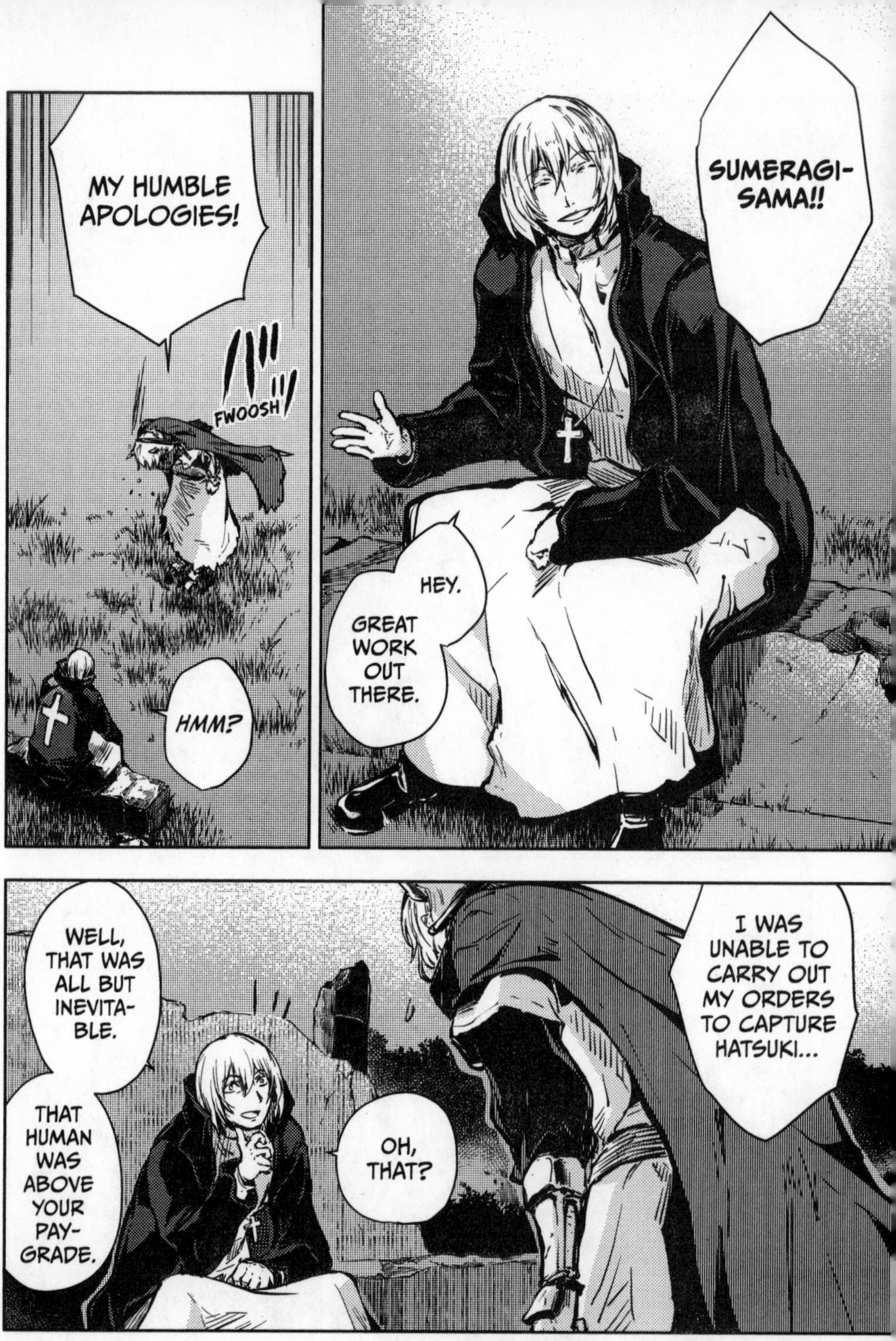
SUMERAGI-SAMA!!
HEY.
GREAT WORK OUT THERE.
MY HUMBLE APOLOGIES!
FWOOSH
HMM?
I WAS UNABLE TO CARRY OUT MY ORDERS TO CAPTURE HATSUKI...
OH, THAT?
WELL, THAT WAS ALL BUT INEVITA-BLE.
THAT HUMAN WAS ABOVE YOUR PAY-GRADE.

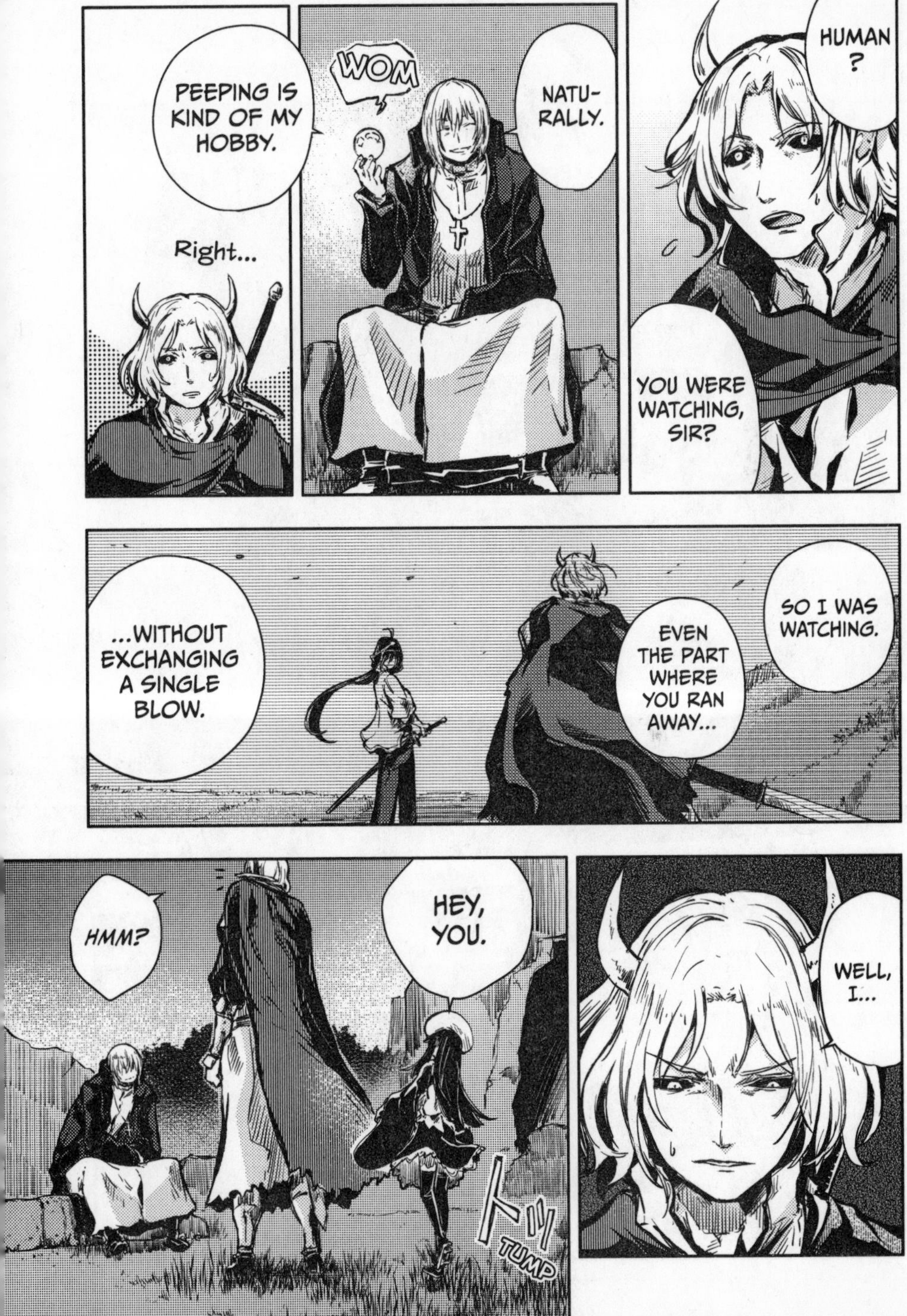
HUMAN?
YOU WERE WATCHING, SIR?
WOM
NATU-RALLY.
PEEPING IS KIND OF MY HOBBY.
Right...
SO I WAS WATCHING.
EVEN THE PART WHERE YOU RAN AWAY...
...WITHOUT EXCHANGING A SINGLE BLOW.
WELL, I...
HEY, YOU.
HMM?
トッ
TUMP

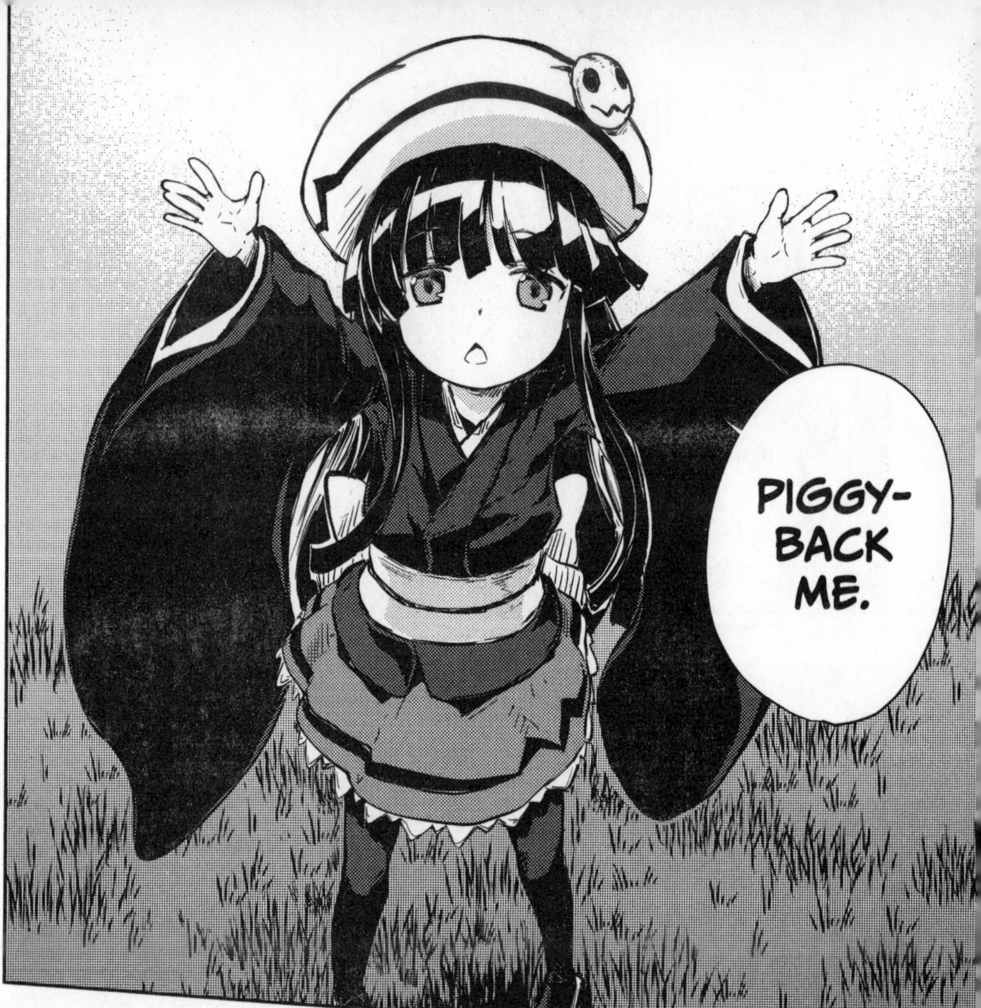
PIGGY-BACK ME.

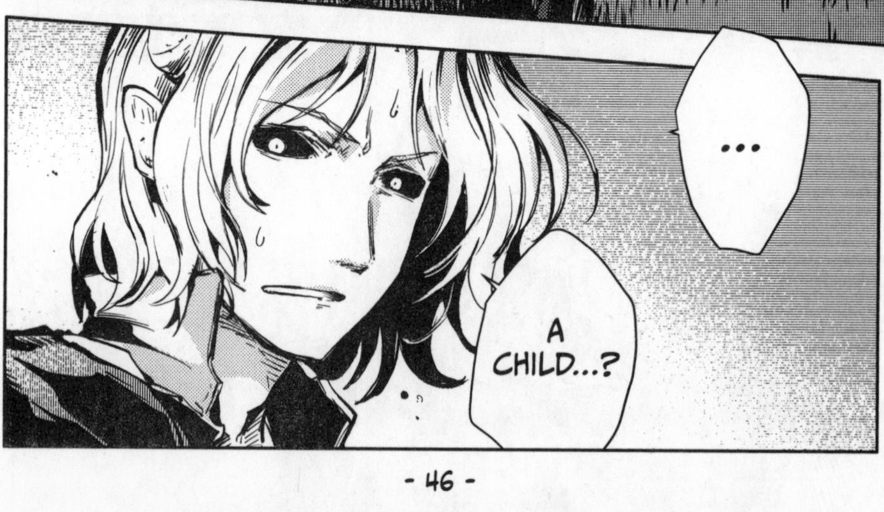
...
A CHILD...?

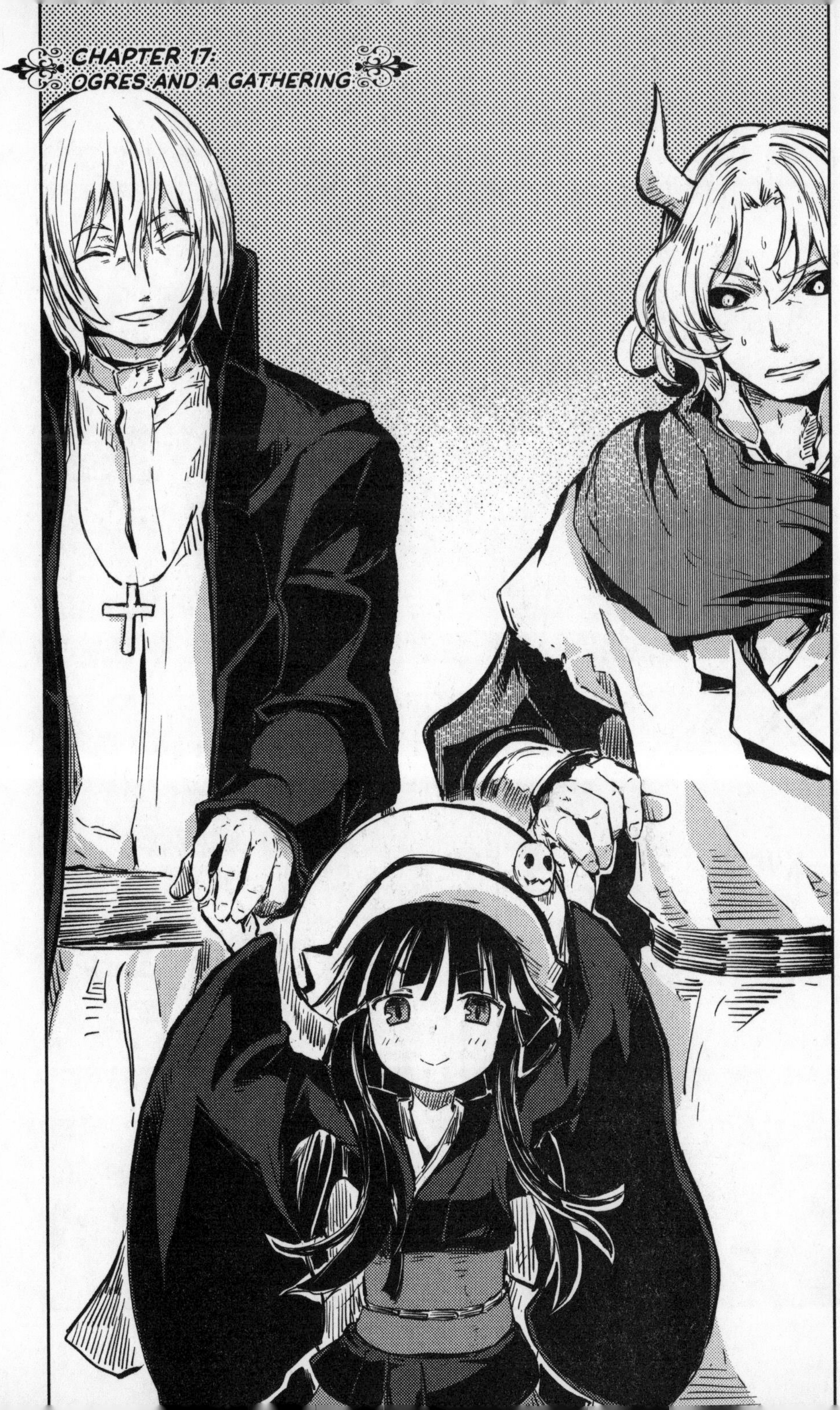
CHAPTER 17:
OGRES AND A GATHERING

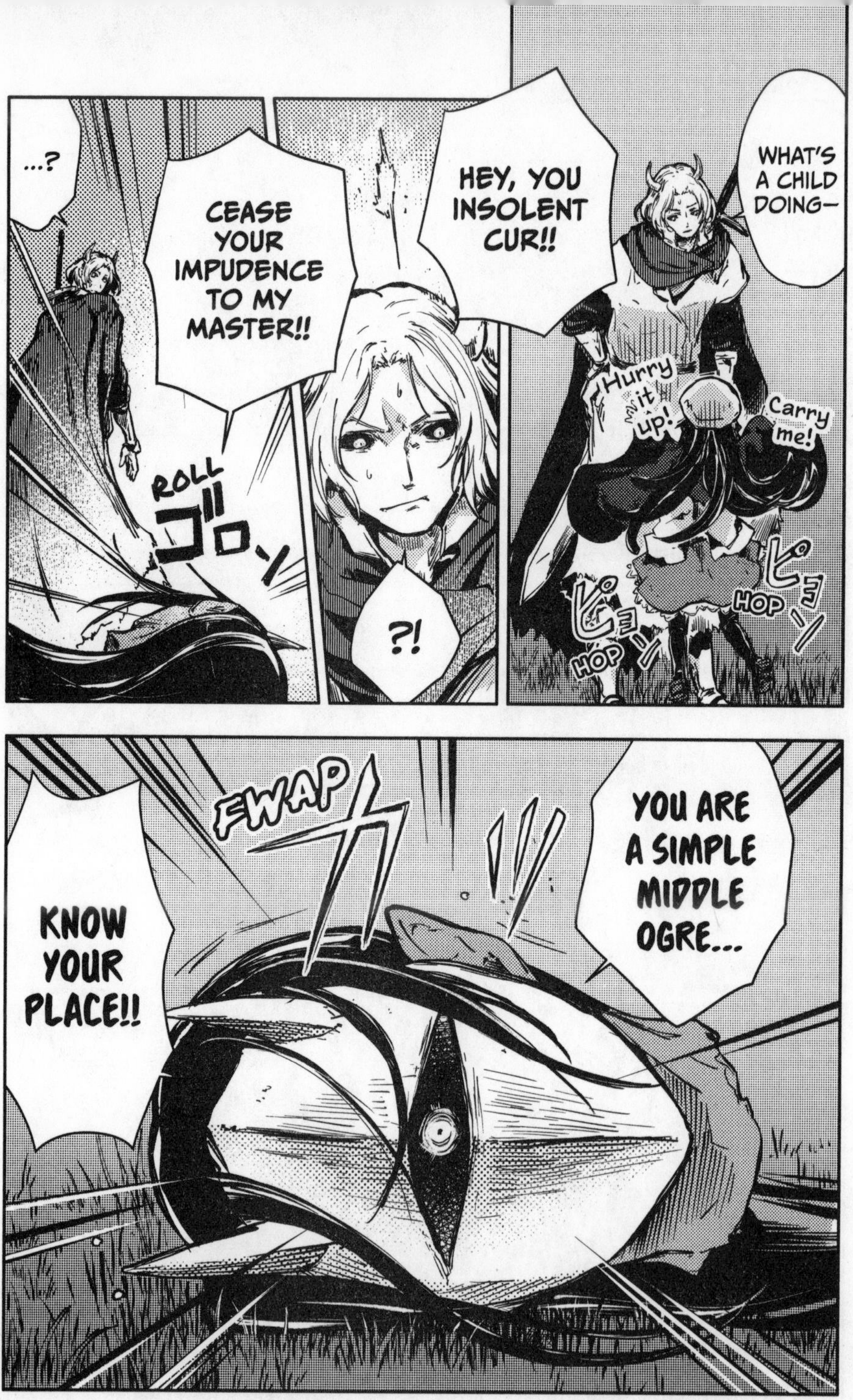
WHAT'S A CHILD DOING—
Carry me!
Hurry it up!
ピョン HOP
ピョン HOP
HEY, YOU INSOLENT CUR!!
?!
CEASE YOUR IMPUDENCE TO MY MASTER!!
...?
ROLL ゴローン
YOU ARE A SIMPLE MIDDLE OGRE...
FWAP ガッ
KNOW YOUR PLACE!!

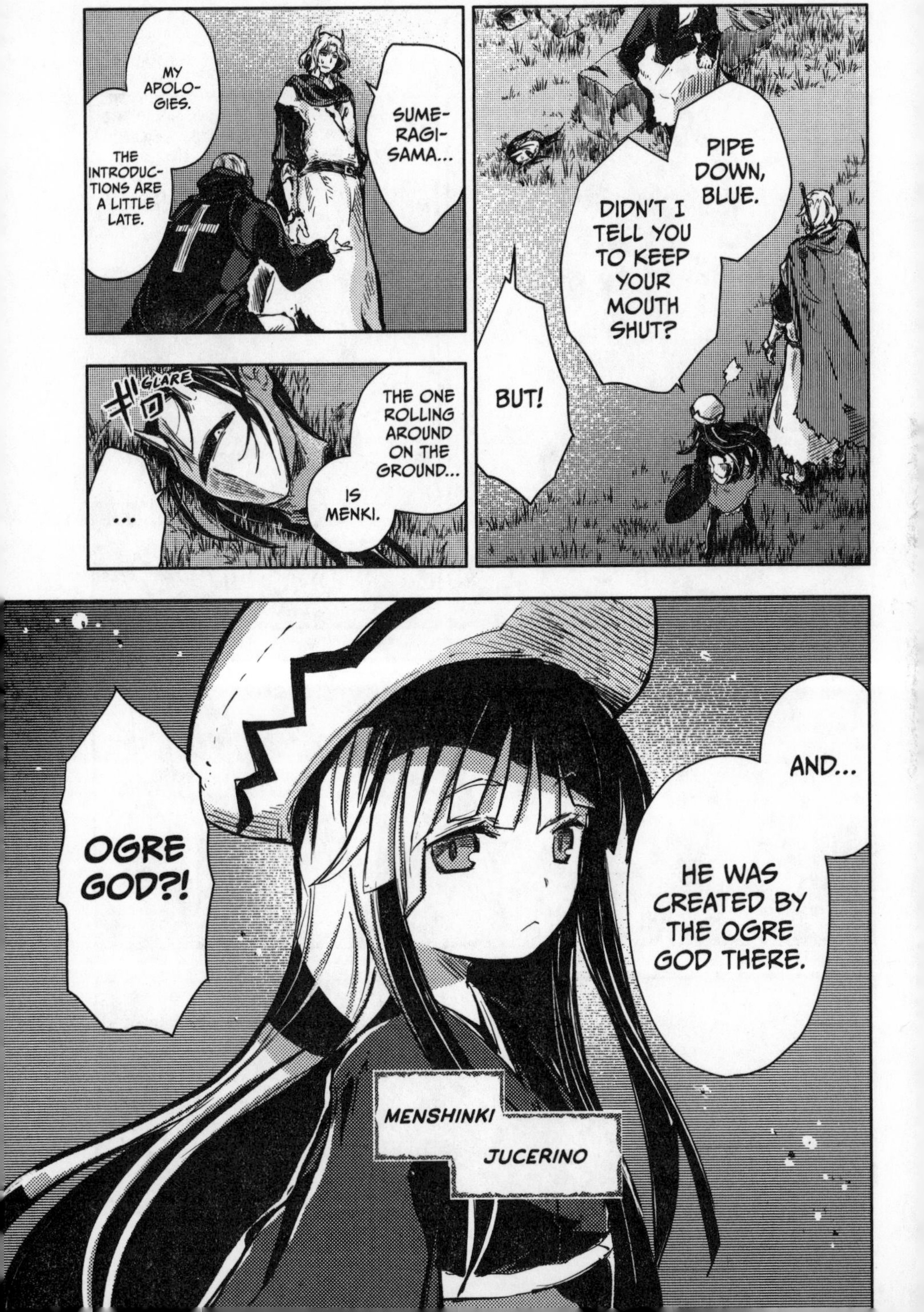
PIPE DOWN, BLUE.
DIDN'T I TELL YOU TO KEEP YOUR MOUTH SHUT?
BUT!
SUME-RAGI-SAMA...
MY APOLO-GIES.
THE INTRODUC-TIONS ARE A LITTLE LATE.
THE ONE ROLLING AROUND ON THE GROUND...
IS MENKI.
GLARE
...
AND...
HE WAS CREATED BY THE OGRE GOD THERE.
OGRE GOD?!
MENSHINKI
JUCERINO

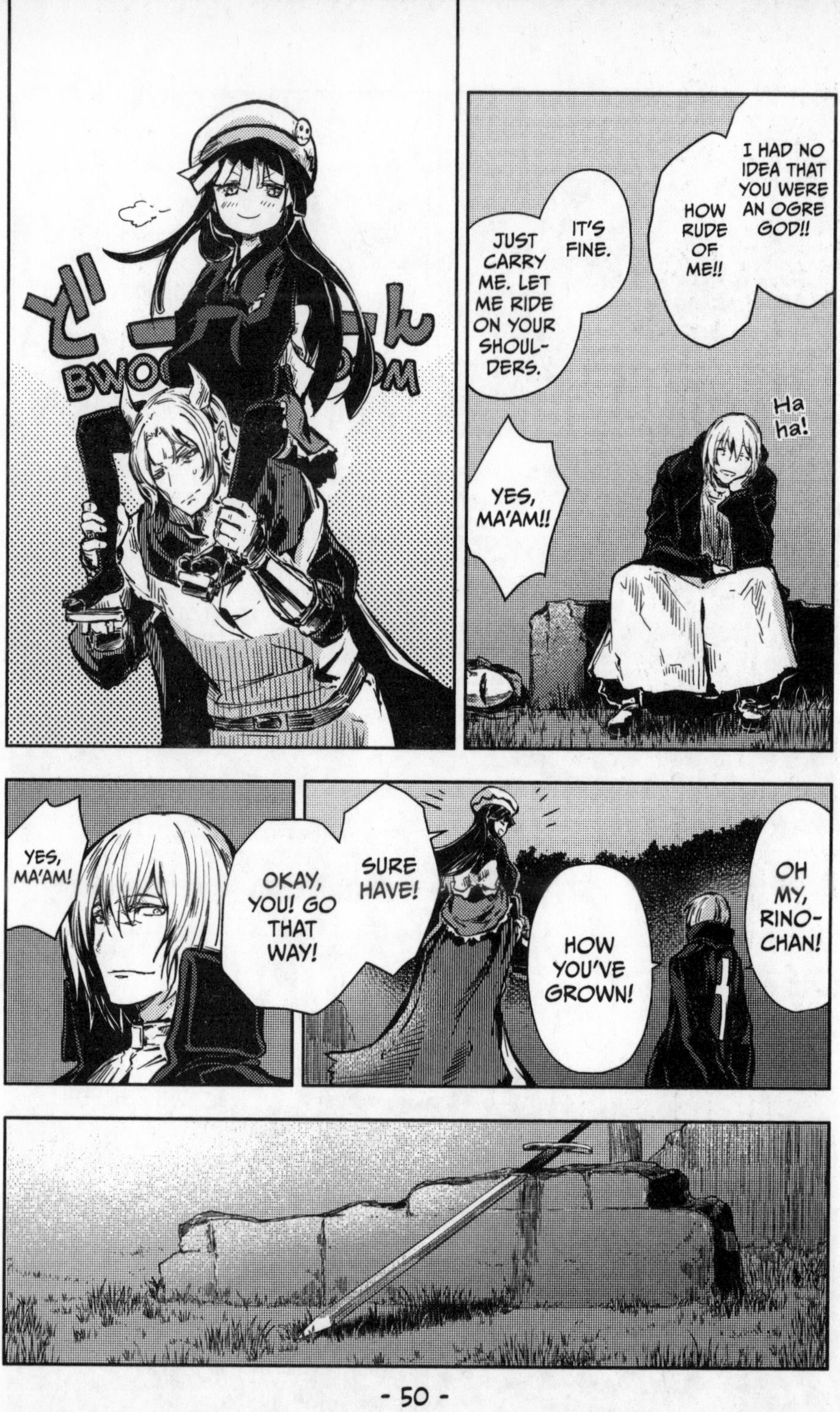
I HAD NO IDEA THAT YOU WERE AN OGRE GOD!! HOW RUDE OF ME!!
IT'S FINE. JUST CARRY ME. LET ME RIDE ON YOUR SHOULDERS.
Ha ha!
YES, MA'AM!!
OH MY, RINO-CHAN!
HOW YOU'VE GROWN!
SURE HAVE!
OKAY, YOU! GO THAT WAY!
YES, MA'AM!

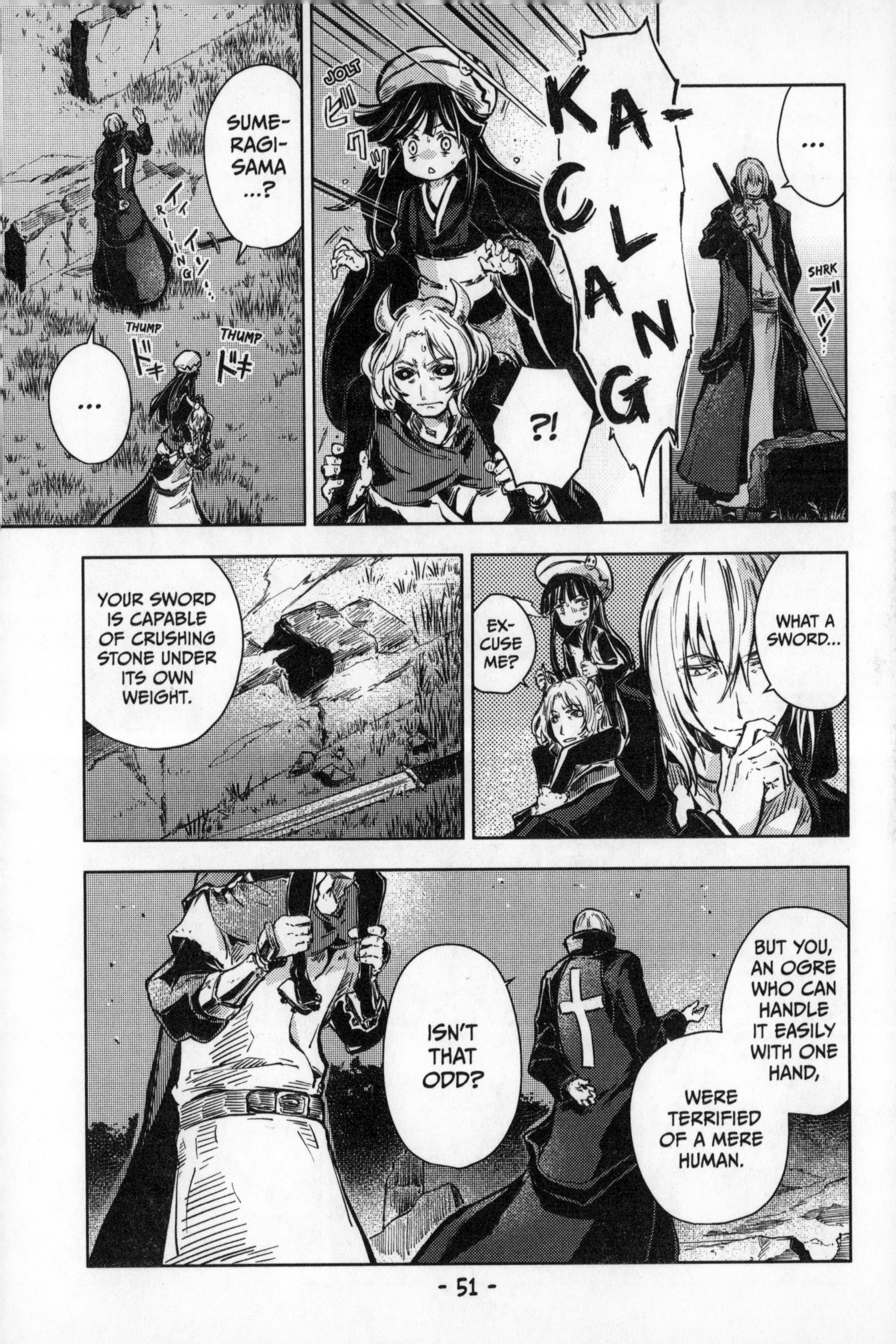
...
SHRK
ズッ…
KA-CLANG
JOLT
ビクッ
?!
SUME-RAGI-SAMA ...?
RIIING
イィィン…
THUMP
ドキ
THUMP
ドキ
...
WHAT A SWORD...
EX-CUSE ME?
YOUR SWORD IS CAPABLE OF CRUSHING STONE UNDER ITS OWN WEIGHT.
BUT YOU, AN OGRE WHO CAN HANDLE IT EASILY WITH ONE HAND,
WERE TERRIFIED OF A MERE HUMAN.
ISN'T THAT ODD?

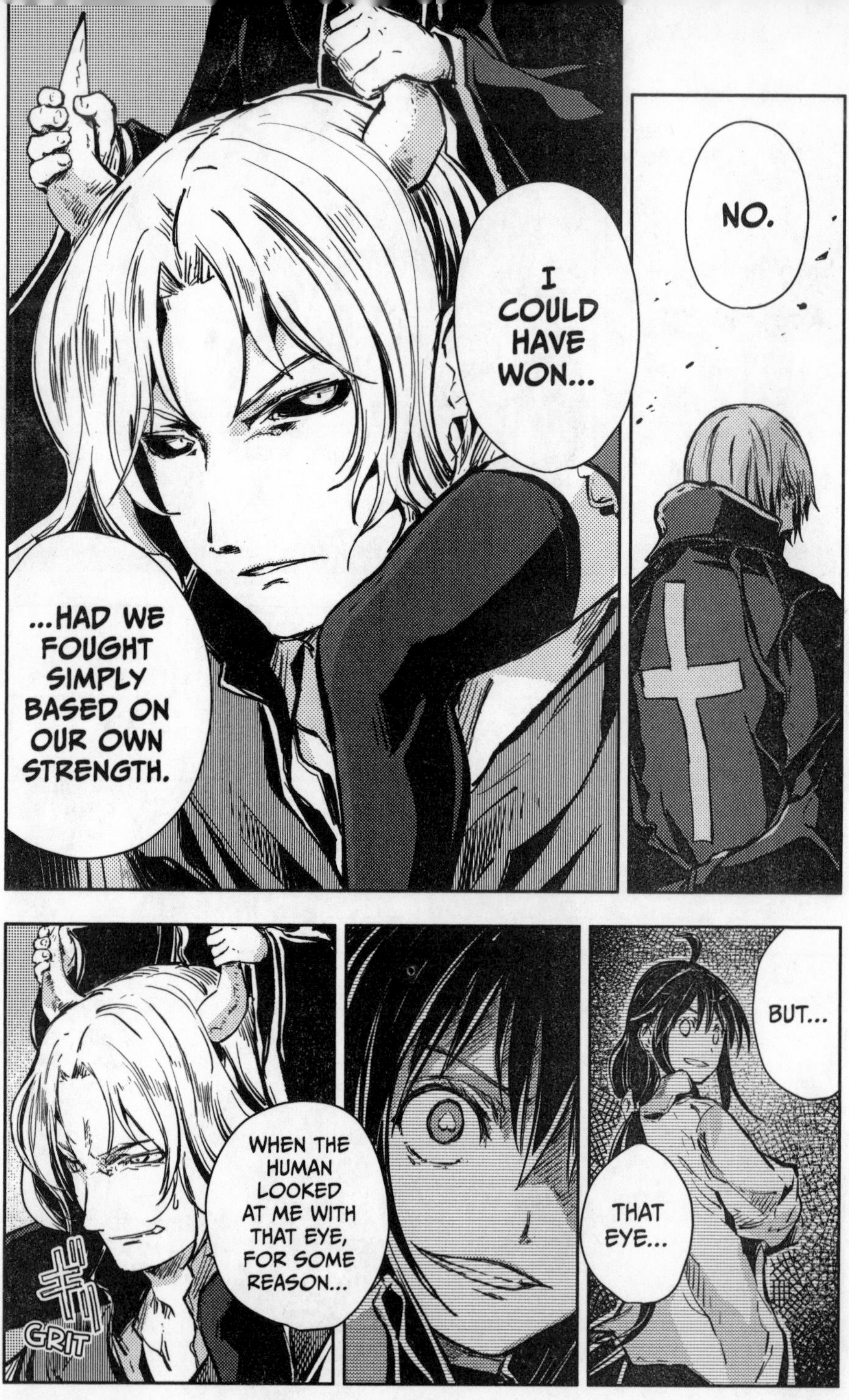
NO.
I COULD HAVE WON...
...HAD WE FOUGHT SIMPLY BASED ON OUR OWN STRENGTH.
BUT...
THAT EYE...
WHEN THE HUMAN LOOKED AT ME WITH THAT EYE, FOR SOME REASON...
ギリ
GRIT

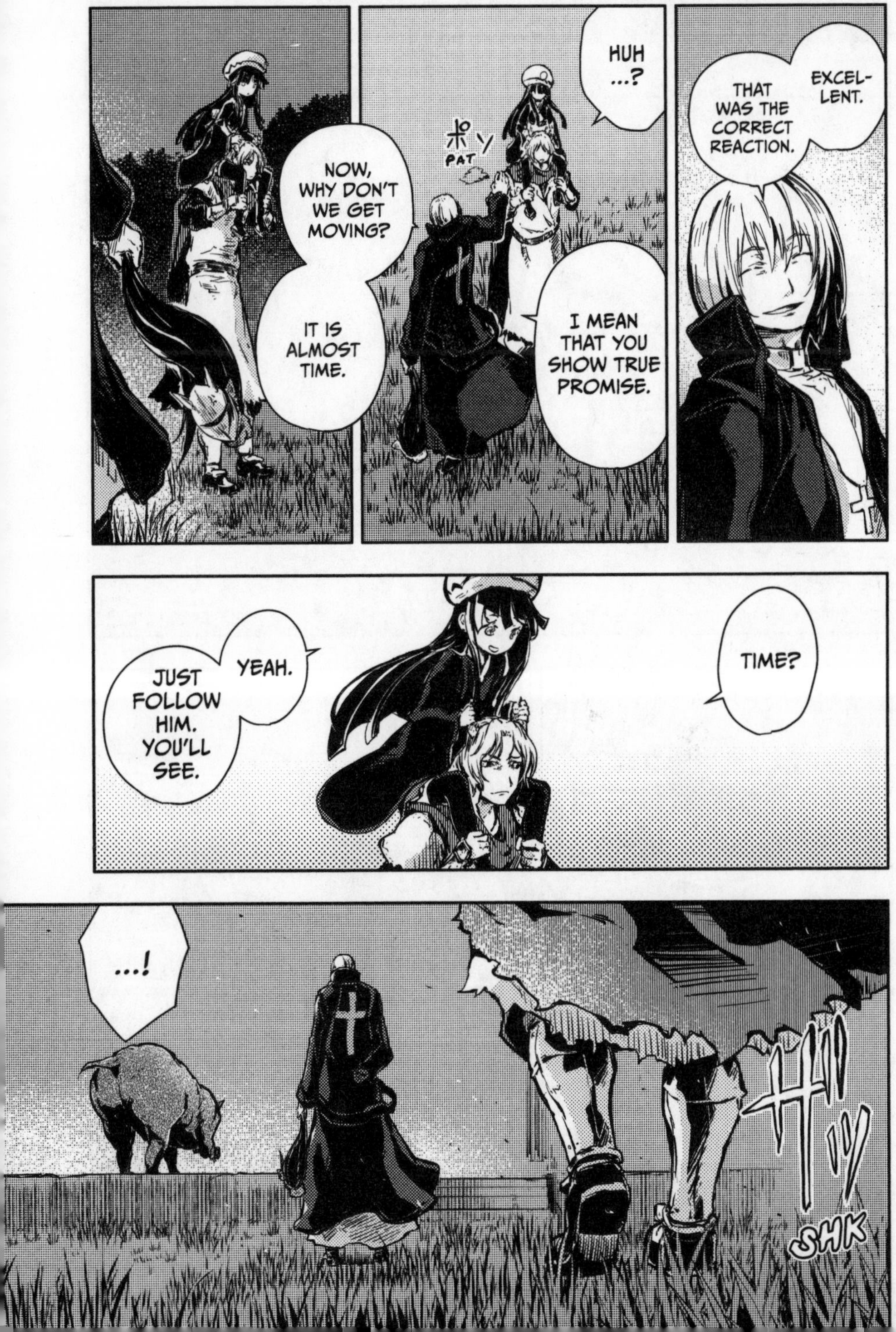
EXCEL-LENT.
THAT WAS THE CORRECT REACTION.
HUH ...?
I MEAN THAT YOU SHOW TRUE PROMISE.
ポン
PAT
NOW, WHY DON'T WE GET MOVING?
IT IS ALMOST TIME.
TIME?
YEAH.
JUST FOLLOW HIM. YOU'LL SEE.
SHK
...!

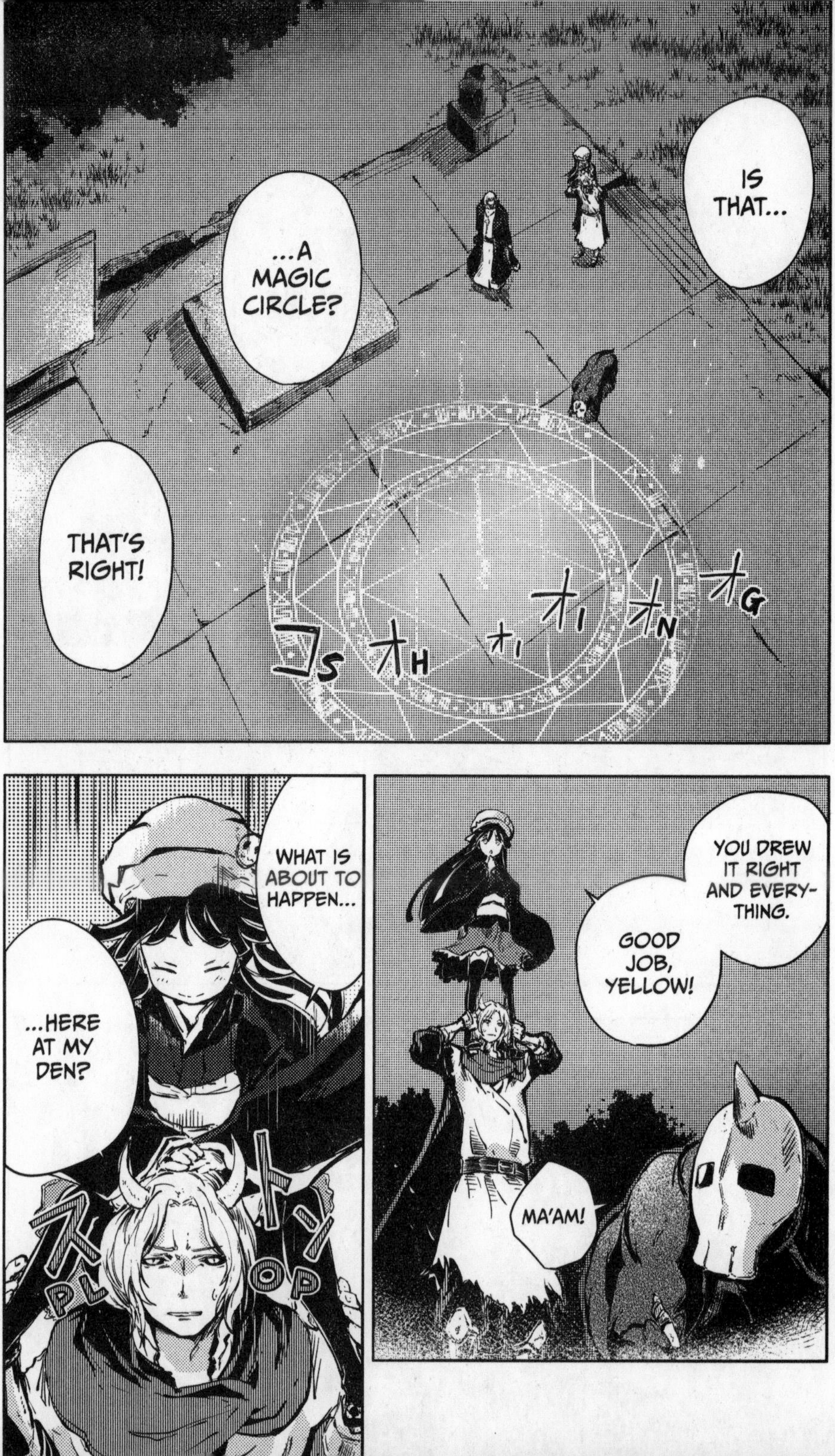

IS THAT...
...A MAGIC CIRCLE?
THAT'S RIGHT!
SHING
YOU DREW IT RIGHT AND EVERY-THING.
GOOD JOB, YELLOW!
MA'AM!
WHAT IS ABOUT TO HAPPEN...
...HERE AT MY DEN?
PLOP

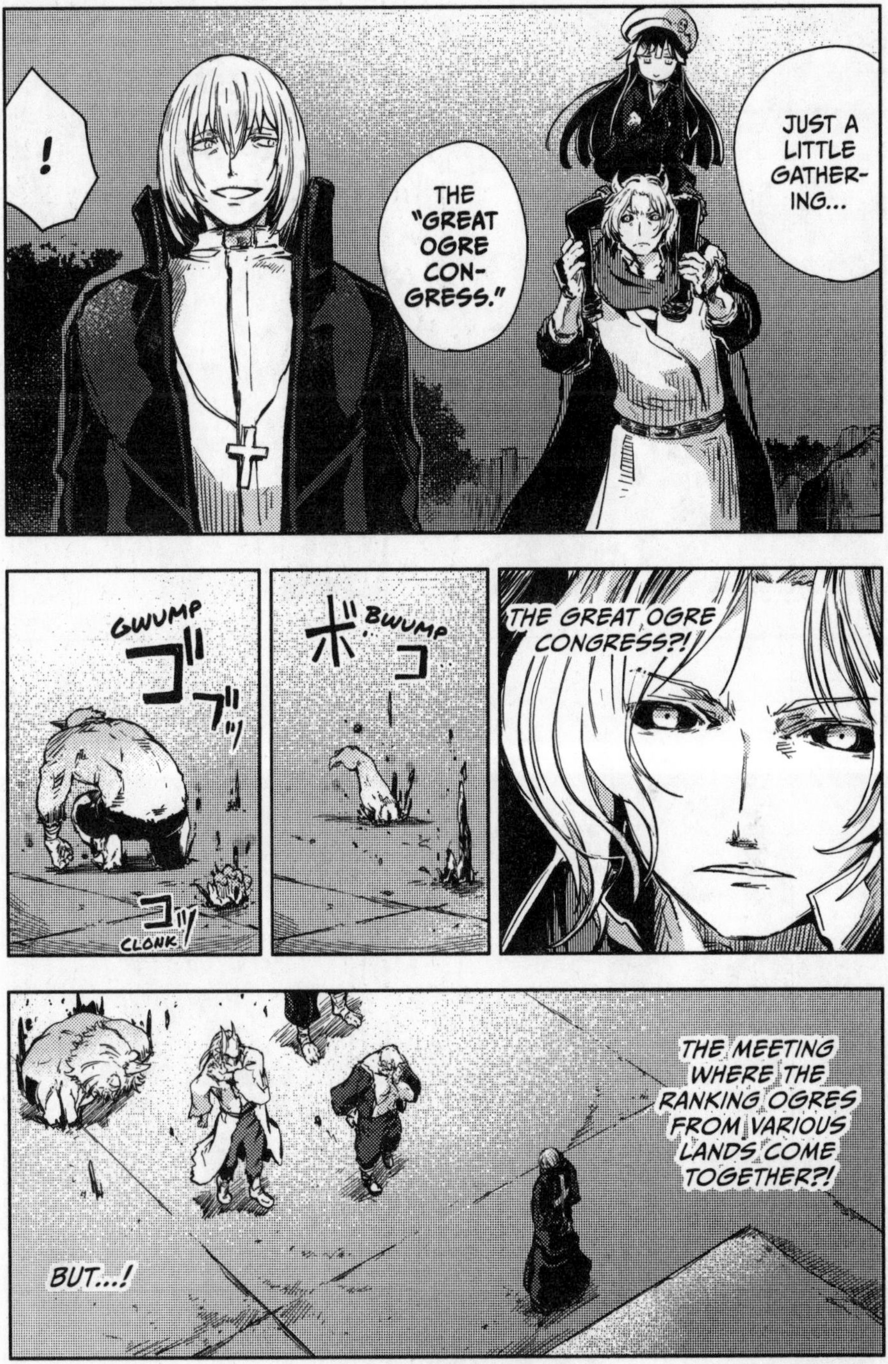
JUST A LITTLE GATHER-ING...
THE "GREAT OGRE CON-GRESS."
!
THE GREAT OGRE CONGRESS?!
ボコ
BWUMP
ゴブッ
GWUMP
ゴッ
CLONK!
THE MEETING WHERE THE RANKING OGRES FROM VARIOUS LANDS COME TOGETHER?!
BUT...!

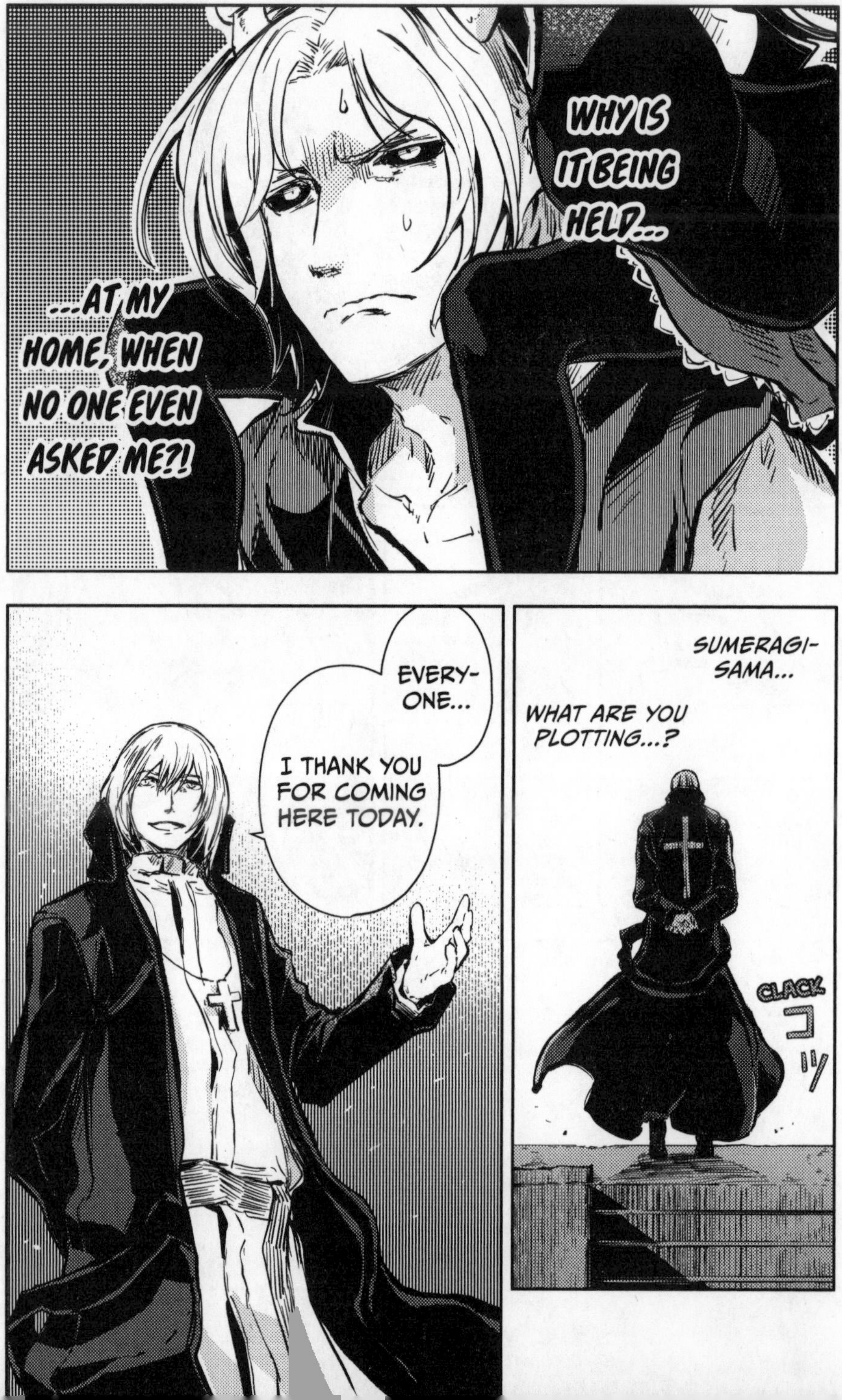
WHY IS IT BEING HELD...
...AT MY HOME, WHEN NO ONE EVEN ASKED ME?!
SUMERAGI-SAMA...
WHAT ARE YOU PLOTTING...?
CLACK
コツ
EVERY-ONE...
I THANK YOU FOR COMING HERE TODAY.

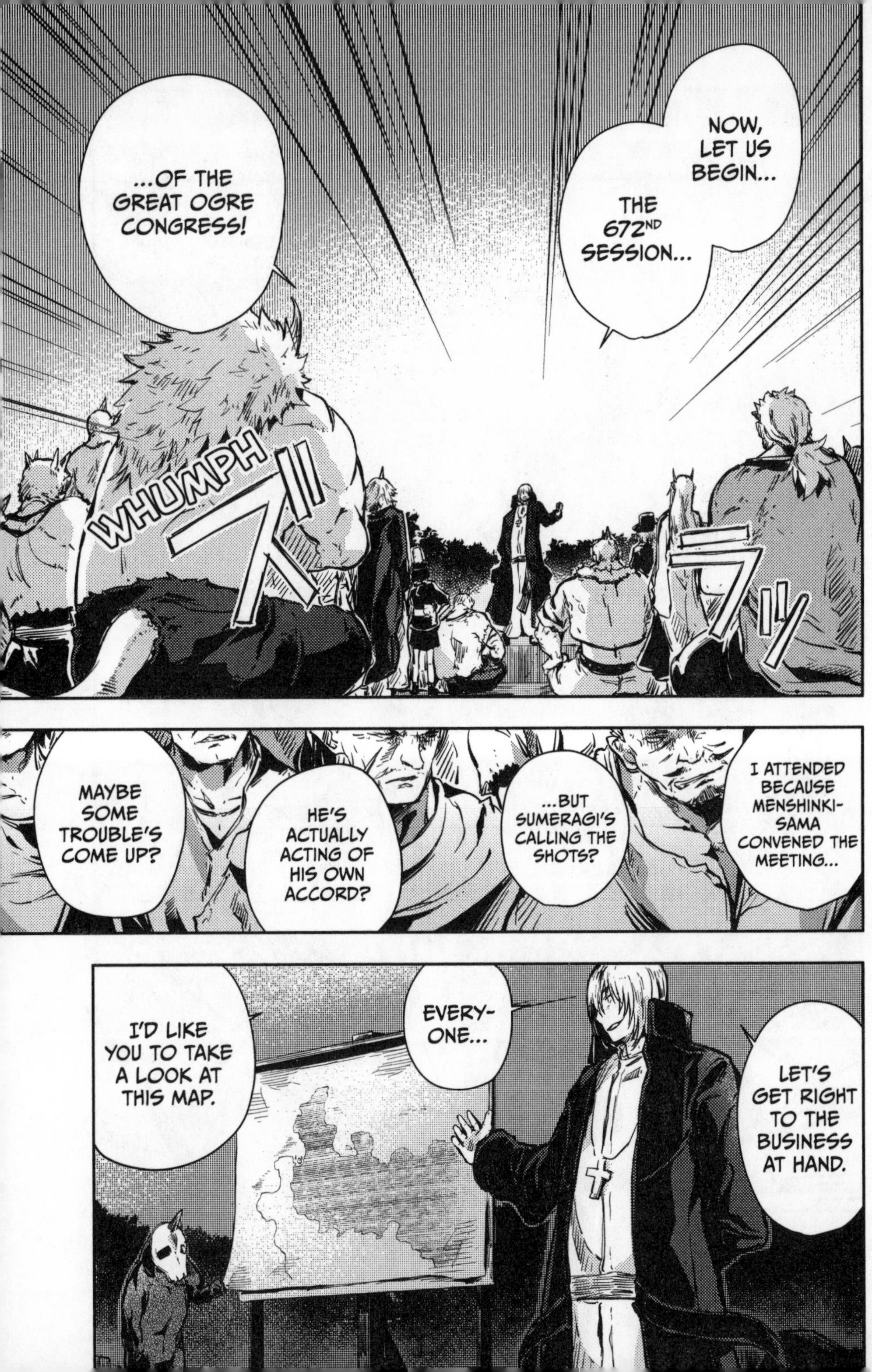
NOW, LET US BEGIN...
THE 672ND SESSION...
...OF THE GREAT OGRE CONGRESS!
ラッ
WHUMPH
I ATTENDED BECAUSE MENSHINKI-SAMA CONVENED THE MEETING...
...BUT SUMERAGI'S CALLING THE SHOTS?
HE'S ACTUALLY ACTING OF HIS OWN ACCORD?
MAYBE SOME TROUBLE'S COME UP?
EVERY-ONE...
LET'S GET RIGHT TO THE BUSINESS AT HAND.
I'D LIKE YOU TO TAKE A LOOK AT THIS MAP.

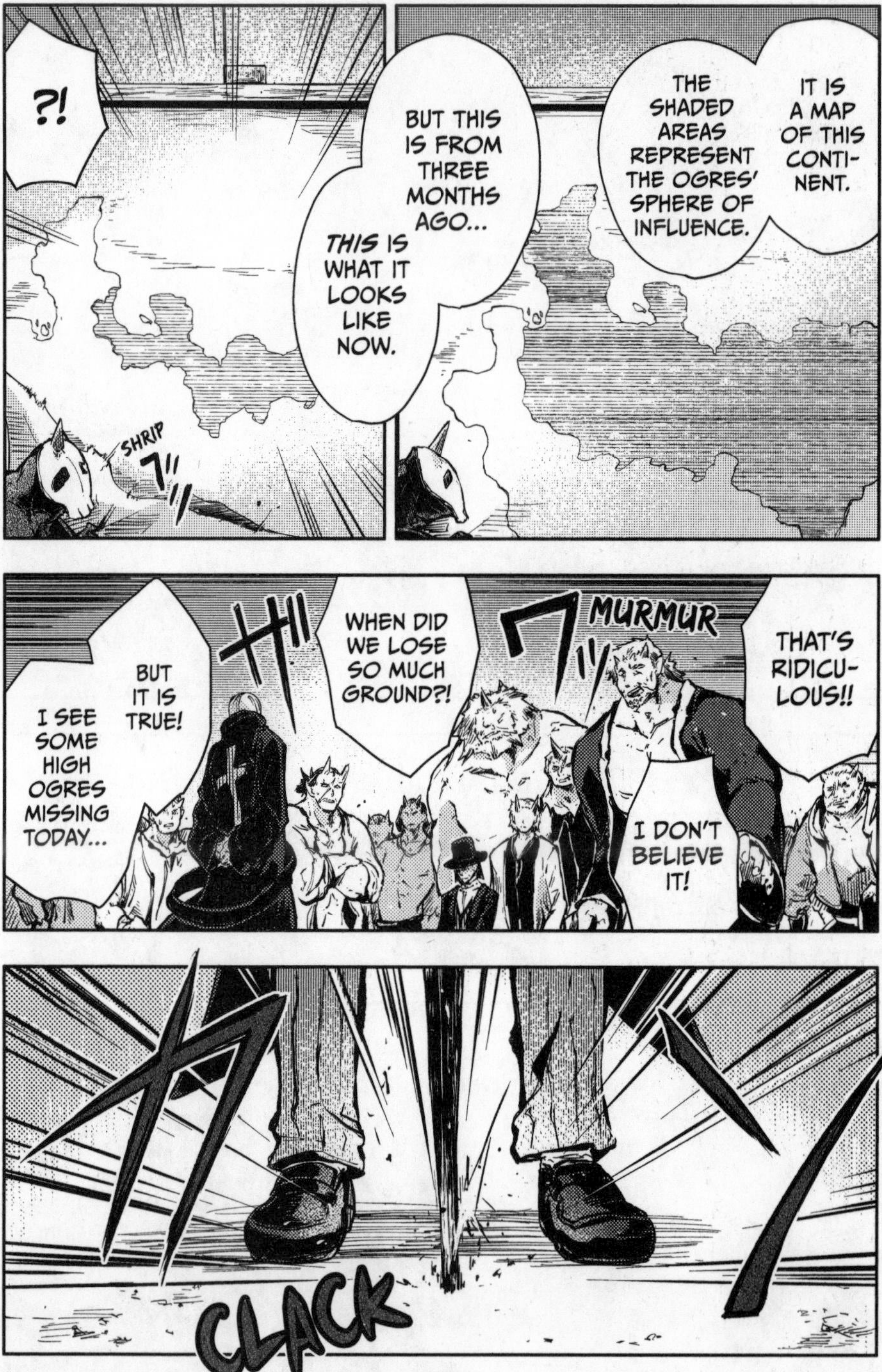
IT IS A MAP OF THIS CONTI-NENT.
THE SHADED AREAS REPRESENT THE OGRES' SPHERE OF INFLUENCE.
BUT THIS IS FROM THREE MONTHS AGO...
THIS IS WHAT IT LOOKS LIKE NOW.
?!
SHRIP
THAT'S RIDICU-LOUS!!
MURMUR
I DON'T BELIEVE IT!
WHEN DID WE LOSE SO MUCH GROUND?!
BUT IT IS TRUE!
I SEE SOME HIGH OGRES MISSING TODAY...
CLACK

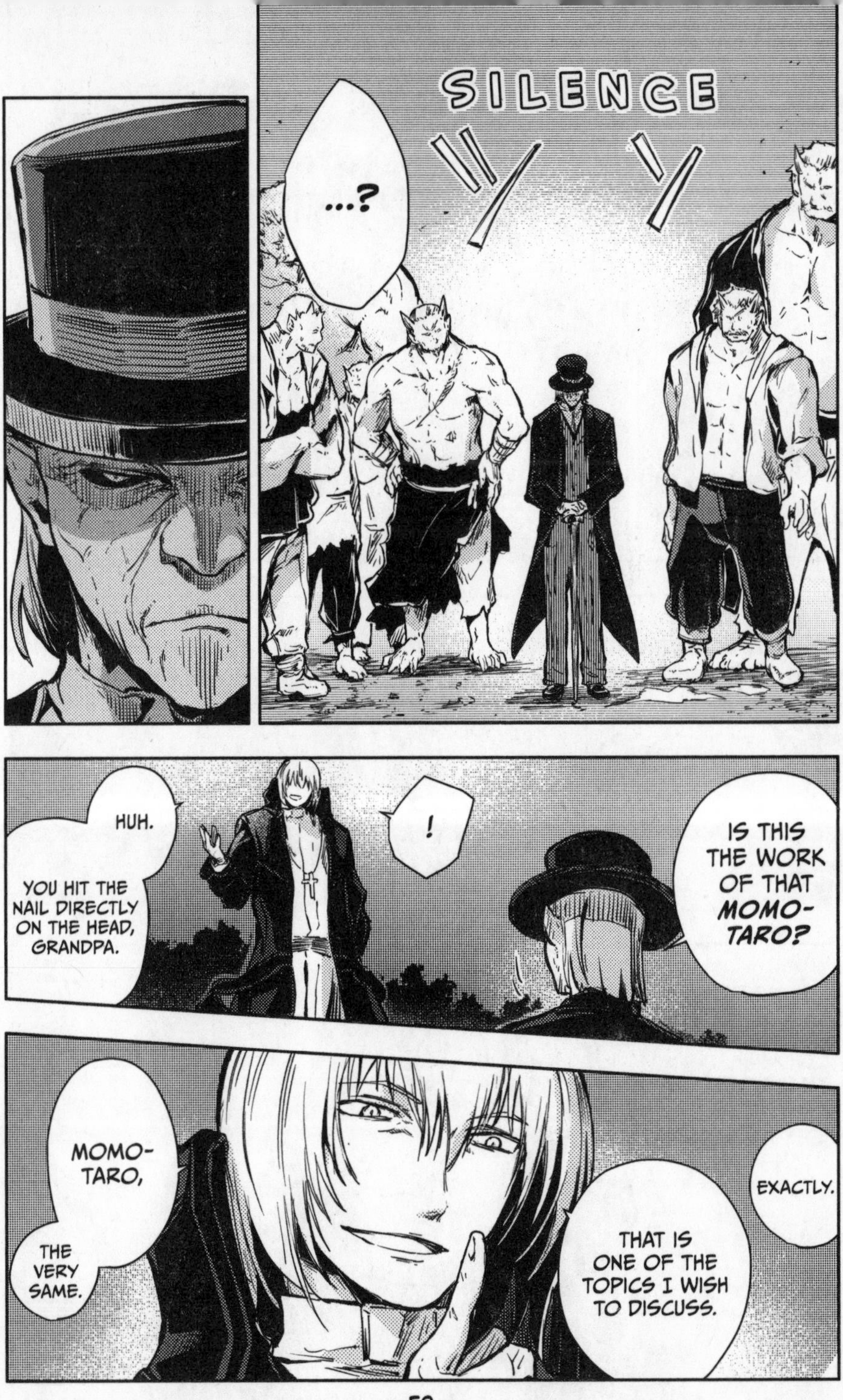
SILENCE
...?
IS THIS THE WORK OF THAT *MOMO-TARO?*
!
HUH.
YOU HIT THE NAIL DIRECTLY ON THE HEAD, GRANDPA.
EXACTLY.
THAT IS ONE OF THE TOPICS I WISH TO DISCUSS.
MOMO-TARO,
THE VERY SAME.

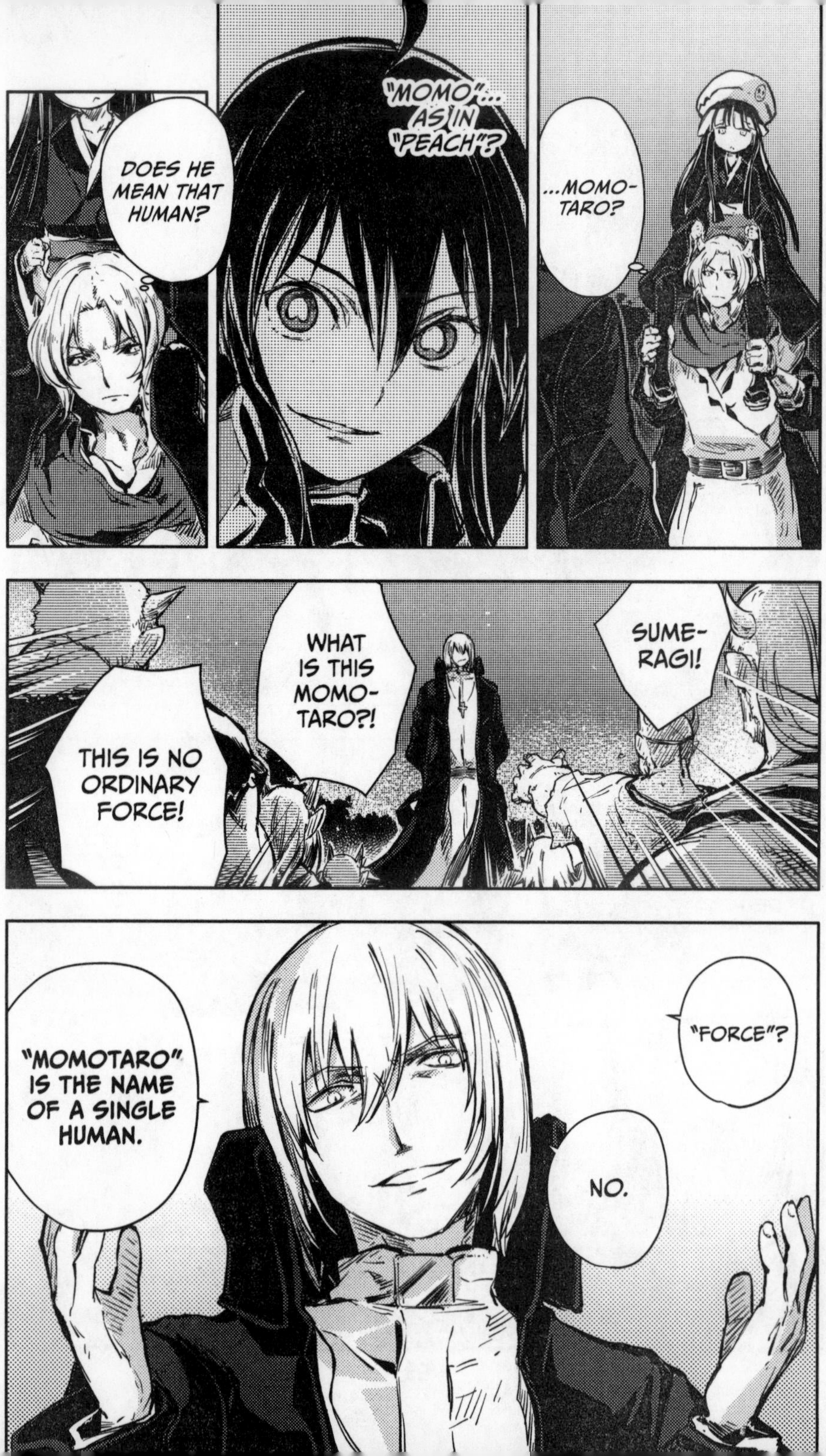
...MOMO-TARO?
"MOMO"... AS IN "PEACH"?
DOES HE MEAN THAT HUMAN?
SUME-RAGI!
WHAT IS THIS MOMO-TARO?!
THIS IS NO ORDINARY FORCE!
"FORCE"?
NO.
"MOMOTARO" IS THE NAME OF A SINGLE HUMAN.

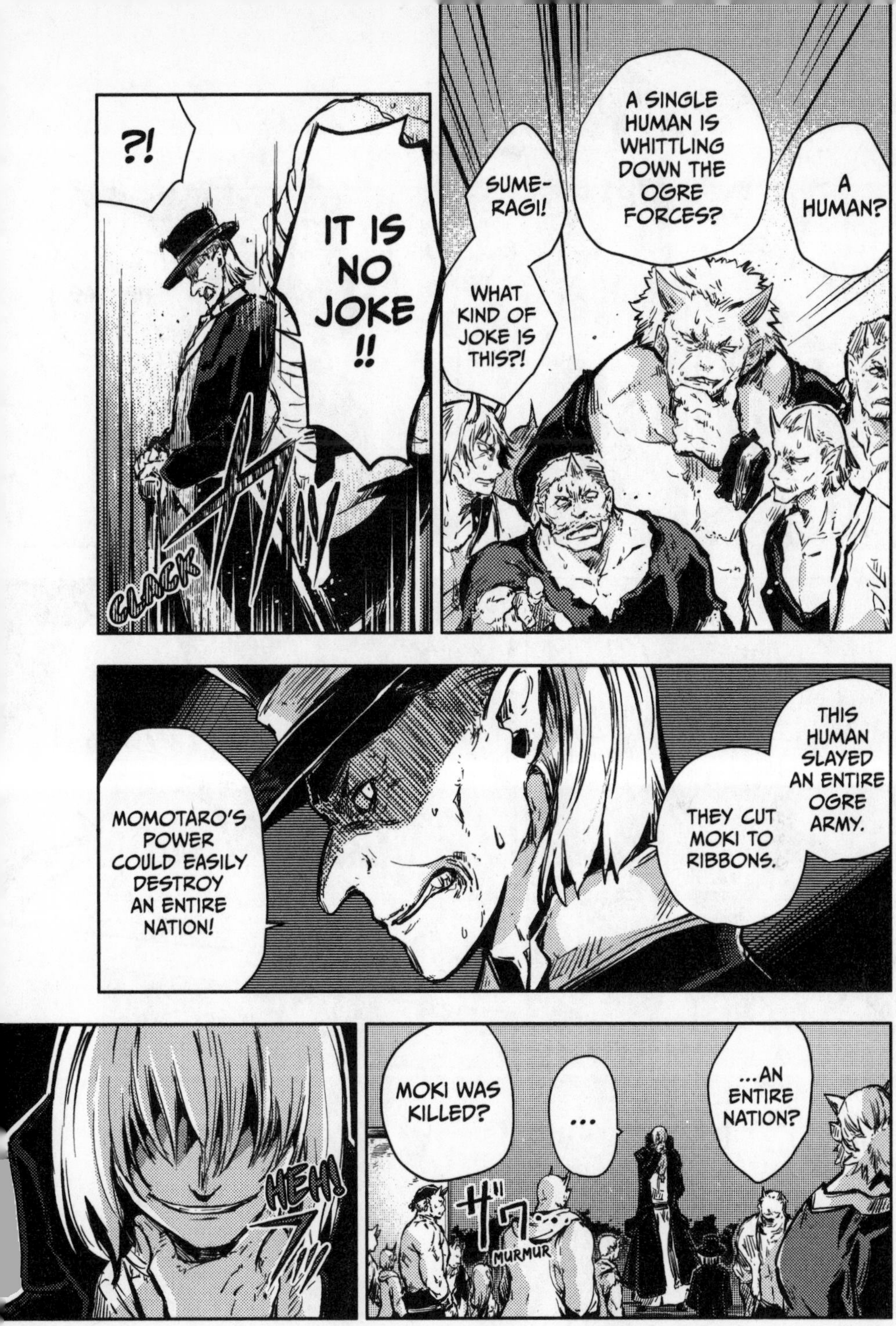
A HUMAN?
A SINGLE HUMAN IS WHITTLING DOWN THE OGRE FORCES?
SUME-RAGI!
WHAT KIND OF JOKE IS THIS?!
IT IS NO JOKE!!
?!
CLACK
THIS HUMAN SLAYED AN ENTIRE OGRE ARMY.
THEY CUT MOKI TO RIBBONS.
MOMOTARO'S POWER COULD EASILY DESTROY AN ENTIRE NATION!
...AN ENTIRE NATION?
...
MOKI WAS KILLED?
MURMUR
HEH!

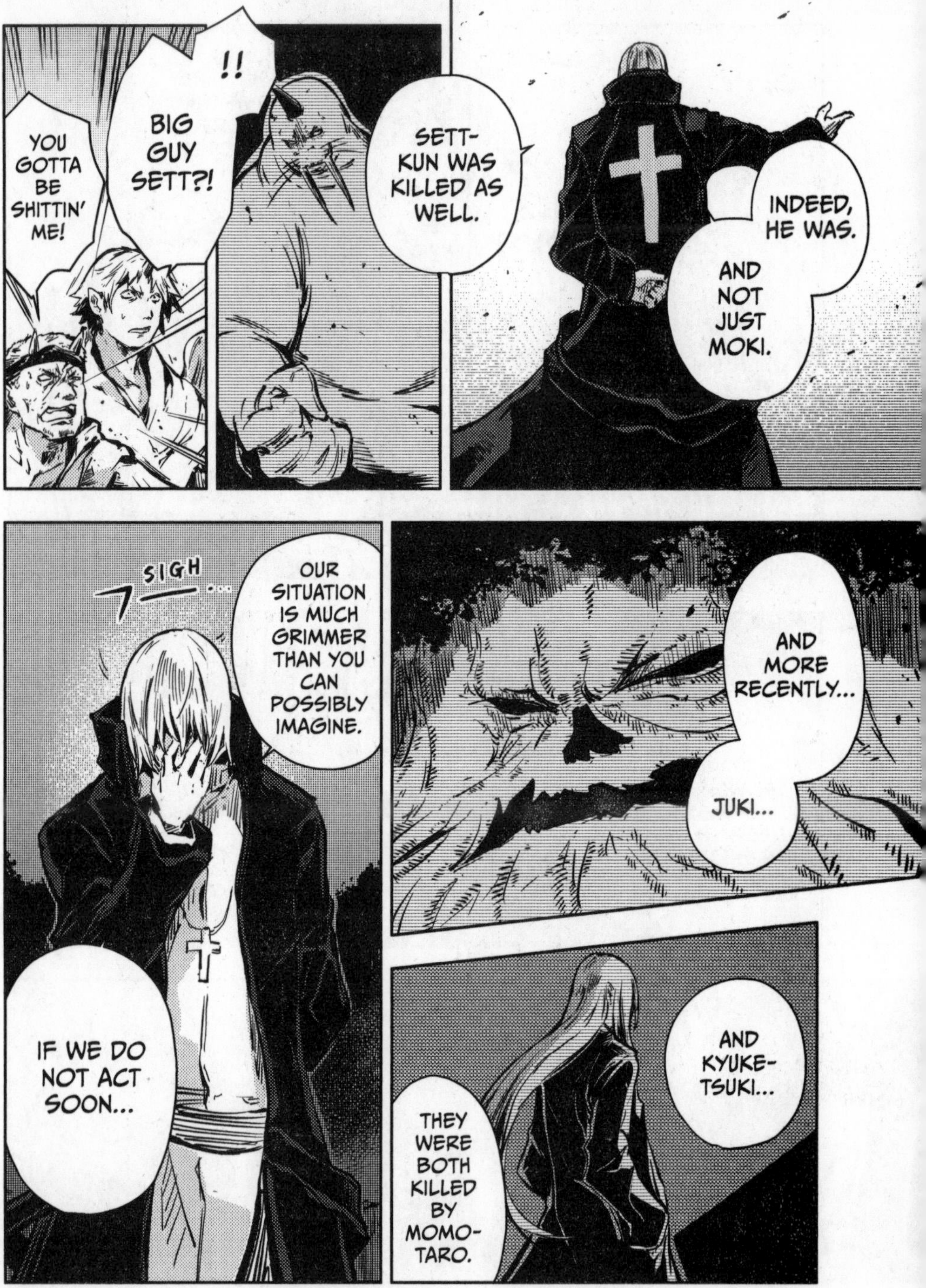
INDEED, HE WAS.
AND NOT JUST MOKI.
SETT-KUN WAS KILLED AS WELL.
!!
BIG GUY SETT?!
YOU GOTTA BE SHITTIN' ME!
AND MORE RECENTLY...
JUKI...
AND KYUKE-TSUKI...
THEY WERE BOTH KILLED BY MOMO-TARO.
SIGH...
OUR SITUATION IS MUCH GRIMMER THAN YOU CAN POSSIBLY IMAGINE.
IF WE DO NOT ACT SOON...

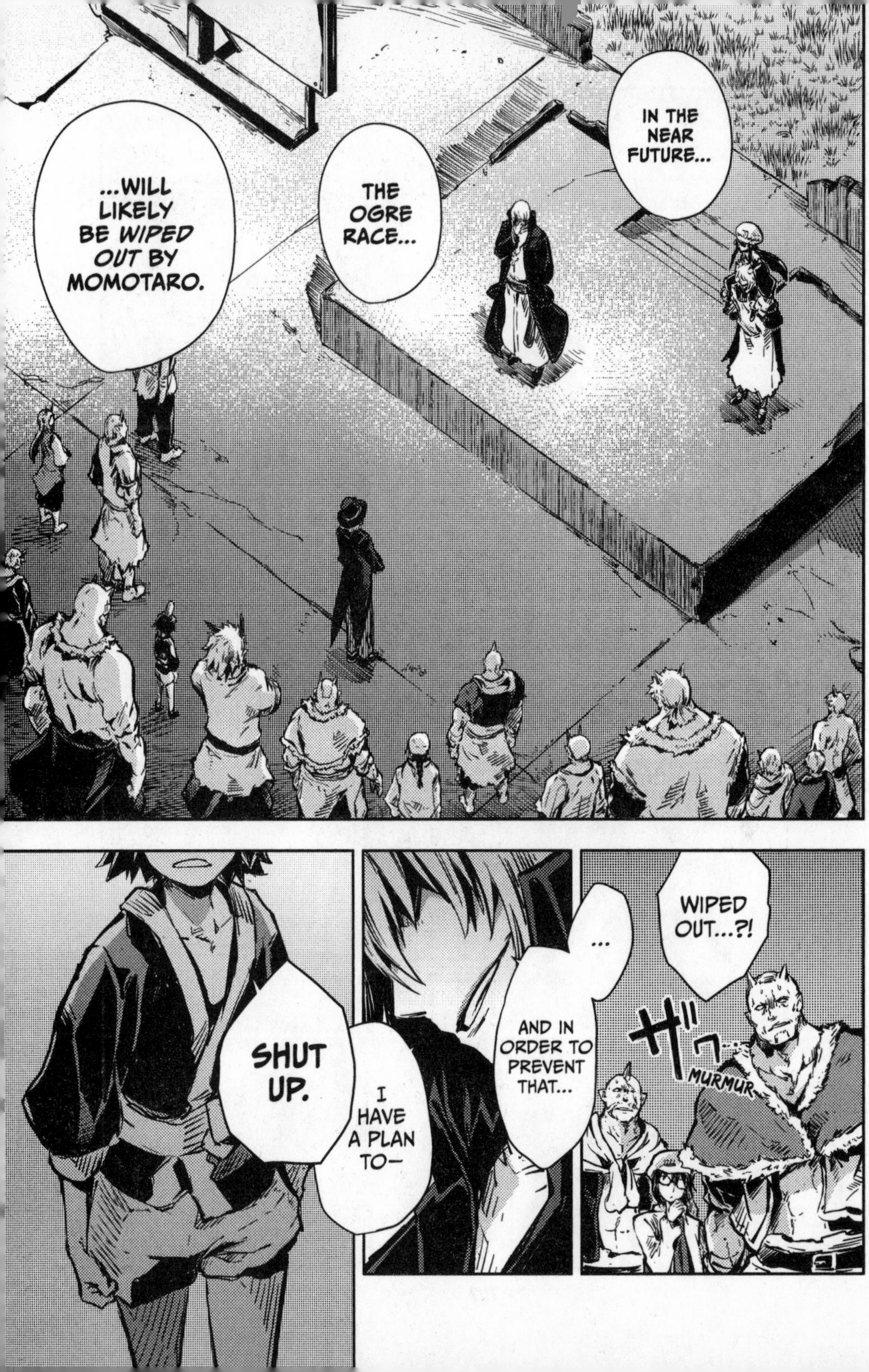
IN THE NEAR FUTURE...
THE OGRE RACE...
...WILL LIKELY BE WIPED OUT BY MOMOTARO.
WIPED OUT...?!
MURMUR
...
AND IN ORDER TO PREVENT THAT...
I HAVE A PLAN TO—
SHUT UP.

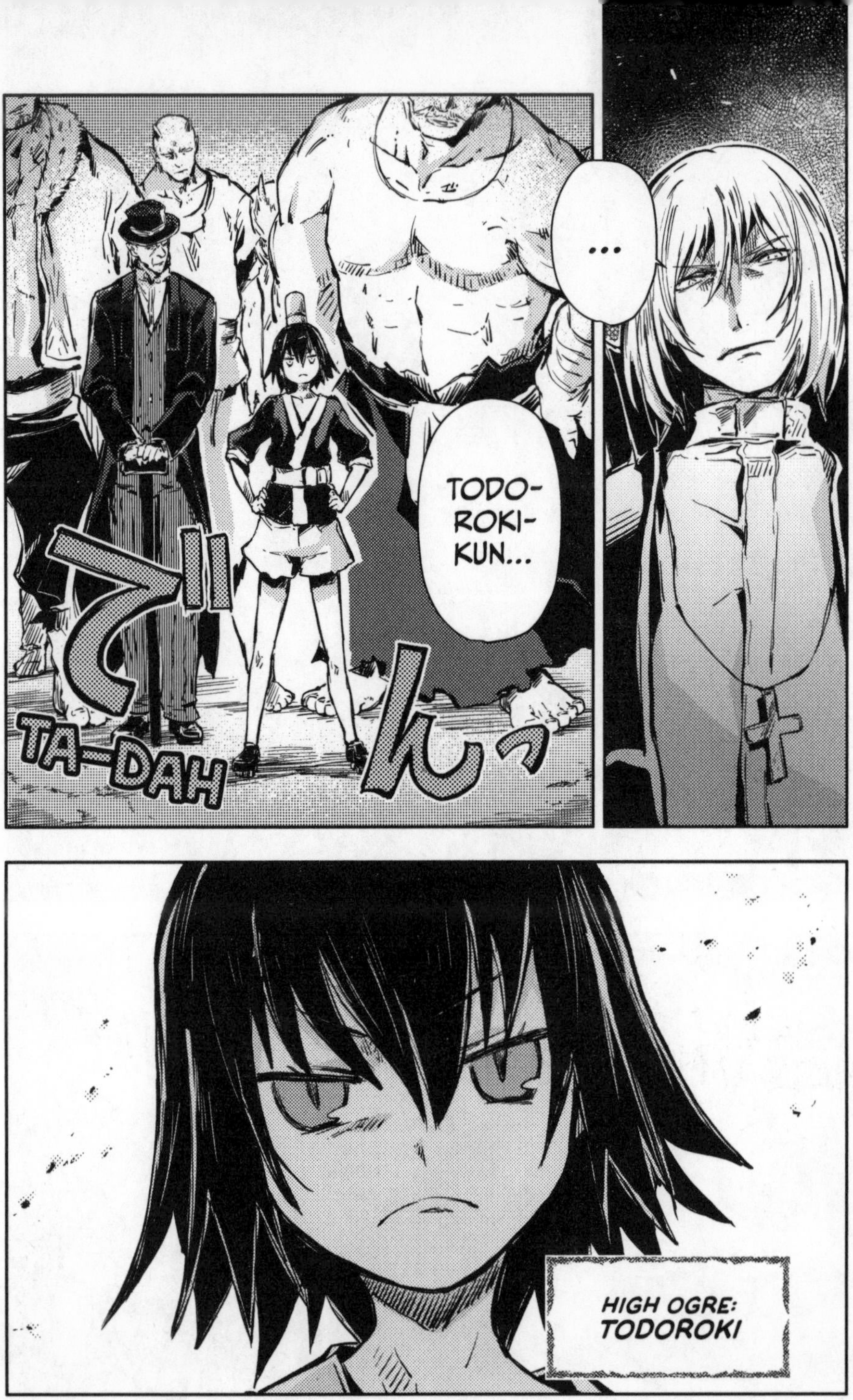
...
TODO-ROKI-KUN...
TA-DAH
HIGH OGRE: TODOROKI

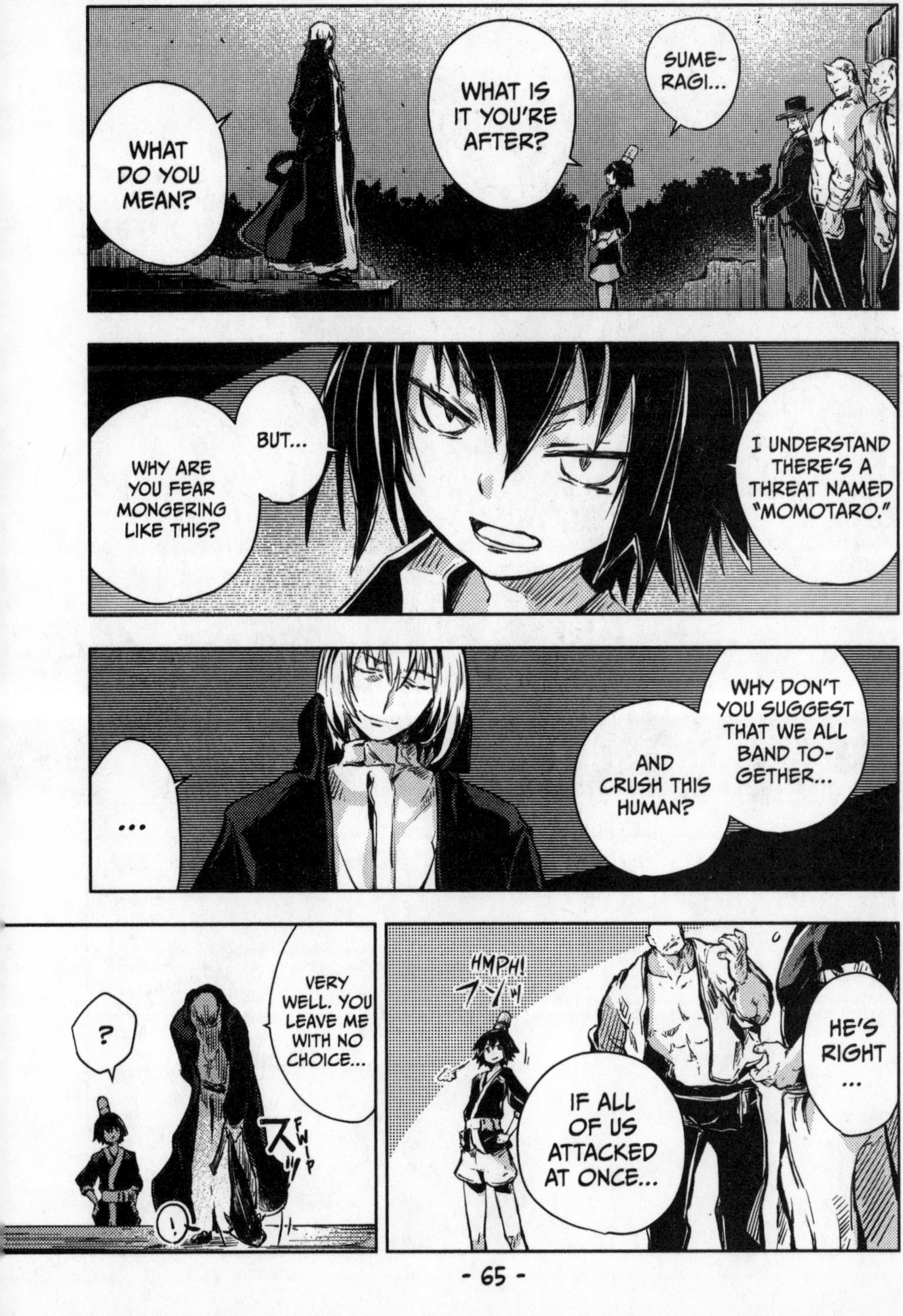
SUME-RAGI...
WHAT IS IT YOU'RE AFTER?
WHAT DO YOU MEAN?
I UNDERSTAND THERE'S A THREAT NAMED "MOMOTARO."
BUT...
WHY ARE YOU FEAR MONGERING LIKE THIS?
WHY DON'T YOU SUGGEST THAT WE ALL BAND TO-GETHER...
AND CRUSH THIS HUMAN?
...
HE'S RIGHT ...
HMPH!
IF ALL OF US ATTACKED AT ONCE...
VERY WELL. YOU LEAVE ME WITH NO CHOICE...
FWIP
?
!

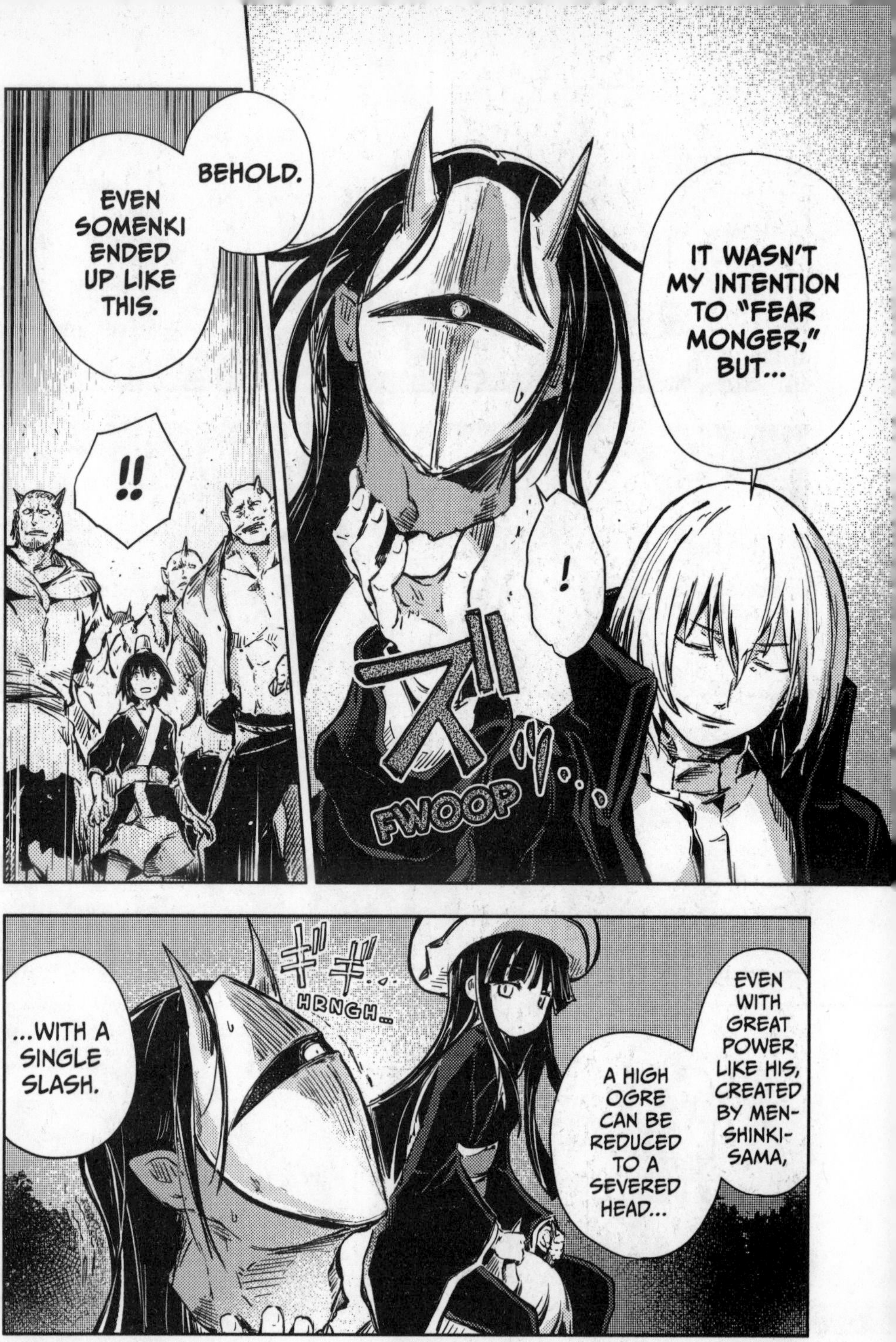
IT WASN'T MY INTENTION TO "FEAR MONGER," BUT...
!
ズ
FWOOP
BEHOLD.
EVEN SOMENKI ENDED UP LIKE THIS.
!!
EVEN WITH GREAT POWER LIKE HIS, CREATED BY MEN-SHINKI-SAMA,
A HIGH OGRE CAN BE REDUCED TO A SEVERED HEAD...
ギギ
HRNGH...
...WITH A SINGLE SLASH.

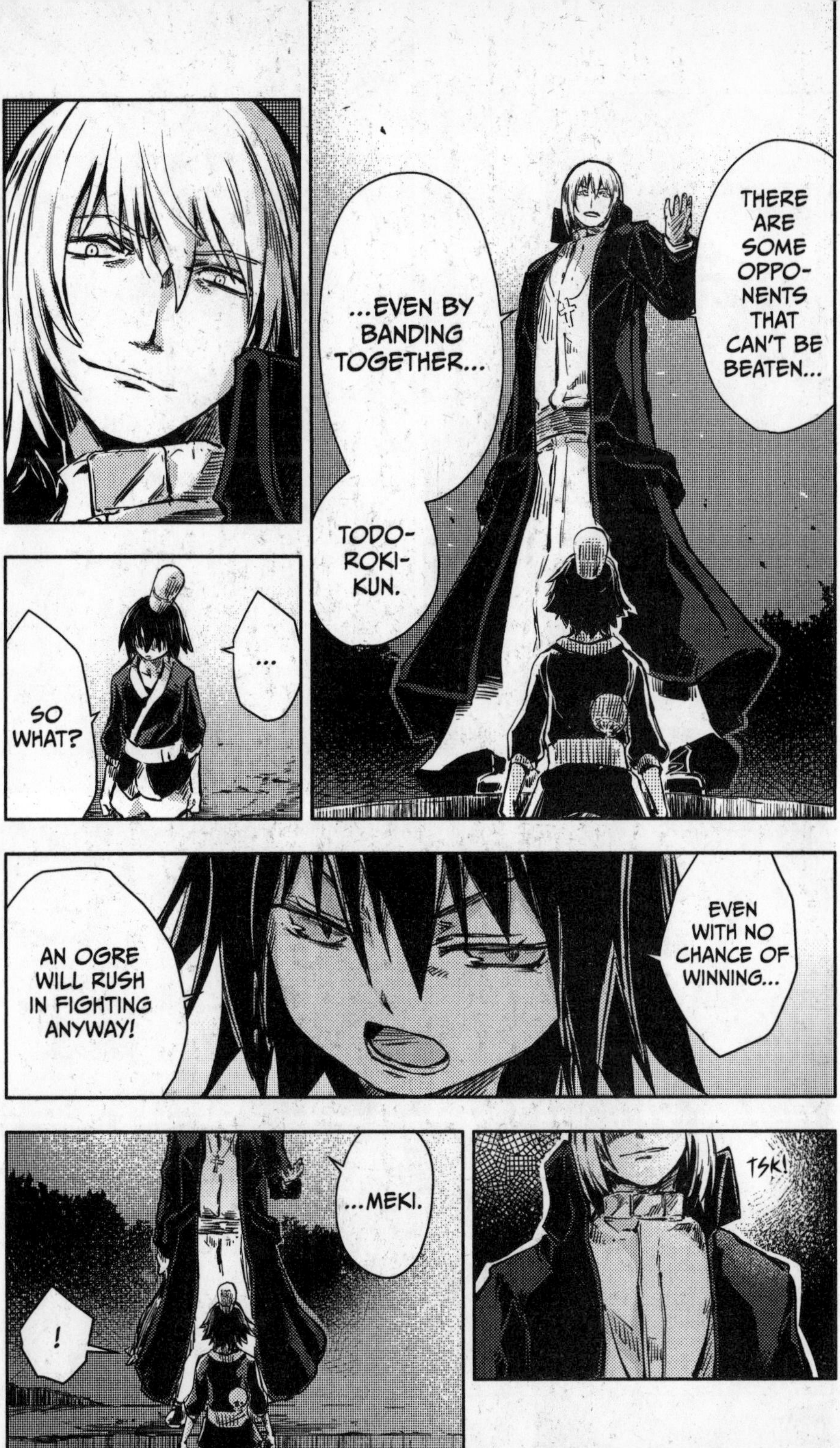
THERE ARE SOME OPPONENTS THAT CAN'T BE BEATEN...
...EVEN BY BANDING TOGETHER...
TODOROKI-KUN.
...
SO WHAT?
EVEN WITH NO CHANCE OF WINNING...
AN OGRE WILL RUSH IN FIGHTING ANYWAY!
TSK!
...MEKI.
!

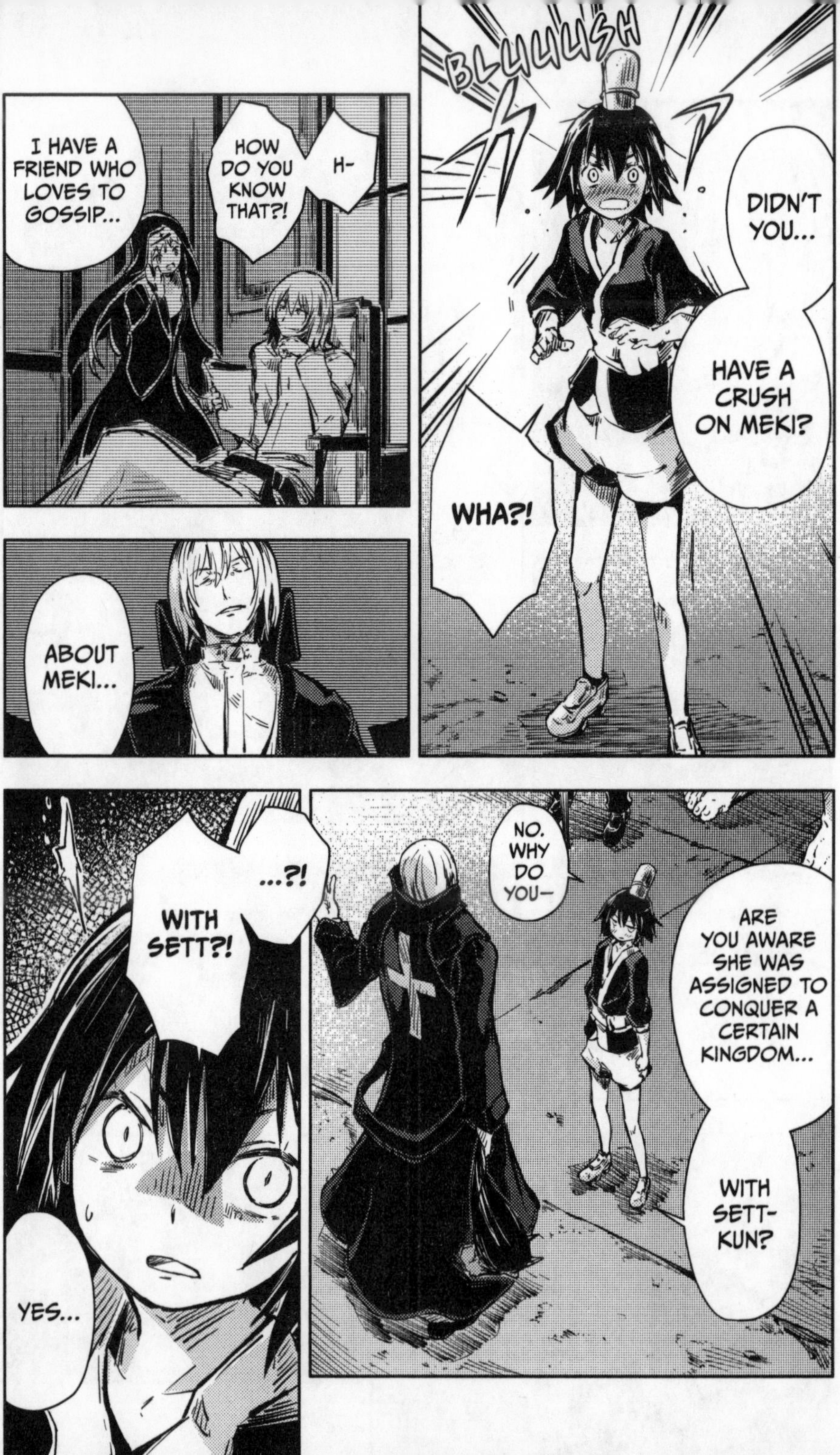
BLULUSH
DIDN'T YOU...
HAVE A CRUSH ON MEKI?
WHA?!
H-
HOW DO YOU KNOW THAT?!
I HAVE A FRIEND WHO LOVES TO GOSSIP...
ABOUT MEKI...
ARE YOU AWARE SHE WAS ASSIGNED TO CONQUER A CERTAIN KINGDOM...
WITH SETT-KUN?
NO. WHY DO YOU—
...?!
WITH SETT?!
YES...

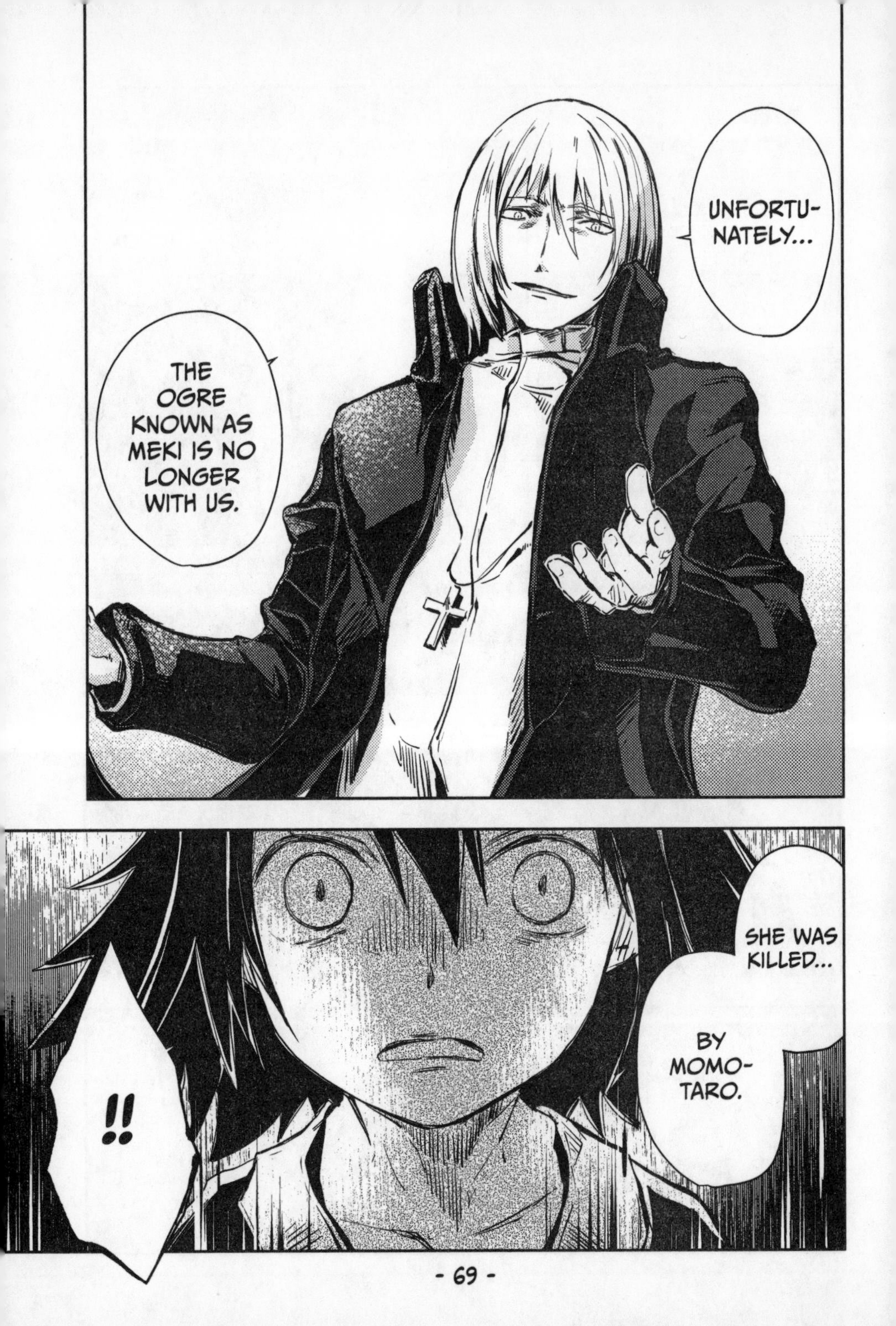
UNFORTU-
NATELY...
THE OGRE KNOWN AS MEKI IS NO LONGER WITH US.
SHE WAS KILLED...
BY MOMO-
TARO.
!!

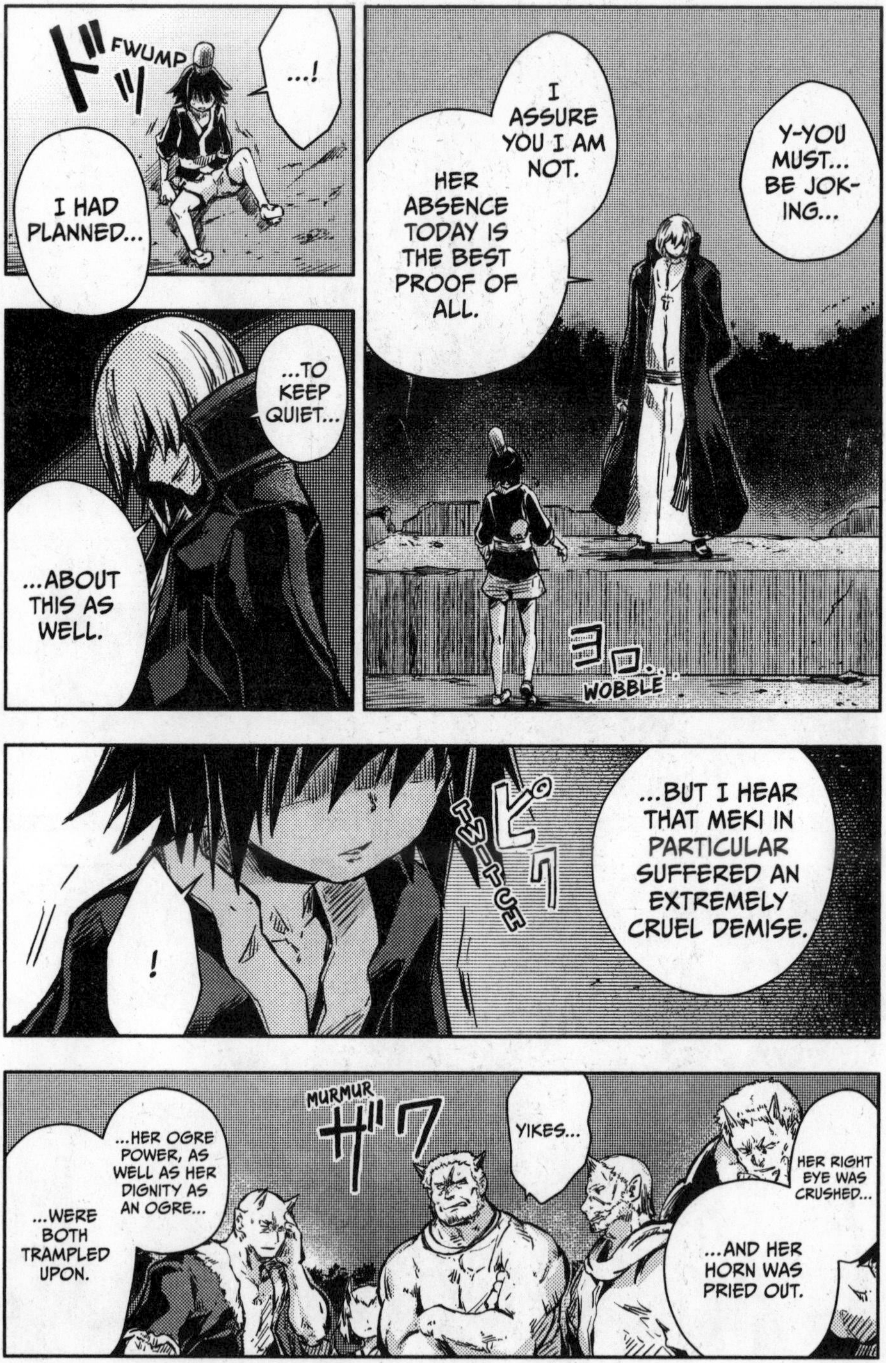
Y-YOU MUST... BE JOKING...
I ASSURE YOU I AM NOT.
HER ABSENCE TODAY IS THE BEST PROOF OF ALL.
ヨロ
WOBBLE
...!
ドッ
FWUMP
I HAD PLANNED...
...TO KEEP QUIET...
...ABOUT THIS AS WELL.
...BUT I HEAR THAT MEKI IN PARTICULAR SUFFERED AN EXTREMELY CRUEL DEMISE.
ピク
TWITCH
!
HER RIGHT EYE WAS CRUSHED...
...AND HER HORN WAS PRIED OUT.
YIKES...
ザワ
MURMUR
...HER OGRE POWER, AS WELL AS HER DIGNITY AS AN OGRE...
...WERE BOTH TRAMPLED UPON.

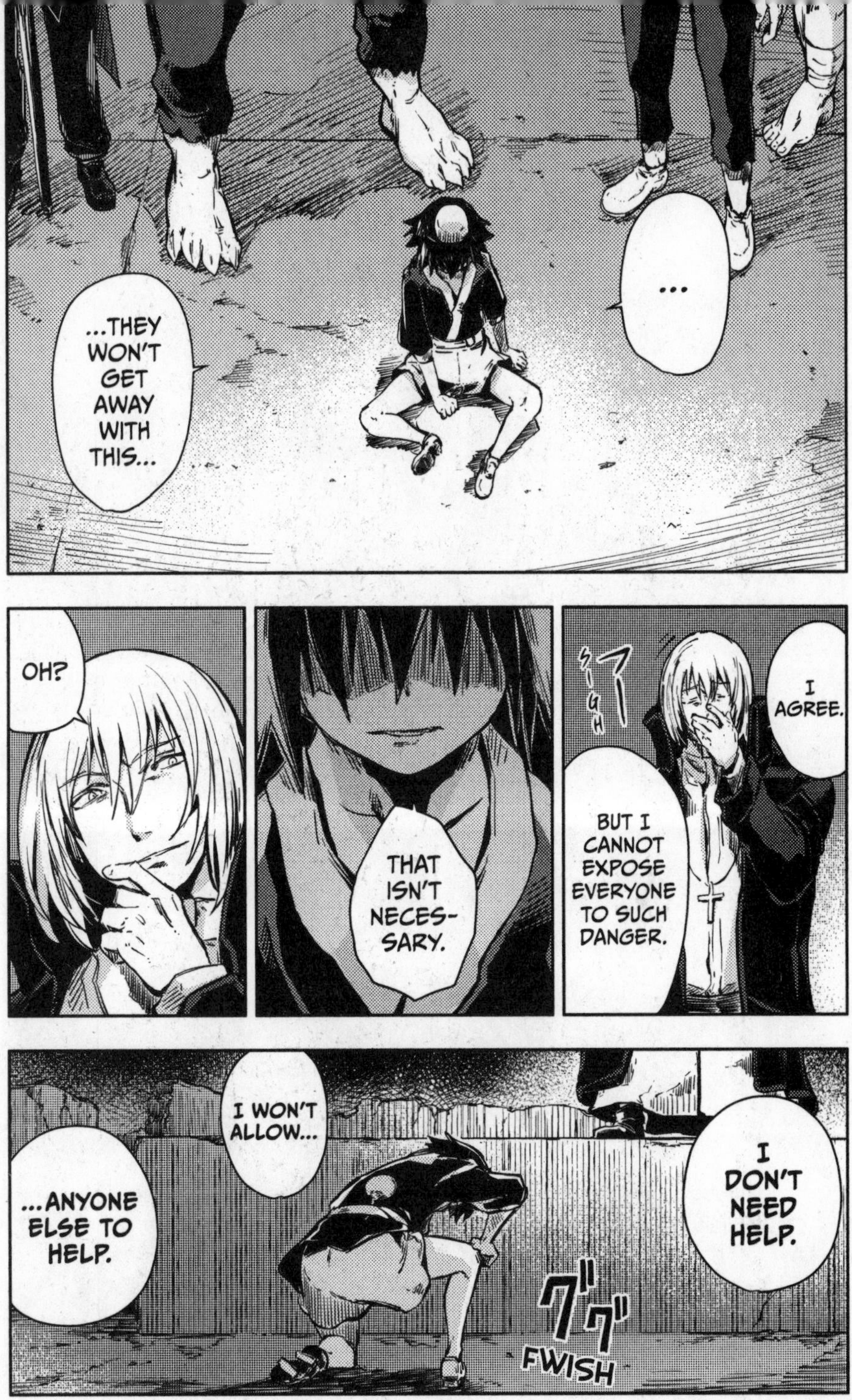
...
...THEY WON'T GET AWAY WITH THIS...
SIGH
I AGREE.
BUT I CANNOT EXPOSE EVERYONE TO SUCH DANGER.
THAT ISN'T NECES-SARY.
OH?
I DON'T NEED HELP.
FWISH
I WON'T ALLOW...
...ANYONE ELSE TO HELP.

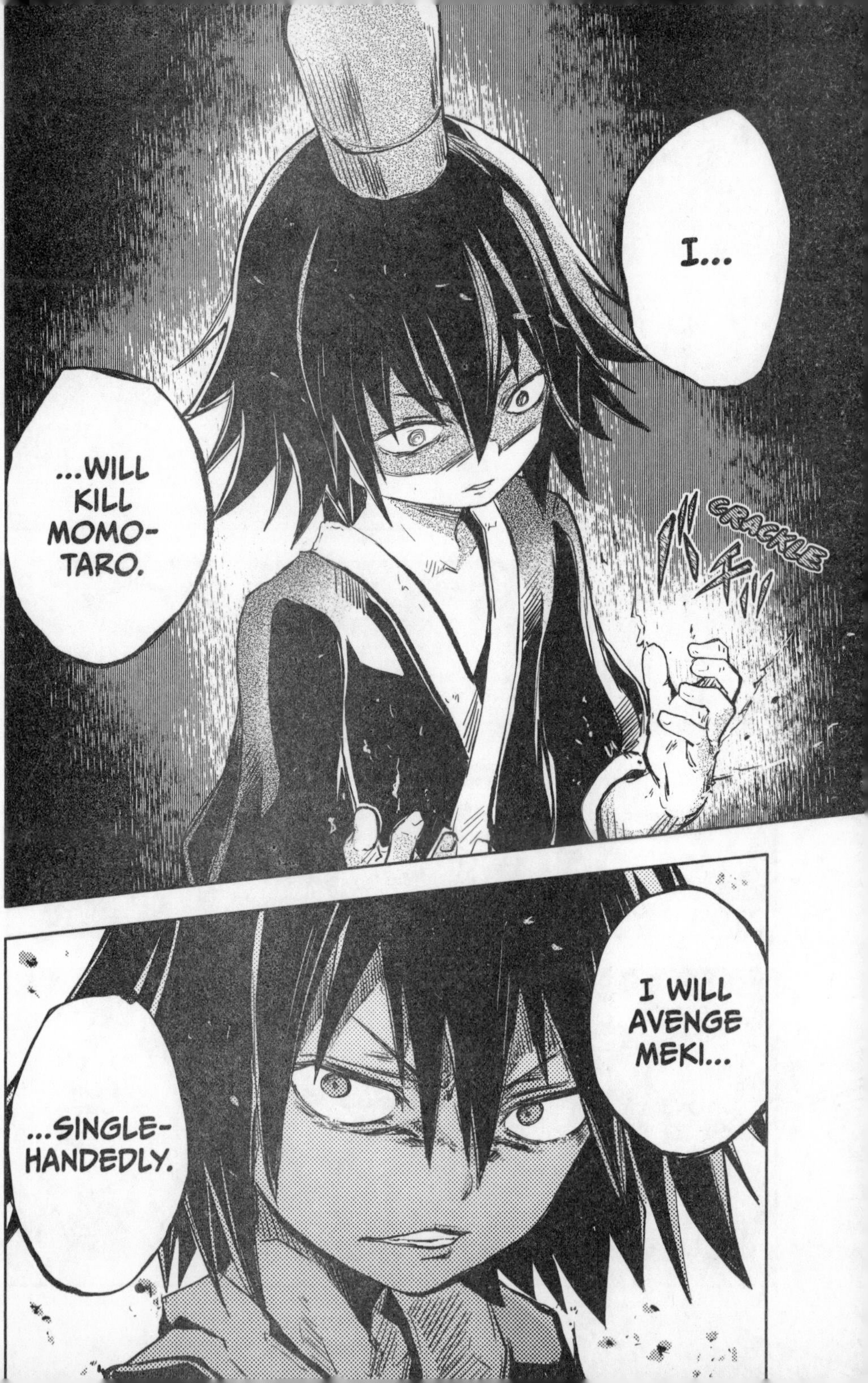
I...
...WILL KILL MOMO-TARO.
CRACKLE
I WILL AVENGE MEKI...
...SINGLE-HANDEDLY.

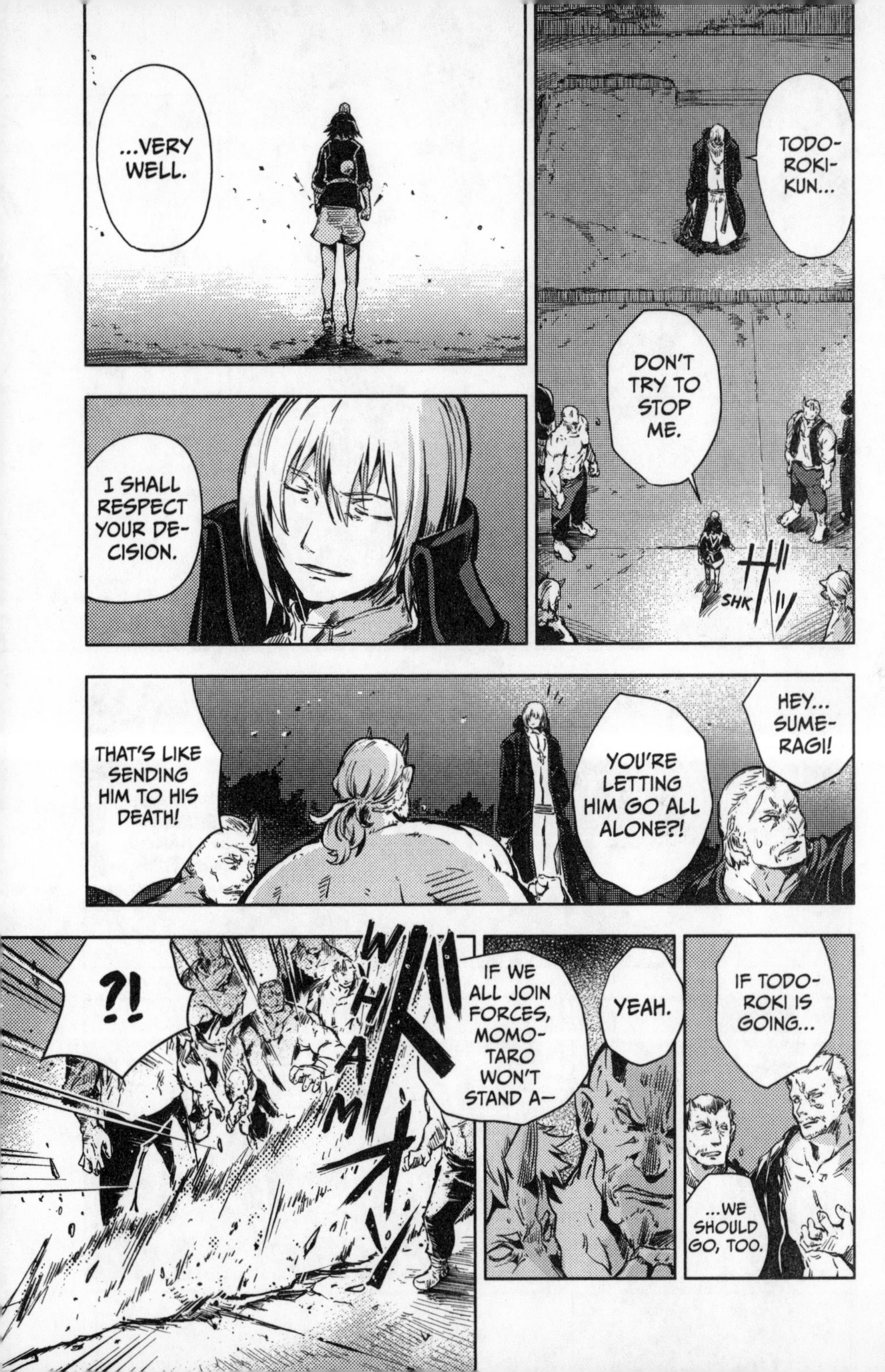
TODO-ROKI-KUN...
DON'T TRY TO STOP ME.
SHK
...VERY WELL.
I SHALL RESPECT YOUR DE-CISION.
HEY... SUME-RAGI!
YOU'RE LETTING HIM GO ALL ALONE?!
THAT'S LIKE SENDING HIM TO HIS DEATH!
IF TODO-ROKI IS GOING...
...WE SHOULD GO, TOO.
YEAH.
IF WE ALL JOIN FORCES, MOMO-TARO WON'T STAND A—
WHAM
?!

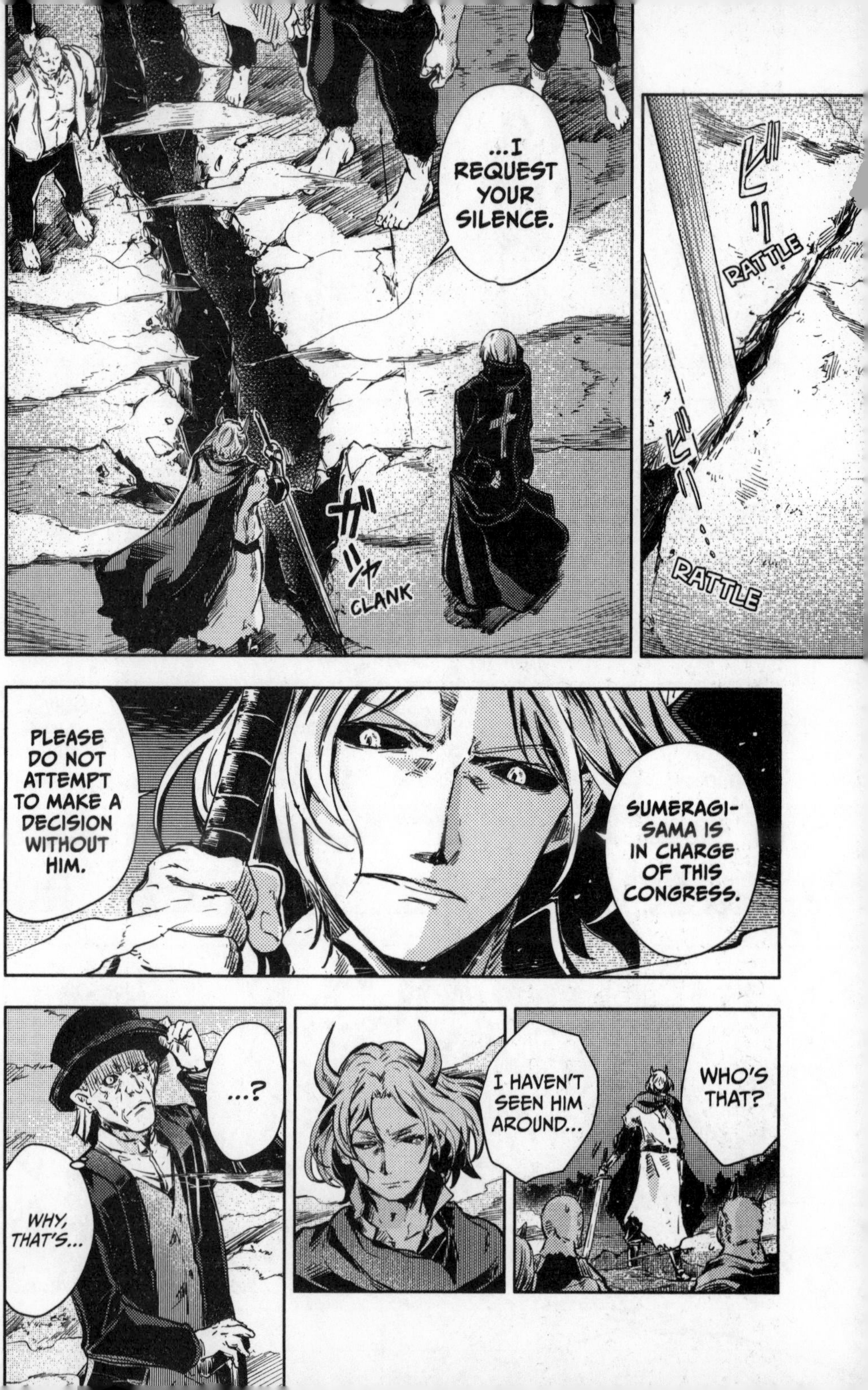
RATTLE
RATTLE
...I REQUEST YOUR SILENCE.
CLANK
SUMERAGI-SAMA IS IN CHARGE OF THIS CONGRESS.
PLEASE DO NOT ATTEMPT TO MAKE A DECISION WITHOUT HIM.
WHO'S THAT?
I HAVEN'T SEEN HIM AROUND...
...?
WHY, THAT'S...

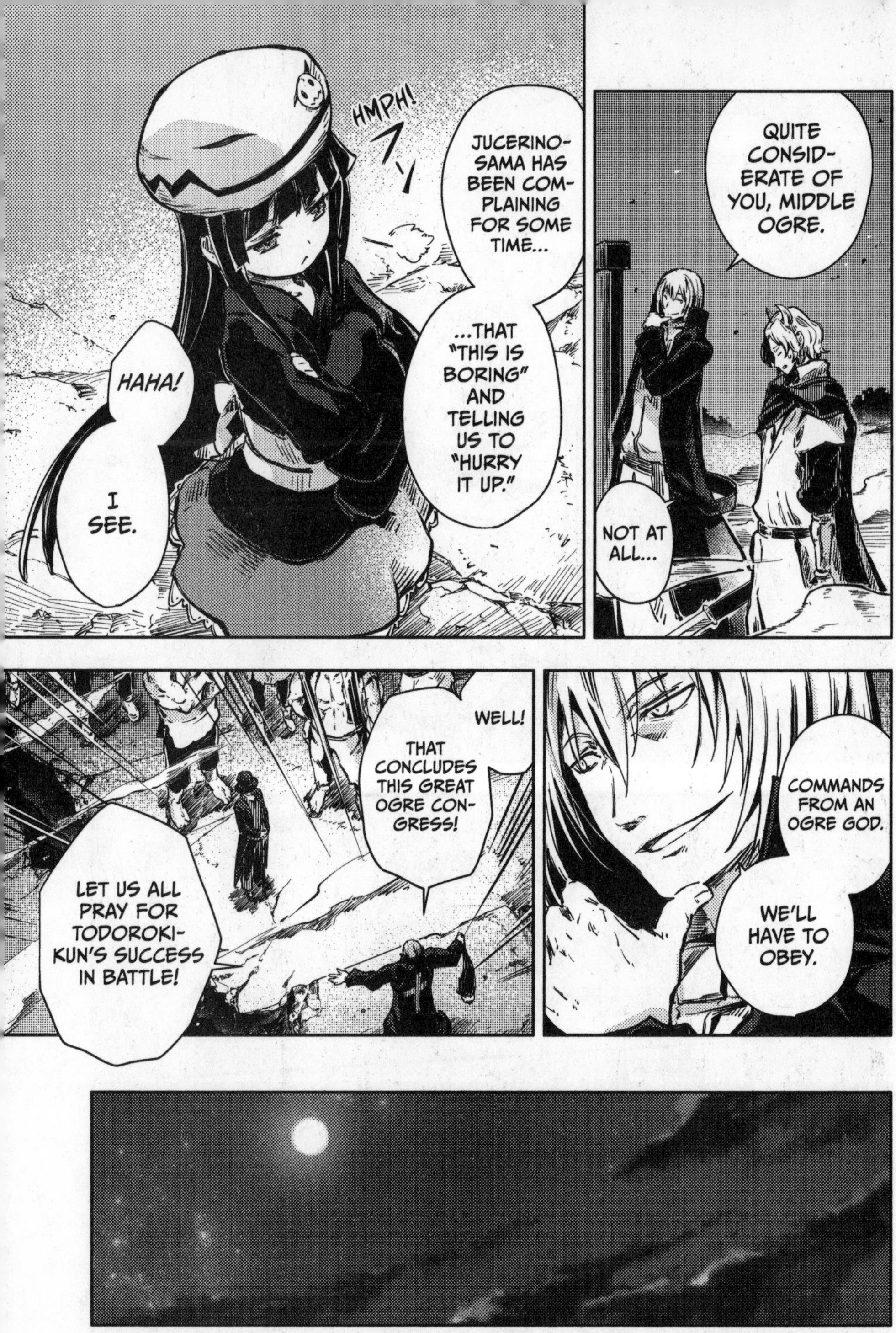
QUITE CONSID-ERATE OF YOU, MIDDLE OGRE.
NOT AT ALL...
JUCERINO-SAMA HAS BEEN COM-PLAINING FOR SOME TIME...
HMPH!
...THAT "THIS IS BORING" AND TELLING US TO "HURRY IT UP."
HAHA! I SEE.
COMMANDS FROM AN OGRE GOD.
WE'LL HAVE TO OBEY.
WELL!
THAT CONCLUDES THIS GREAT OGRE CON-GRESS!
LET US ALL PRAY FOR TODOROKI-KUN'S SUCCESS IN BATTLE!

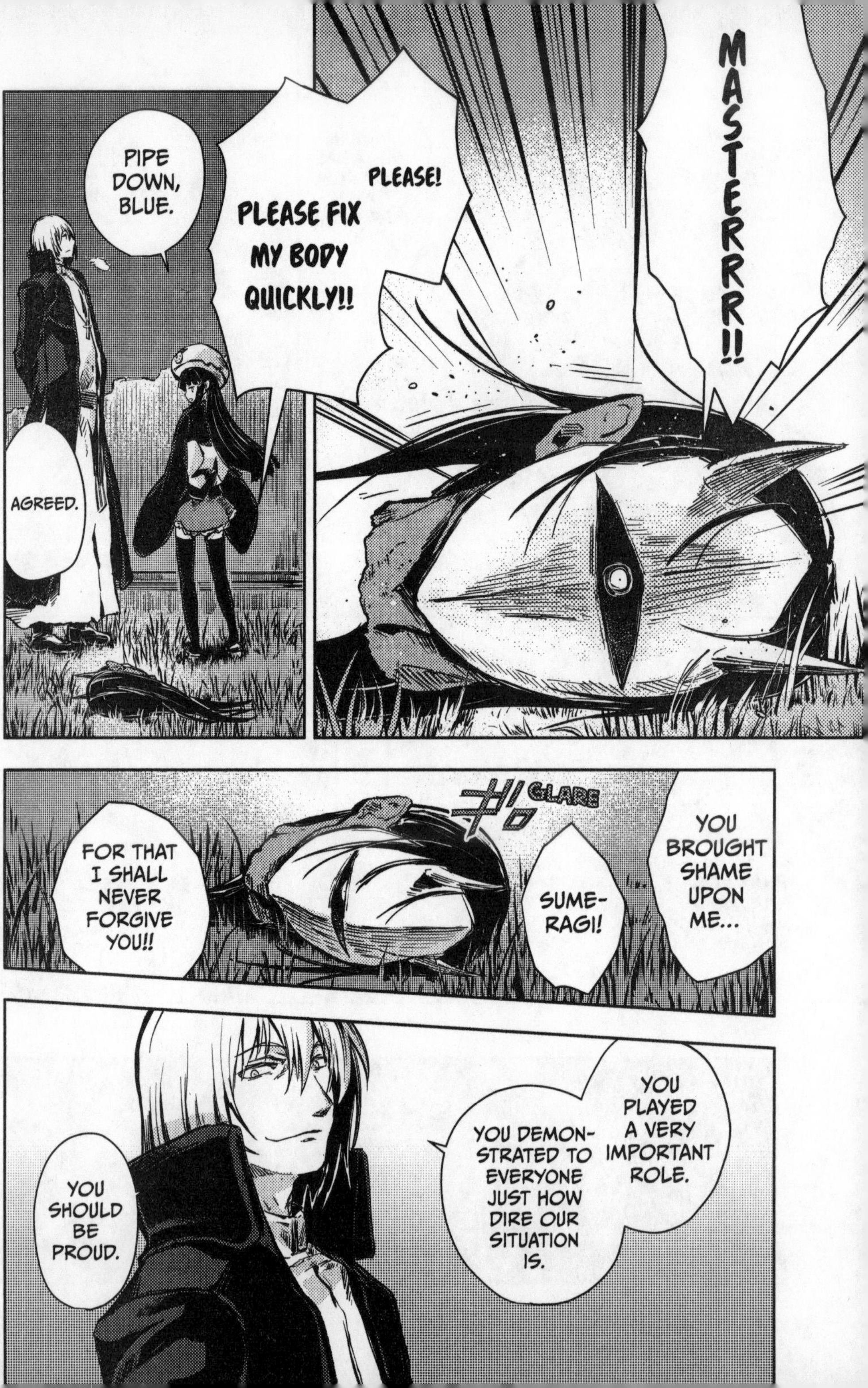
MASTERRRR!!
PLEASE!
PLEASE FIX MY BODY QUICKLY!!
PIPE DOWN, BLUE.
AGREED.
YOU BROUGHT SHAME UPON ME...
SUME-RAGI!
ギロ GLARE
FOR THAT I SHALL NEVER FORGIVE YOU!!
YOU PLAYED A VERY IMPORTANT ROLE.
YOU DEMON-STRATED TO EVERYONE JUST HOW DIRE OUR SITUATION IS.
YOU SHOULD BE PROUD.

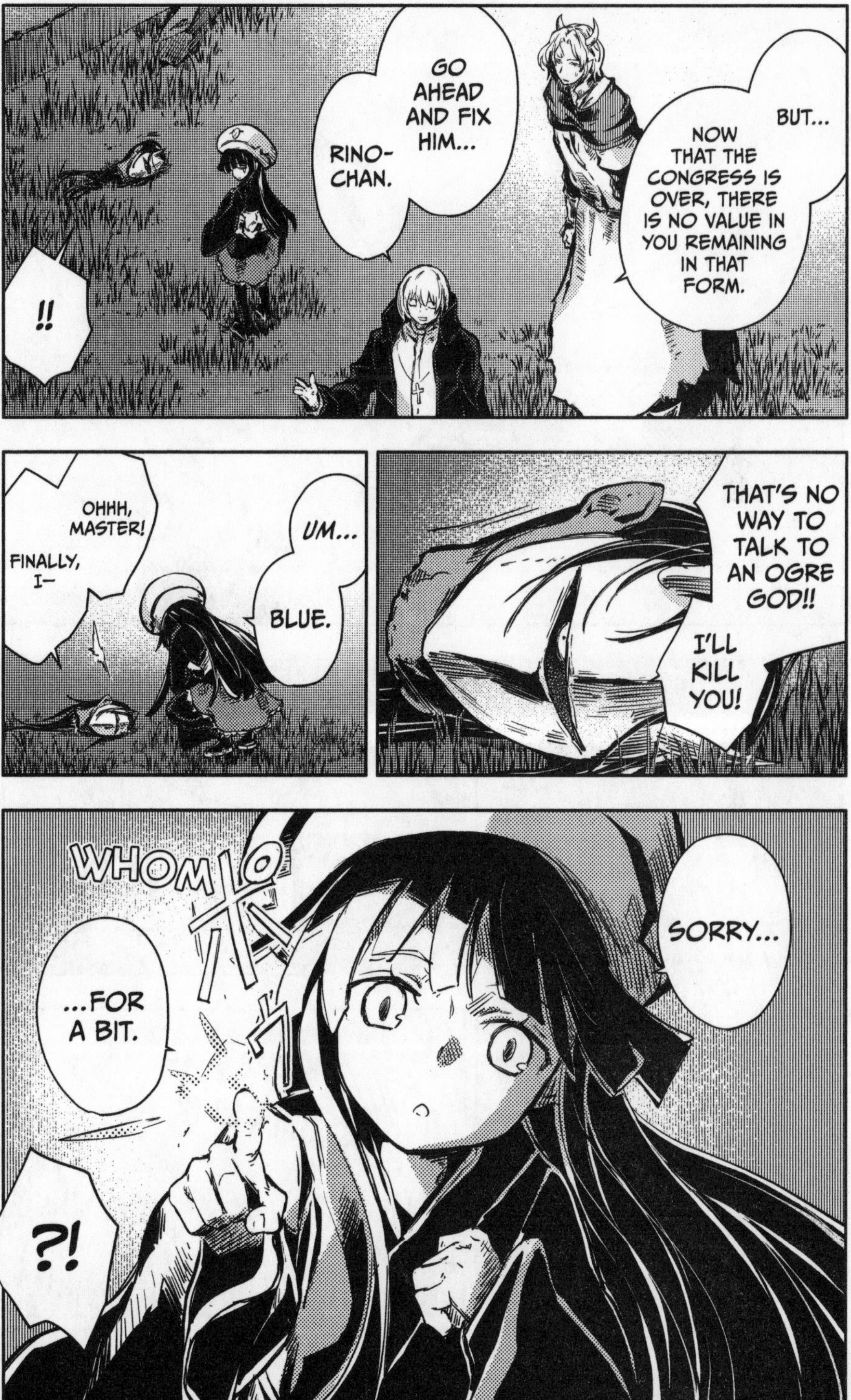
BUT... NOW THAT THE CONGRESS IS OVER, THERE IS NO VALUE IN YOU REMAINING IN THAT FORM.
GO AHEAD AND FIX HIM... RINO-CHAN.
!!
THAT'S NO WAY TO TALK TO AN OGRE GOD!!
I'LL KILL YOU!
UM... BLUE.
OHHH, MASTER! FINALLY, I—
SORRY...
WHOMP
...FOR A BIT.
?!

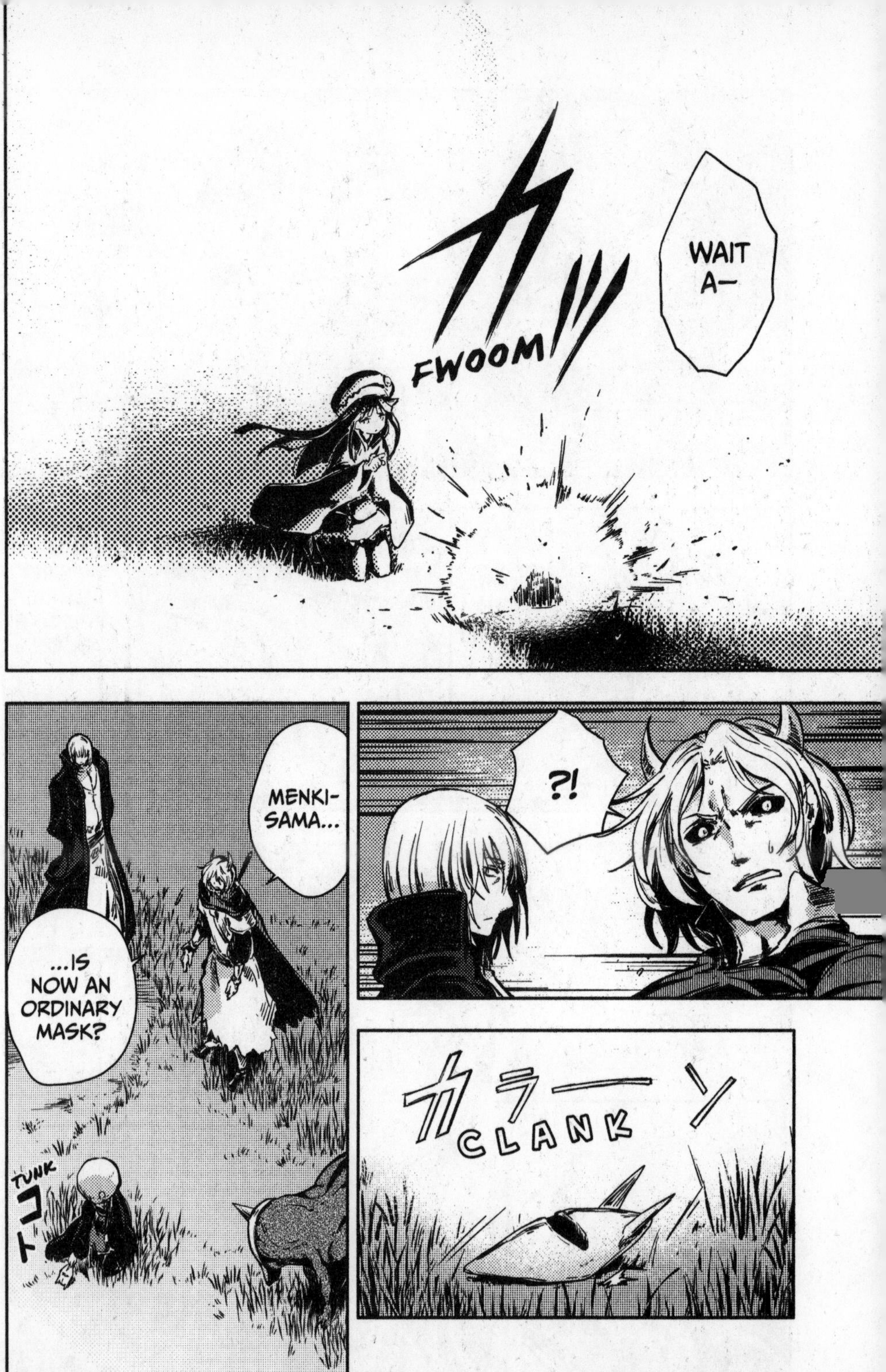
WAIT A—
FWOOM
?!
カラーン
CLANK
MENKI-SAMA...
...IS NOW AN ORDINARY MASK?
TUNK

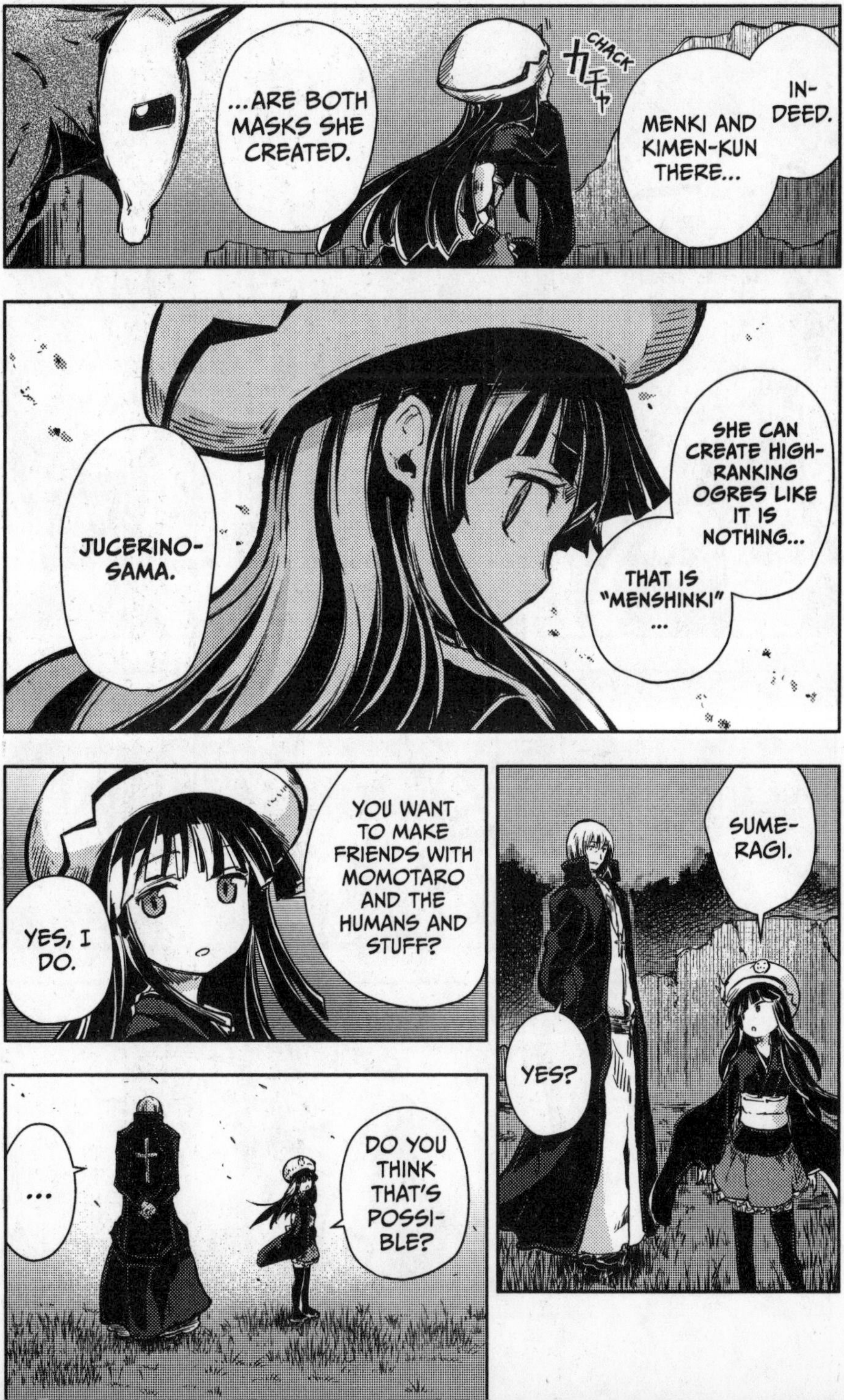
IN-DEED.
MENKI AND KIMEN-KUN THERE...
CHACK
カチャ
...ARE BOTH MASKS SHE CREATED.
SHE CAN CREATE HIGH-RANKING OGRES LIKE IT IS NOTHING...
THAT IS "MENSHINKI" ...
JUCERINO-SAMA.
SUME-RAGI.
YES?
YOU WANT TO MAKE FRIENDS WITH MOMOTARO AND THE HUMANS AND STUFF?
YES, I DO.
DO YOU THINK THAT'S POSSIBLE?
...

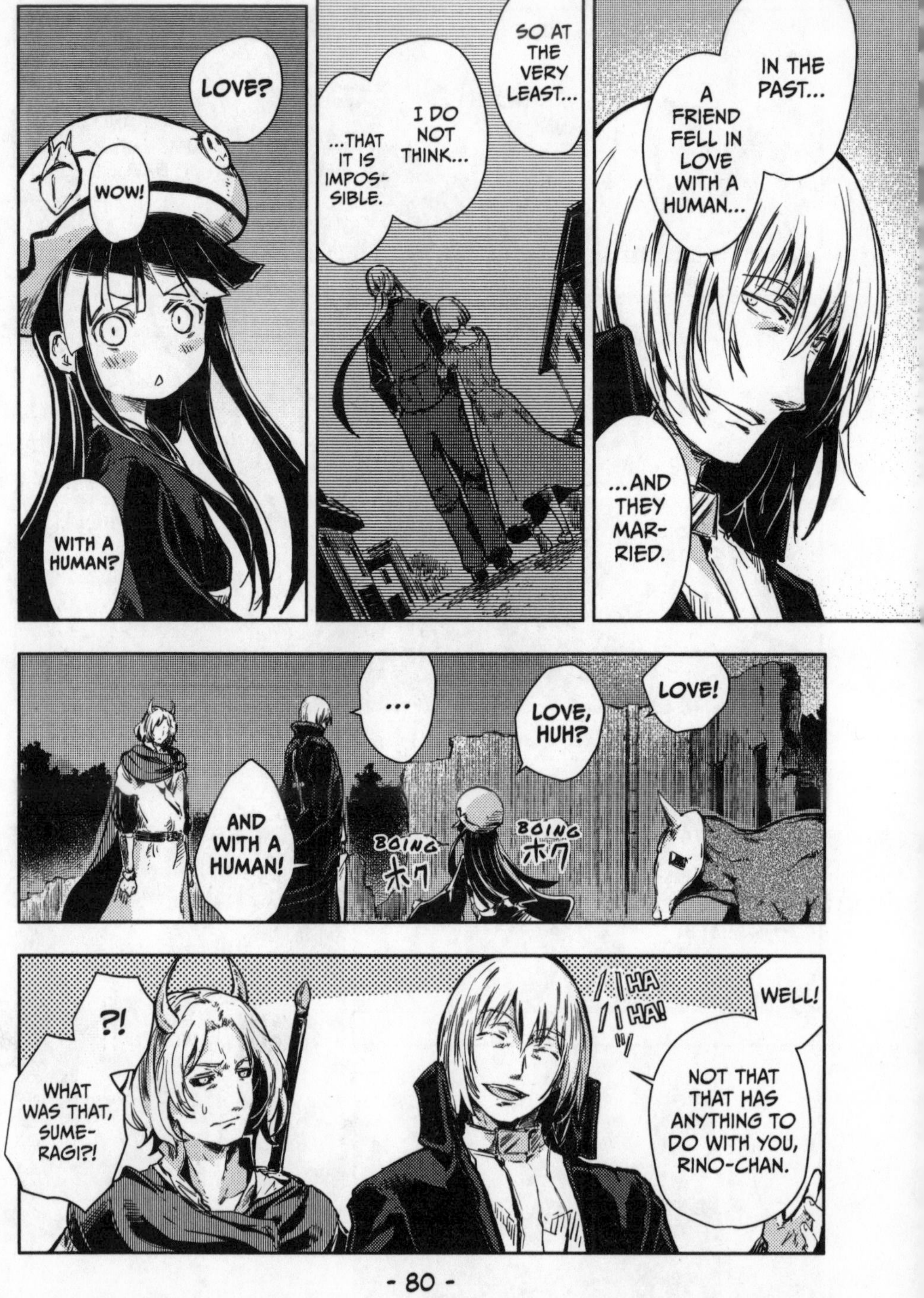
IN THE PAST...
A FRIEND FELL IN LOVE WITH A HUMAN...
...AND THEY MARRIED.
SO AT THE VERY LEAST...
I DO NOT THINK...
...THAT IT IS IMPOSSIBLE.
LOVE?
WOW!
WITH A HUMAN?
LOVE!
LOVE, HUH?
...
BOING ホク
BOING ホク
AND WITH A HUMAN!
WELL!
HA HA!
NOT THAT THAT HAS ANYTHING TO DO WITH YOU, RINO-CHAN.
?!
WHAT WAS THAT, SUMERAGI?!

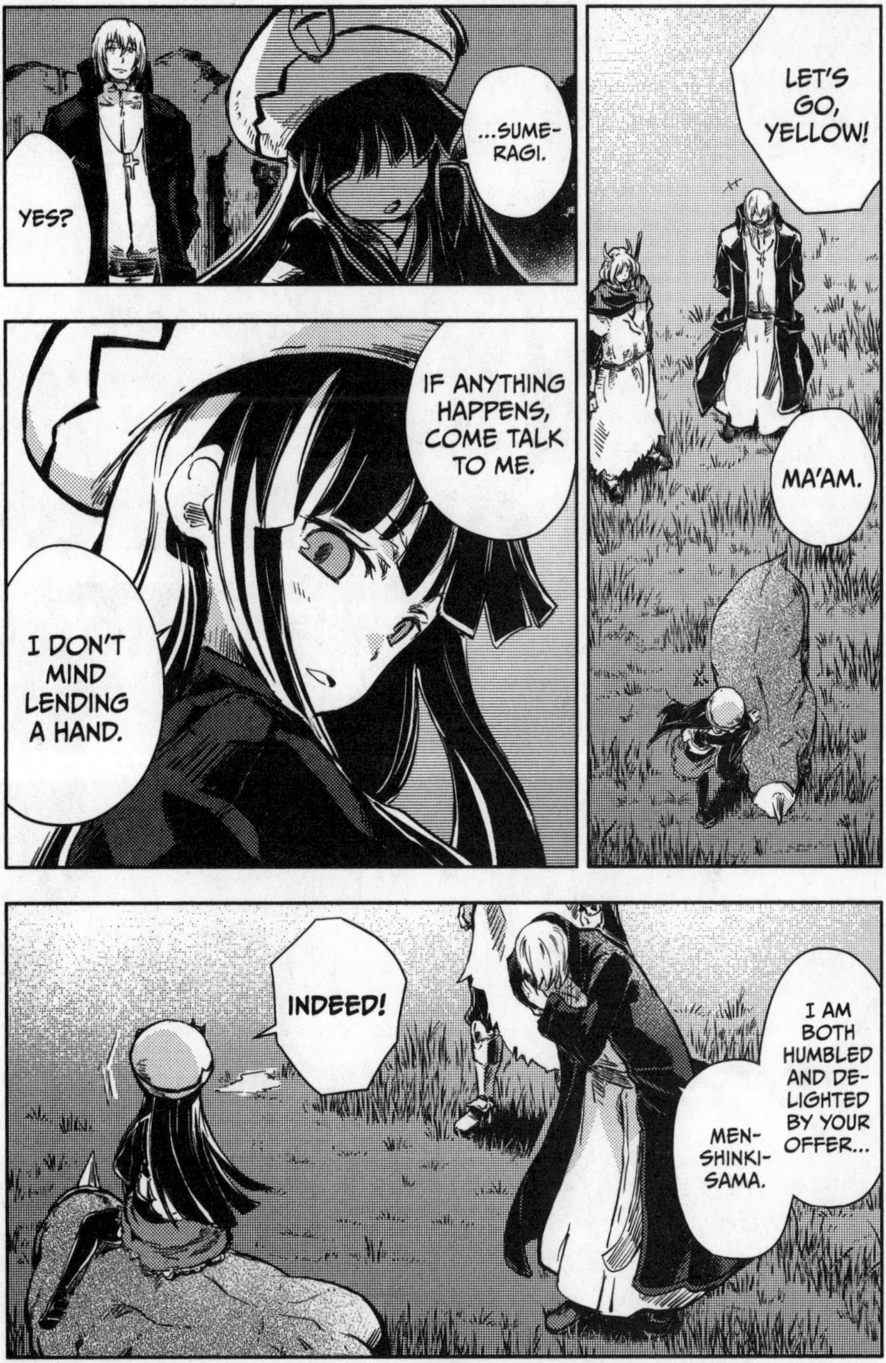
LET'S GO, YELLOW!
MA'AM.
...SUME-RAGI.
YES?
IF ANYTHING HAPPENS, COME TALK TO ME.
I DON'T MIND LENDING A HAND.
I AM BOTH HUMBLED AND DE-LIGHTED BY YOUR OFFER...
MEN-SHINKI-SAMA.
INDEED!

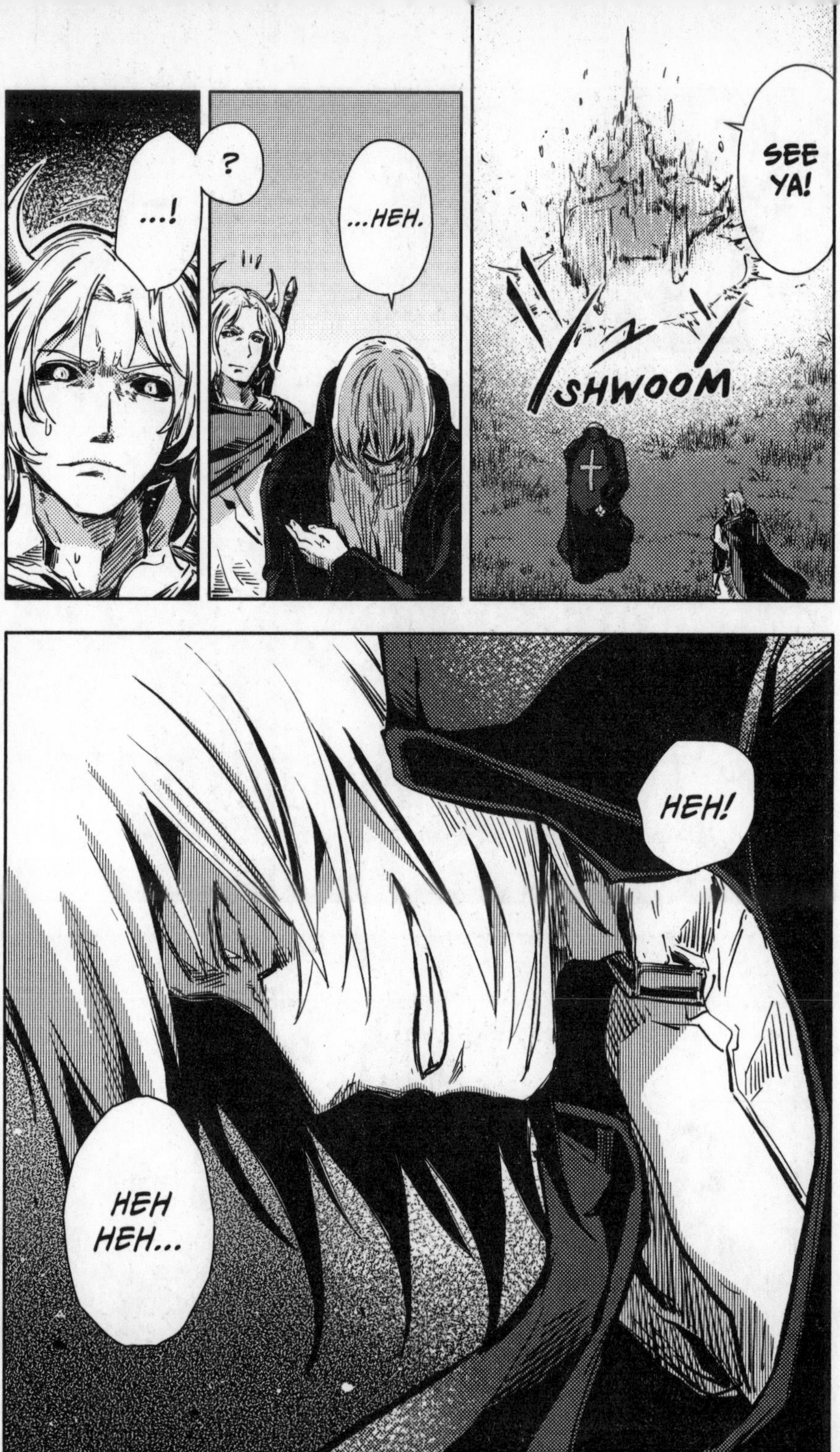
SEE YA!
SHWOOM
...HEH.
?
...!
HEH!
HEH HEH...

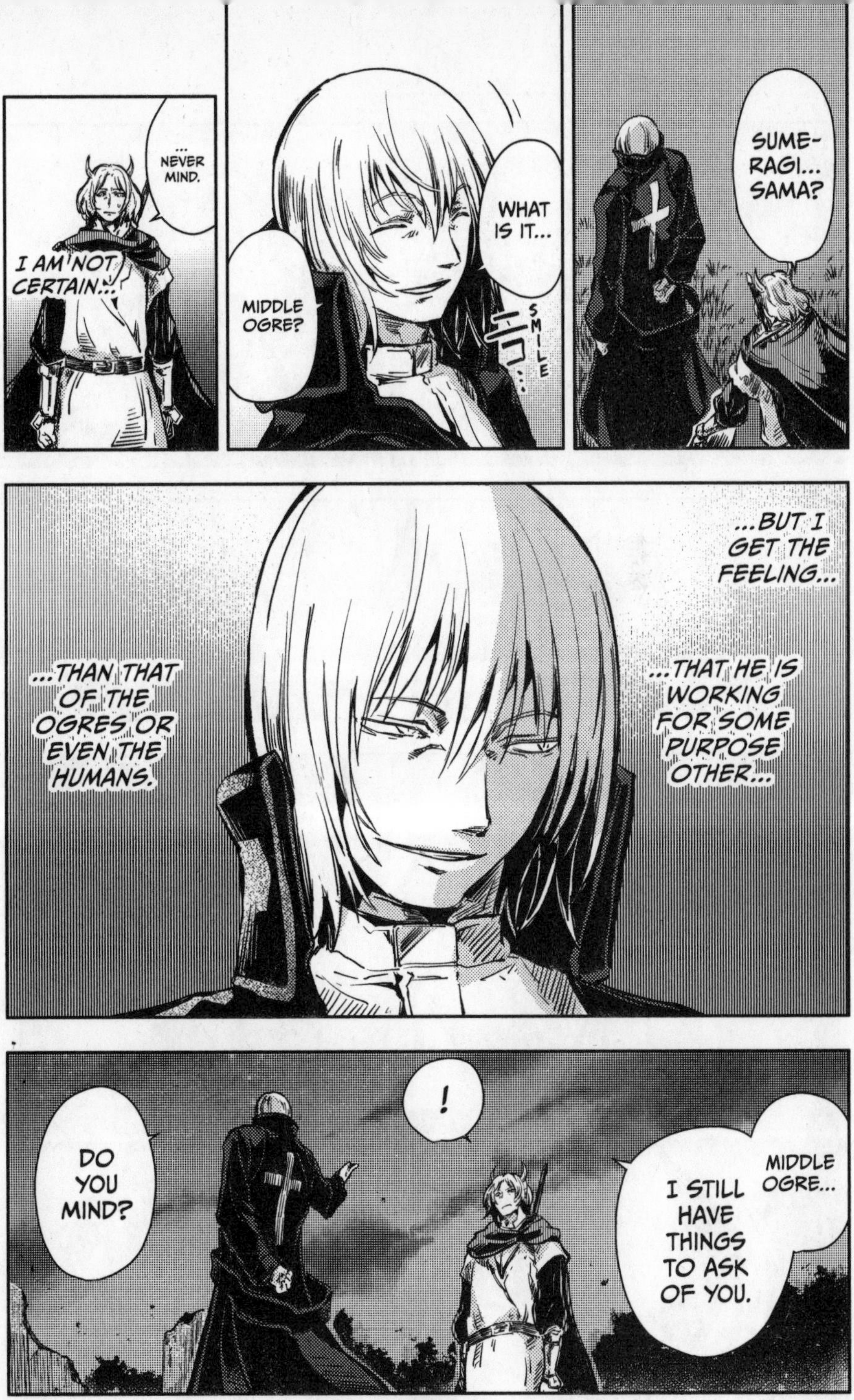
SUME-RAGI... SAMA?
WHAT IS IT...
MIDDLE OGRE?
SMILE
... NEVER MIND.
I AM NOT CERTAIN...
...BUT I GET THE FEELING...
...THAT HE IS WORKING FOR SOME PURPOSE OTHER...
...THAN THAT OF THE OGRES OR EVEN THE HUMANS.
MIDDLE OGRE...
I STILL HAVE THINGS TO ASK OF YOU.
!
DO YOU MIND?

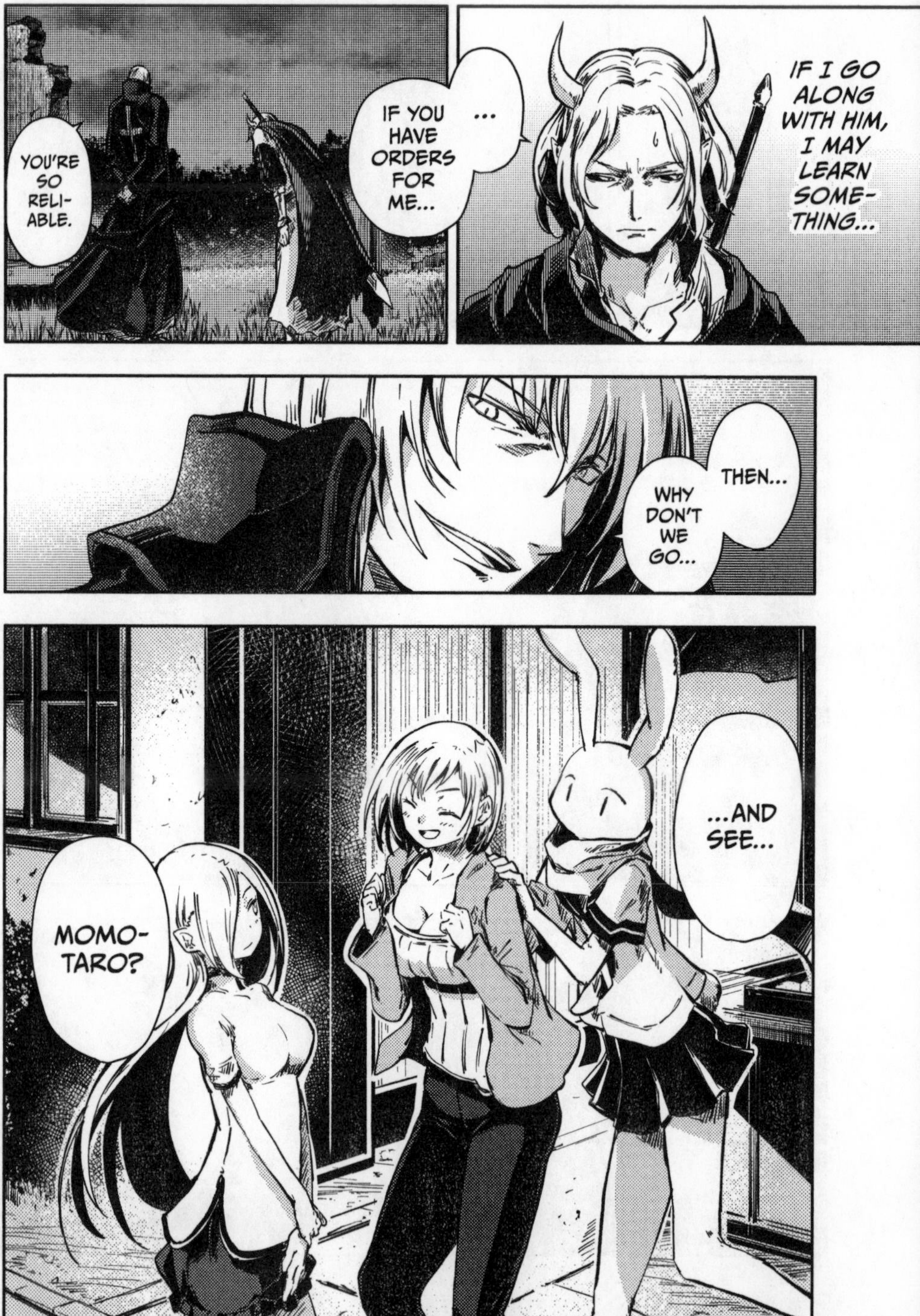
IF I GO ALONG WITH HIM, I MAY LEARN SOME-THING...
...
IF YOU HAVE ORDERS FOR ME...
YOU'RE SO RELI-ABLE.
THEN...
WHY DON'T WE GO...
...AND SEE...
MOMO-TARO?

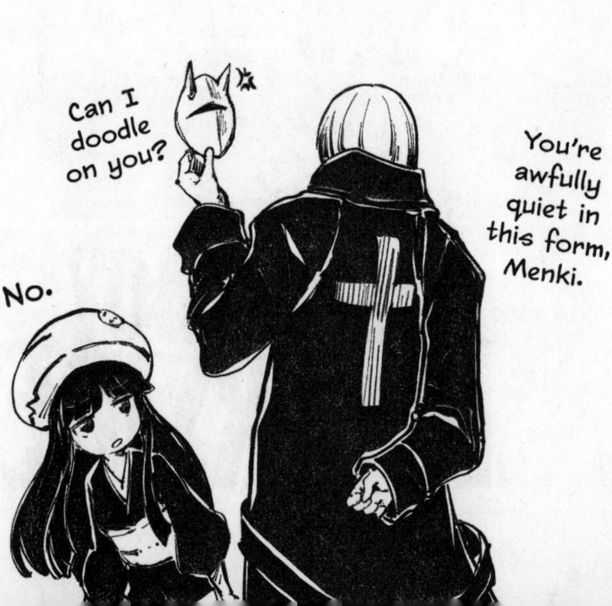

You're awfully quiet in this form, Menki.
Can I doodle on you?
No.

PEACH BOY
RIVERSIDE

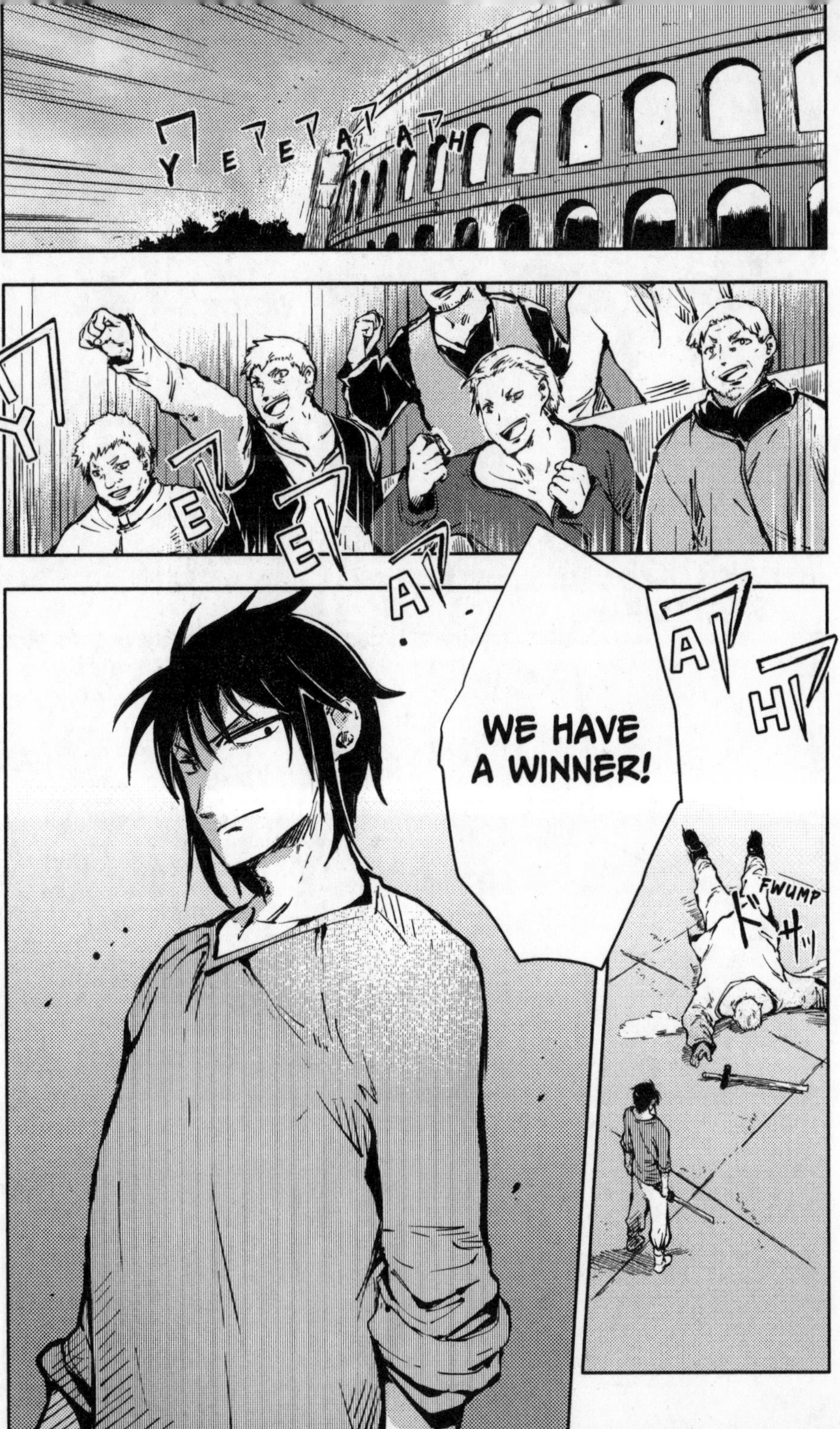
YEEEAAAH
YEEEA
AH
WE HAVE A WINNER!
FWUMP

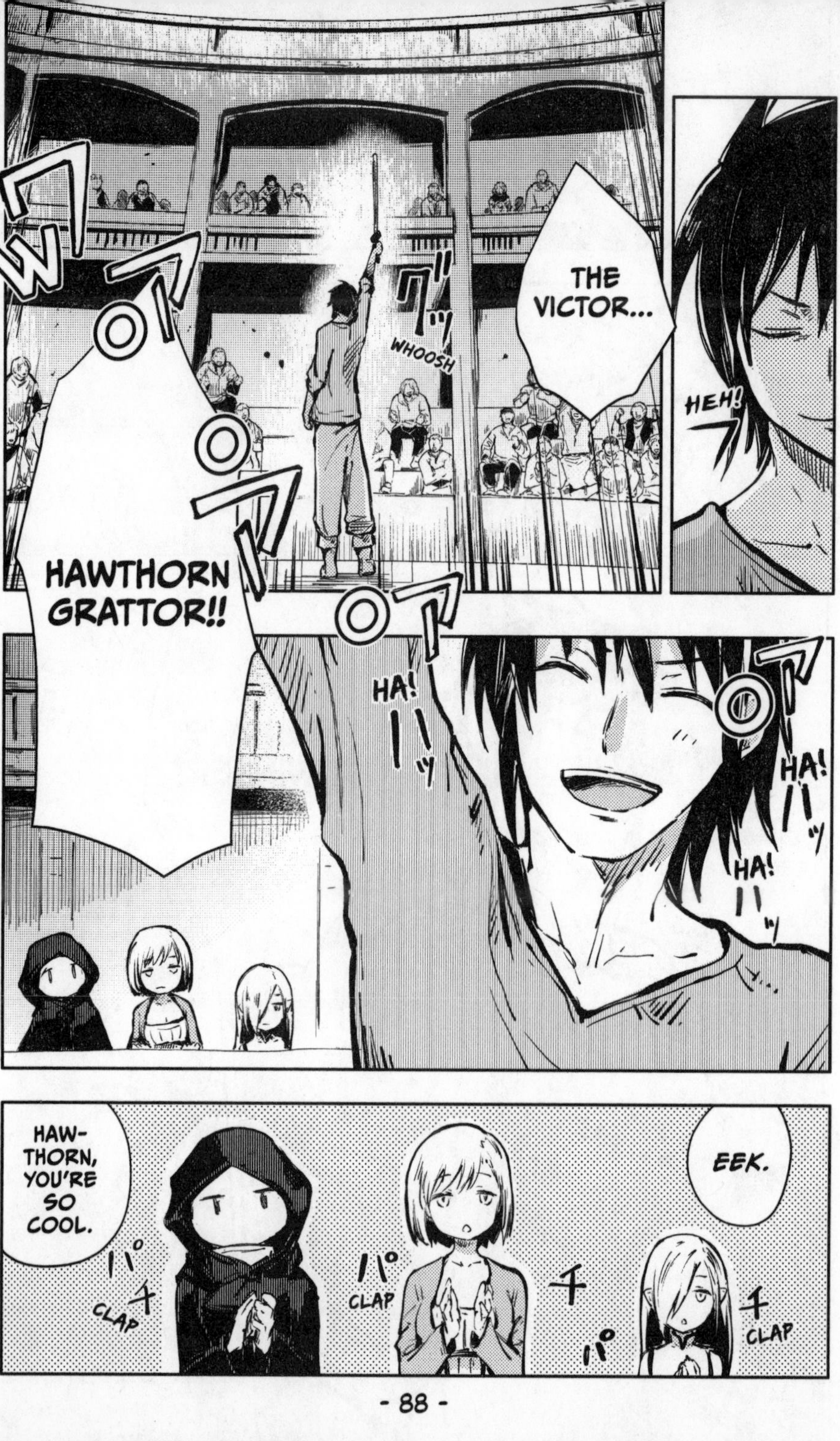
HEH!
THE VICTOR...
HAWTHORN GRATTOR!!
WHOOSH
HA!
HA!
HA!
EEK.
CLAP
CLAP
HAW-THORN, YOU'RE SO COOL.
CLAP

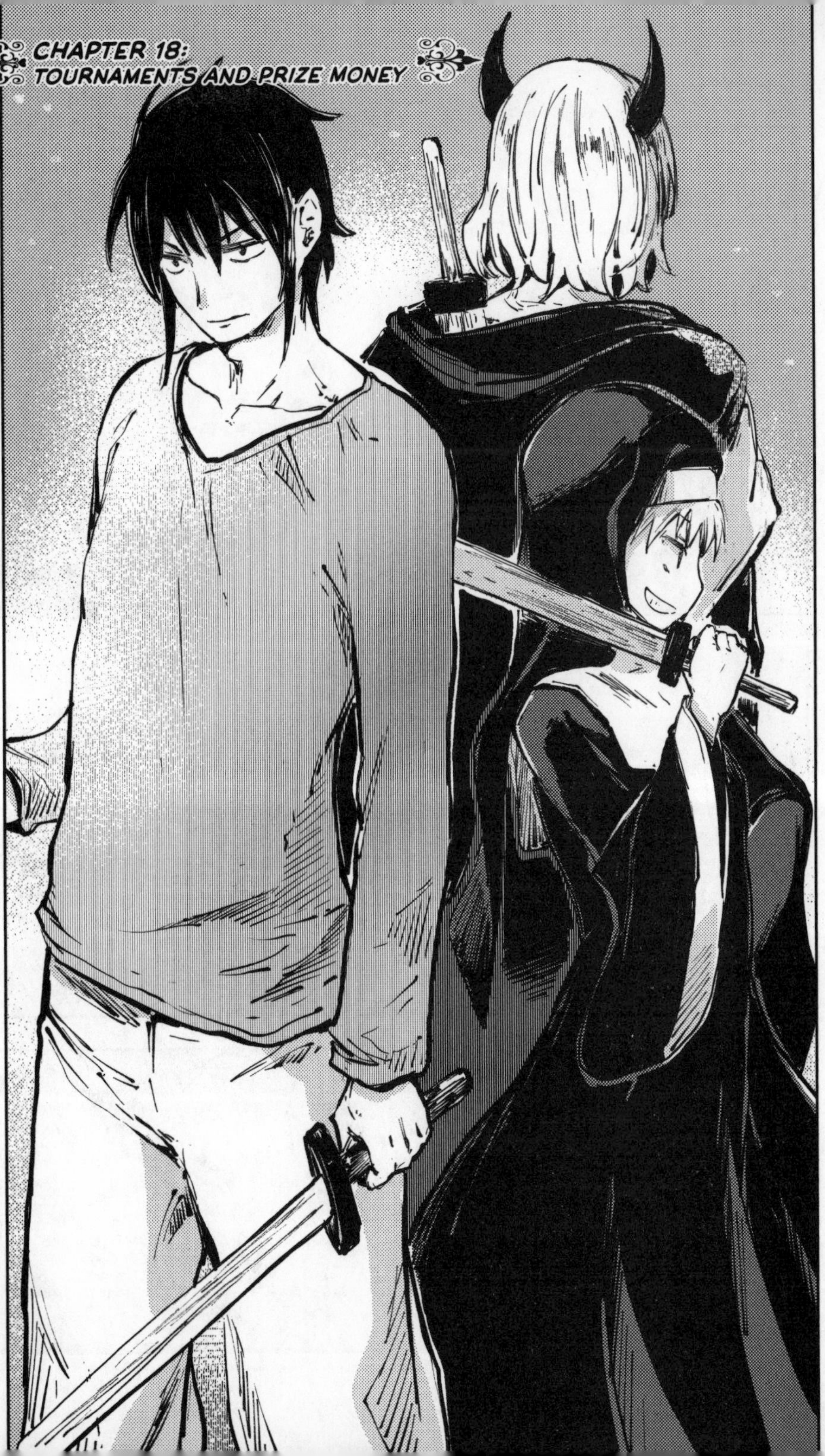
CHAPTER 18:
TOURNAMENTS AND PRIZE MONEY

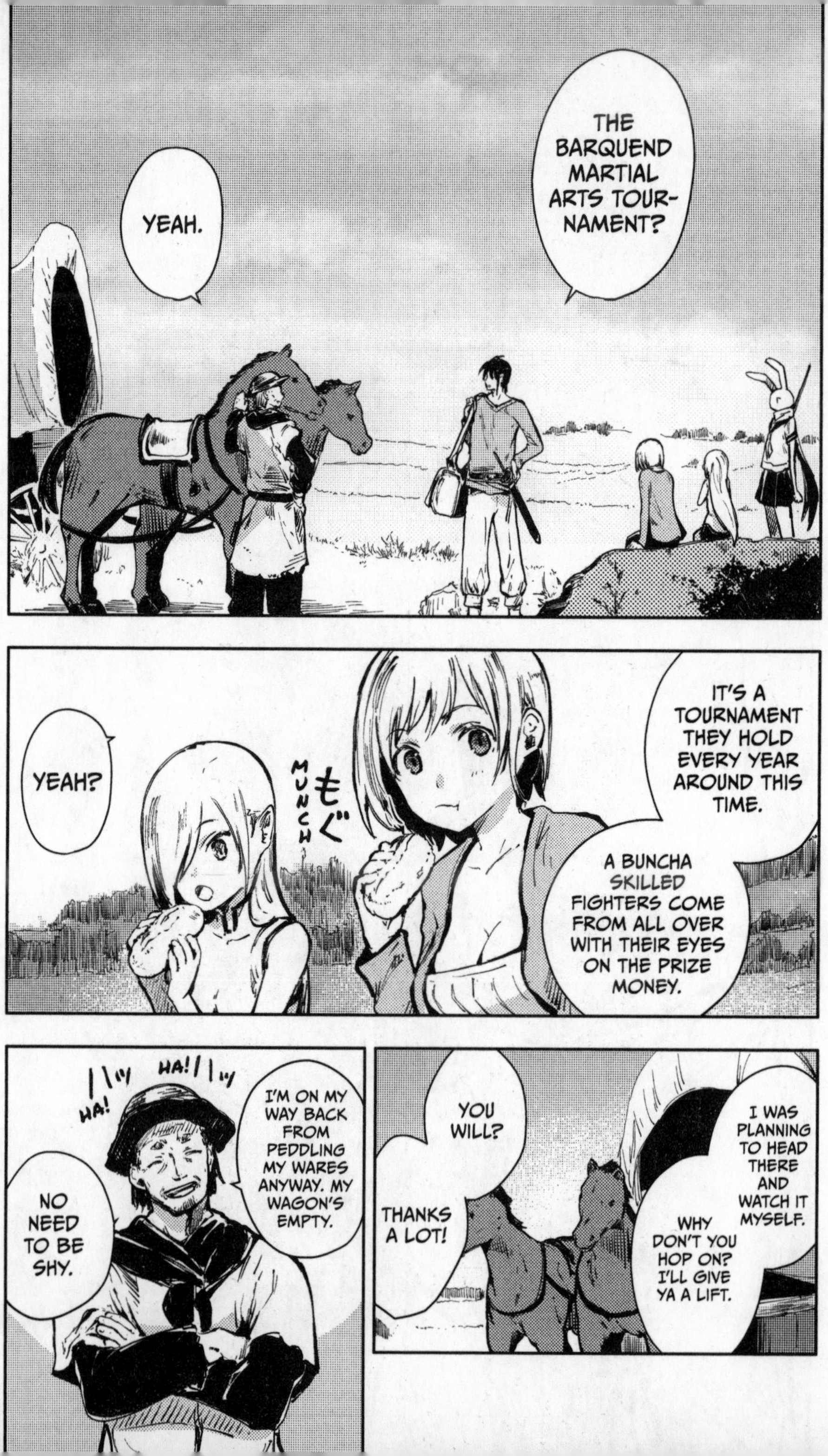
THE BARQUEND MARTIAL ARTS TOURNAMENT?
YEAH.
IT'S A TOURNAMENT THEY HOLD EVERY YEAR AROUND THIS TIME.
A BUNCHA SKILLED FIGHTERS COME FROM ALL OVER WITH THEIR EYES ON THE PRIZE MONEY.
もぐ MUNCH
YEAH?
I WAS PLANNING TO HEAD THERE AND WATCH IT MYSELF.
WHY DON'T YOU HOP ON? I'LL GIVE YA A LIFT.
YOU WILL?
THANKS A LOT!
ハッ HA! ハッ HA!
I'M ON MY WAY BACK FROM PEDDLING MY WARES ANYWAY. MY WAGON'S EMPTY.
NO NEED TO BE SHY.

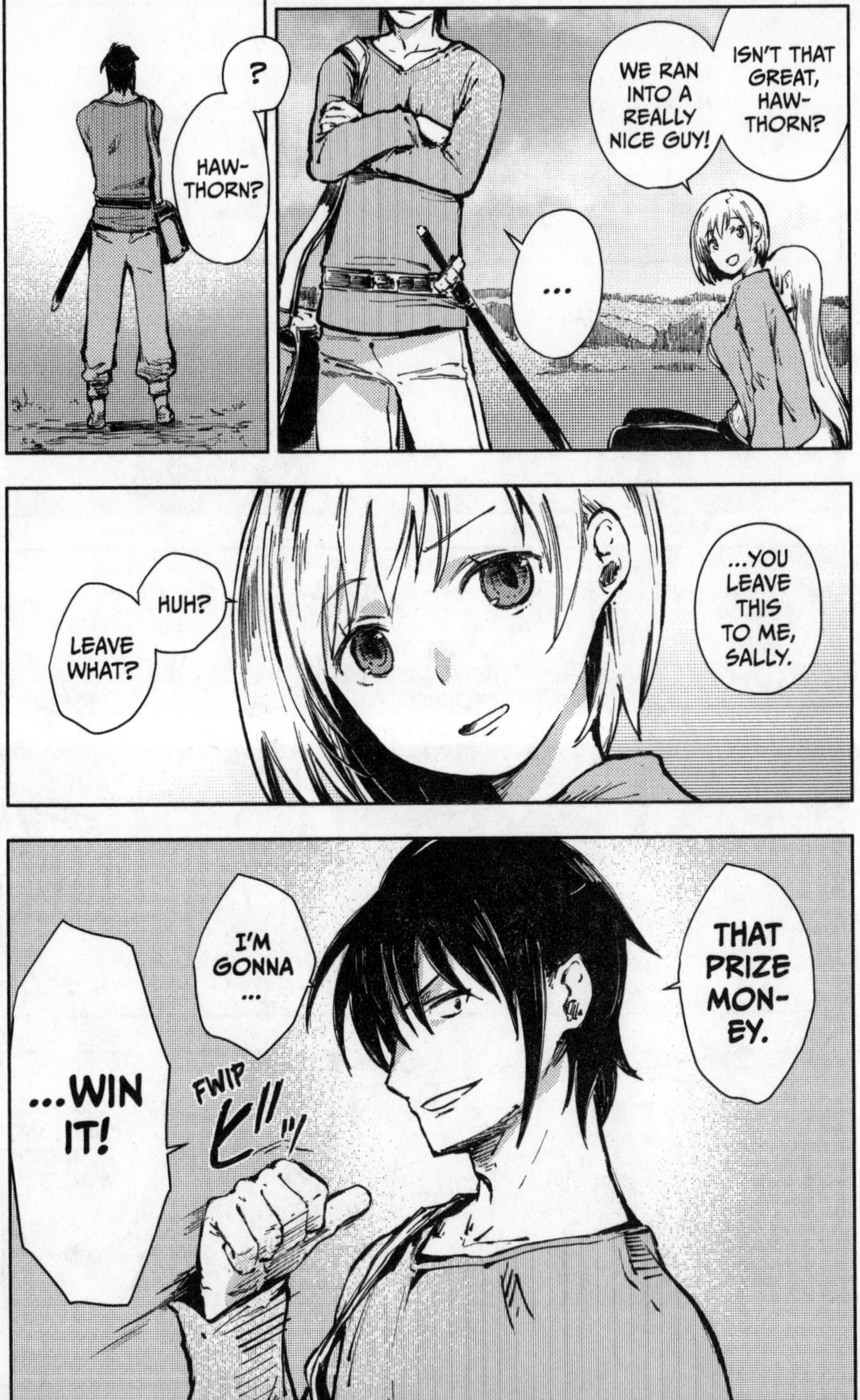
ISN'T THAT GREAT, HAW-THORN?
WE RAN INTO A REALLY NICE GUY!
...
?
HAW-THORN?
...YOU LEAVE THIS TO ME, SALLY.
HUH?
LEAVE WHAT?
THAT PRIZE MON-EY.
I'M GONNA ...
FWIP
...WIN IT!

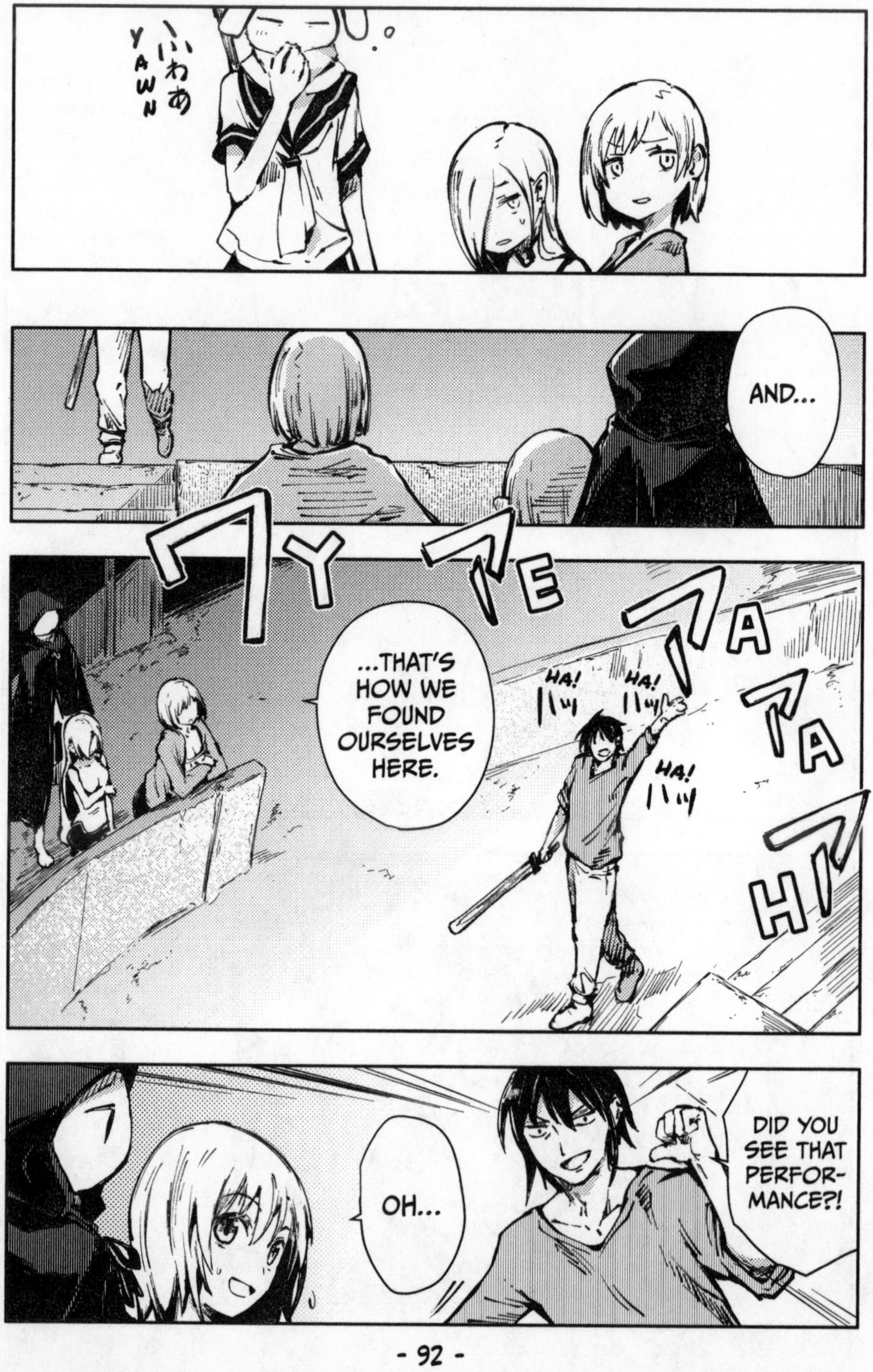
ふわあ YAWN
AND...
WYEAAAH
HA! バッ
HA! バッ
HA! バッ
...THAT'S HOW WE FOUND OURSELVES HERE.
DID YOU SEE THAT PERFORMANCE?!
OH...

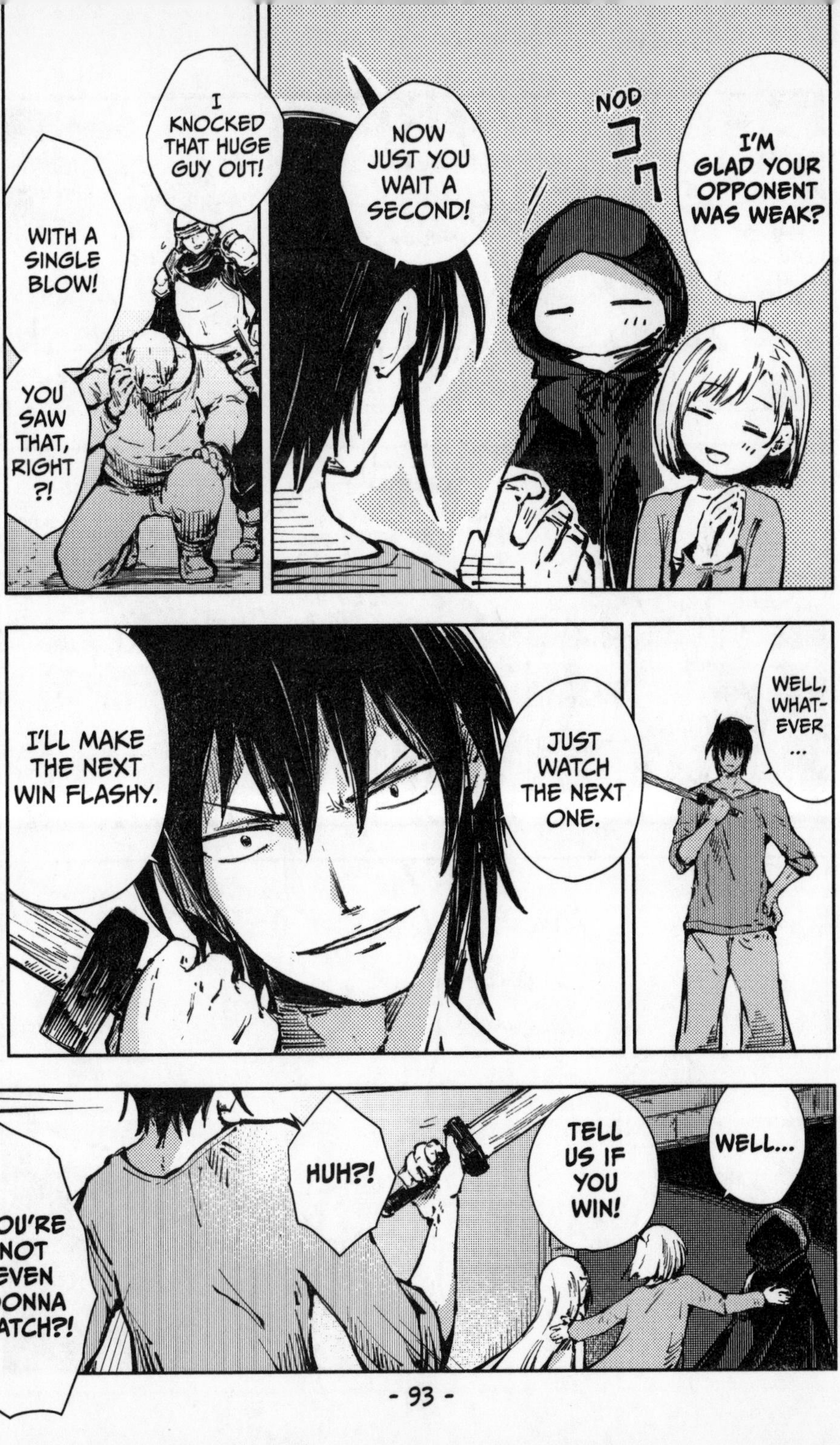
I'M GLAD YOUR OPPONENT WAS WEAK?
NOD
NOW JUST YOU WAIT A SECOND!
I KNOCKED THAT HUGE GUY OUT!
WITH A SINGLE BLOW!
YOU SAW THAT, RIGHT?!
WELL, WHAT-EVER...
JUST WATCH THE NEXT ONE.
I'LL MAKE THE NEXT WIN FLASHY.
WELL...
TELL US IF YOU WIN!
HUH?!
YOU'RE NOT EVEN GONNA WATCH?!

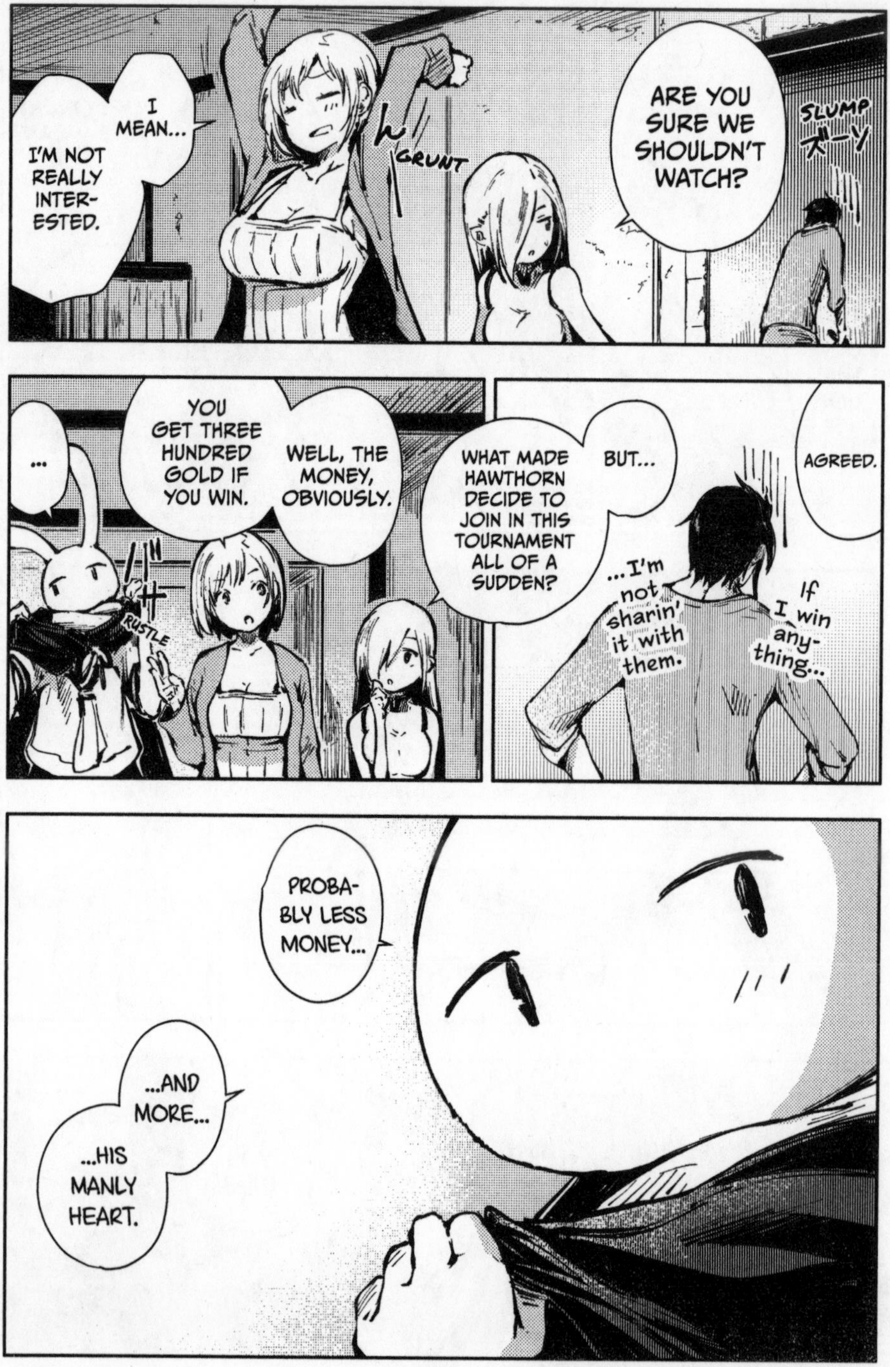
SLUMP
ズーン
ARE YOU SURE WE SHOULDN'T WATCH?
GRUNT
I MEAN...
I'M NOT REALLY INTER-ESTED.
AGREED.
BUT...
If I win any-thing...
...I'm not sharin' it with them.
WHAT MADE HAWTHORN DECIDE TO JOIN IN THIS TOURNAMENT ALL OF A SUDDEN?
WELL, THE MONEY, OBVIOUSLY.
YOU GET THREE HUNDRED GOLD IF YOU WIN.
...
RUSTLE
PROBA-BLY LESS MONEY...
...AND MORE...
...HIS MANLY HEART.

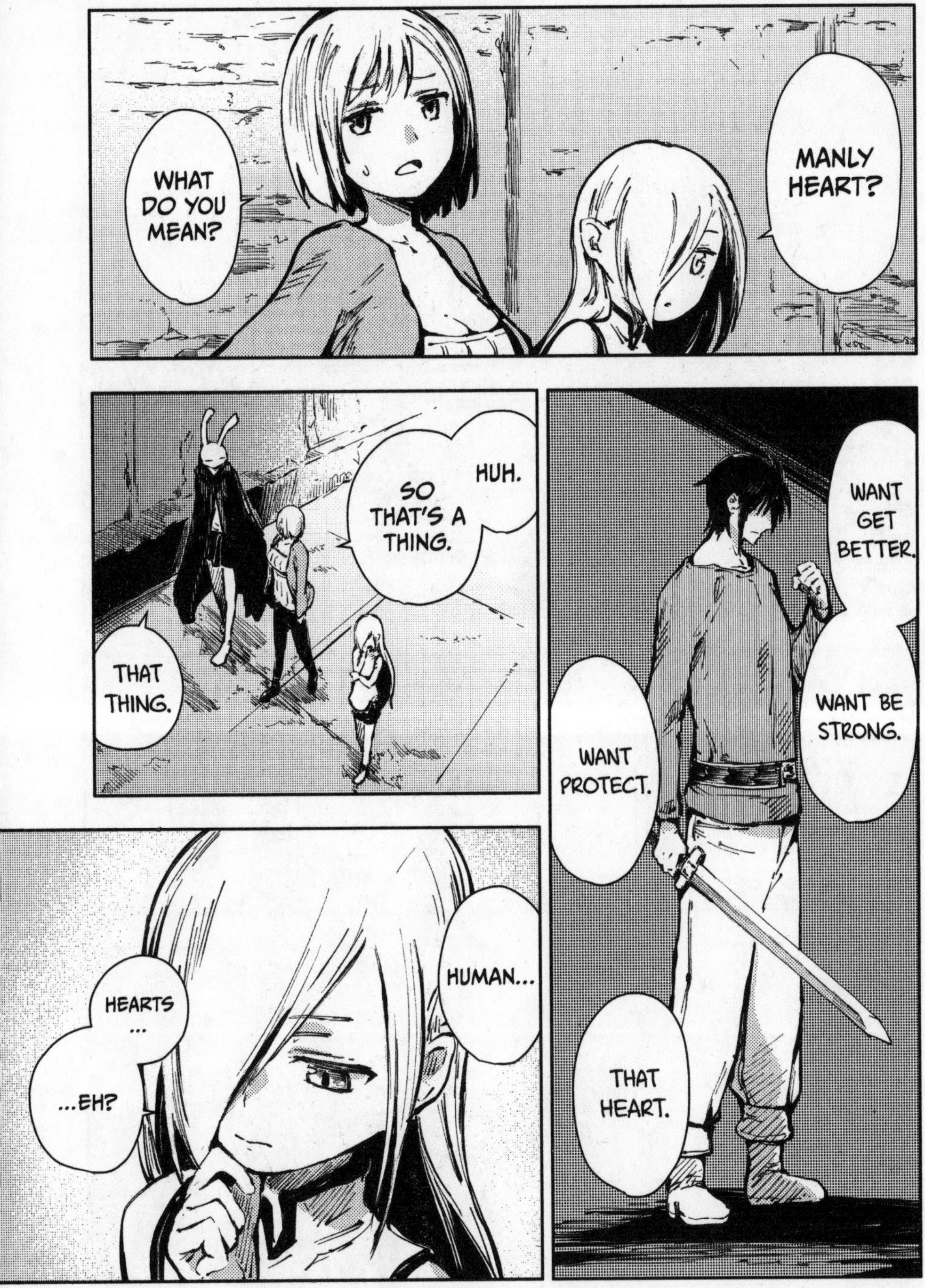
MANLY HEART?
WHAT DO YOU MEAN?
WANT GET BETTER.
WANT BE STRONG.
WANT PROTECT.
THAT HEART.
HUH. SO THAT'S A THING.
THAT THING.
HUMAN...
HEARTS ...
...EH?

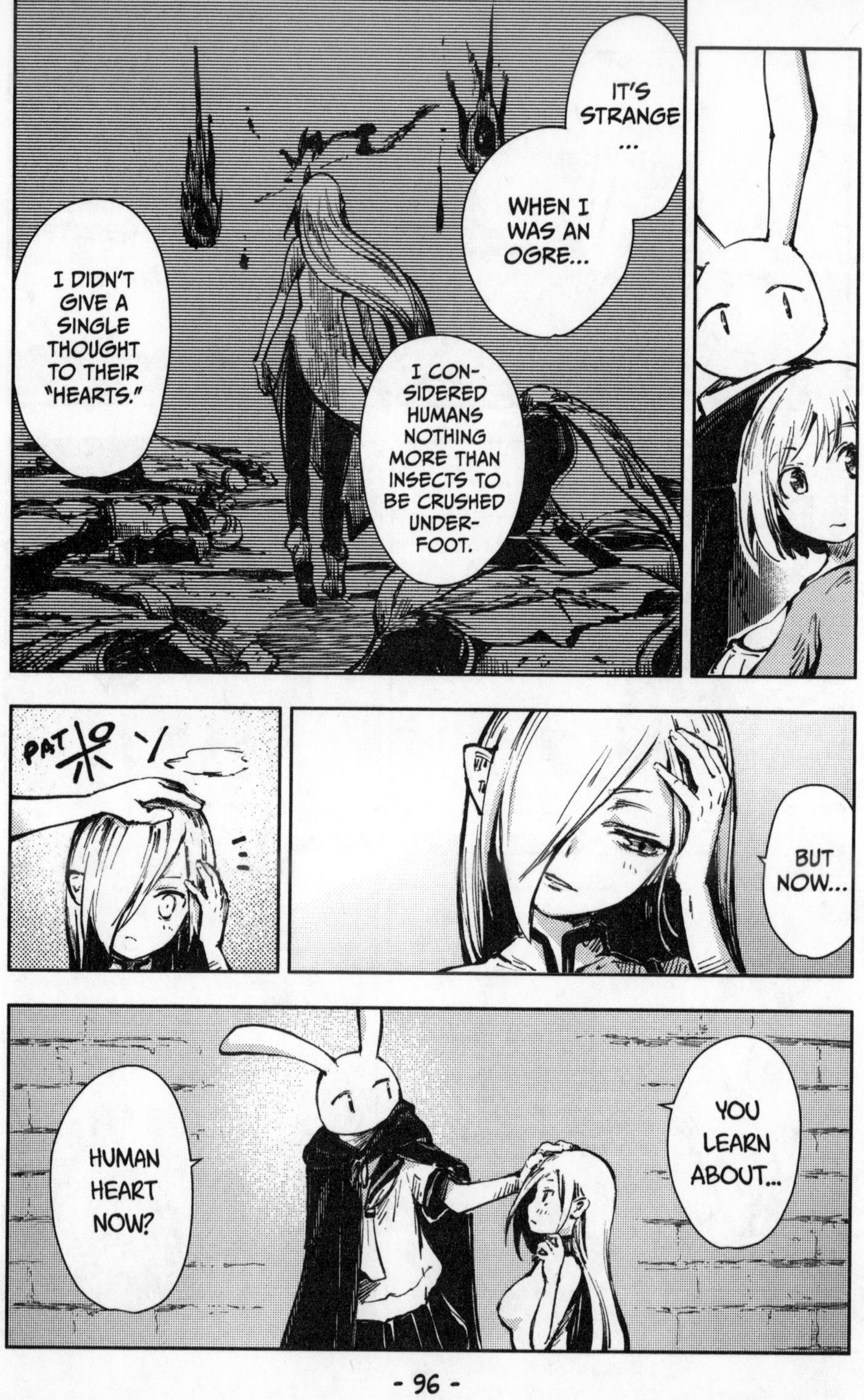
IT'S STRANGE ...
WHEN I WAS AN OGRE...
I CONSIDERED HUMANS NOTHING MORE THAN INSECTS TO BE CRUSHED UNDERFOOT.
I DIDN'T GIVE A SINGLE THOUGHT TO THEIR "HEARTS."
BUT NOW...
PAT
YOU LEARN ABOUT...
HUMAN HEART NOW?

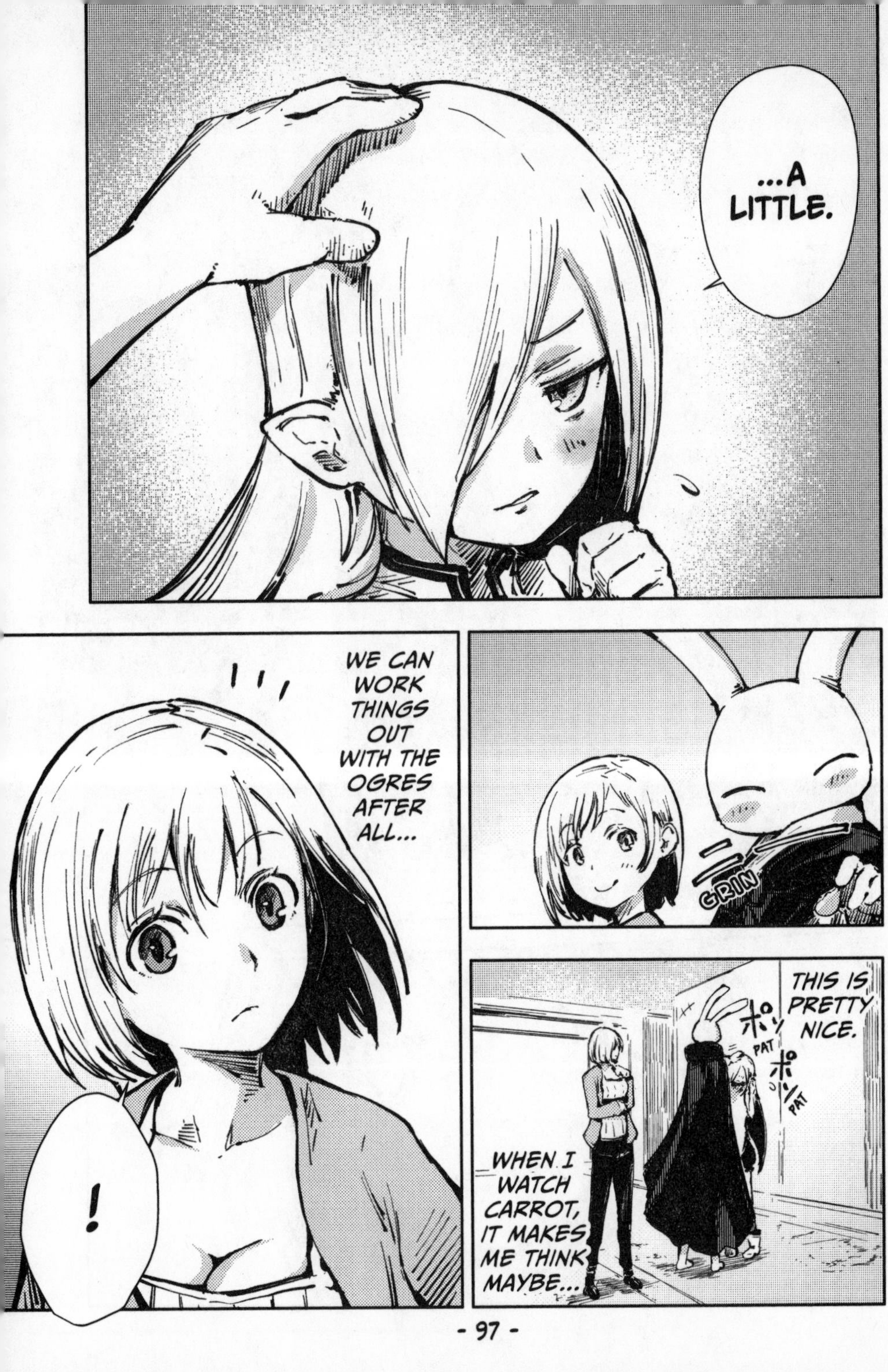
...A LITTLE.
GRIN
THIS IS PRETTY NICE.
ポン
PAT
ポン
PAT
WHEN I WATCH CARROT, IT MAKES ME THINK MAYBE...
WE CAN WORK THINGS OUT WITH THE OGRES AFTER ALL...
!

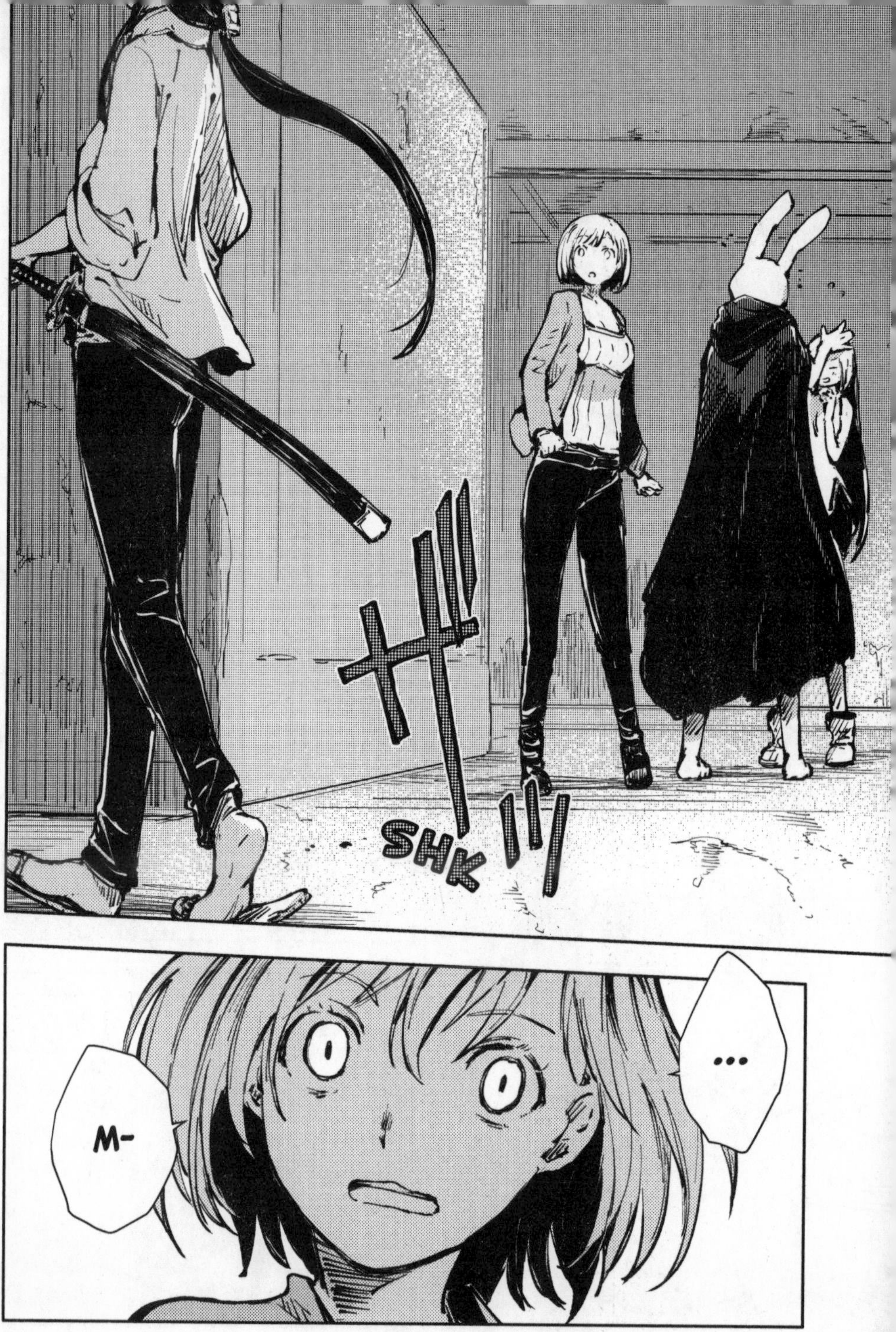
SHK
...
M-

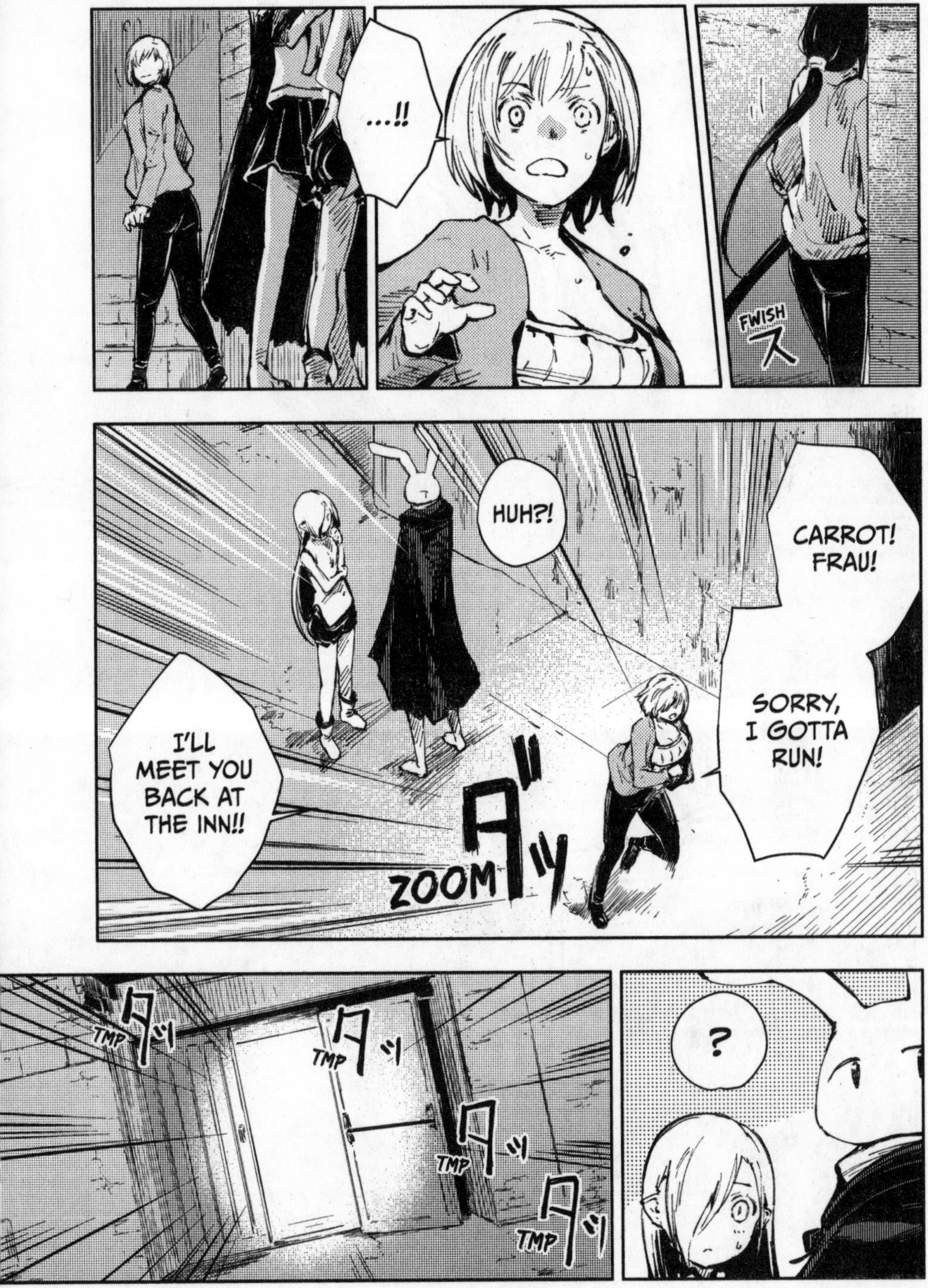
FWISH
ス
...!!
CARROT! FRAU!
SORRY, I GOTTA RUN!
HUH?!
I'LL MEET YOU BACK AT THE INN!!
ZOOM
ダッ
?
TMP
タッ
TMP
タッ
TMP
タッ
TMP
ダッ

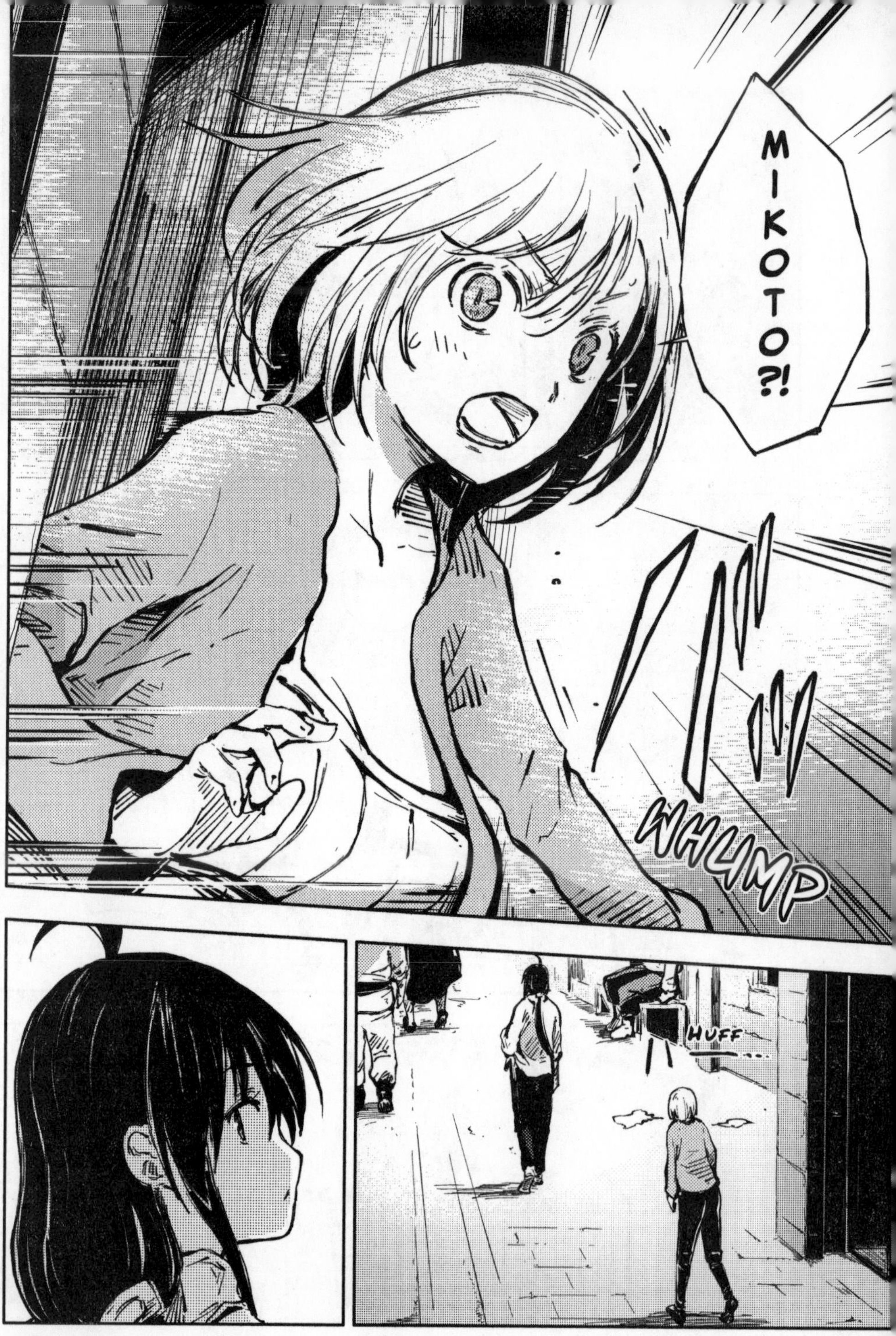
MIKOTO?!
WHUMP
HUFF...

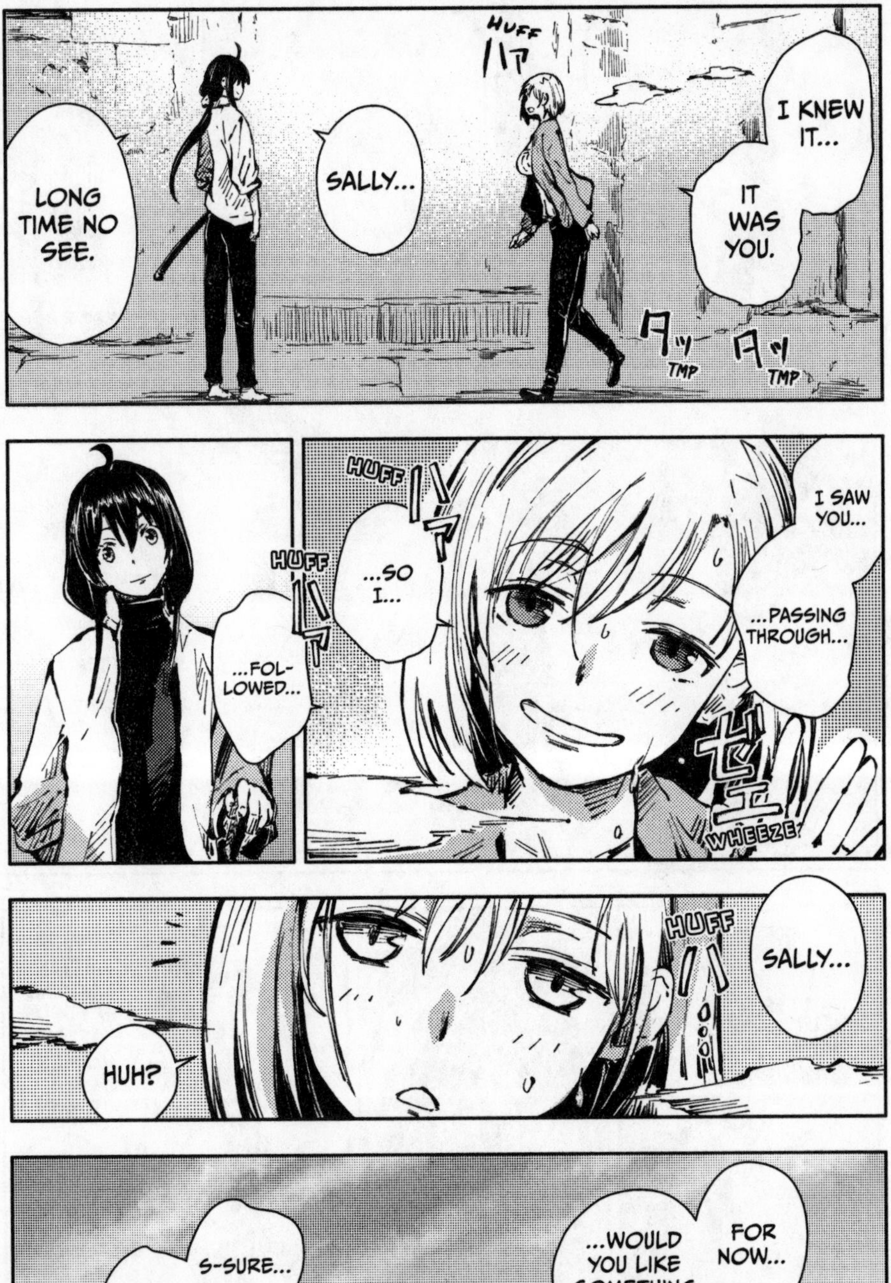
I KNEW IT...
IT WAS YOU.
HUFF ハァ
SALLY...
LONG TIME NO SEE.
タッ TMP
タッ TMP
I SAW YOU...
...PASSING THROUGH...
ゼェ WHEEZE
HUFF ハァ
...SO I...
HUFF ハァ
...FOL-LOWED...
SALLY...
HUFF ハ
HUH?
FOR NOW...
...WOULD YOU LIKE SOMETHING TO DRINK?
S-SURE...
THAT'S A GOOD IDEA...

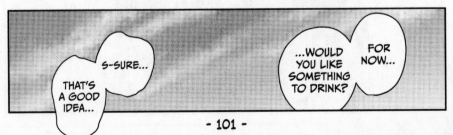

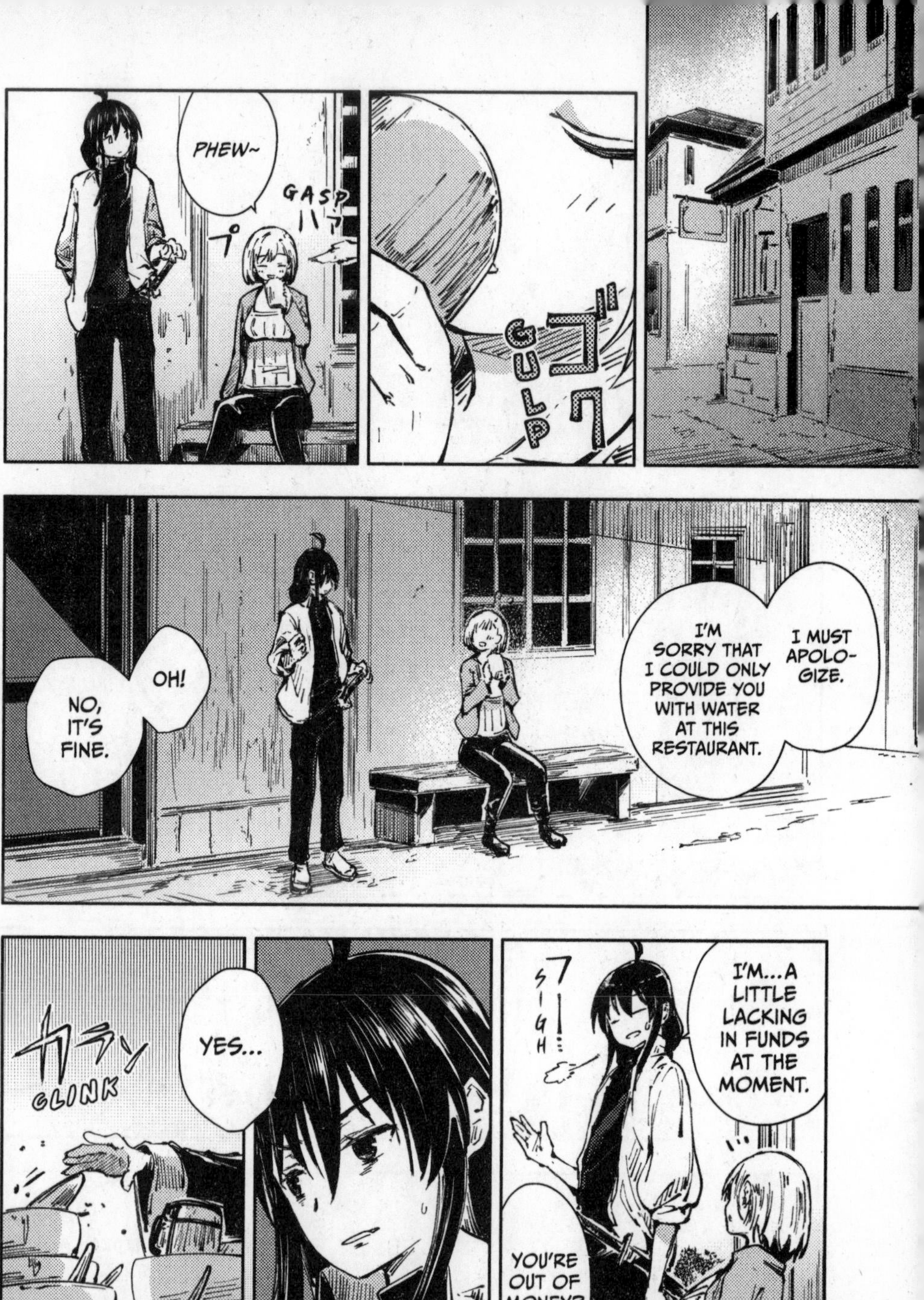
GULP
ゴク
PHEW~
GASP
ハァ
ぷ
I MUST APOLOGIZE.
I'M SORRY THAT I COULD ONLY PROVIDE YOU WITH WATER AT THIS RESTAURANT.
OH!
NO, IT'S FINE.
I'M...A LITTLE LACKING IN FUNDS AT THE MOMENT.
SIGH
フー
YOU'RE OUT OF MONEY?
YES...
カラン
CLINK

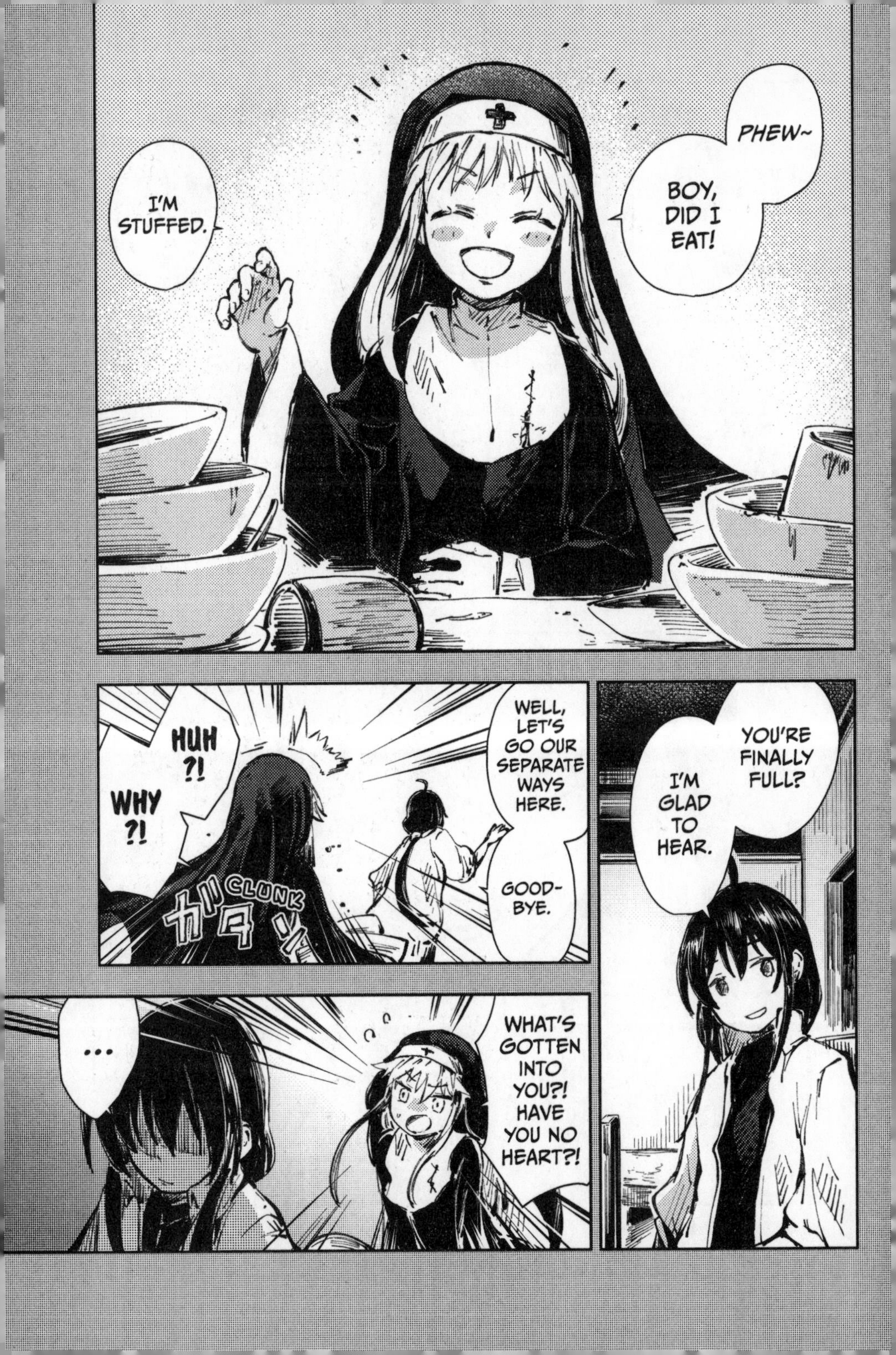
PHEW~
BOY, DID I EAT!
I'M STUFFED.
YOU'RE FINALLY FULL?
I'M GLAD TO HEAR.
WELL, LET'S GO OUR SEPARATE WAYS HERE.
GOOD-BYE.
HUH?!
WHY?!
CLUNK
カタン
WHAT'S GOTTEN INTO YOU?! HAVE YOU NO HEART?!
...

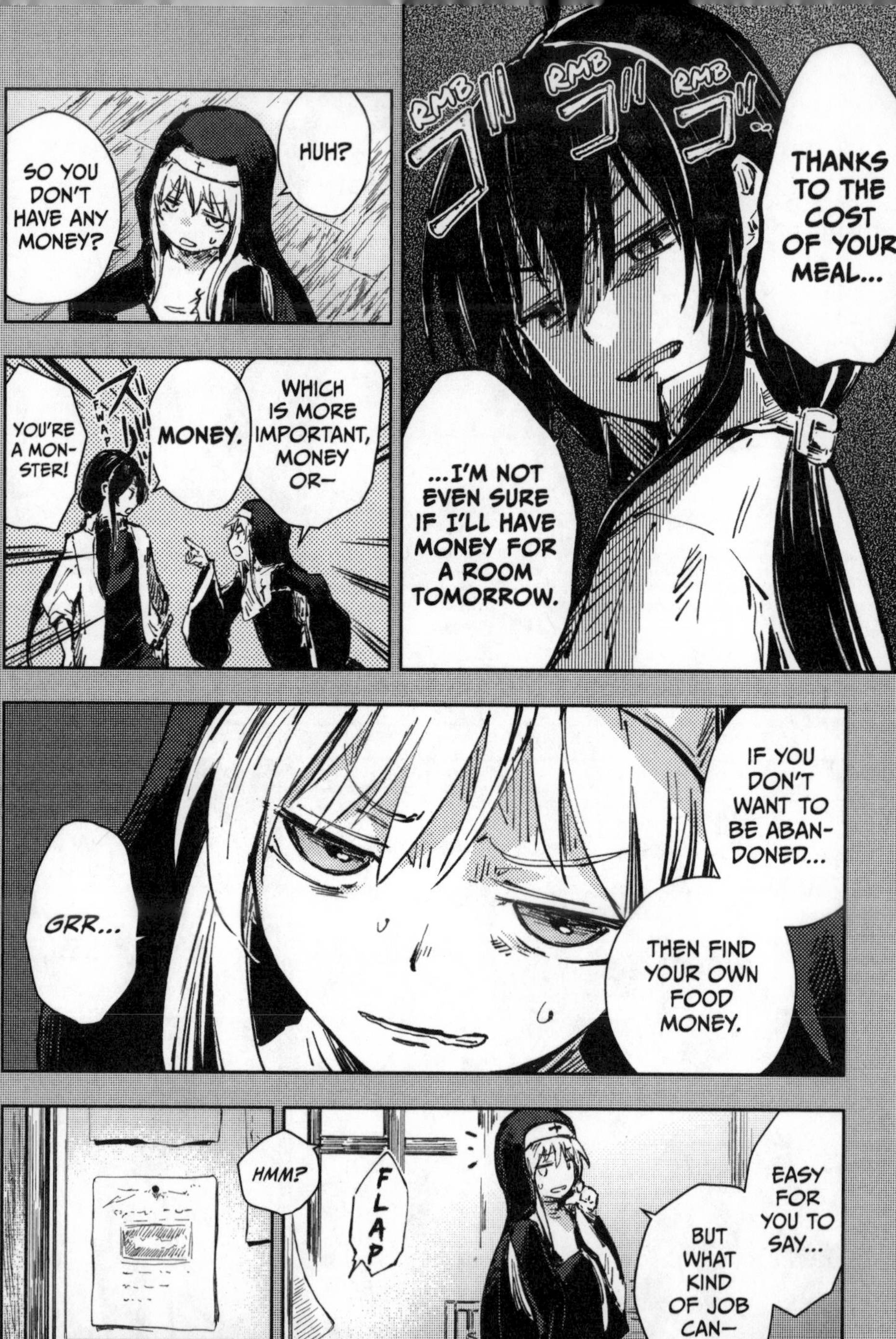
RMB RMB RMB
THANKS TO THE COST OF YOUR MEAL...
...I'M NOT EVEN SURE IF I'LL HAVE MONEY FOR A ROOM TOMORROW.
HUH?
SO YOU DON'T HAVE ANY MONEY?
WHICH IS MORE IMPORTANT, MONEY OR—
MONEY.
FWAP
YOU'RE A MON-STER!
IF YOU DON'T WANT TO BE ABAN-DONED...
THEN FIND YOUR OWN FOOD MONEY.
GRR...
EASY FOR YOU TO SAY...
BUT WHAT KIND OF JOB CAN—
FLAP
HMM?

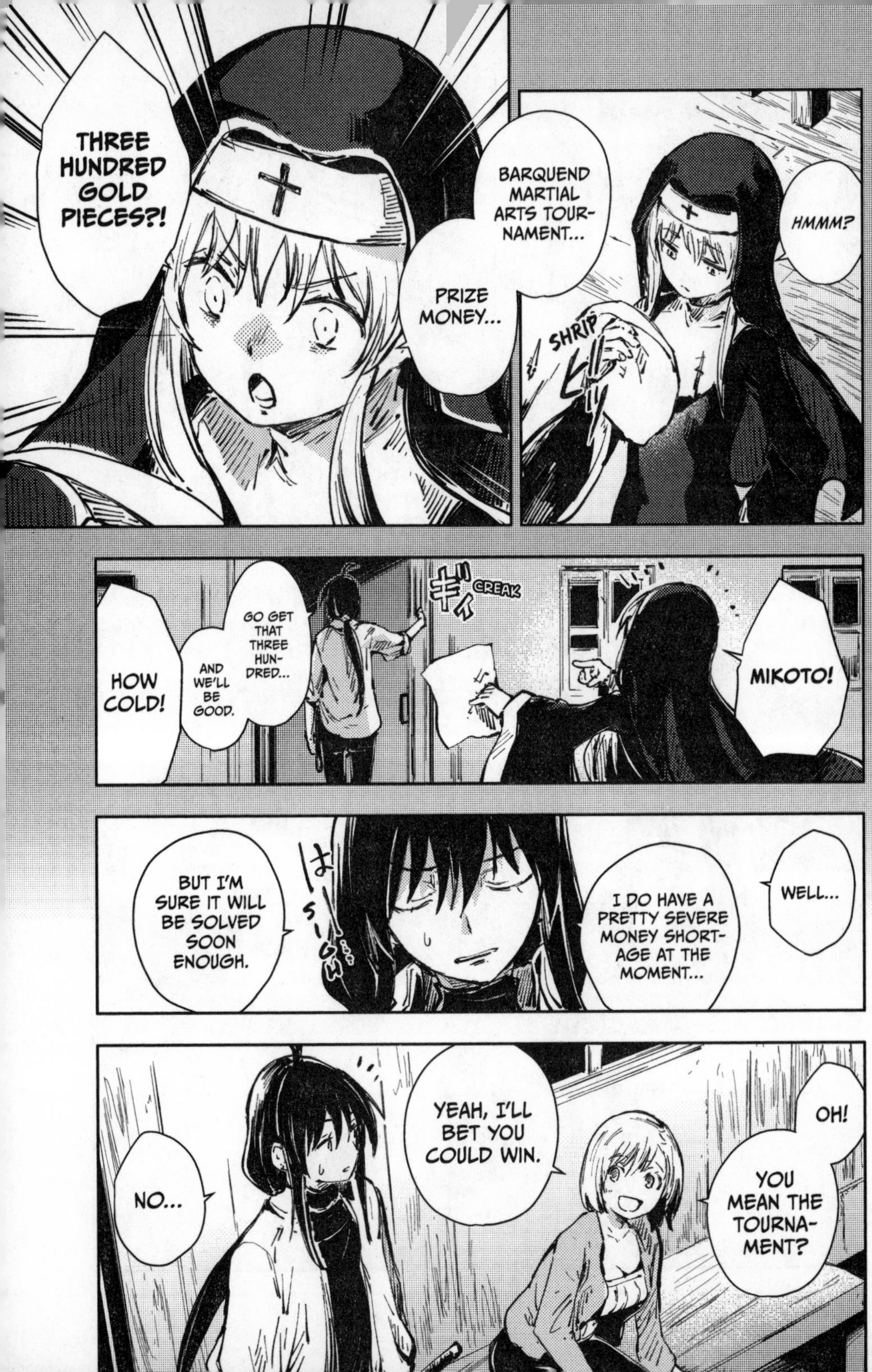
HMMM?
BARQUEND MARTIAL ARTS TOUR-NAMENT...
PRIZE MONEY...
SHRIP
THREE HUNDRED GOLD PIECES?!
MIKOTO!
CREAK
GO GET THAT THREE HUN-DRED...
AND WE'LL BE GOOD.
HOW COLD!
WELL...
I DO HAVE A PRETTY SEVERE MONEY SHORT-AGE AT THE MOMENT...
BUT I'M SURE IT WILL BE SOLVED SOON ENOUGH.
OH!
YOU MEAN THE TOURNA-MENT?
YEAH, I'LL BET YOU COULD WIN.
NO...

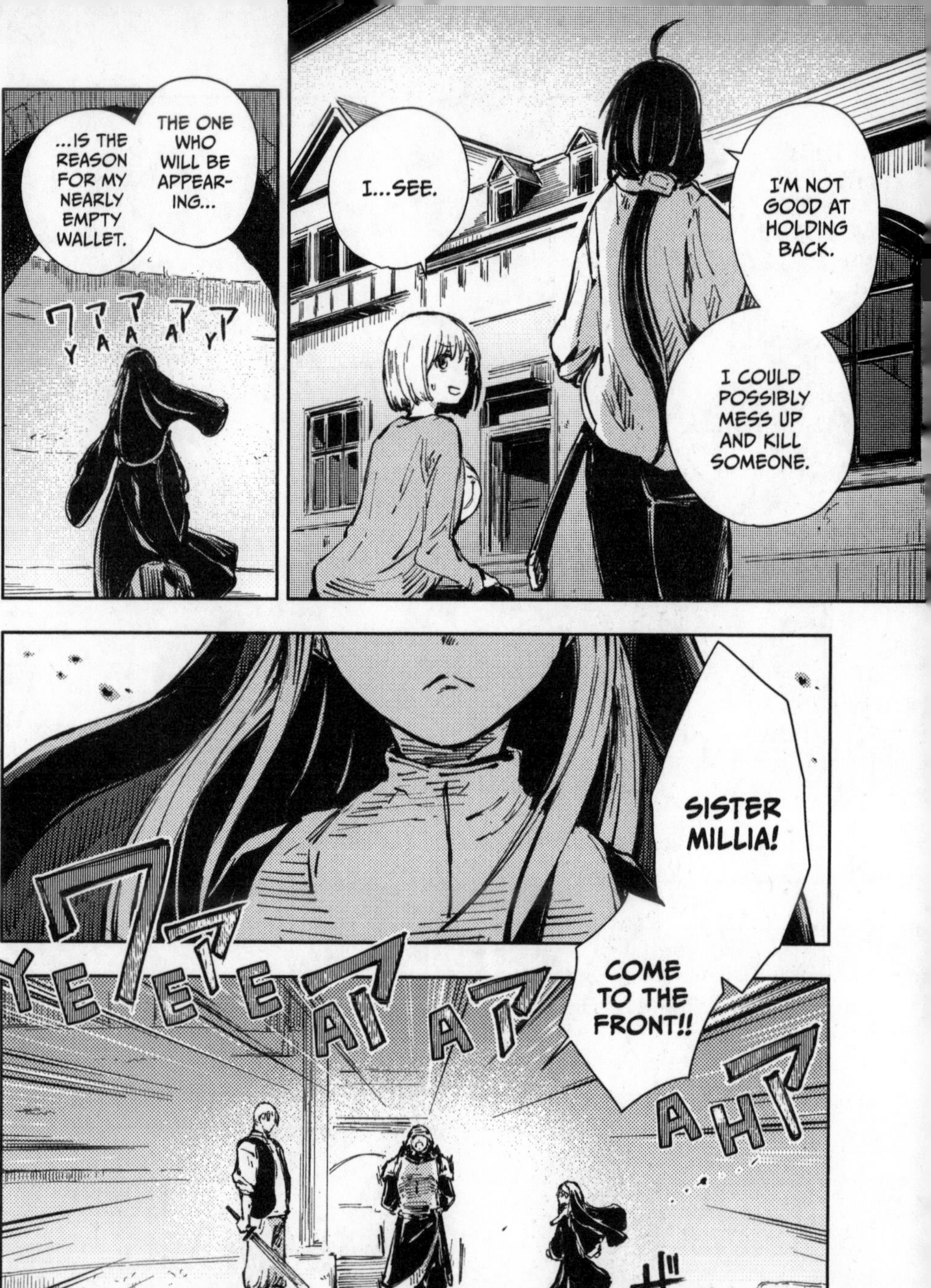
I'M NOT GOOD AT HOLDING BACK.
I COULD POSSIBLY MESS UP AND KILL SOMEONE.
I...SEE.
THE ONE WHO WILL BE APPEARING...
...IS THE REASON FOR MY NEARLY EMPTY WALLET.
YAAAY
SISTER MILLIA!
COME TO THE FRONT!!
YEEEAAAH
SHK

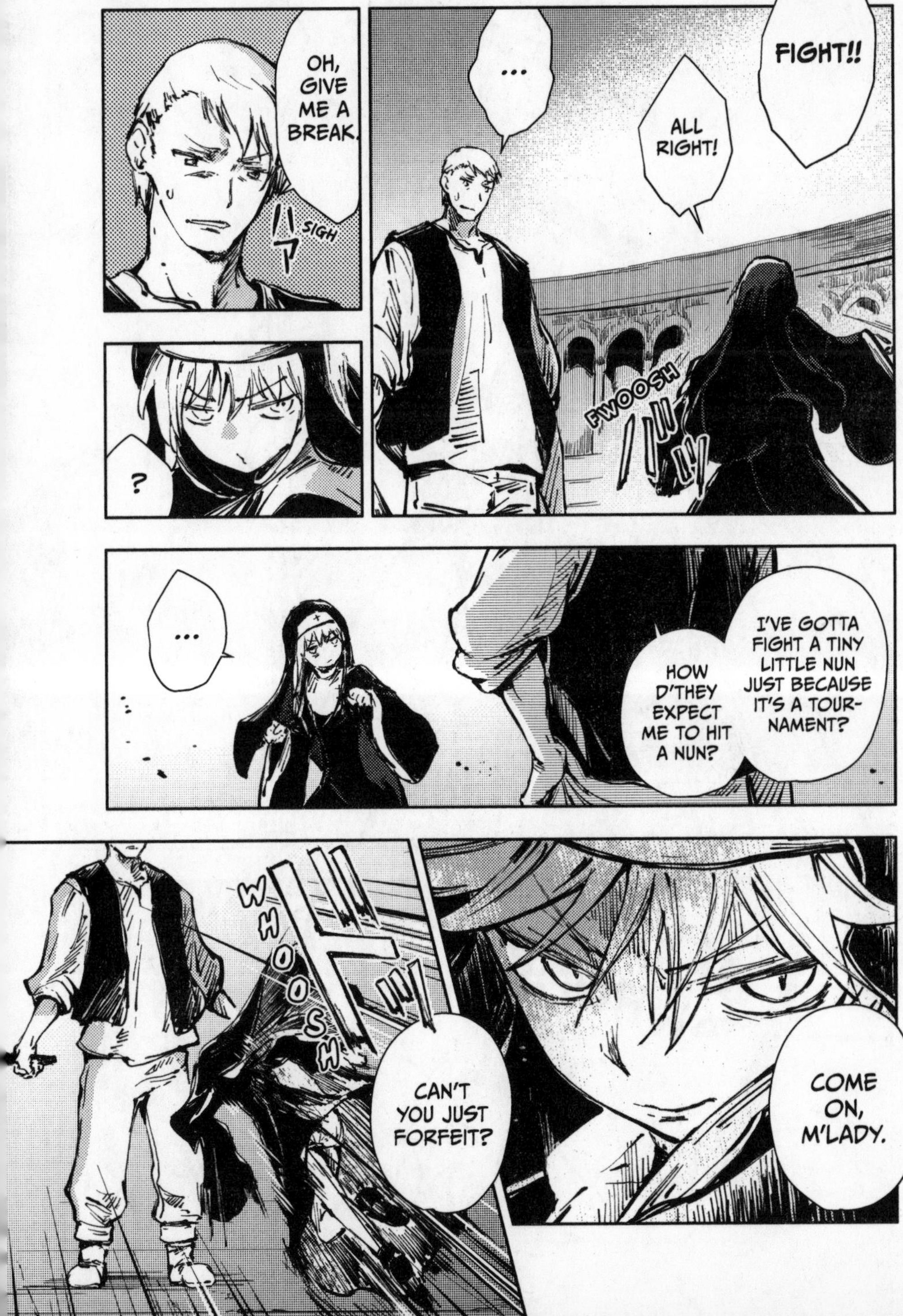
FIGHT!!
ALL RIGHT!
...
FWOOSH
OH, GIVE ME A BREAK.
SIGH
?
I'VE GOTTA FIGHT A TINY LITTLE NUN JUST BECAUSE IT'S A TOUR-NAMENT?
HOW D'THEY EXPECT ME TO HIT A NUN?
...
COME ON, M'LADY.
CAN'T YOU JUST FORFEIT?
WHOOSH

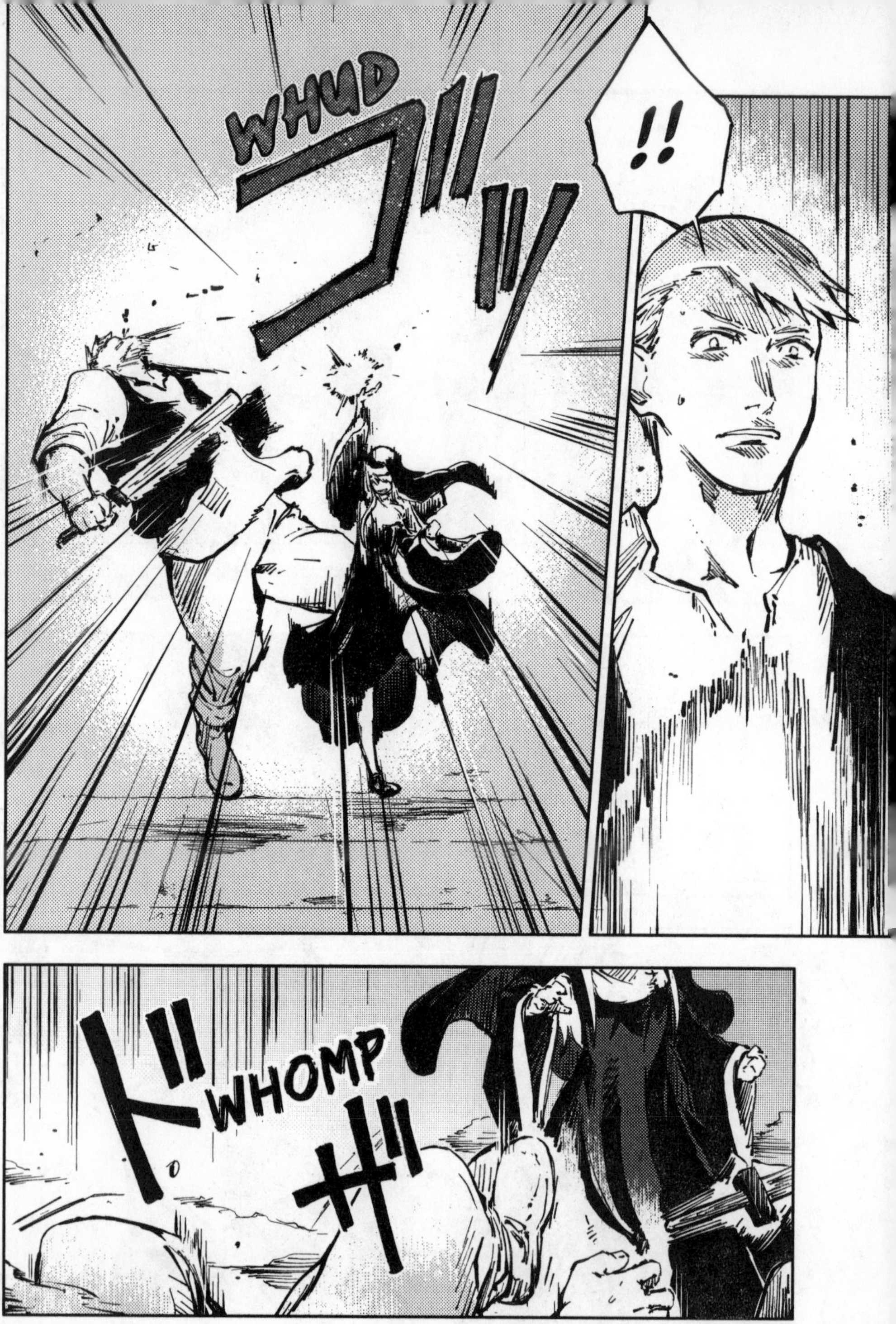
!!
WHUD
ゴッ
WHOMP
ドザッ

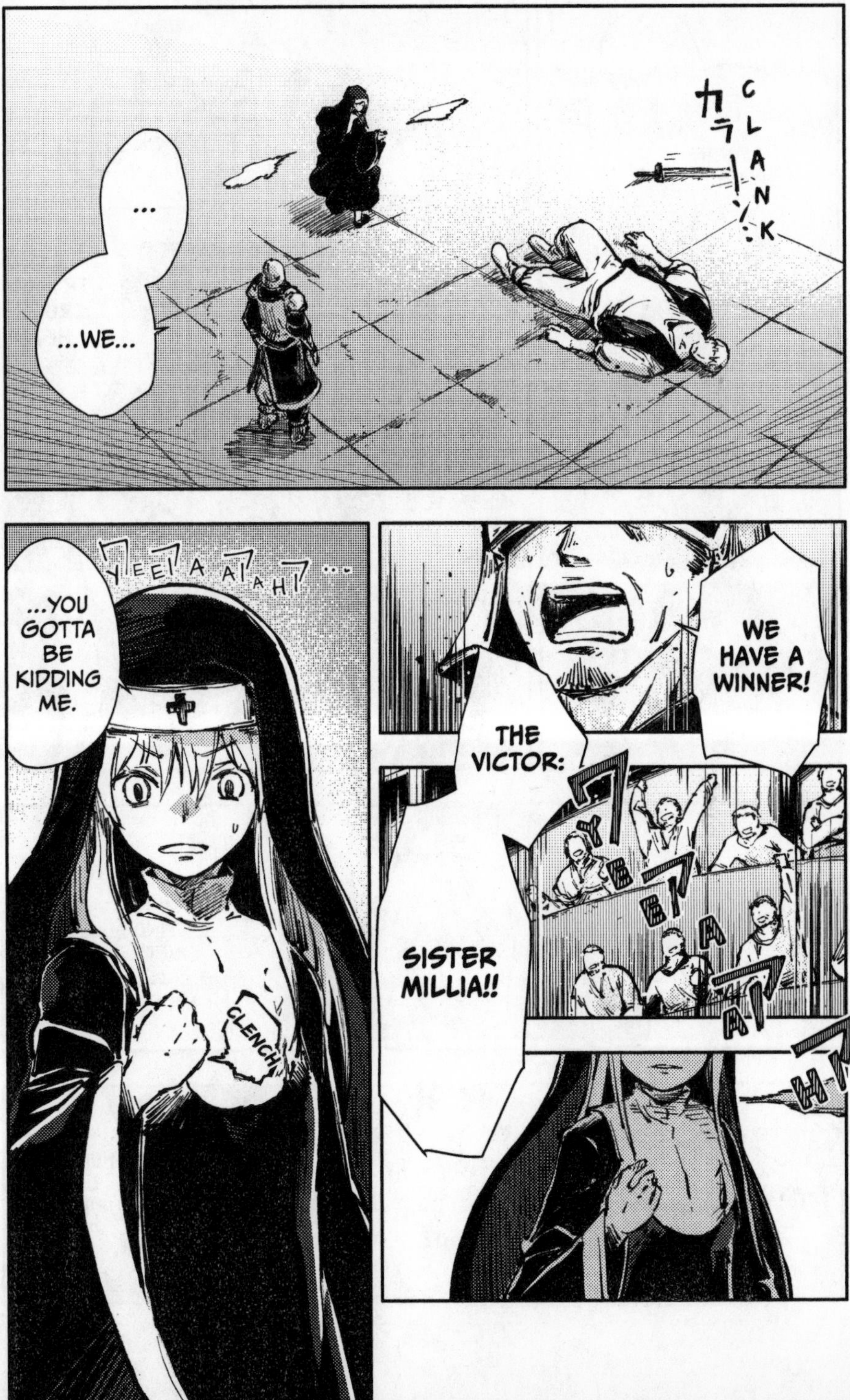
CLANK
...
...WE...
WE HAVE A WINNER!
THE VICTOR:
SISTER MILLIA!!
YEEAAAH
YEEAAAH...
...YOU GOTTA BE KIDDING ME.
CLENCH

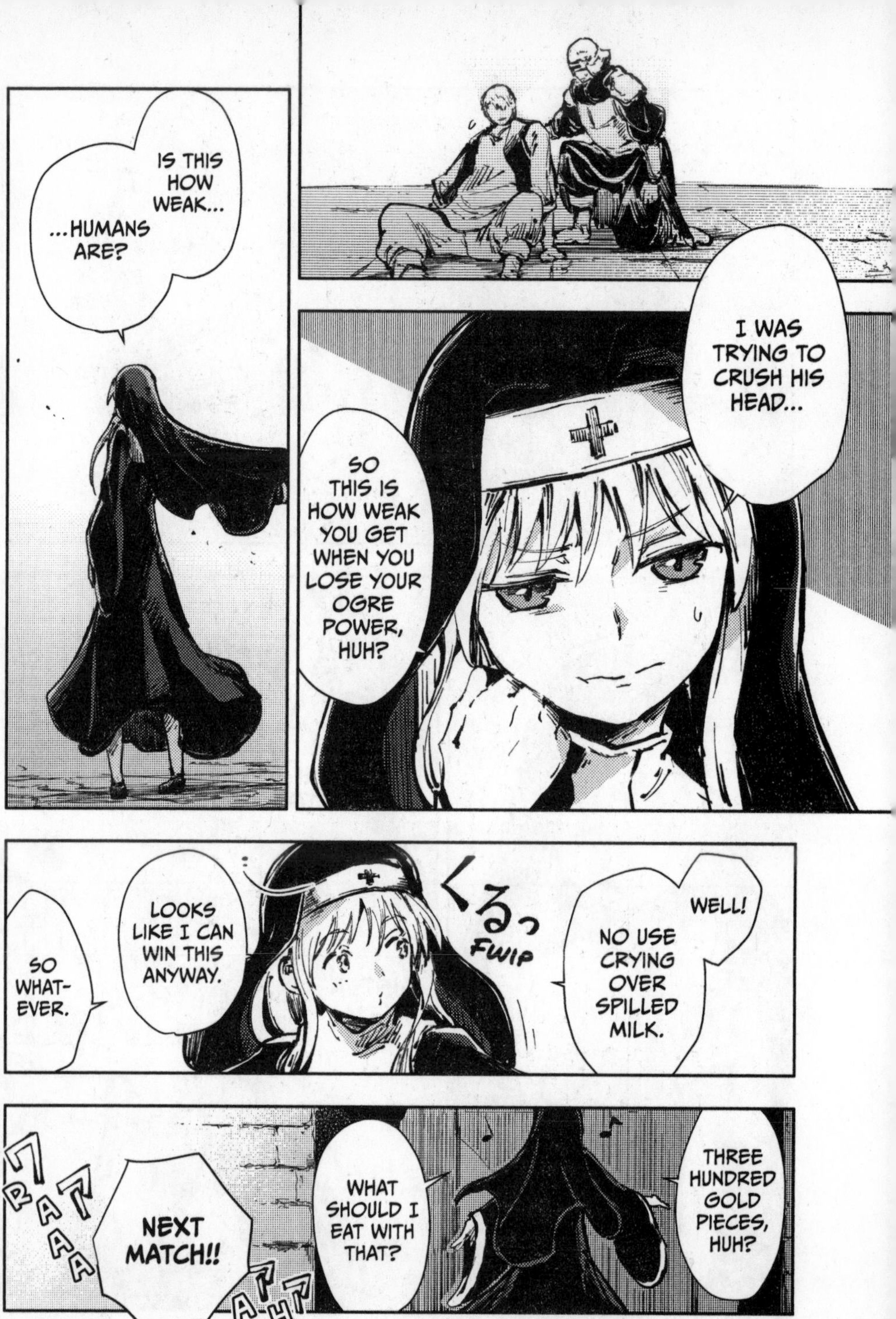

I WAS TRYING TO CRUSH HIS HEAD...
SO THIS IS HOW WEAK YOU GET WHEN YOU LOSE YOUR OGRE POWER, HUH?
IS THIS HOW WEAK...
...HUMANS ARE?
WELL!
NO USE CRYING OVER SPILLED MILK.
くるっ
FWIP
LOOKS LIKE I CAN WIN THIS ANYWAY.
SO WHATEVER.
THREE HUNDRED GOLD PIECES, HUH?
WHAT SHOULD I EAT WITH THAT?
AH
NEXT MATCH!!
RAAA

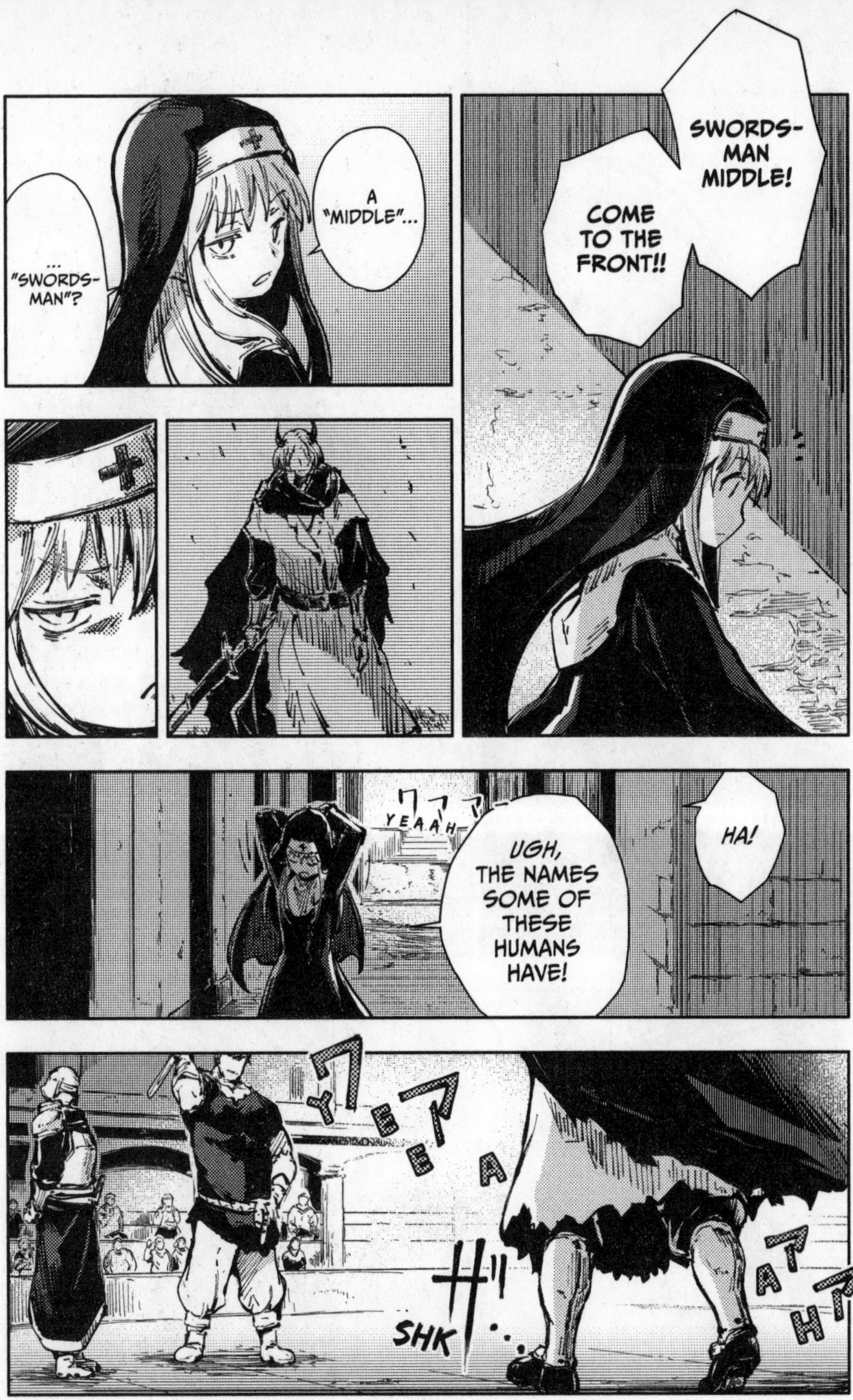
SWORDS-MAN MIDDLE!
COME TO THE FRONT!!
A "MIDDLE"...
... "SWORDS-MAN"?
HA!
UGH, THE NAMES SOME OF THESE HUMANS HAVE!
YEAAAH
AAAHH
YEAA
SHK

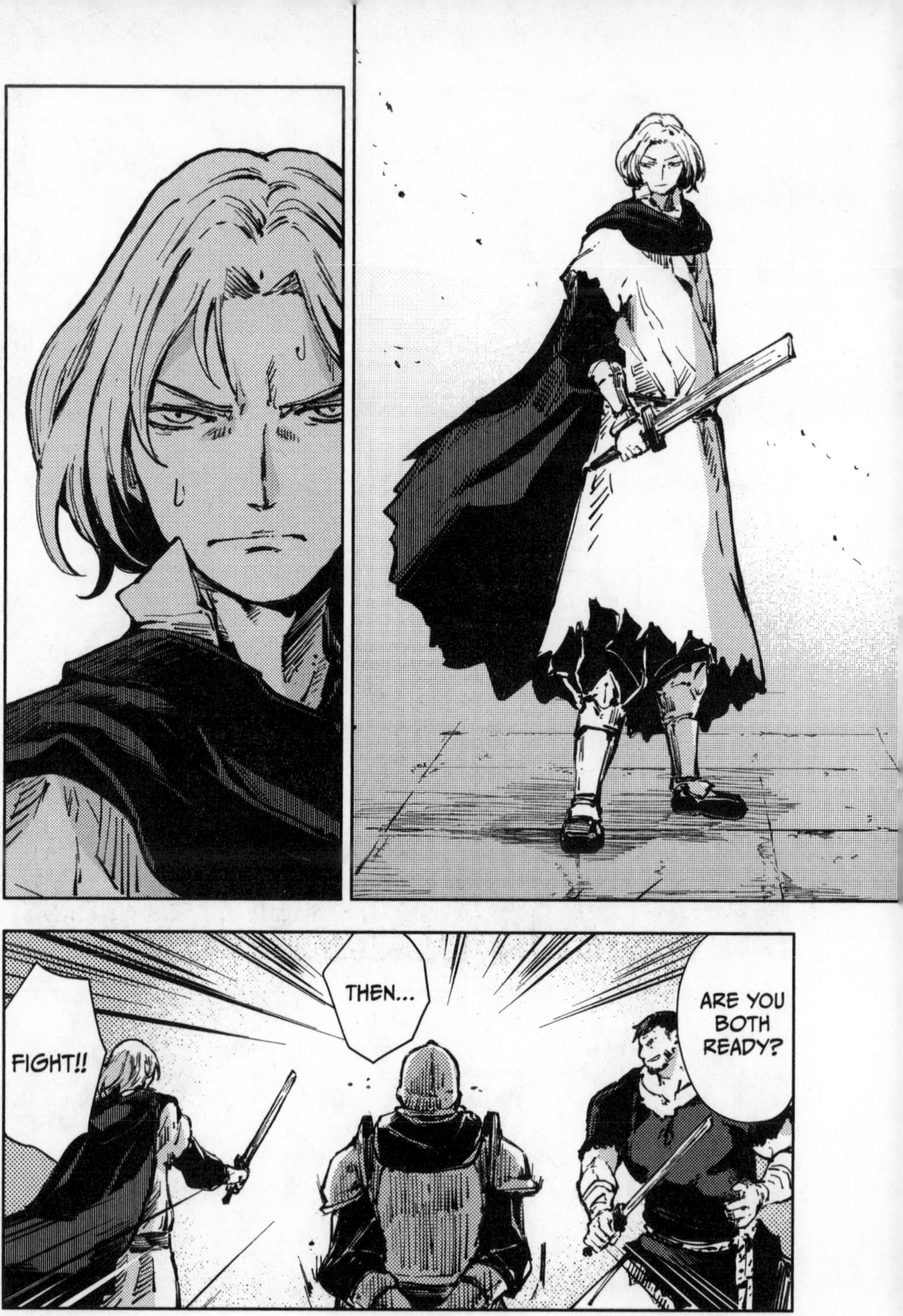
ARE YOU BOTH READY?
THEN...
FIGHT!!

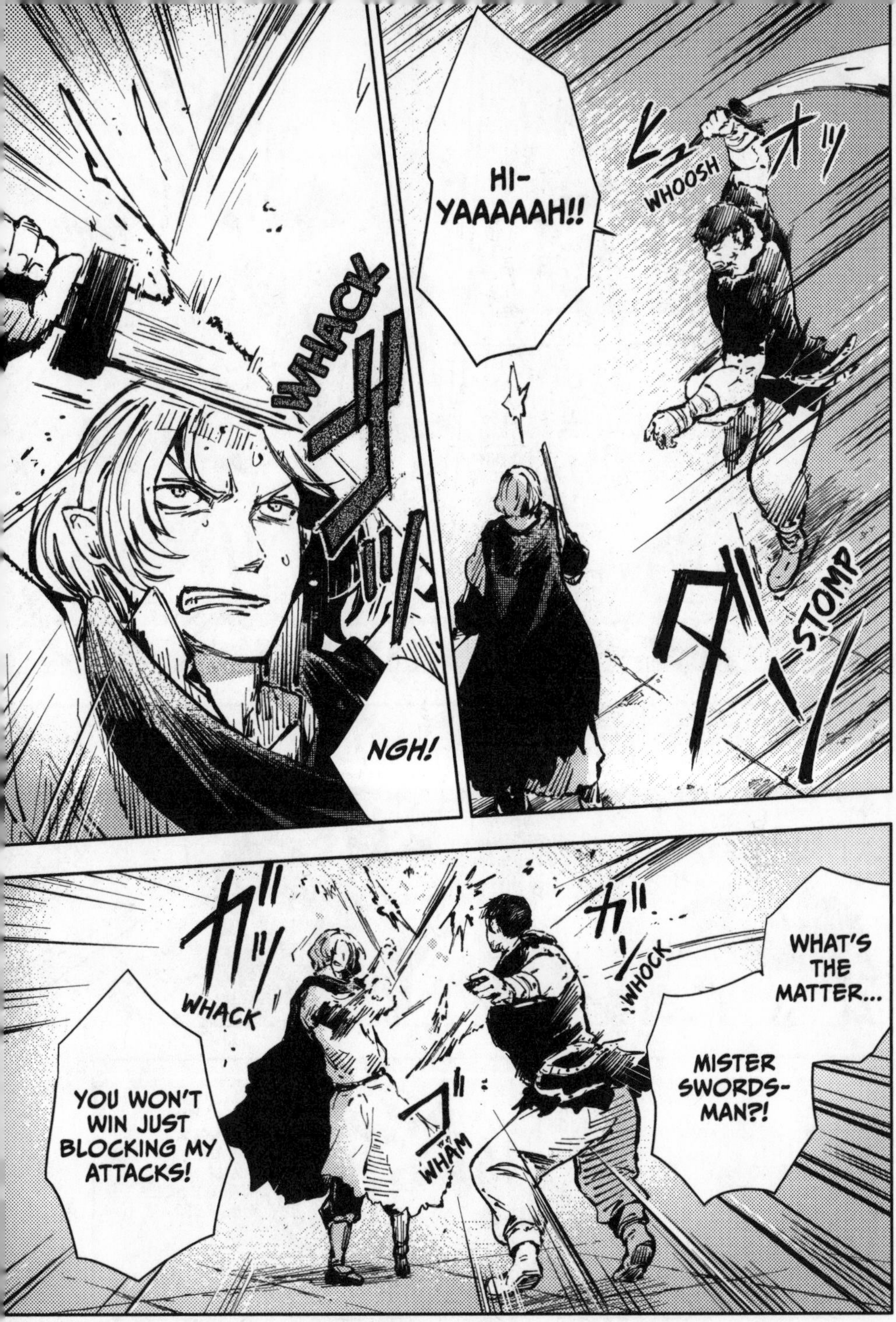
WHOOSH
HI-YAAAAAH!!
STOMP
WHACK
NGH!
WHAT'S THE MATTER...
MISTER SWORDSMAN?!
WHOCK
WHAM
WHACK
YOU WON'T WIN JUST BLOCKING MY ATTACKS!

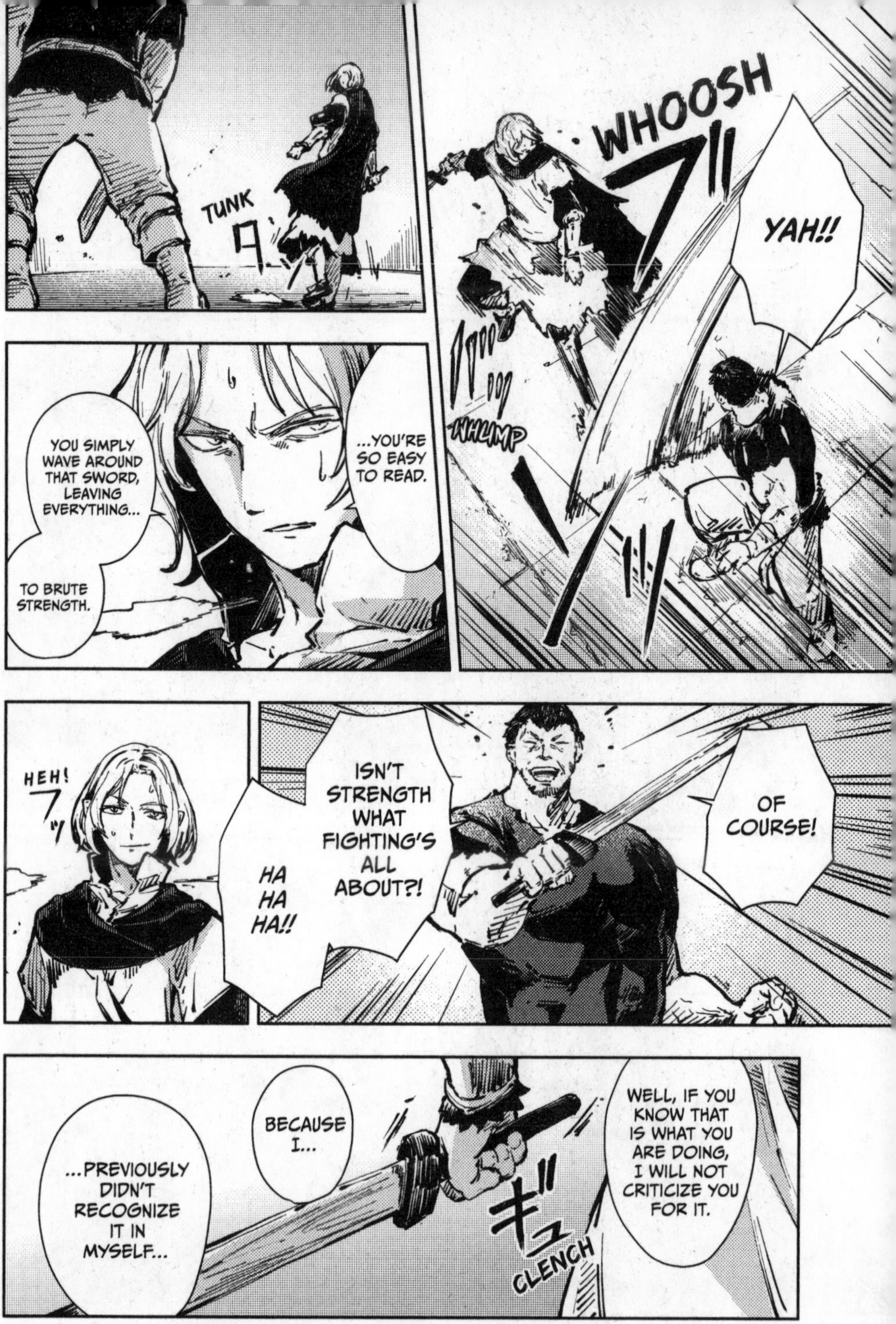
WHOOSH
YAH!!
WHUMP
TUNK
...YOU'RE SO EASY TO READ.
YOU SIMPLY WAVE AROUND THAT SWORD, LEAVING EVERYTHING...
TO BRUTE STRENGTH.
OF COURSE!
ISN'T STRENGTH WHAT FIGHTING'S ALL ABOUT?!
HA HA HA!!
HEH!
WELL, IF YOU KNOW THAT IS WHAT YOU ARE DOING, I WILL NOT CRITICIZE YOU FOR IT.
CLENCH
BECAUSE I...
...PREVIOUSLY DIDN'T RECOGNIZE IT IN MYSELF...

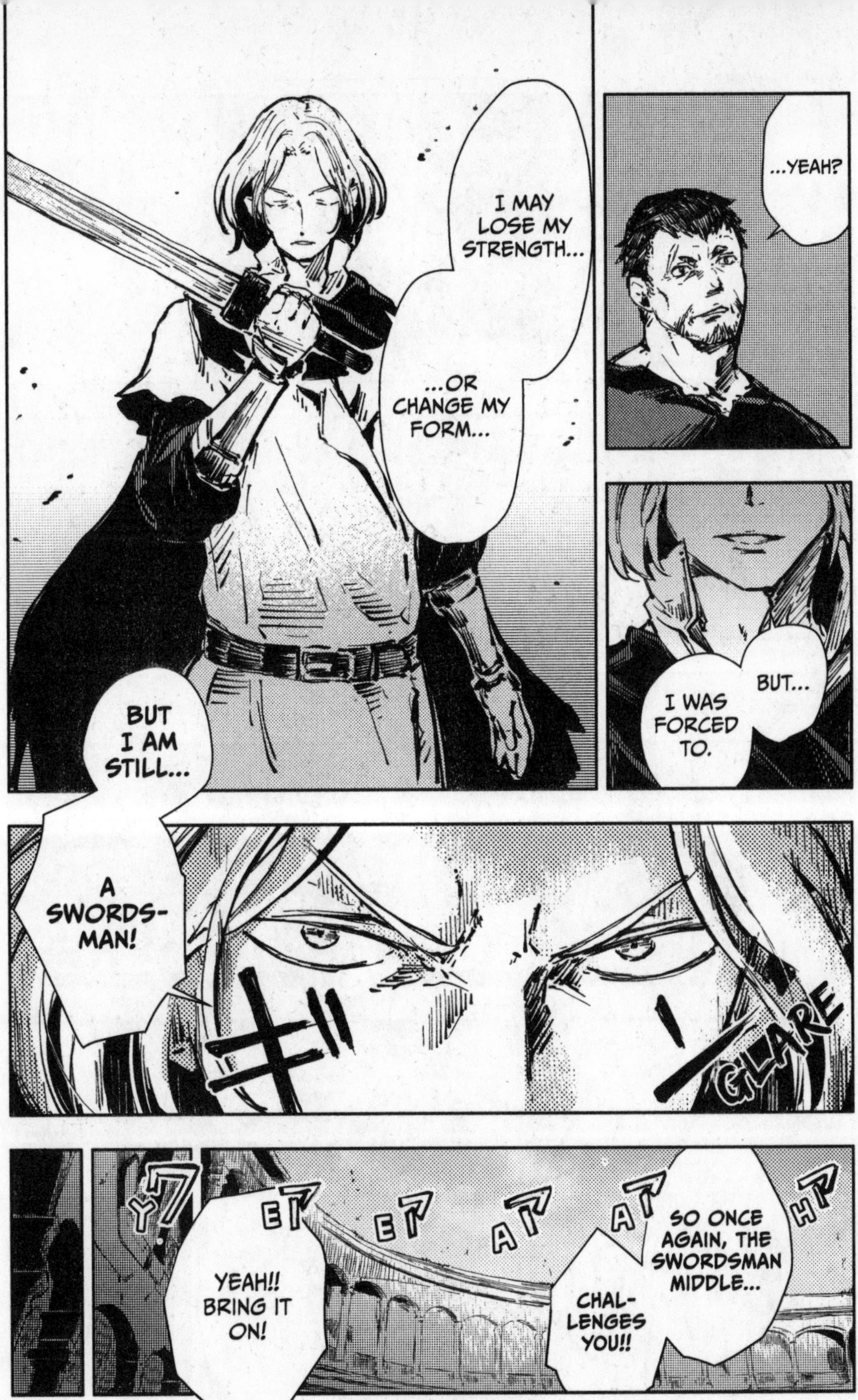

...YEAH?
BUT...
I WAS FORCED TO.
I MAY LOSE MY STRENGTH...
...OR CHANGE MY FORM...
BUT I AM STILL...
A SWORDS-MAN!
GLARE
HA
SO ONCE AGAIN, THE SWORDSMAN MIDDLE...
CHAL-LENGES YOU!!
YEAH!! BRING IT ON!

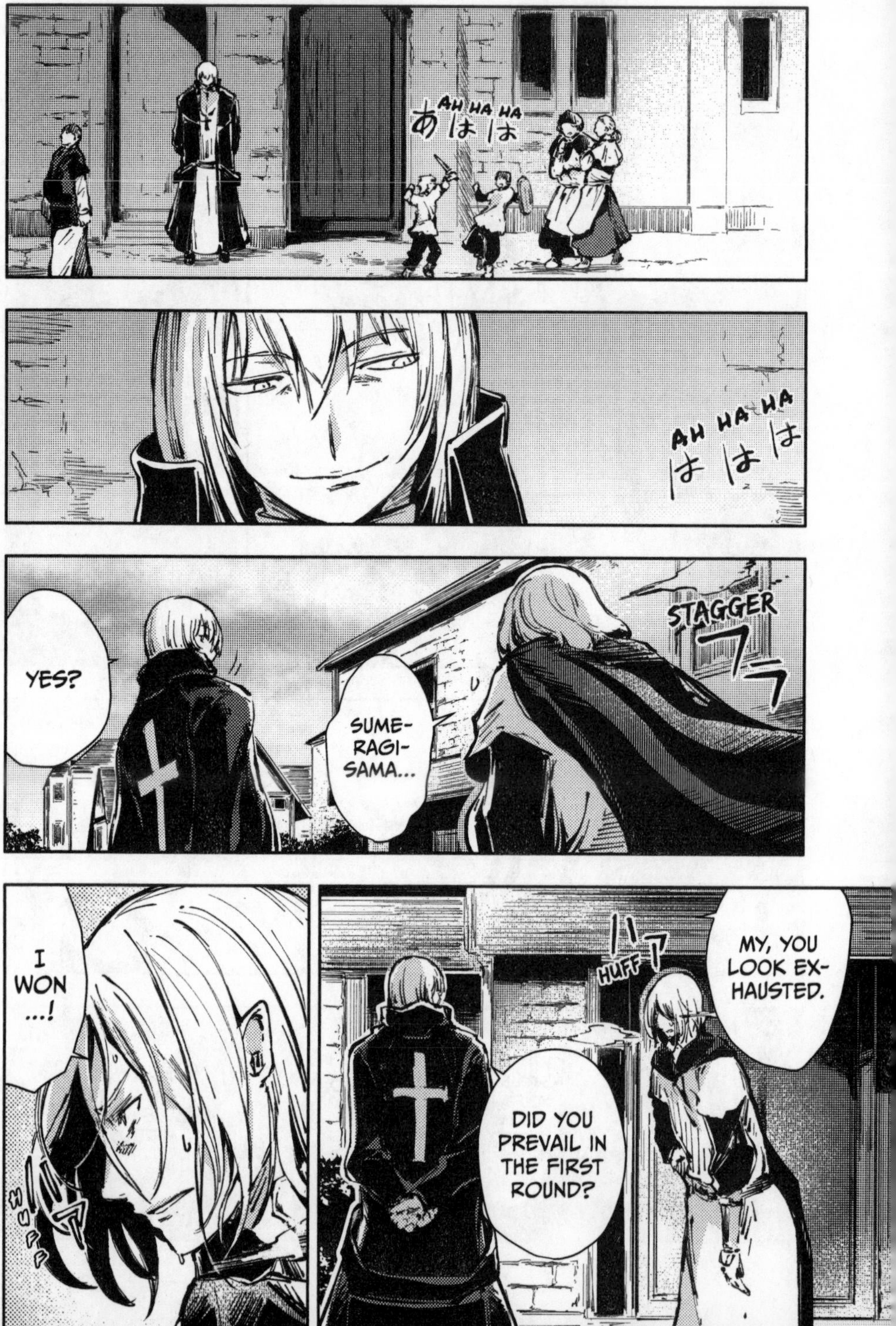

AH HA HA
あはは
AH HA HA
ははは
STAGGER
フラ
SUME-RAGI-SAMA...
YES?
MY, YOU LOOK EX-HAUSTED.
HUFF
ハァ
DID YOU PREVAIL IN THE FIRST ROUND?
I WON ...!
HUFF
ハァ

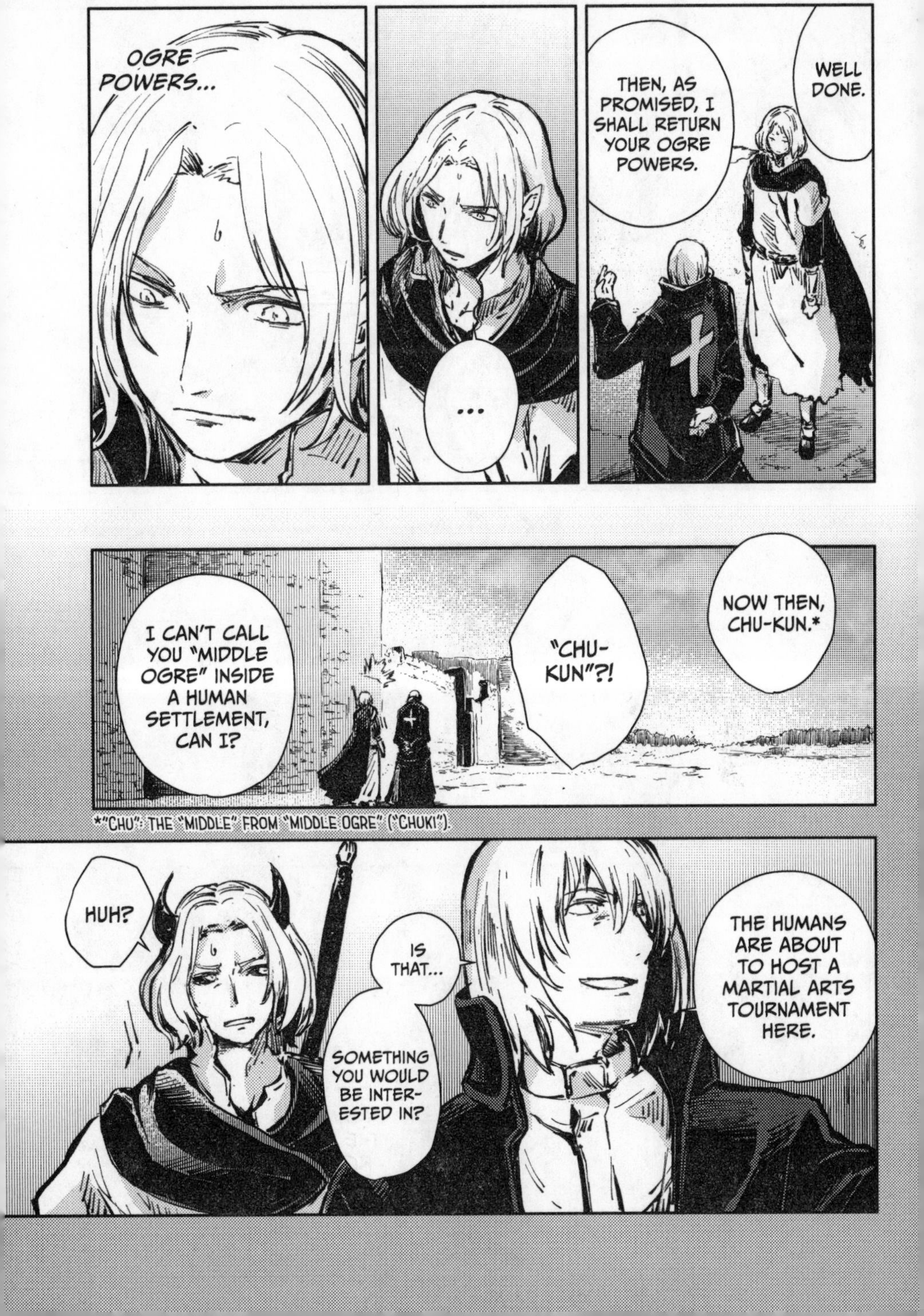
WELL DONE.
THEN, AS PROMISED, I SHALL RETURN YOUR OGRE POWERS.
...
OGRE POWERS...
NOW THEN, CHU-KUN.*
"CHU-KUN"?!
I CAN'T CALL YOU "MIDDLE OGRE" INSIDE A HUMAN SETTLEMENT, CAN I?
THE HUMANS ARE ABOUT TO HOST A MARTIAL ARTS TOURNAMENT HERE.
IS THAT...
SOMETHING YOU WOULD BE INTER-ESTED IN?
HUH?

*"CHU": THE "MIDDLE" FROM "MIDDLE OGRE" ("CHUKI").

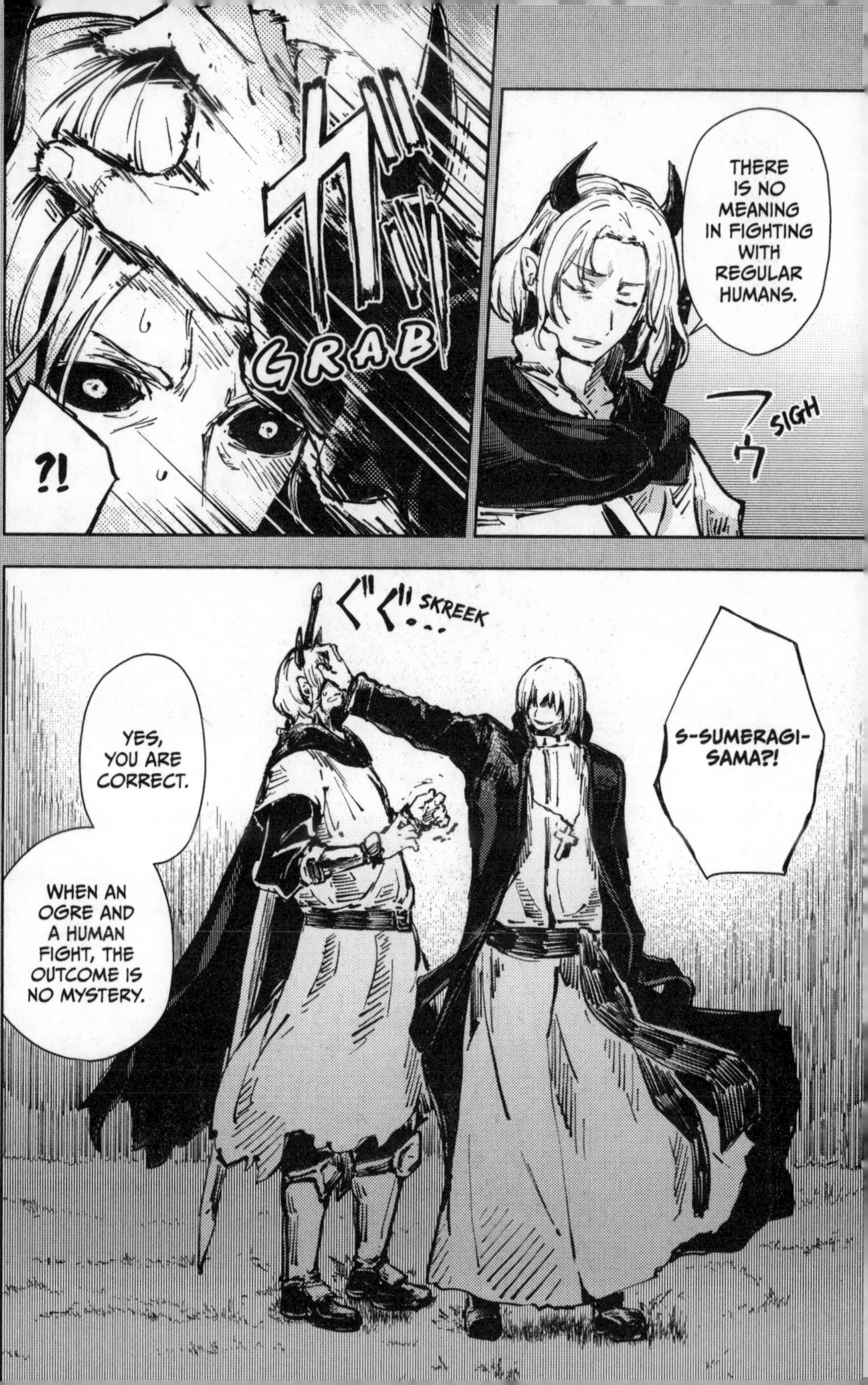
THERE IS NO MEANING IN FIGHTING WITH REGULAR HUMANS.
SIGH
GRAB
?!
S-SUMERAGI-SAMA?!
SKREEK
YES, YOU ARE CORRECT.
WHEN AN OGRE AND A HUMAN FIGHT, THE OUTCOME IS NO MYSTERY.

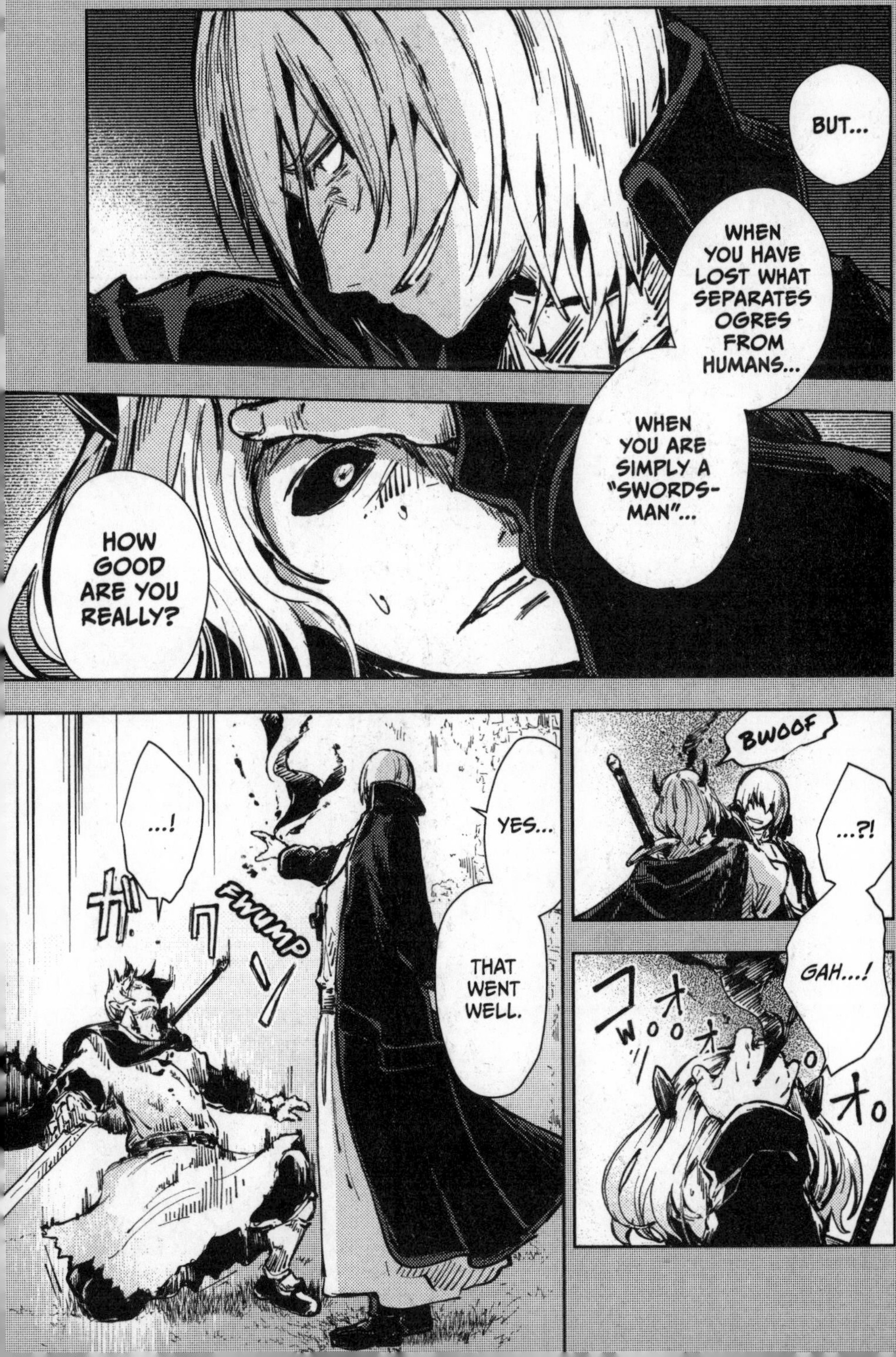
BUT...
WHEN YOU HAVE LOST WHAT SEPARATES OGRES FROM HUMANS...
WHEN YOU ARE SIMPLY A "SWORDS-MAN"...
HOW GOOD ARE YOU REALLY?
BWOOF
...?!
GAH...!
WOOO
YES...
THAT WENT WELL.
...!
FWUMP

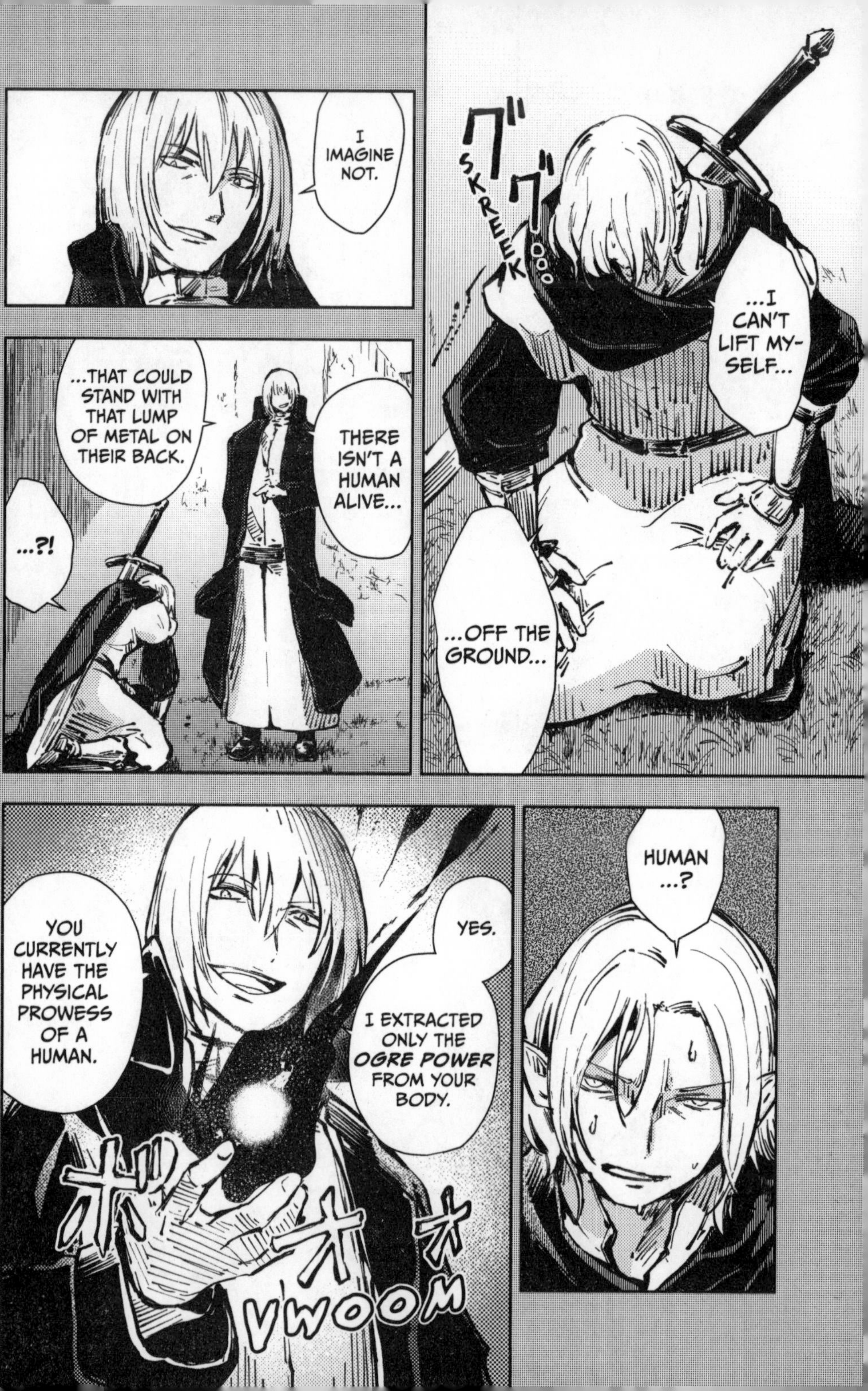
SKREEK
...I CAN'T LIFT MY-SELF...
...OFF THE GROUND...
I IMAGINE NOT.
THERE ISN'T A HUMAN ALIVE...
...THAT COULD STAND WITH THAT LUMP OF METAL ON THEIR BACK.
...?!
HUMAN ...?
YES.
YOU CURRENTLY HAVE THE PHYSICAL PROWESS OF A HUMAN.
I EXTRACTED ONLY THE *OGRE POWER* FROM YOUR BODY.
VWOOM

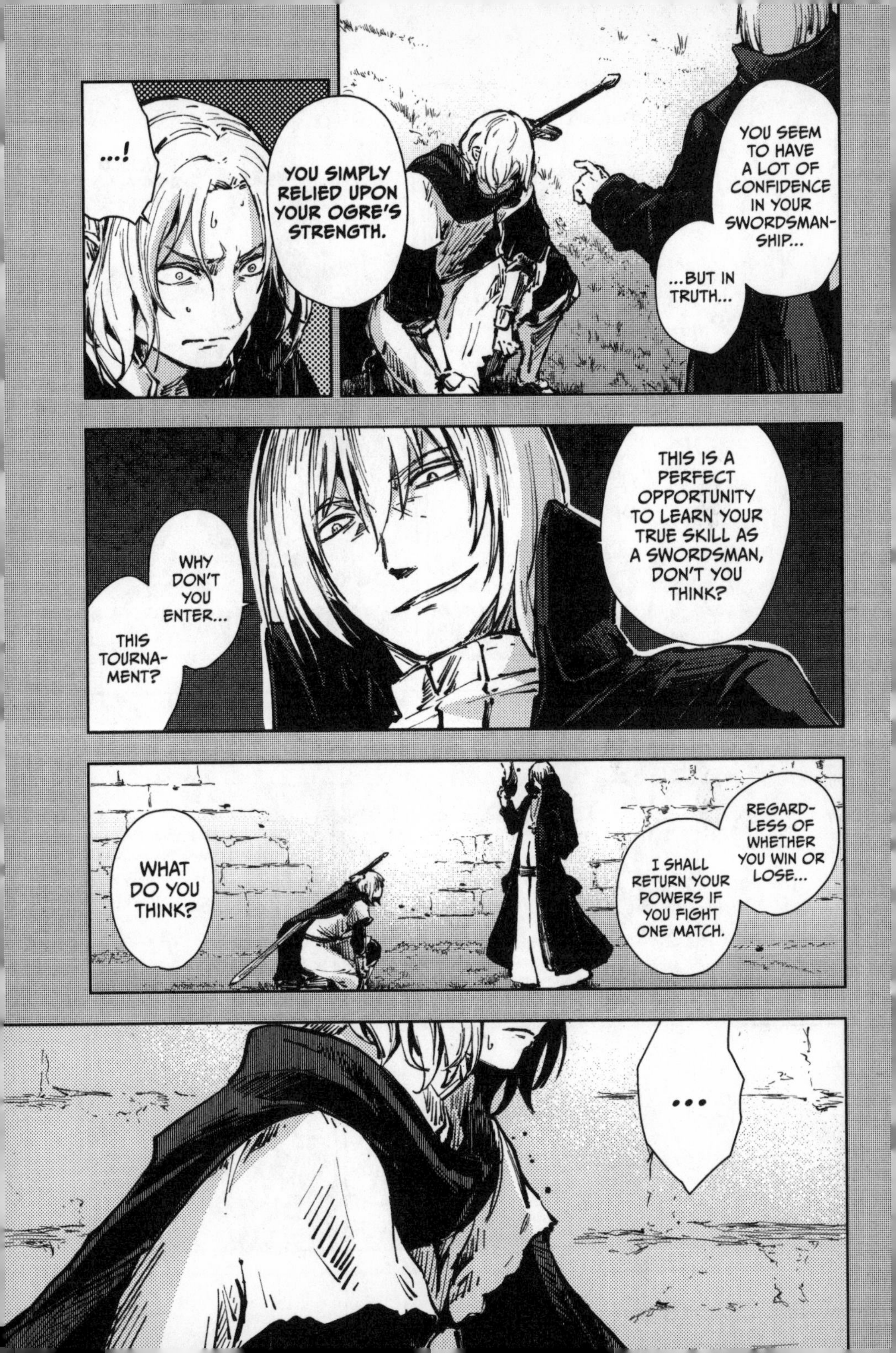
YOU SEEM TO HAVE A LOT OF CONFIDENCE IN YOUR SWORDSMANSHIP...
...BUT IN TRUTH...
YOU SIMPLY RELIED UPON YOUR OGRE'S STRENGTH.
...!
THIS IS A PERFECT OPPORTUNITY TO LEARN YOUR TRUE SKILL AS A SWORDSMAN, DON'T YOU THINK?
WHY DON'T YOU ENTER...
THIS TOURNAMENT?
REGARDLESS OF WHETHER YOU WIN OR LOSE...
I SHALL RETURN YOUR POWERS IF YOU FIGHT ONE MATCH.
WHAT DO YOU THINK?
...

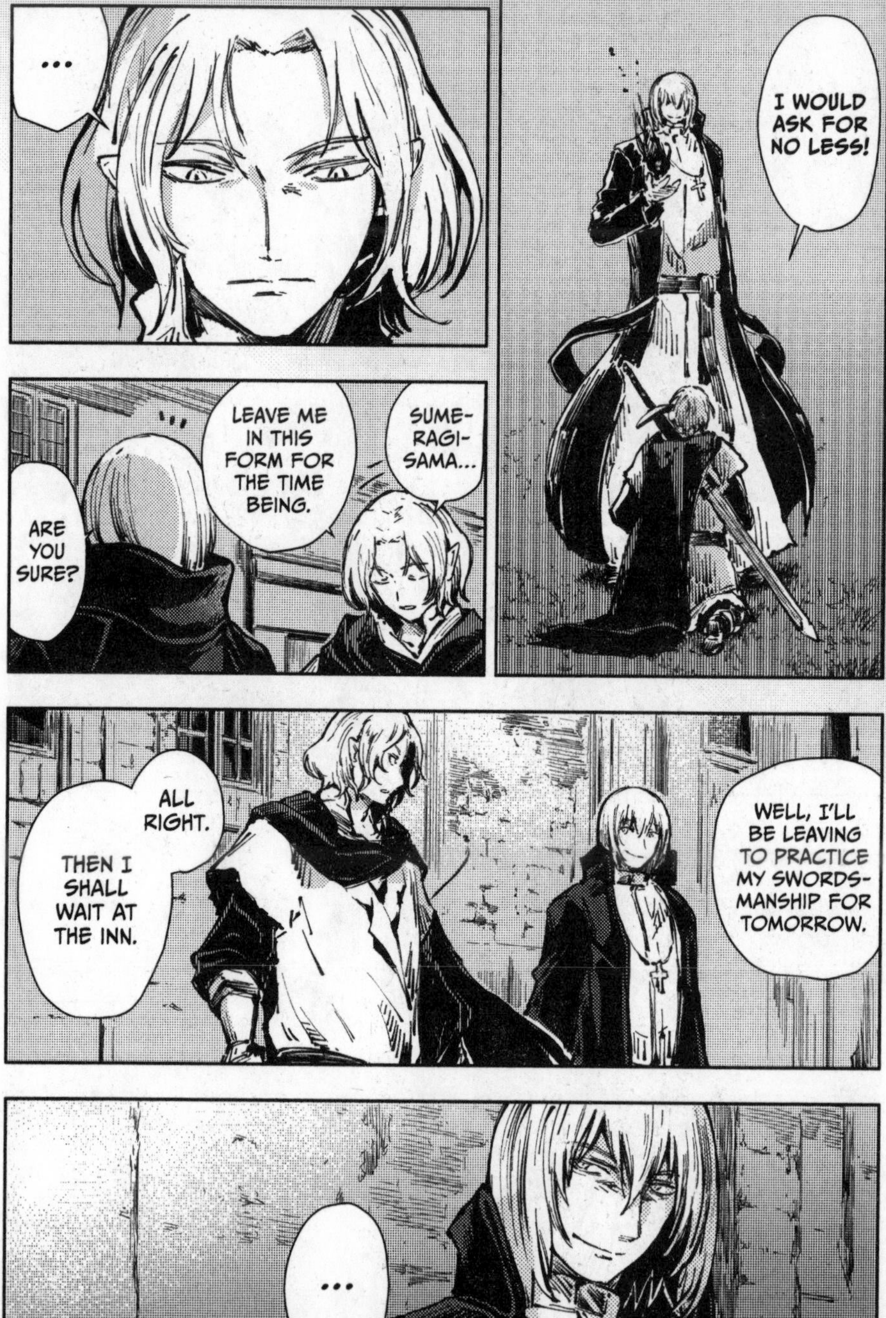
I WOULD ASK FOR NO LESS!
...
SUME-RAGI-SAMA...
LEAVE ME IN THIS FORM FOR THE TIME BEING.
ARE YOU SURE?
WELL, I'LL BE LEAVING TO PRACTICE MY SWORDS-MANSHIP FOR TOMORROW.
ALL RIGHT.
THEN I SHALL WAIT AT THE INN.
...

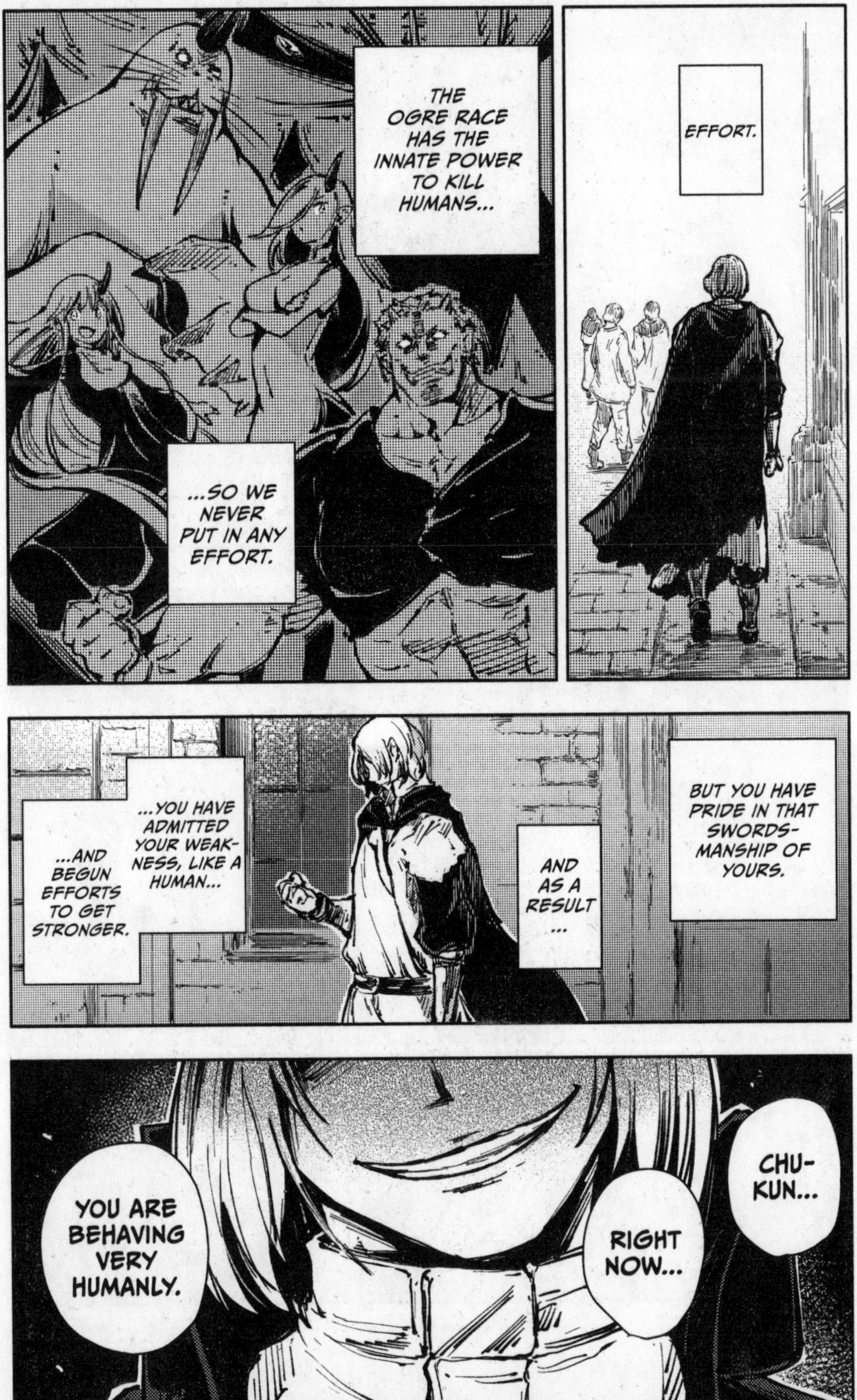
EFFORT.
THE OGRE RACE HAS THE INNATE POWER TO KILL HUMANS...
...SO WE NEVER PUT IN ANY EFFORT.
BUT YOU HAVE PRIDE IN THAT SWORDS-MANSHIP OF YOURS.
AND AS A RESULT ...
...YOU HAVE ADMITTED YOUR WEAK-NESS, LIKE A HUMAN...
...AND BEGUN EFFORTS TO GET STRONGER.
CHU-KUN...
RIGHT NOW...
YOU ARE BEHAVING VERY HUMANLY.

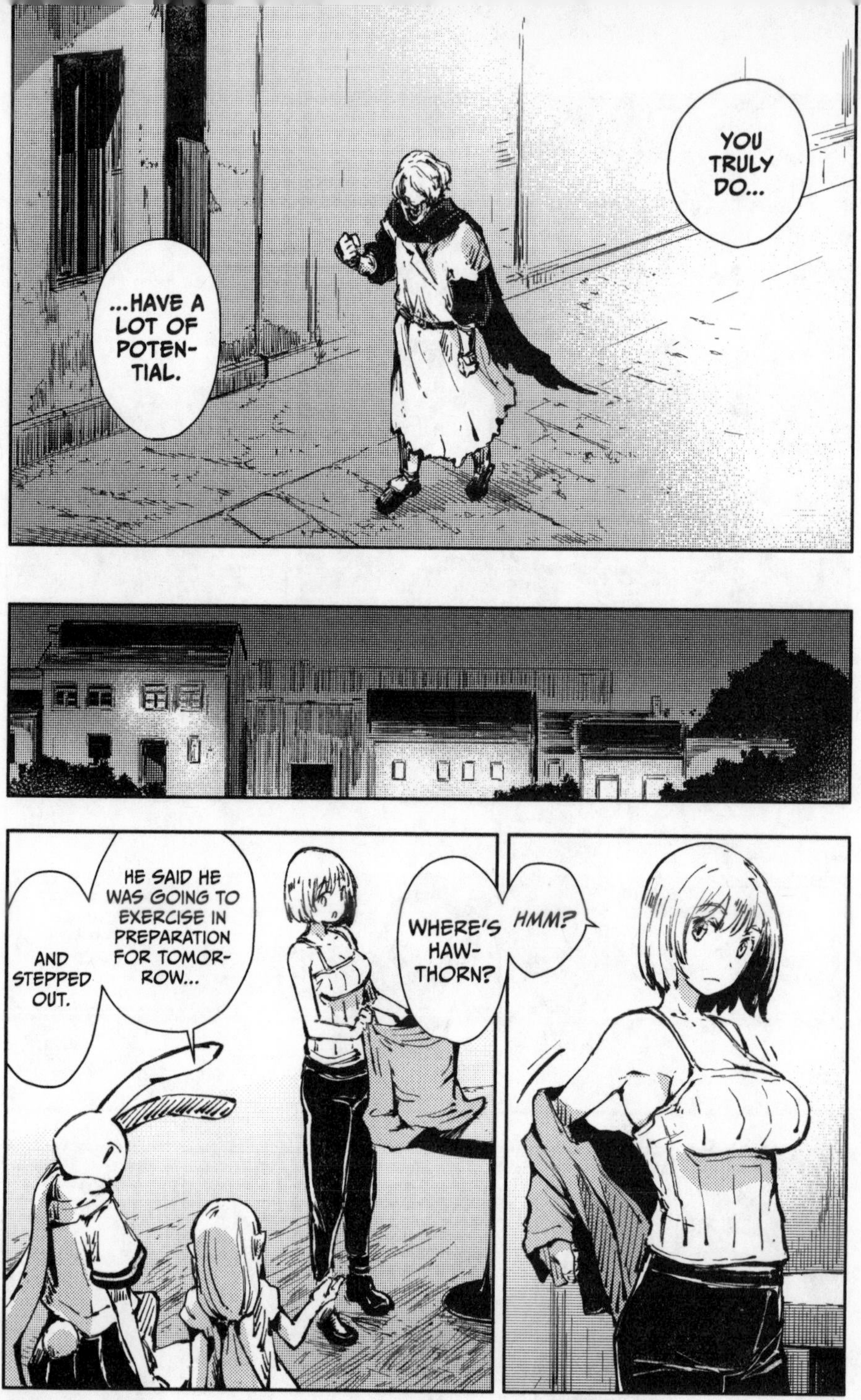
YOU TRULY DO...
...HAVE A LOT OF POTEN-TIAL.
HMM?
WHERE'S HAW-THORN?
HE SAID HE WAS GOING TO EXERCISE IN PREPARATION FOR TOMOR-ROW...
AND STEPPED OUT.

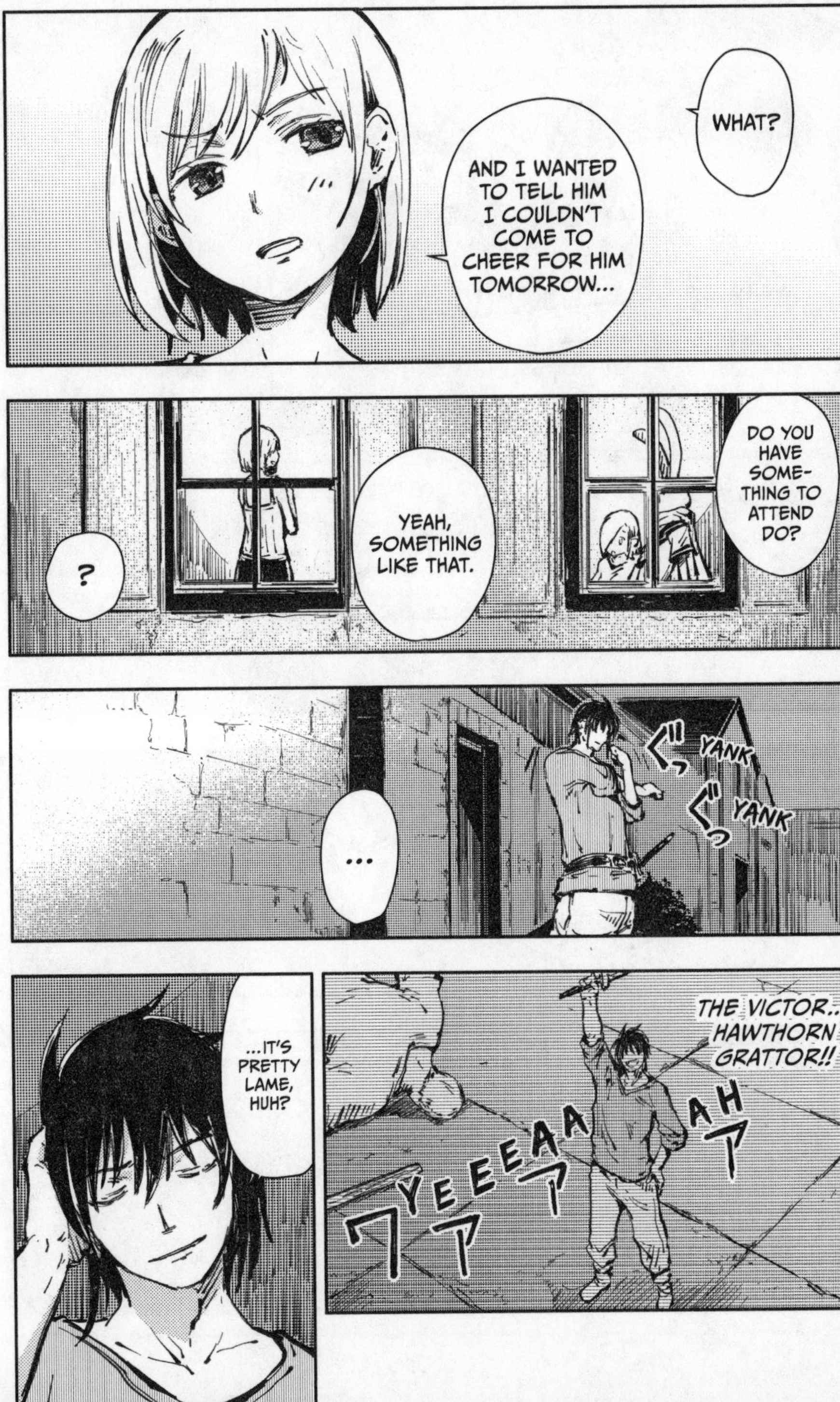
WHAT?
AND I WANTED TO TELL HIM I COULDN'T COME TO CHEER FOR HIM TOMORROW...
DO YOU HAVE SOME-THING TO ATTEND DO?
YEAH, SOMETHING LIKE THAT.
?
YANK
YANK
...
THE VICTOR... HAWTHORN GRATTOR!!
YEEEAAAH
...IT'S PRETTY LAME, HUH?

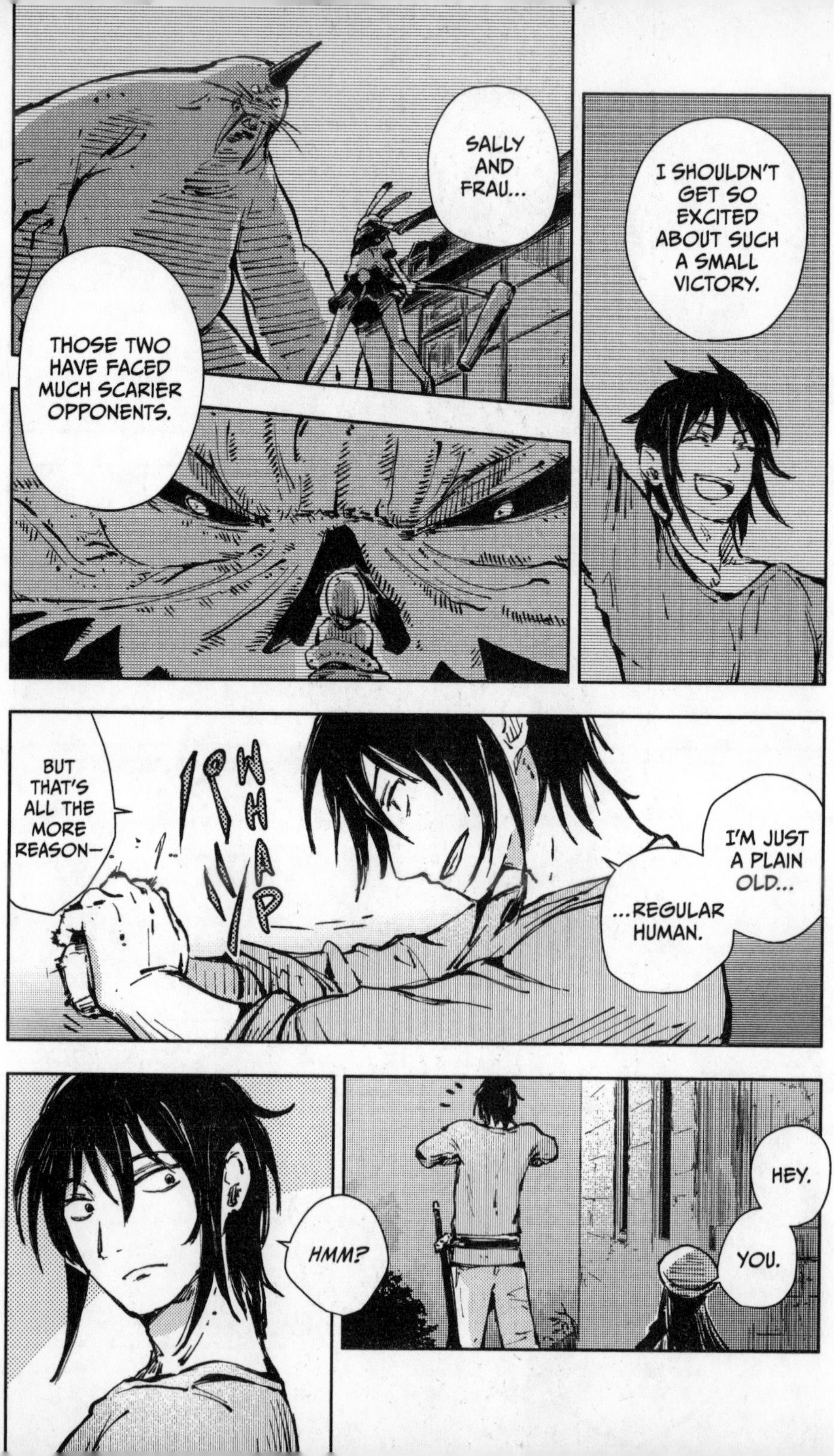
I SHOULDN'T GET SO EXCITED ABOUT SUCH A SMALL VICTORY.
SALLY AND FRAU...
THOSE TWO HAVE FACED MUCH SCARIER OPPONENTS.
I'M JUST A PLAIN OLD...
...REGULAR HUMAN.
WHAP
BUT THAT'S ALL THE MORE REASON—
HEY.
YOU.
HMM?

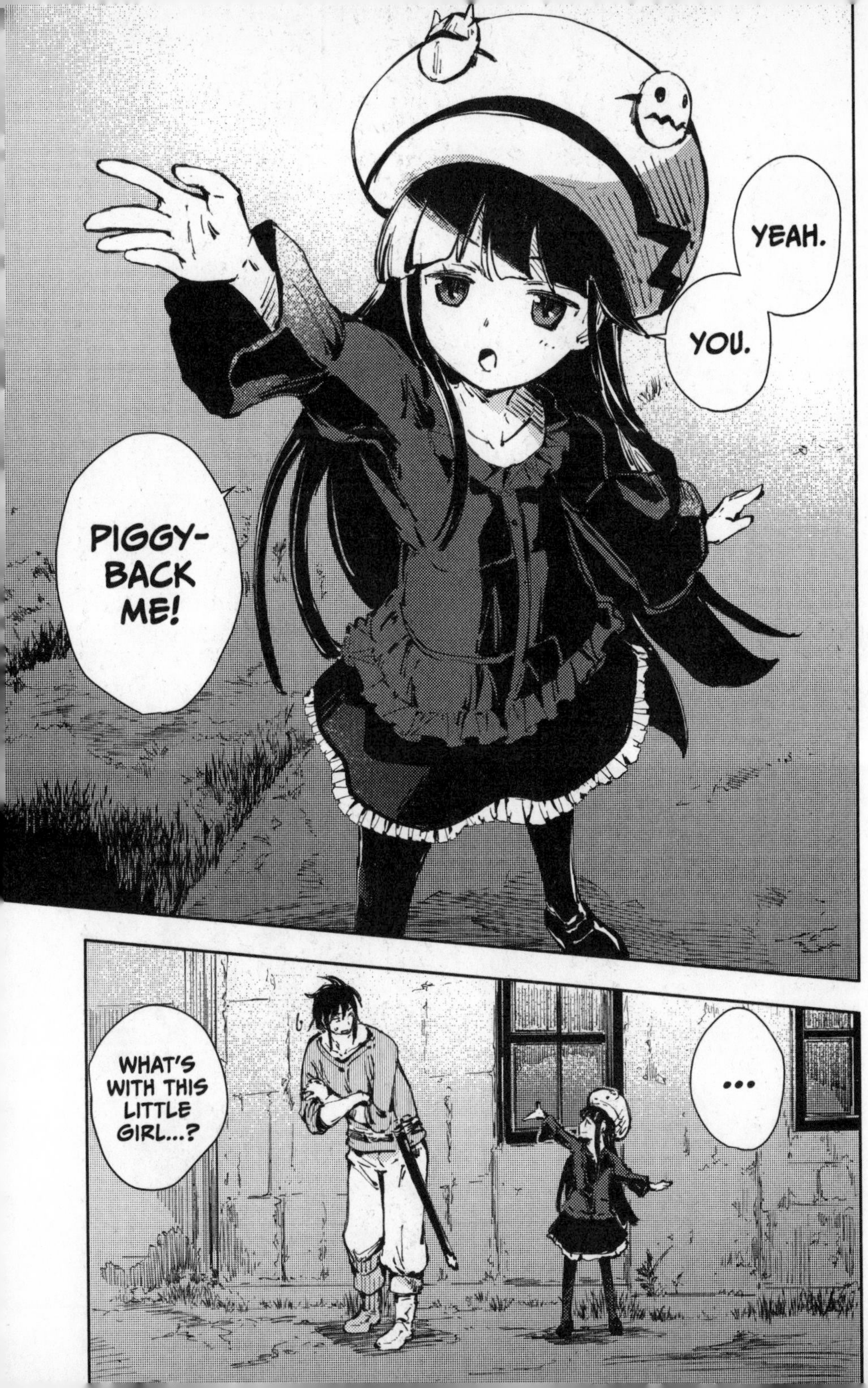
YEAH.
YOU.
PIGGY-BACK ME!
...
WHAT'S WITH THIS LITTLE GIRL...?

I changed clothes!

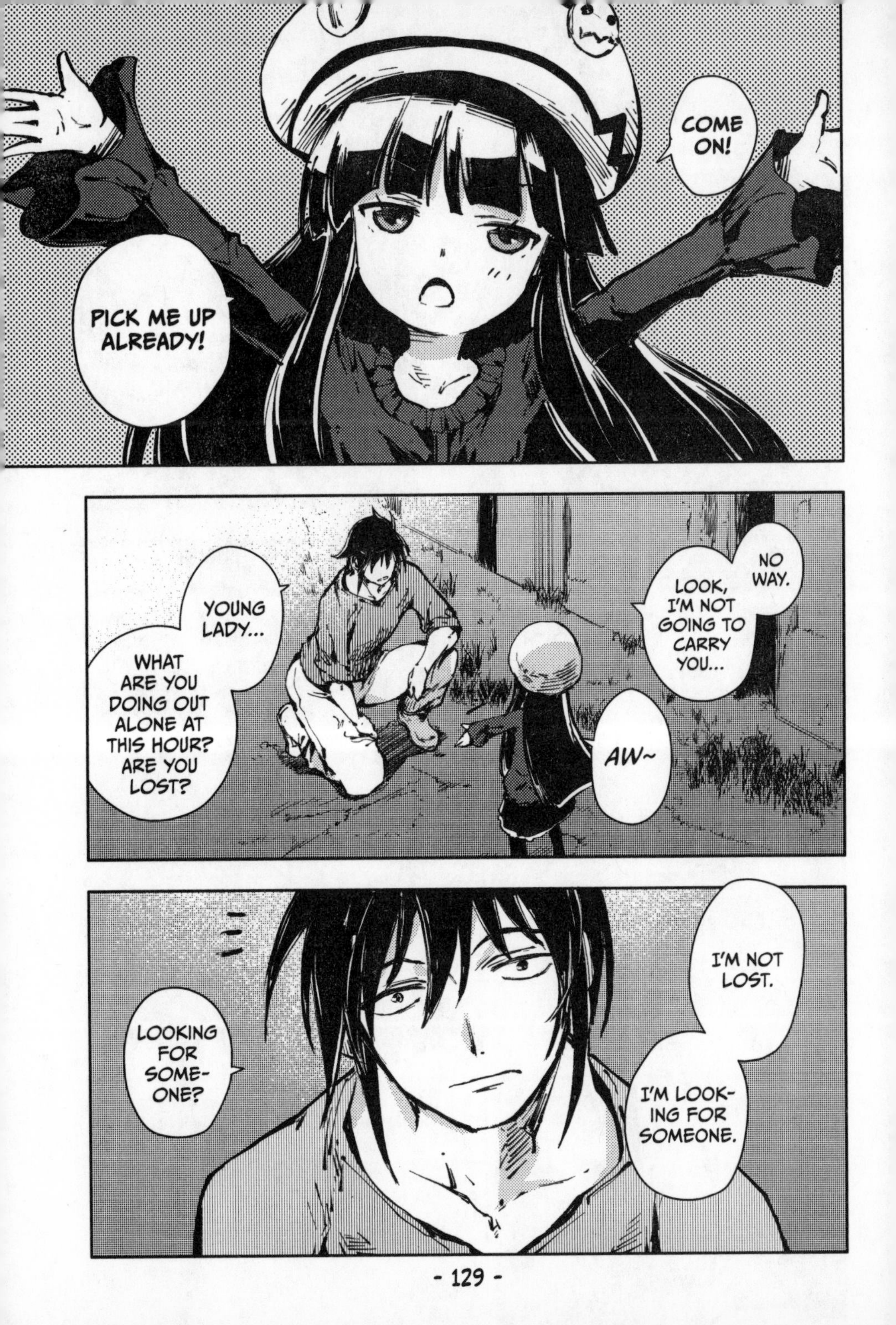
COME ON!
PICK ME UP ALREADY!
NO WAY.
LOOK, I'M NOT GOING TO CARRY YOU...
AW~
YOUNG LADY...
WHAT ARE YOU DOING OUT ALONE AT THIS HOUR? ARE YOU LOST?
I'M NOT LOST.
I'M LOOKING FOR SOMEONE.
LOOKING FOR SOMEONE?

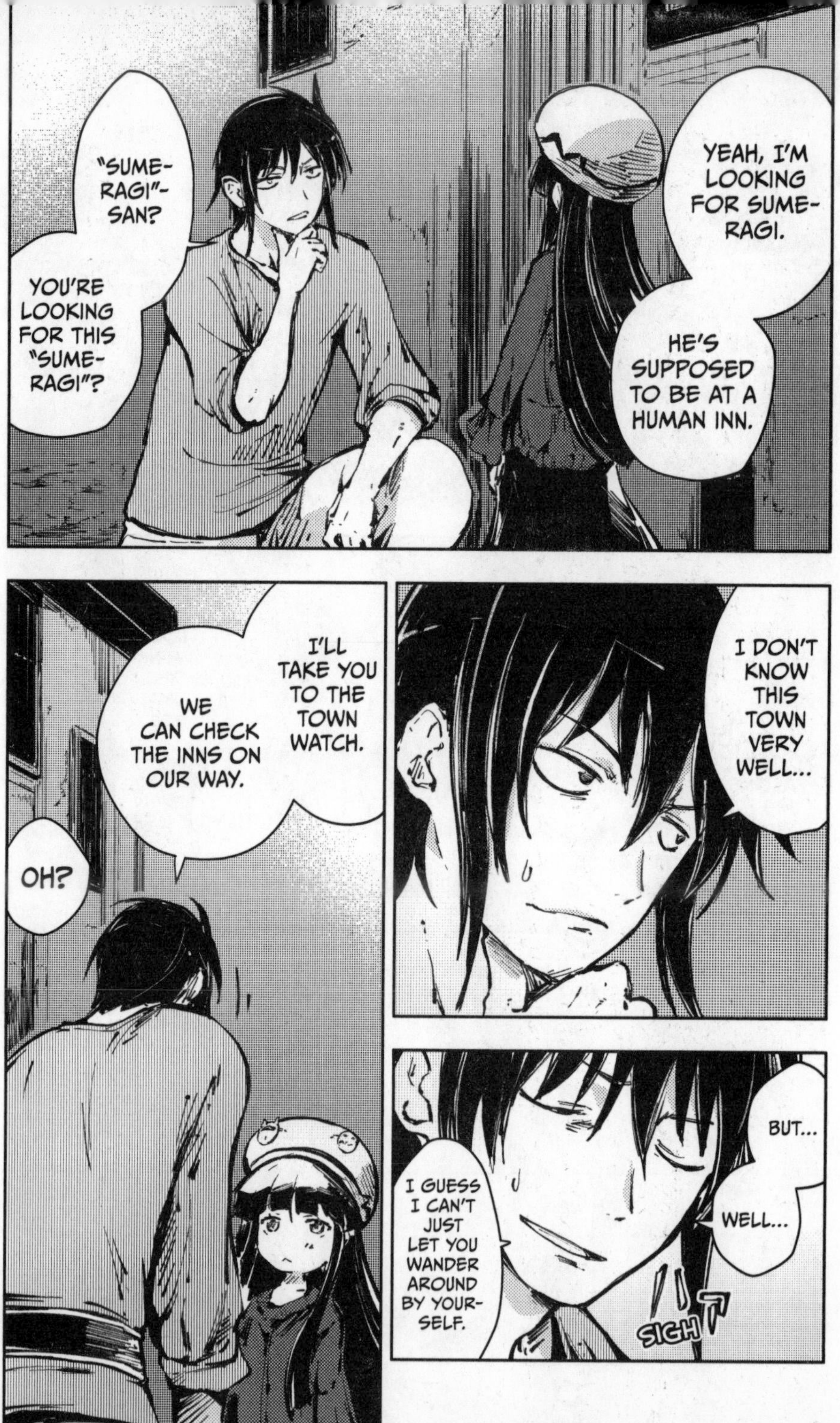
YEAH, I'M LOOKING FOR SUME-RAGI.
HE'S SUPPOSED TO BE AT A HUMAN INN.
"SUME-RAGI"-SAN?
YOU'RE LOOKING FOR THIS "SUME-RAGI"?
I DON'T KNOW THIS TOWN VERY WELL...
BUT...
WELL...
SIGH
I GUESS I CAN'T JUST LET YOU WANDER AROUND BY YOUR-SELF.
I'LL TAKE YOU TO THE TOWN WATCH.
WE CAN CHECK THE INNS ON OUR WAY.
OH?

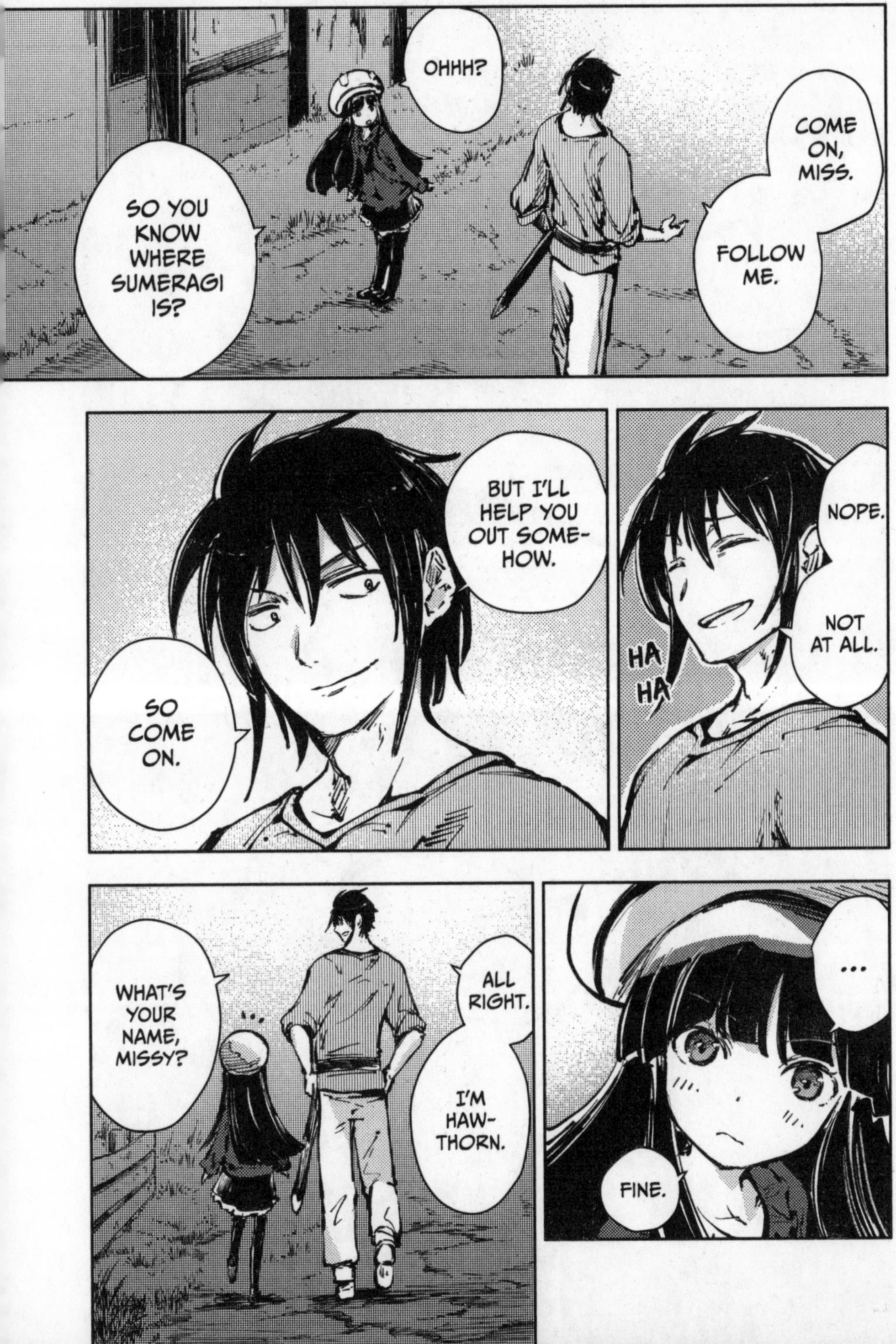
OHHH?
SO YOU KNOW WHERE SUMERAGI IS?
COME ON, MISS.
FOLLOW ME.
NOPE.
NOT AT ALL.
HA HA
BUT I'LL HELP YOU OUT SOME-HOW.
SO COME ON.
...
FINE.
ALL RIGHT.
I'M HAW-THORN.
WHAT'S YOUR NAME, MISSY?
...

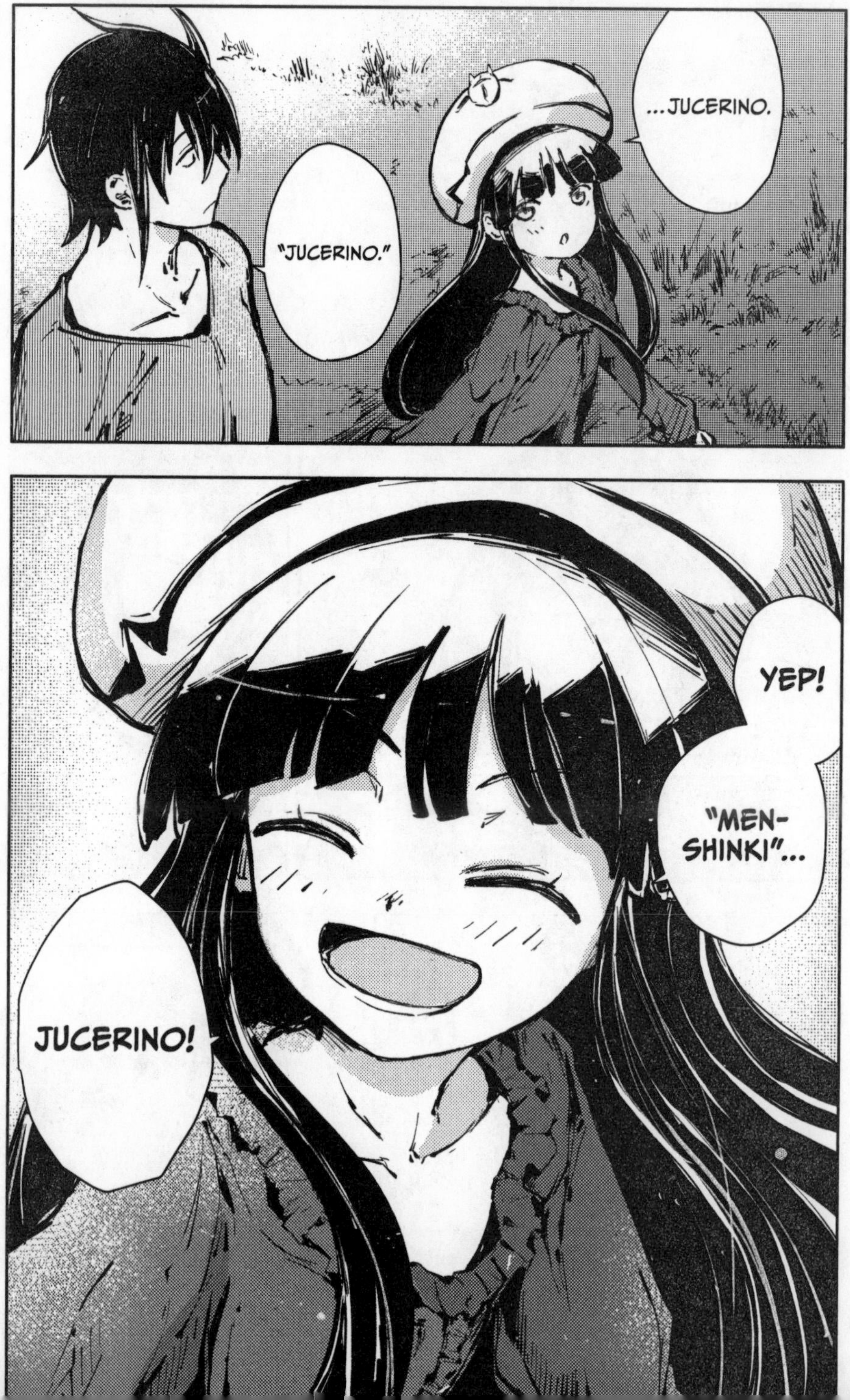
...JUCERINO.
"JUCERINO."
YEP!
"MEN-SHINKI"...
JUCERINO!

CHAPTER 19: SALLY AND THE CROSSROADS

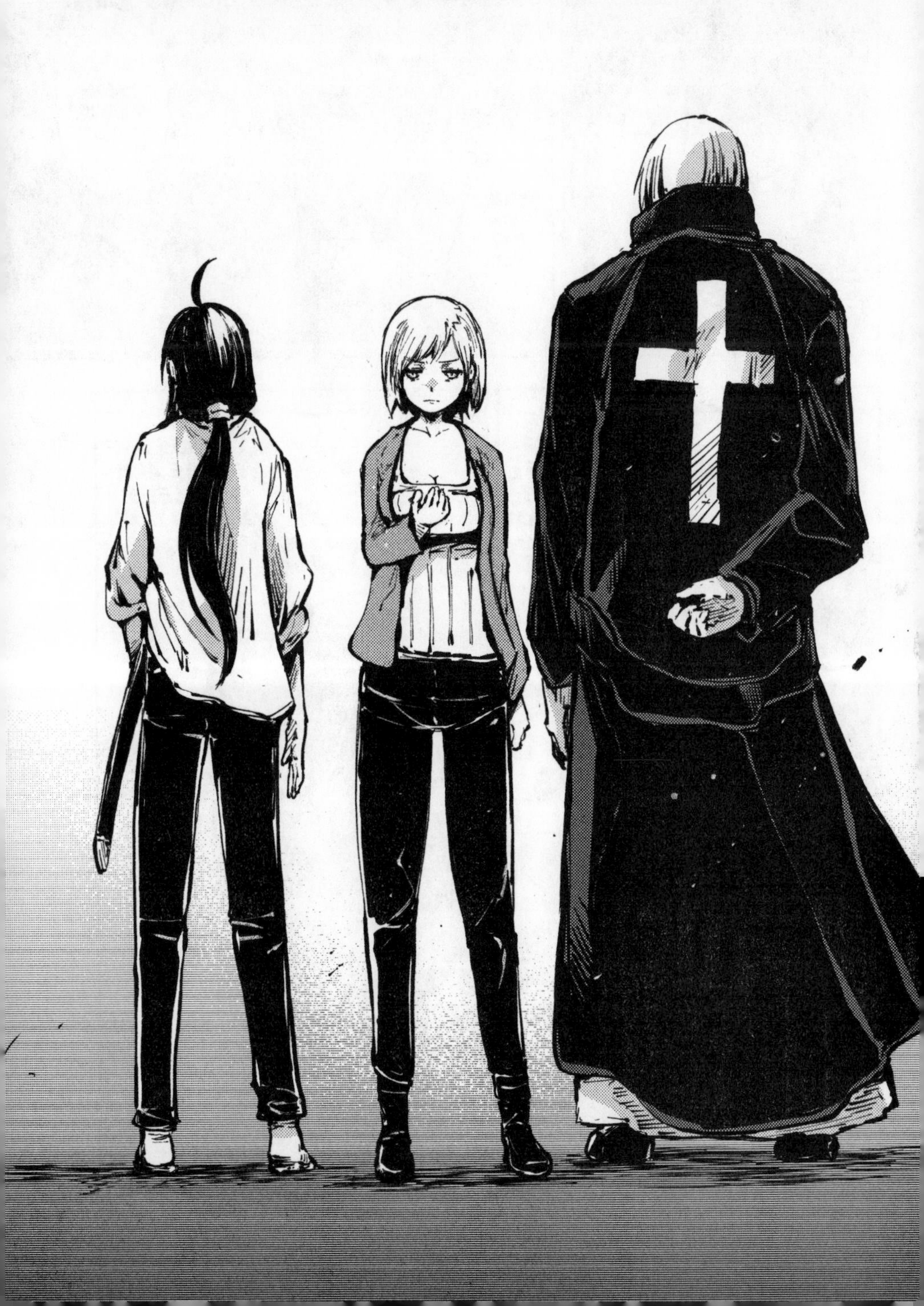

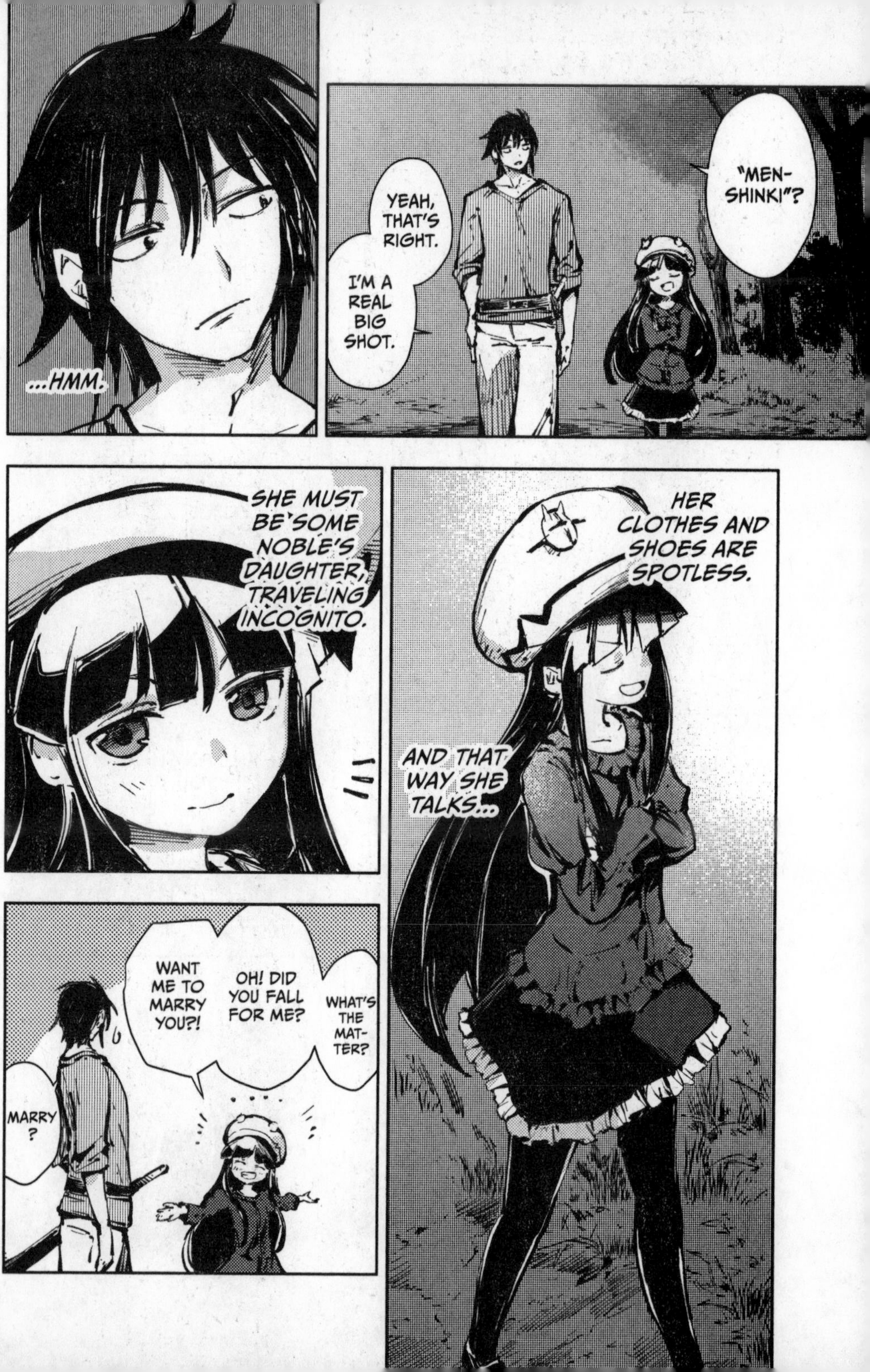
"MEN-SHINKI"?
YEAH, THAT'S RIGHT.
I'M A REAL BIG SHOT.
...HMM.
HER CLOTHES AND SHOES ARE SPOTLESS.
AND THAT WAY SHE TALKS...
SHE MUST BE SOME NOBLE'S DAUGHTER, TRAVELING INCOGNITO.
WHAT'S THE MAT-TER?
OH! DID YOU FALL FOR ME?
WANT ME TO MARRY YOU?!
MARRY?

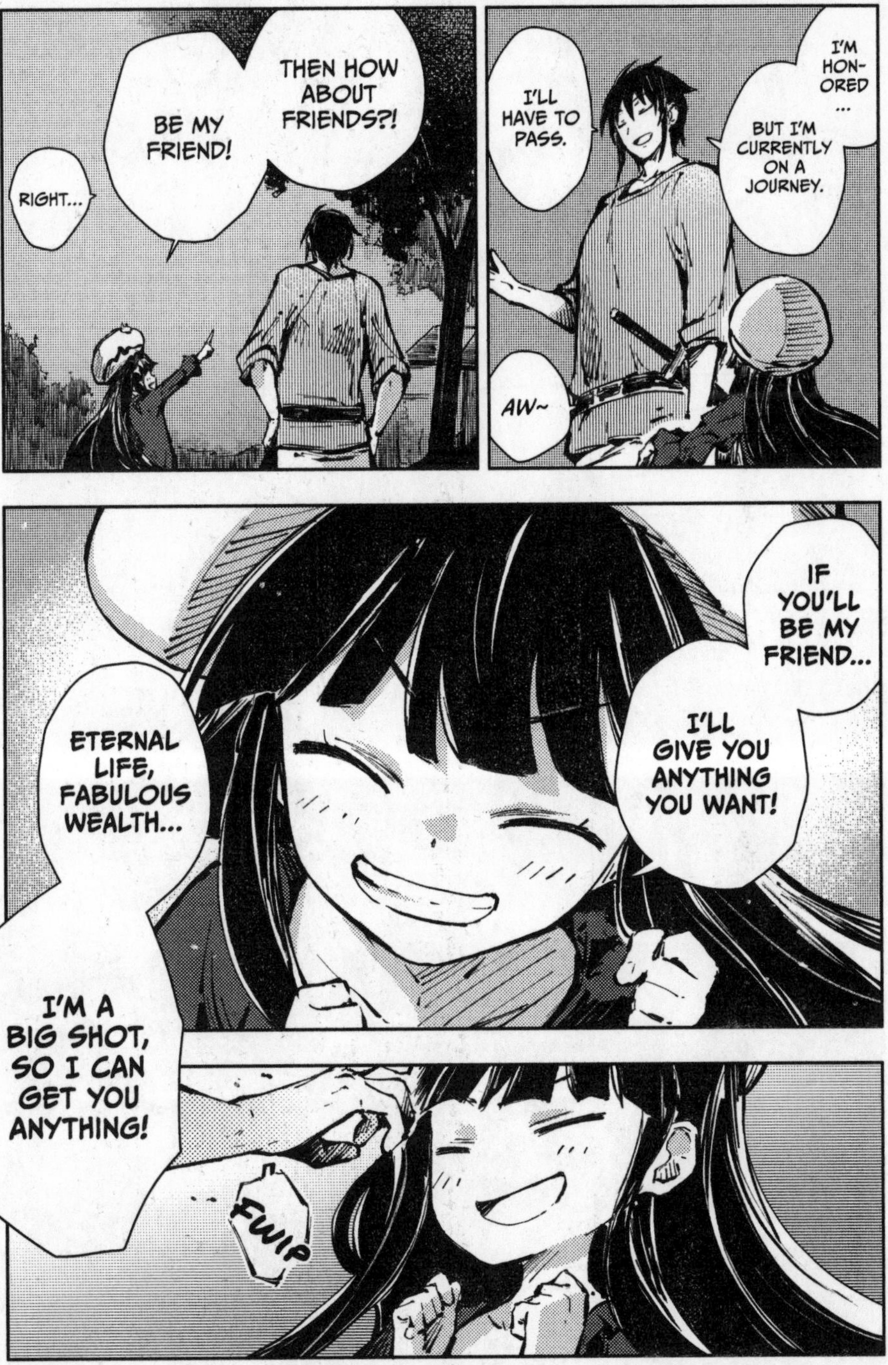
I'M HON-ORED ...
BUT I'M CURRENTLY ON A JOURNEY.
I'LL HAVE TO PASS.
AW~
THEN HOW ABOUT FRIENDS?!
BE MY FRIEND!
RIGHT...
IF YOU'LL BE MY FRIEND...
I'LL GIVE YOU ANYTHING YOU WANT!
ETERNAL LIFE, FABULOUS WEALTH...
I'M A BIG SHOT, SO I CAN GET YOU ANYTHING!
FWIP

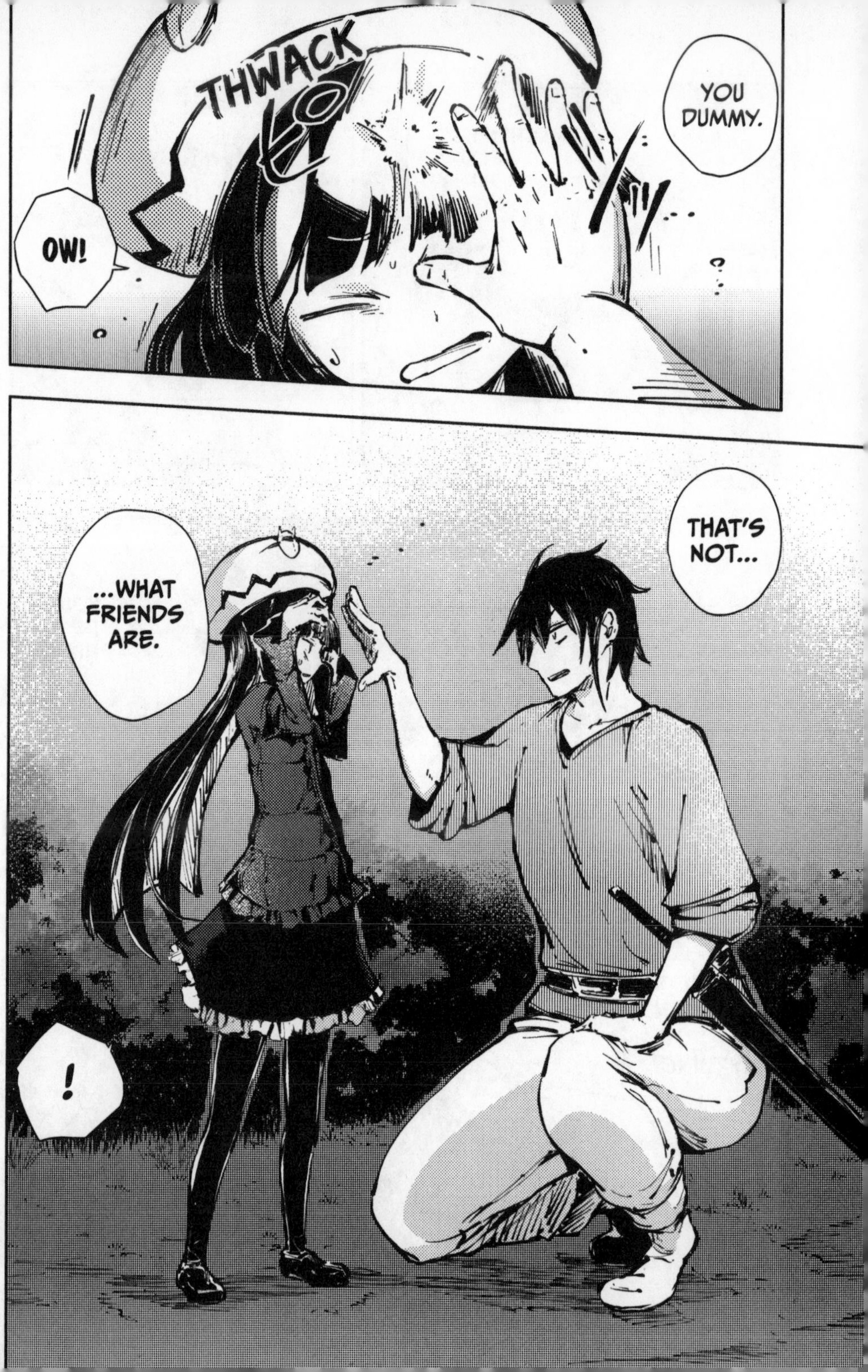
YOU DUMMY.
THWACK
OW!
THAT'S NOT...
...WHAT FRIENDS ARE.
!

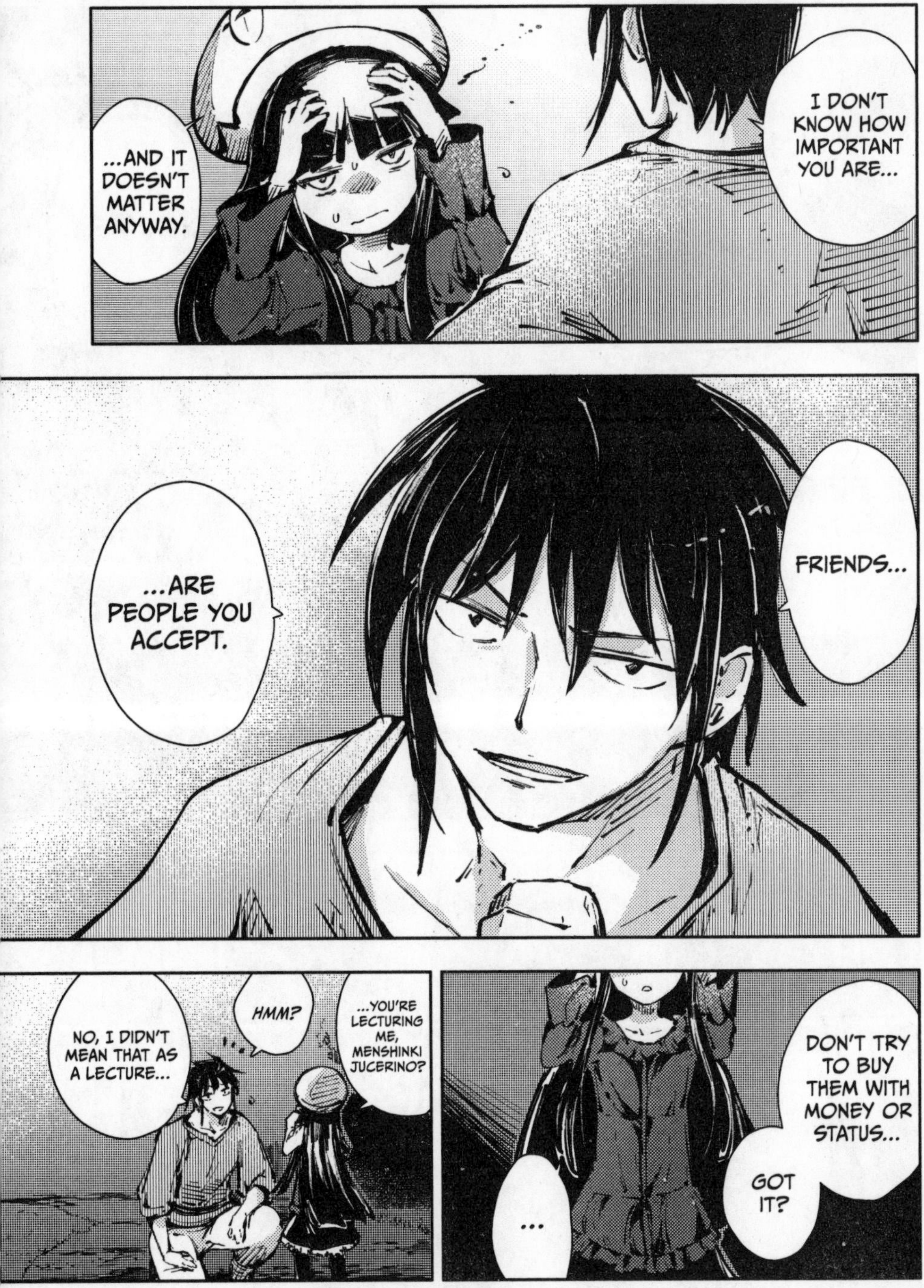
I DON'T KNOW HOW IMPORTANT YOU ARE...
...AND IT DOESN'T MATTER ANYWAY.
FRIENDS...
...ARE PEOPLE YOU ACCEPT.
DON'T TRY TO BUY THEM WITH MONEY OR STATUS...
GOT IT?
...
...YOU'RE LECTURING ME, MENSHINKI JUCERINO?
HMM?
NO, I DIDN'T MEAN THAT AS A LECTURE...

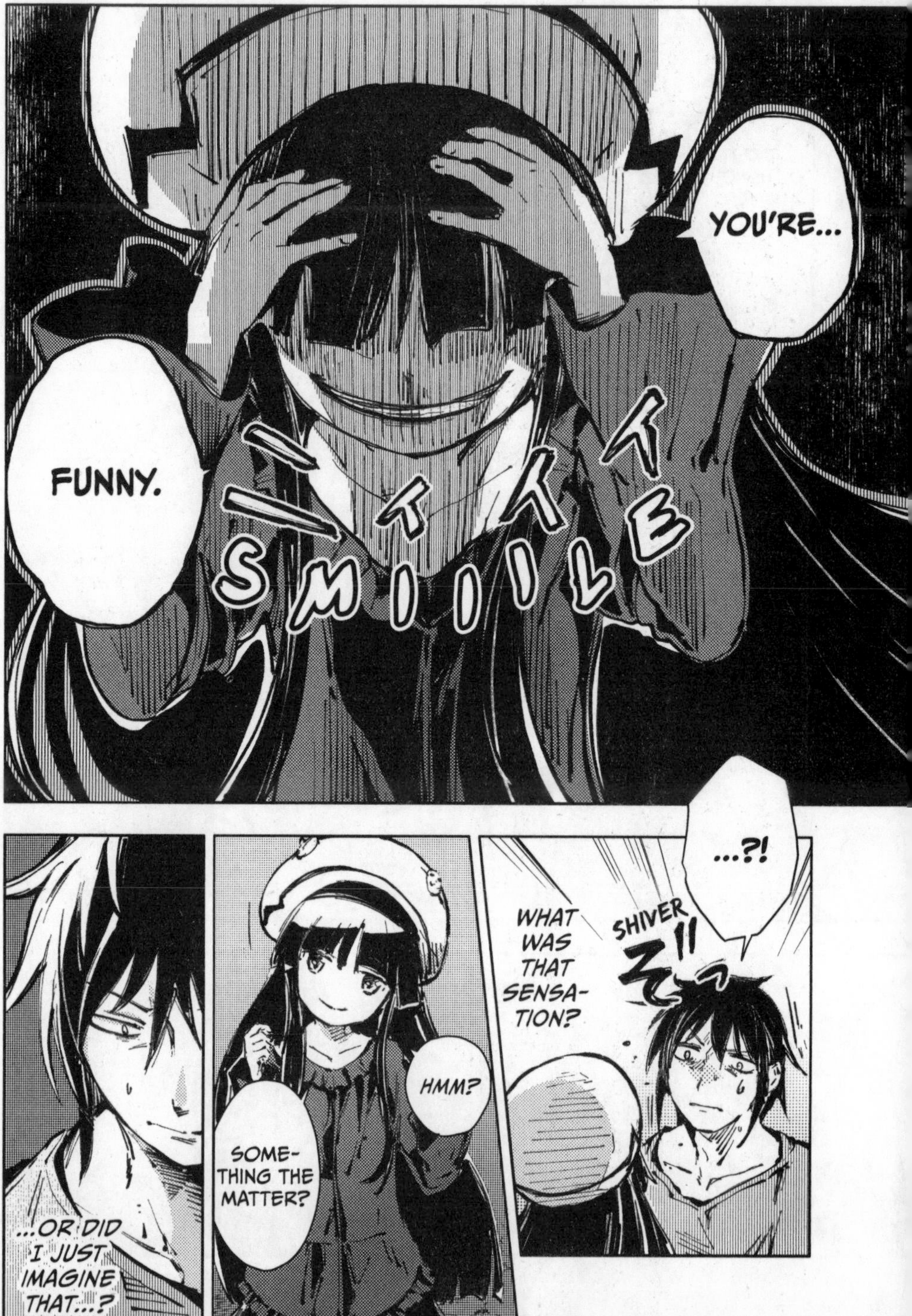
YOU'RE...
FUNNY.
SMIIILE
...?!
SHIVER
WHAT WAS THAT SENSATION?
HMM?
SOME-THING THE MATTER?
...OR DID I JUST IMAGINE THAT...?

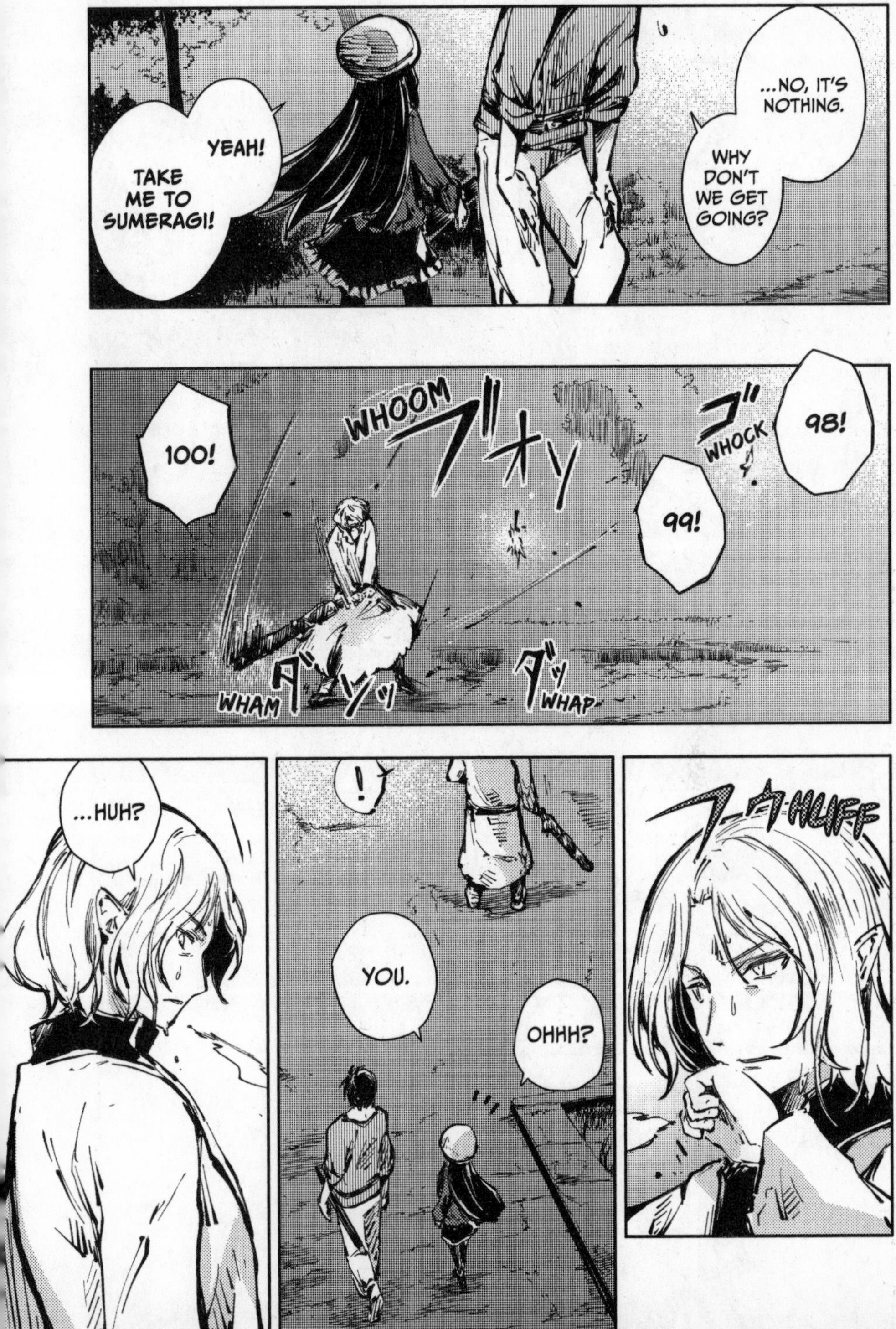
...NO, IT'S NOTHING.
WHY DON'T WE GET GOING?
YEAH! TAKE ME TO SUMERAGI!
98!
WHOCK
99!
WHOOM
100!
WHAP
WHAM
HUFF
!
YOU.
OHHH?
...HUH?

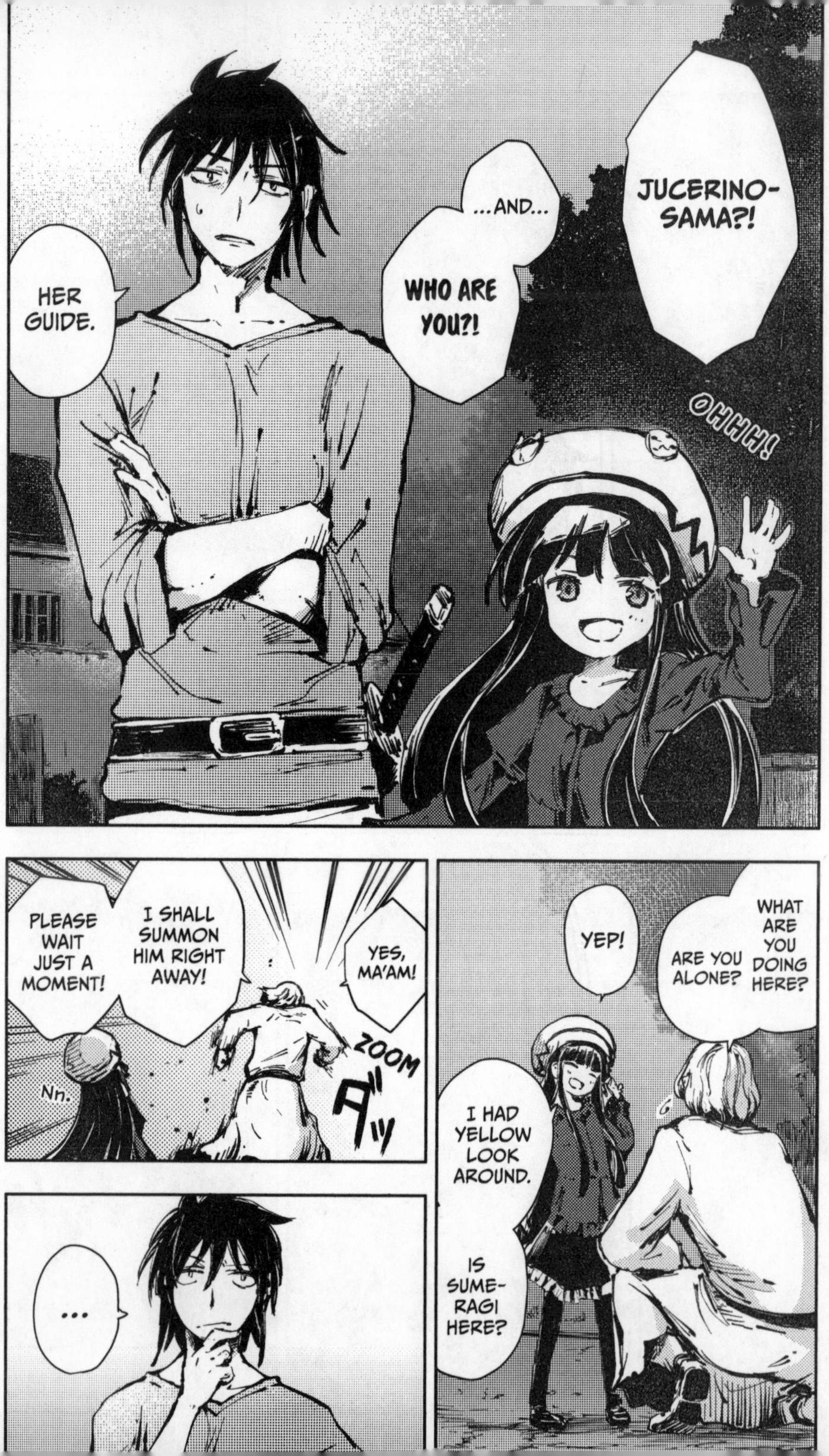
JUCERINO-SAMA?!
OHHHH!
...AND...
WHO ARE YOU?!
HER GUIDE.
WHAT ARE YOU DOING HERE?
ARE YOU ALONE?
YEP!
I HAD YELLOW LOOK AROUND.
IS SUMERAGI HERE?
YES, MA'AM!
I SHALL SUMMON HIM RIGHT AWAY!
PLEASE WAIT JUST A MOMENT!
ZOOM
Nn.
...

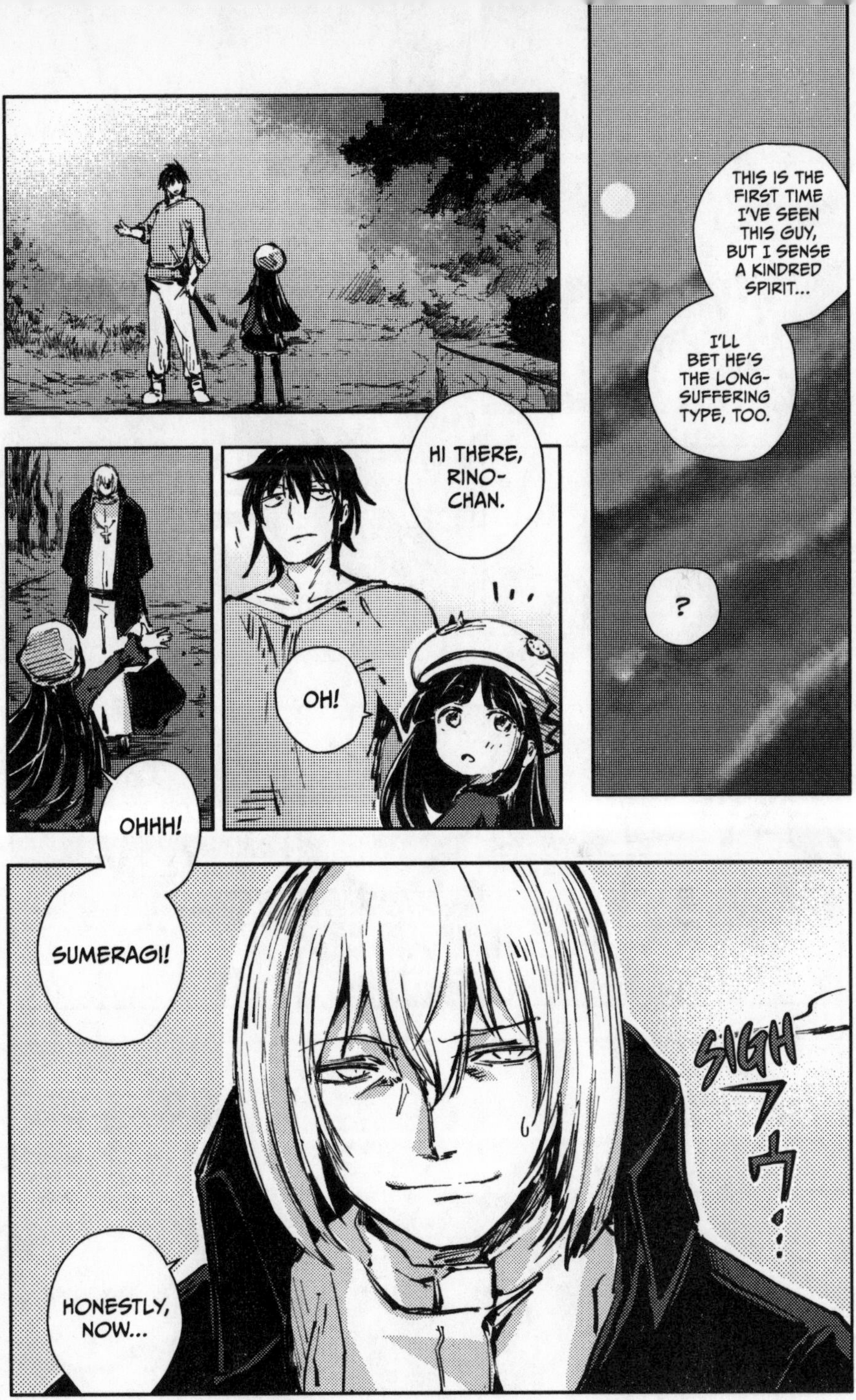
THIS IS THE FIRST TIME I'VE SEEN THIS GUY, BUT I SENSE A KINDRED SPIRIT...
I'LL BET HE'S THE LONG-SUFFERING TYPE, TOO.
?
HI THERE, RINO-CHAN.
OH!
OHHH!
SUMERAGI!
SIGH
フゥ…
HONESTLY, NOW...

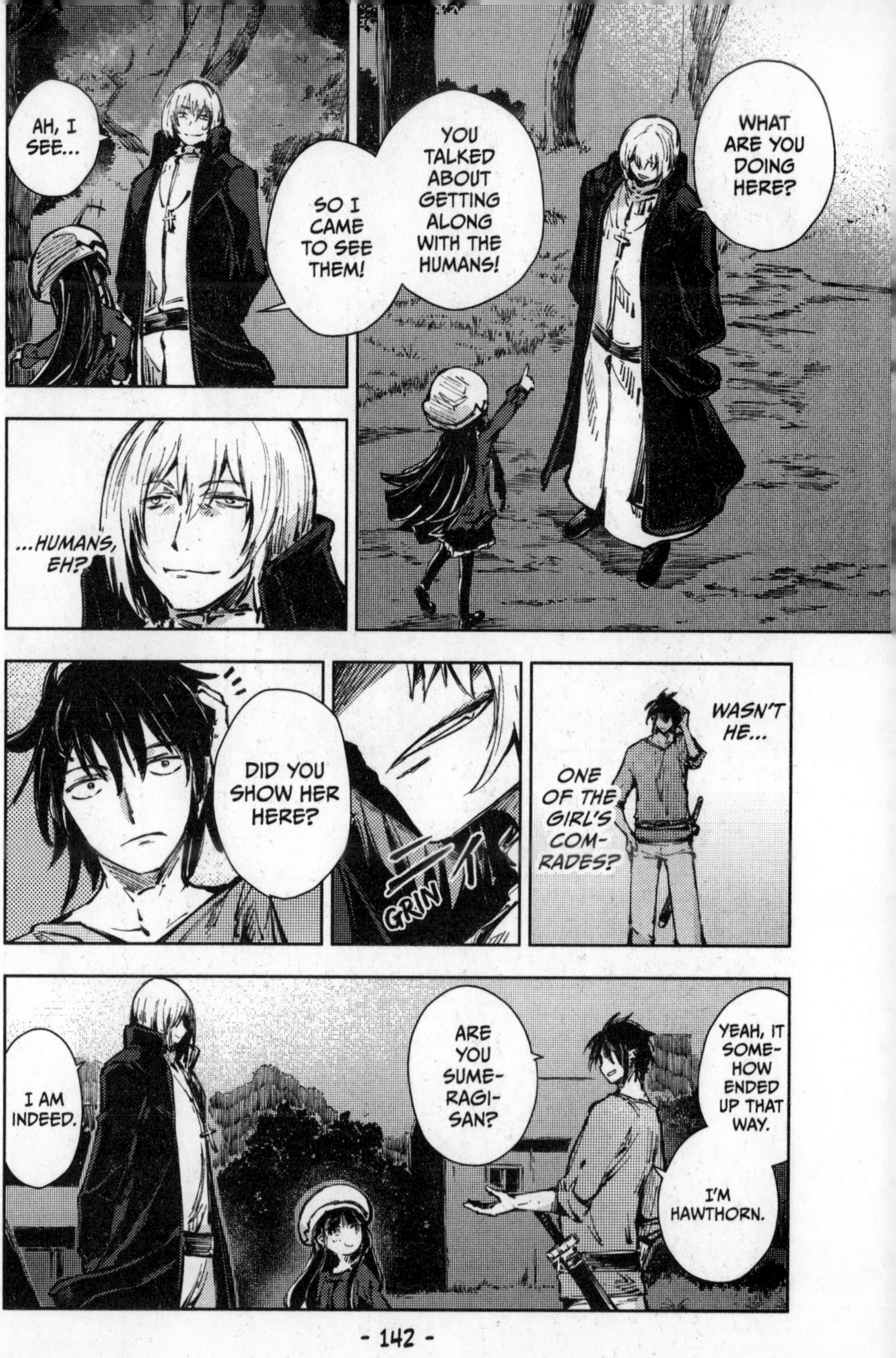
WHAT ARE YOU DOING HERE?
YOU TALKED ABOUT GETTING ALONG WITH THE HUMANS!
SO I CAME TO SEE THEM!
AH, I SEE...
...HUMANS, EH?
WASN'T HE...
ONE OF THE GIRL'S COM-RADES?
GRIN
DID YOU SHOW HER HERE?
YEAH, IT SOME-HOW ENDED UP THAT WAY.
I'M HAWTHORN.
ARE YOU SUME-RAGI-SAN?
I AM INDEED.

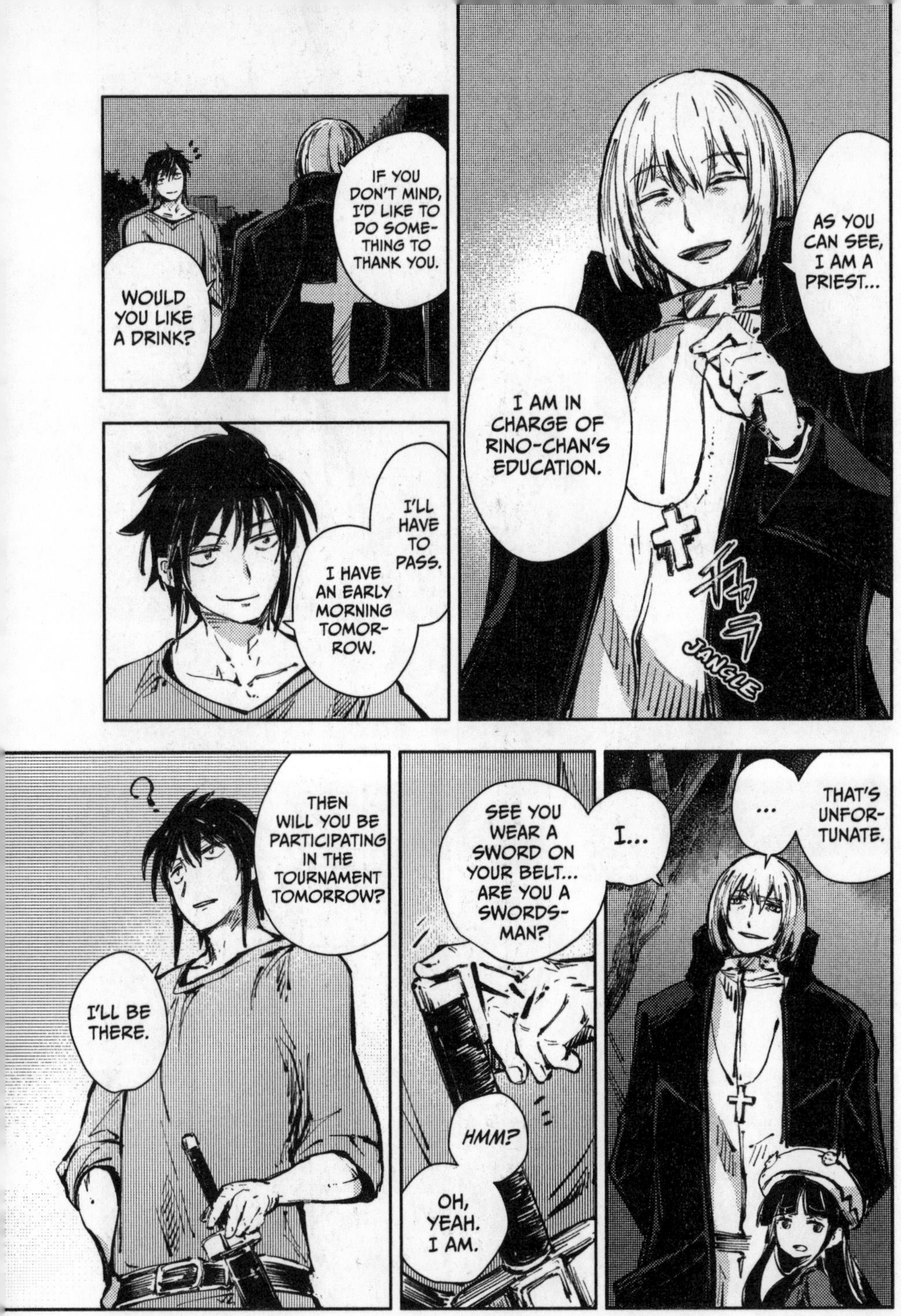
AS YOU CAN SEE, I AM A PRIEST...
I AM IN CHARGE OF RINO-CHAN'S EDUCATION.
チャラ
JANGLE
IF YOU DON'T MIND, I'D LIKE TO DO SOME-THING TO THANK YOU.
WOULD YOU LIKE A DRINK?
I'LL HAVE TO PASS.
I HAVE AN EARLY MORNING TOMOR-ROW.
THAT'S UNFOR-TUNATE.
...
I...
SEE YOU WEAR A SWORD ON YOUR BELT... ARE YOU A SWORDS-MAN?
HMM?
OH, YEAH. I AM.
THEN WILL YOU BE PARTICIPATING IN THE TOURNAMENT TOMORROW?
I'LL BE THERE.

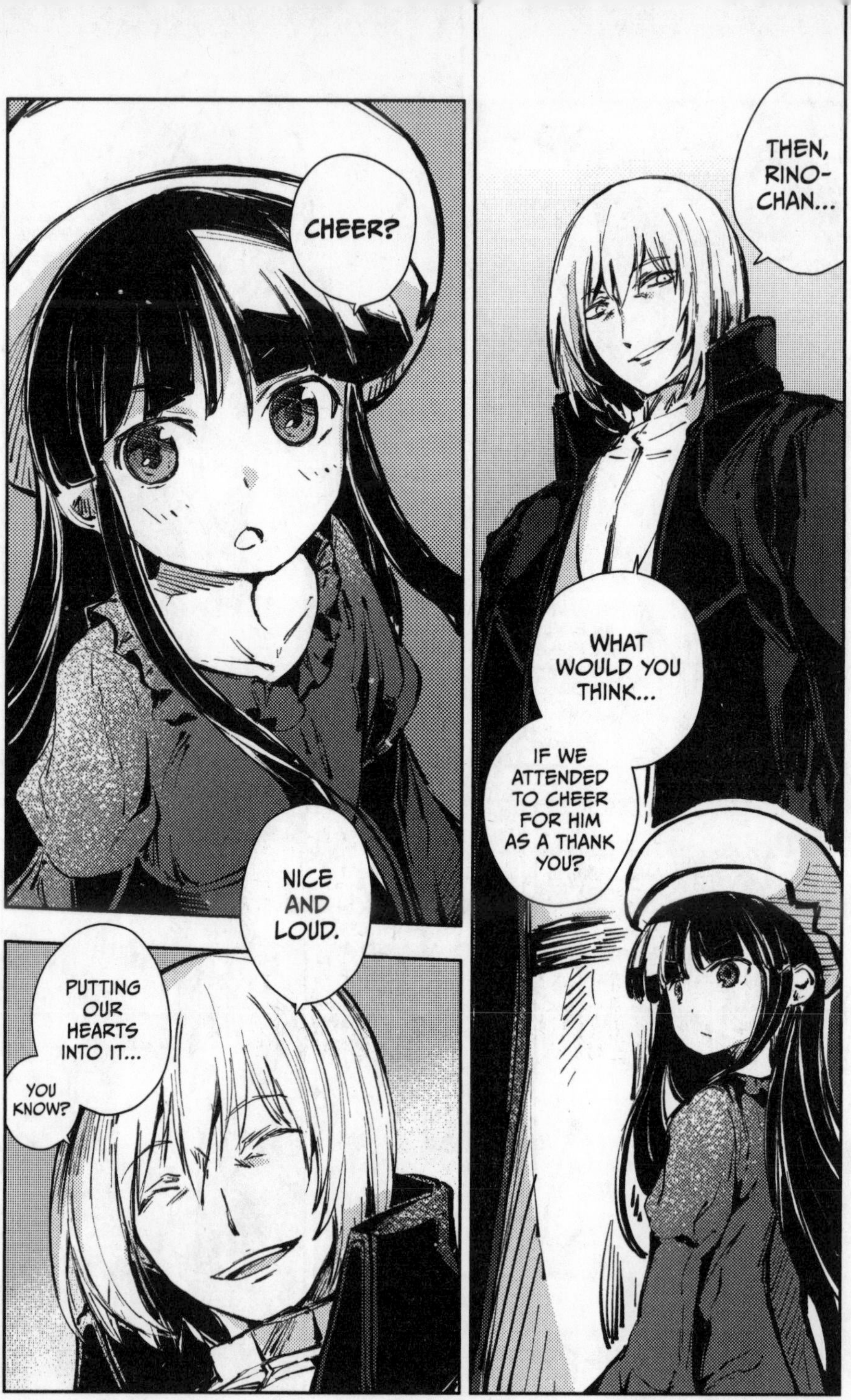
THEN, RINO-CHAN...
WHAT WOULD YOU THINK...
IF WE ATTENDED TO CHEER FOR HIM AS A THANK YOU?
CHEER?
NICE AND LOUD.
PUTTING OUR HEARTS INTO IT...
YOU KNOW?

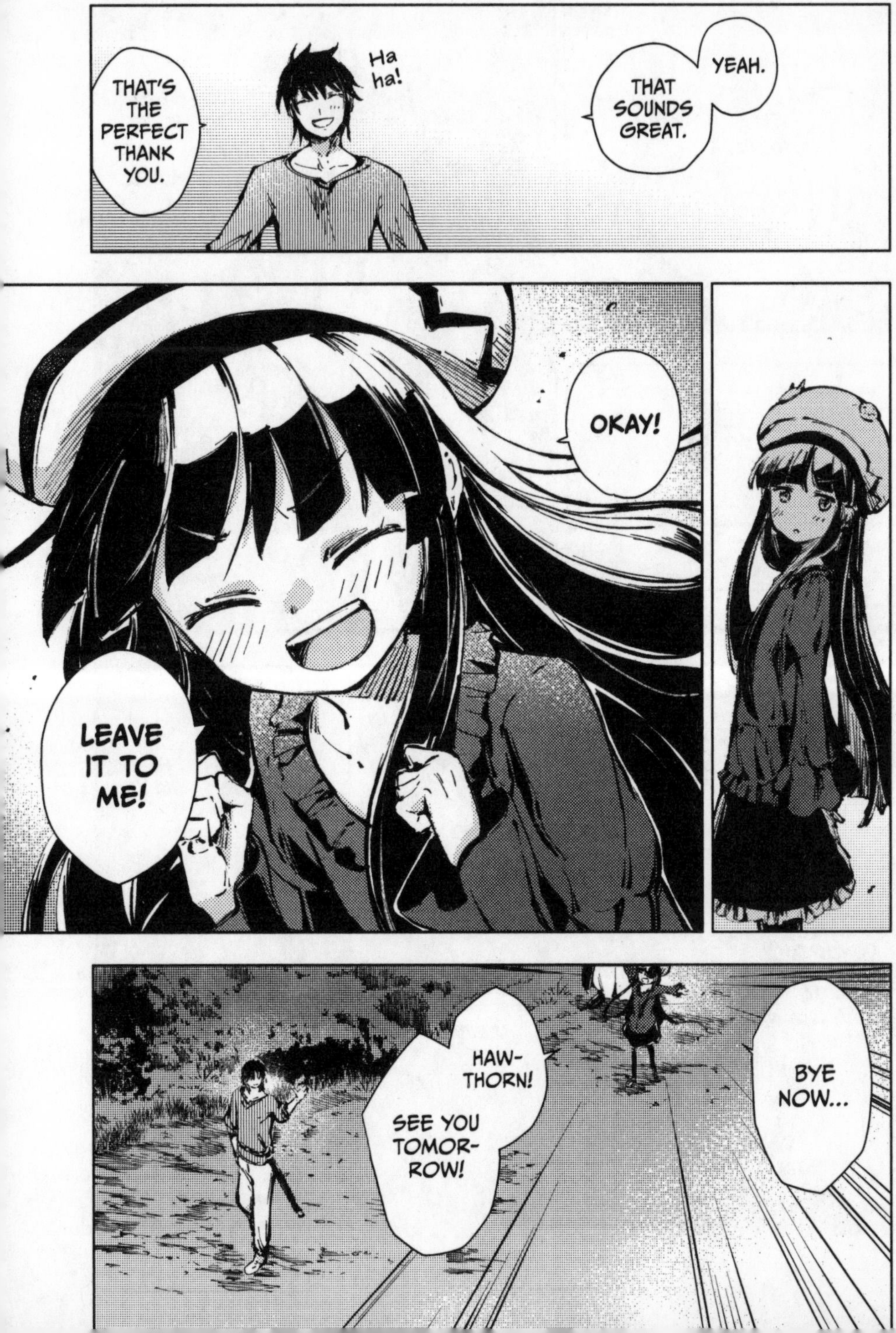
YEAH.
THAT SOUNDS GREAT.
Ha ha!
THAT'S THE PERFECT THANK YOU.
OKAY!
LEAVE IT TO ME!
BYE NOW...
HAW-THORN!
SEE YOU TOMOR-ROW!

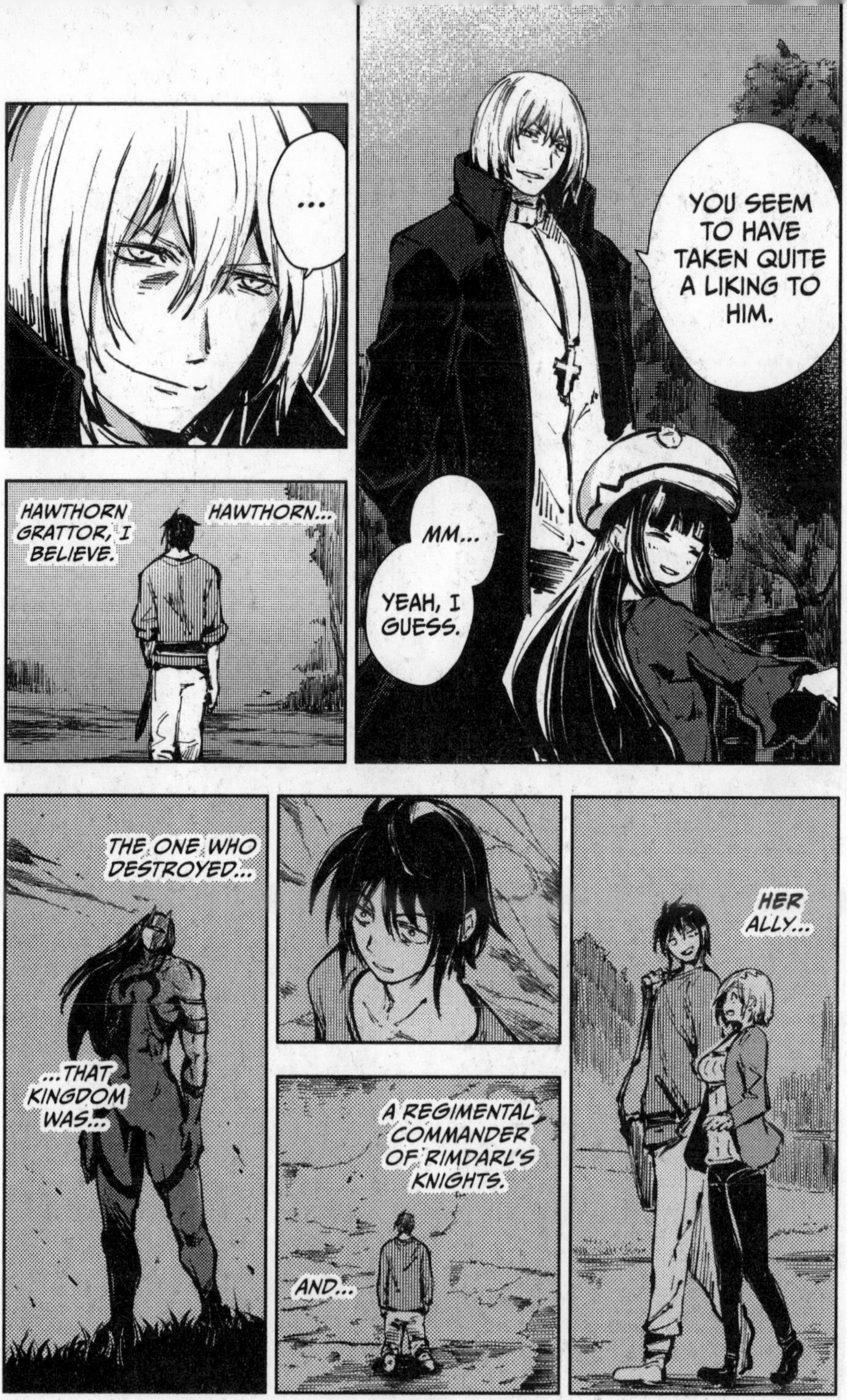
YOU SEEM TO HAVE TAKEN QUITE A LIKING TO HIM.
MM...
YEAH, I GUESS.
...
HAWTHORN...
HAWTHORN GRATTOR, I BELIEVE.
HER ALLY...
A REGIMENTAL COMMANDER OF RIMDARL'S KNIGHTS.
AND...
THE ONE WHO DESTROYED...
...THAT KINGDOM WAS...

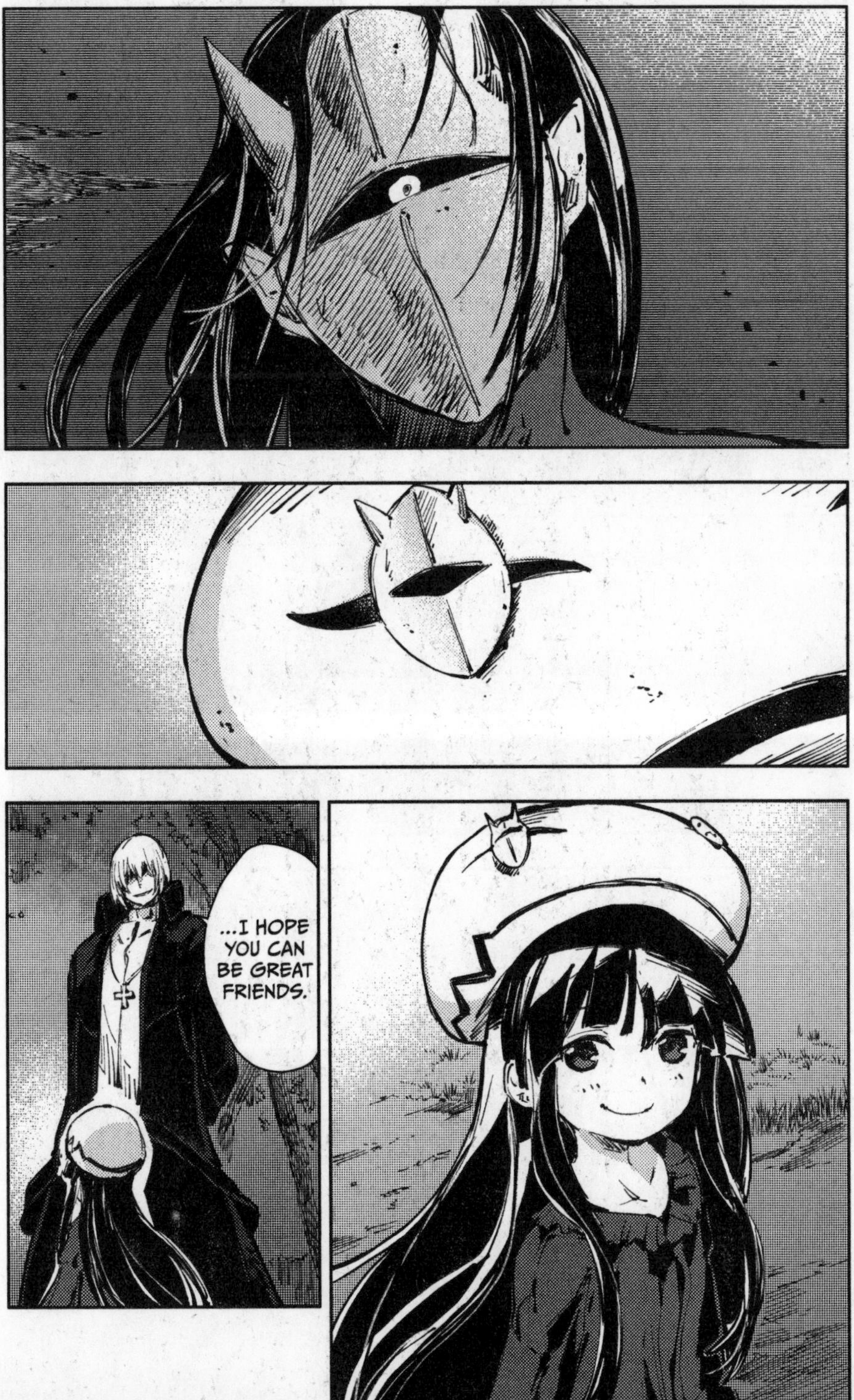
...I HOPE YOU CAN BE GREAT FRIENDS.

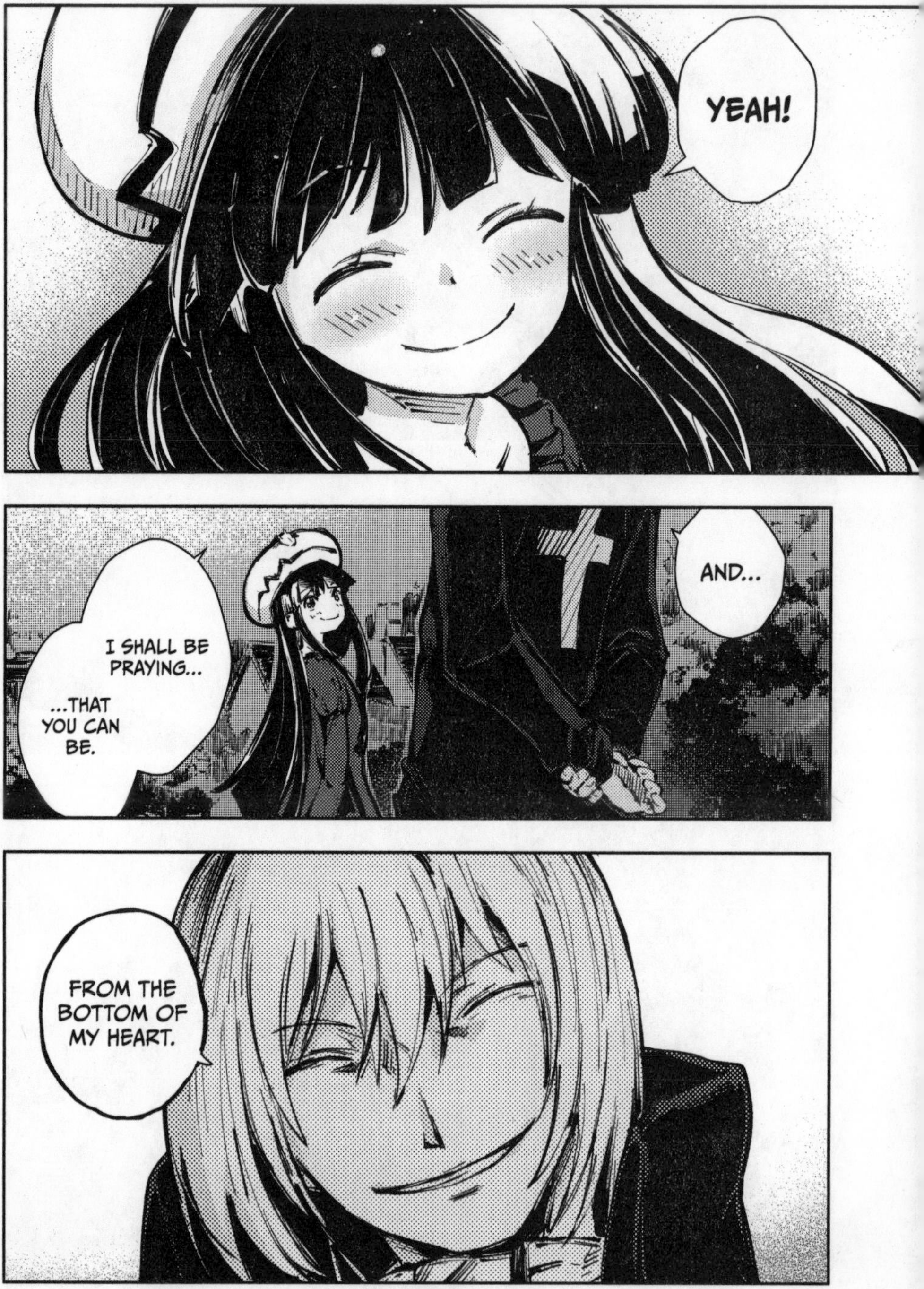
YEAH!
AND...
I SHALL BE PRAYING...
...THAT YOU CAN BE.
FROM THE BOTTOM OF MY HEART.

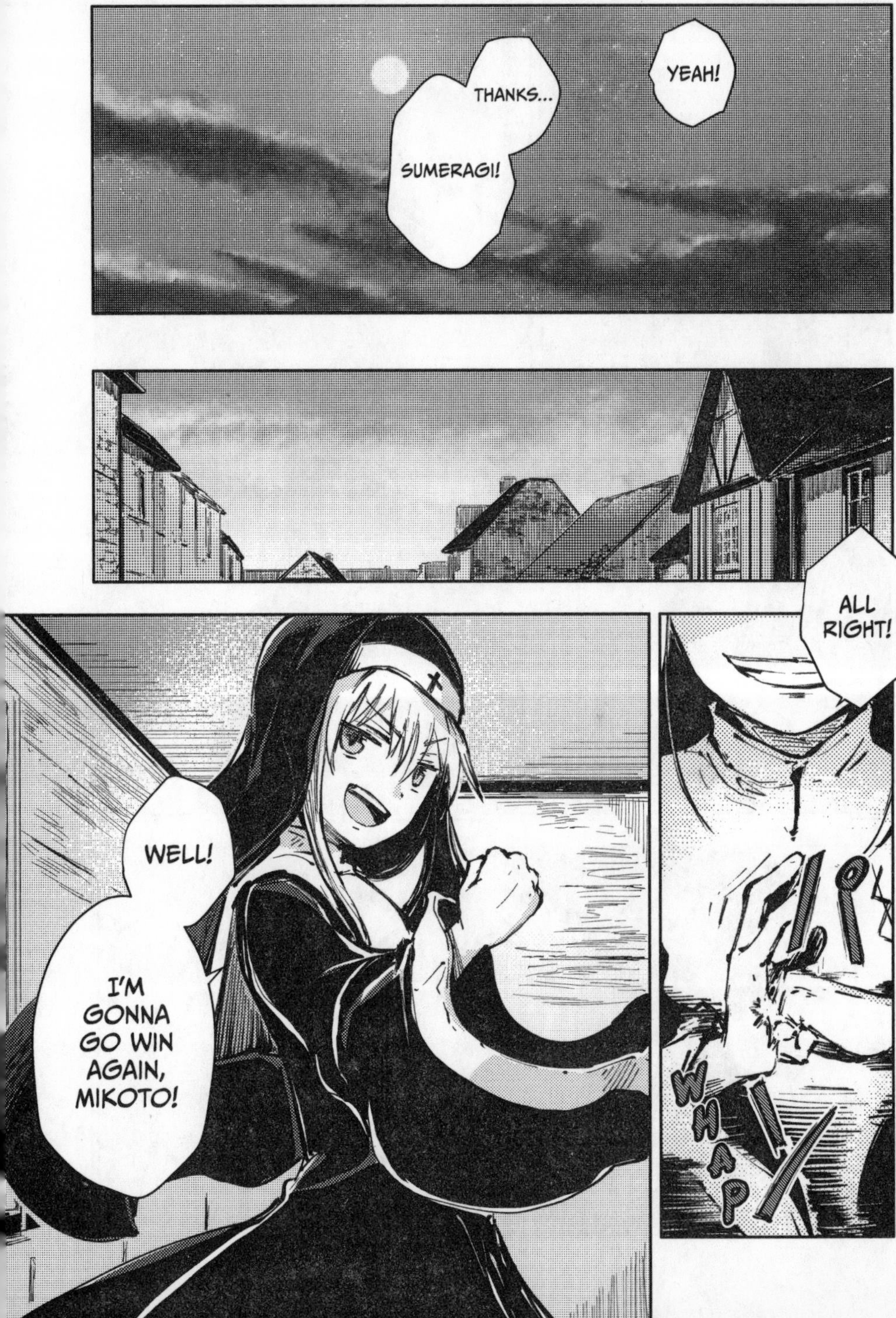
YEAH!
THANKS... SUMERAGI!
ALL RIGHT!
WHAP
WELL!
I'M GONNA GO WIN AGAIN, MIKOTO!

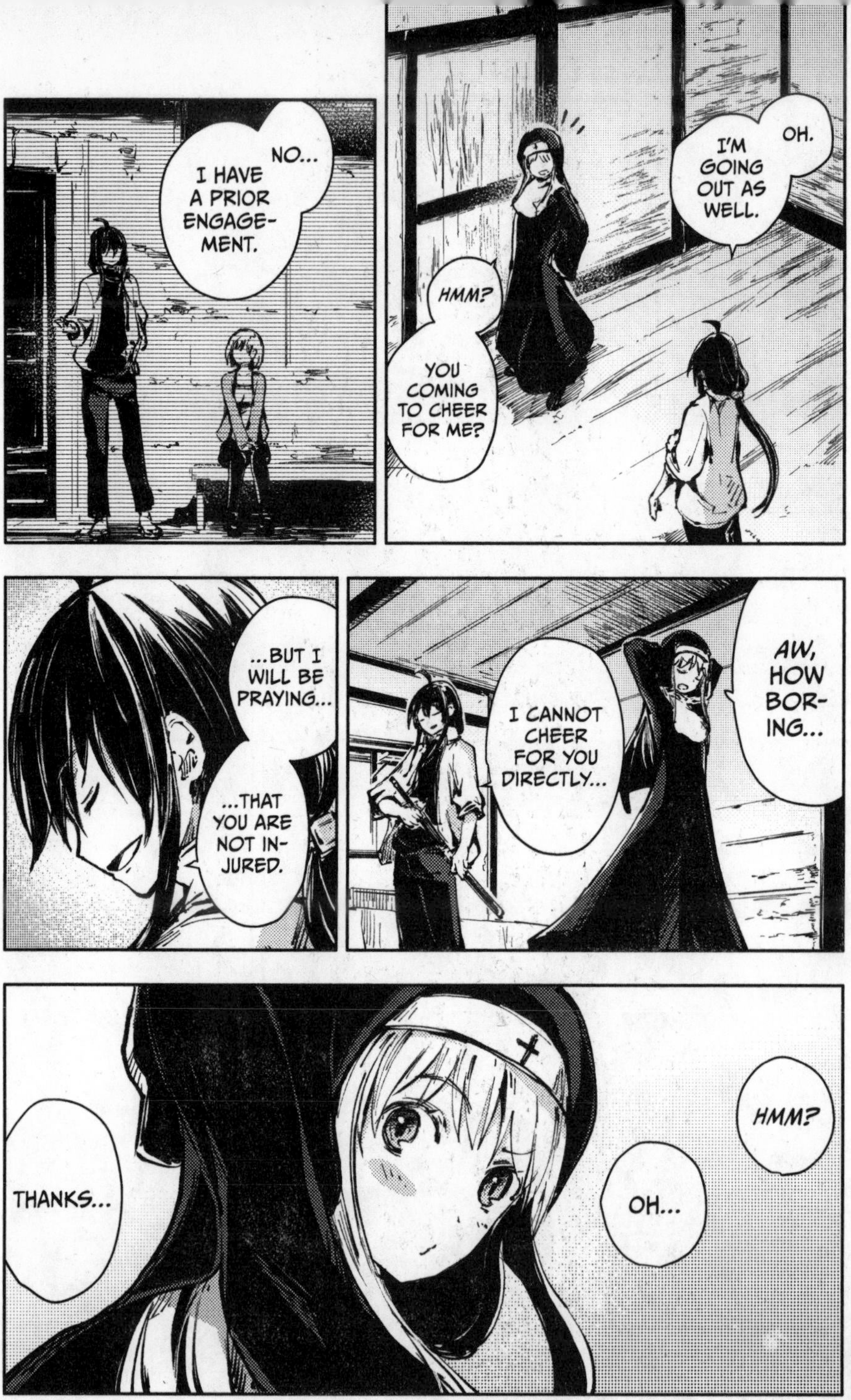
OH. I'M GOING OUT AS WELL.
HMM?
YOU COMING TO CHEER FOR ME?
NO... I HAVE A PRIOR ENGAGE-MENT.
AW, HOW BOR-ING...
I CANNOT CHEER FOR YOU DIRECTLY...
...BUT I WILL BE PRAYING...
...THAT YOU ARE NOT IN-JURED.
HMM?
OH...
THANKS...

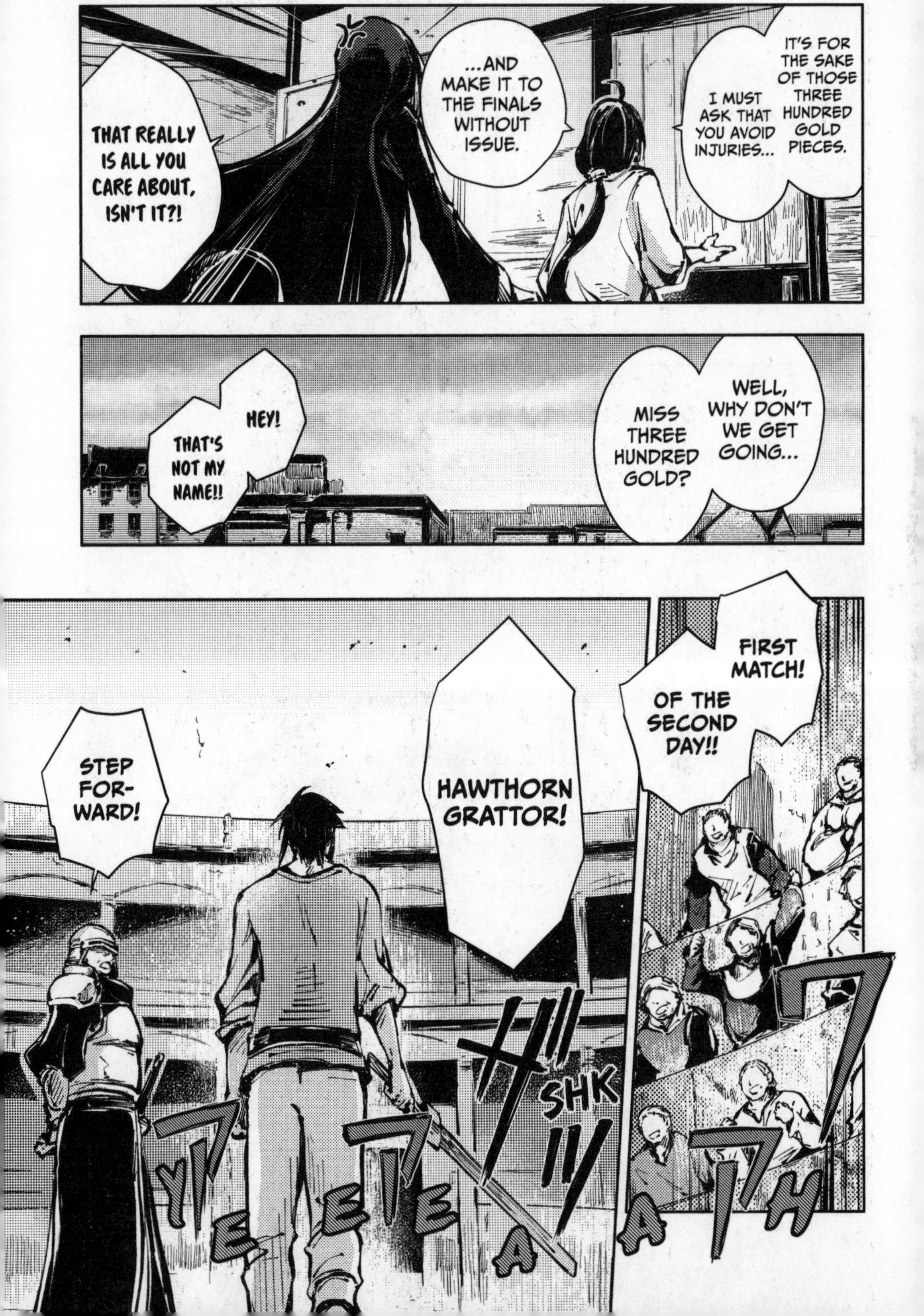
IT'S FOR THE SAKE OF THOSE THREE HUNDRED GOLD PIECES.
I MUST ASK THAT YOU AVOID INJURIES...
...AND MAKE IT TO THE FINALS WITHOUT ISSUE.
THAT REALLY IS ALL YOU CARE ABOUT, ISN'T IT?!
WELL, WHY DON'T WE GET GOING...
MISS THREE HUNDRED GOLD?
HEY!
THAT'S NOT MY NAME!!
FIRST MATCH!
OF THE SECOND DAY!!
HAWTHORN GRATTOR!
STEP FOR-WARD!
SHK
YEEEEAAH

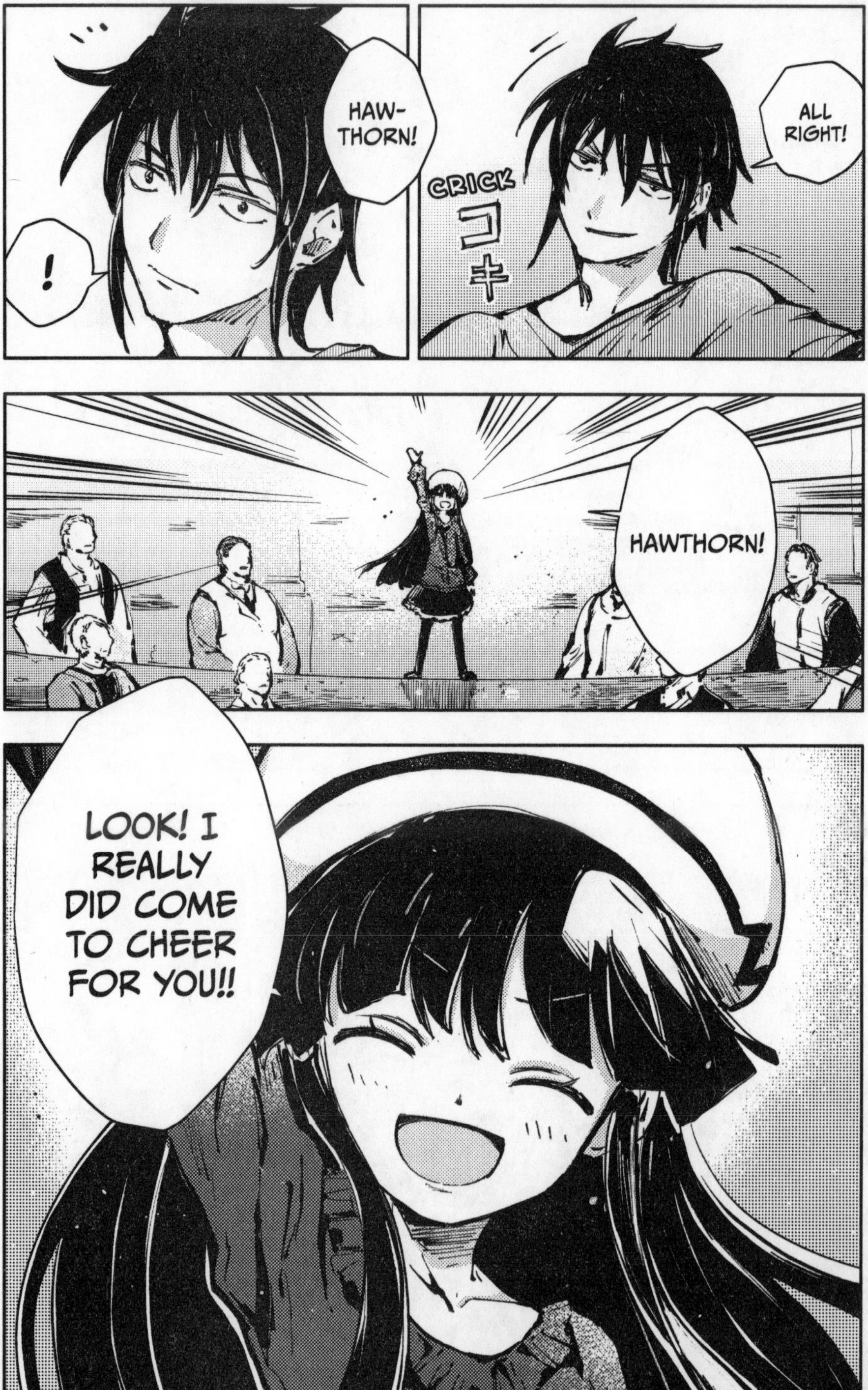

ALL RIGHT!
CRICK
コキ
...
HAW-THORN!
!
HAWTHORN!
LOOK! I REALLY DID COME TO CHEER FOR YOU!!

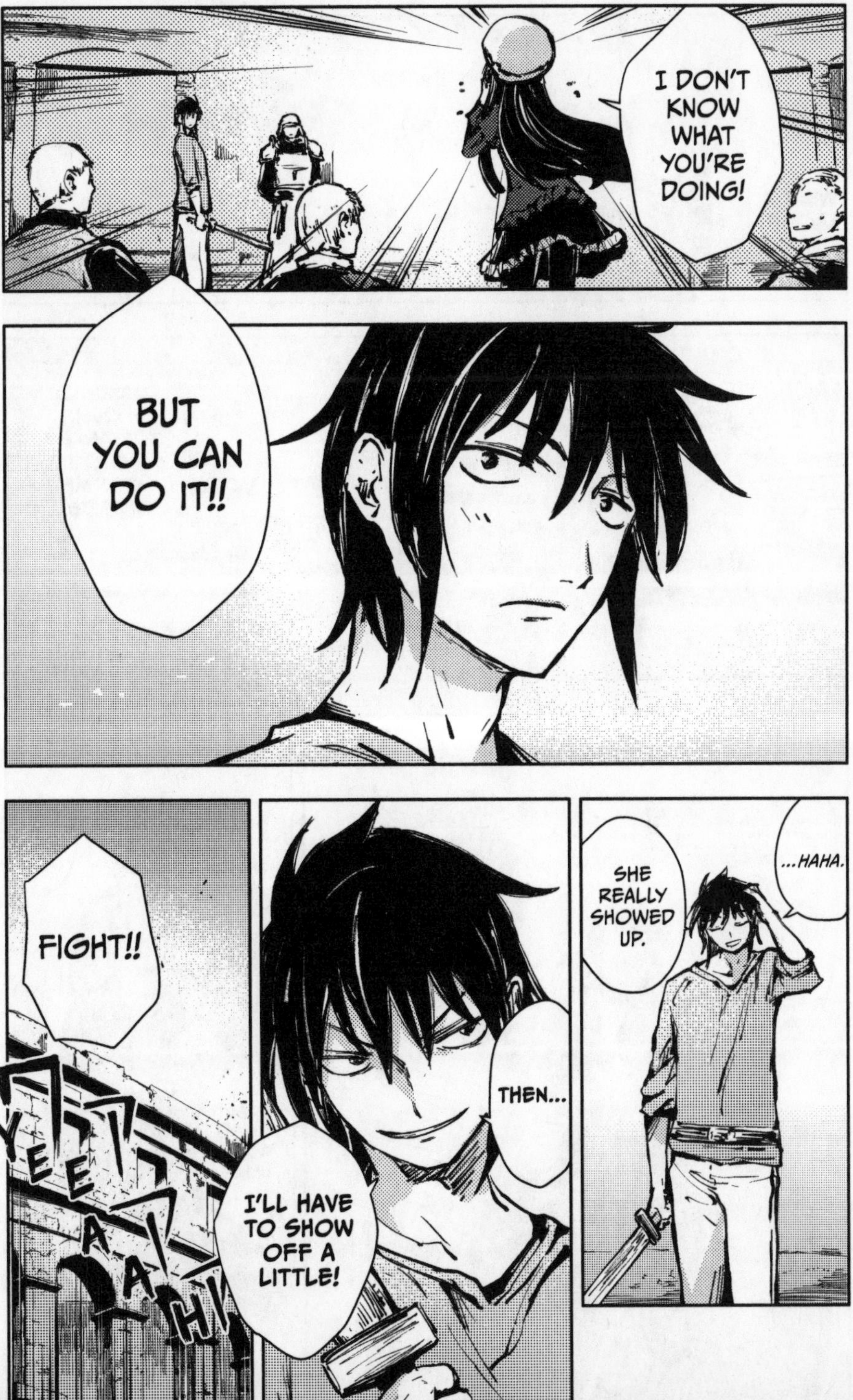
I DON'T KNOW WHAT YOU'RE DOING!
BUT YOU CAN DO IT!!
...HAHA.
SHE REALLY SHOWED UP.
THEN...
I'LL HAVE TO SHOW OFF A LITTLE!
FIGHT!!
YEEAAH!

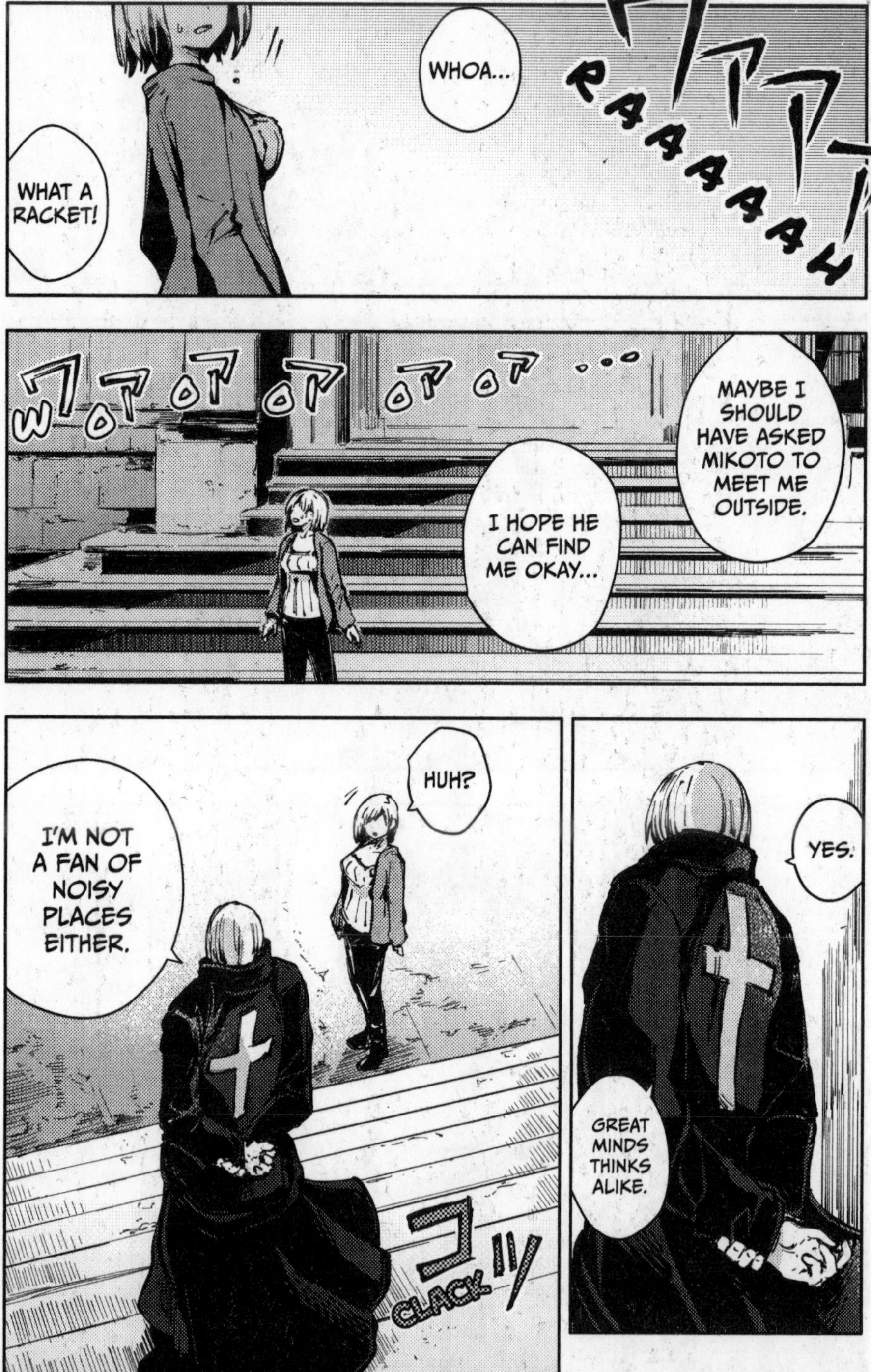
RAAAAAAH
WHOA...
WHAT A RACKET!
MAYBE I SHOULD HAVE ASKED MIKOTO TO MEET ME OUTSIDE.
I HOPE HE CAN FIND ME OKAY...
WOOOOO...
YES.
GREAT MINDS THINKS ALIKE.
HUH?
I'M NOT A FAN OF NOISY PLACES EITHER.
CLACK

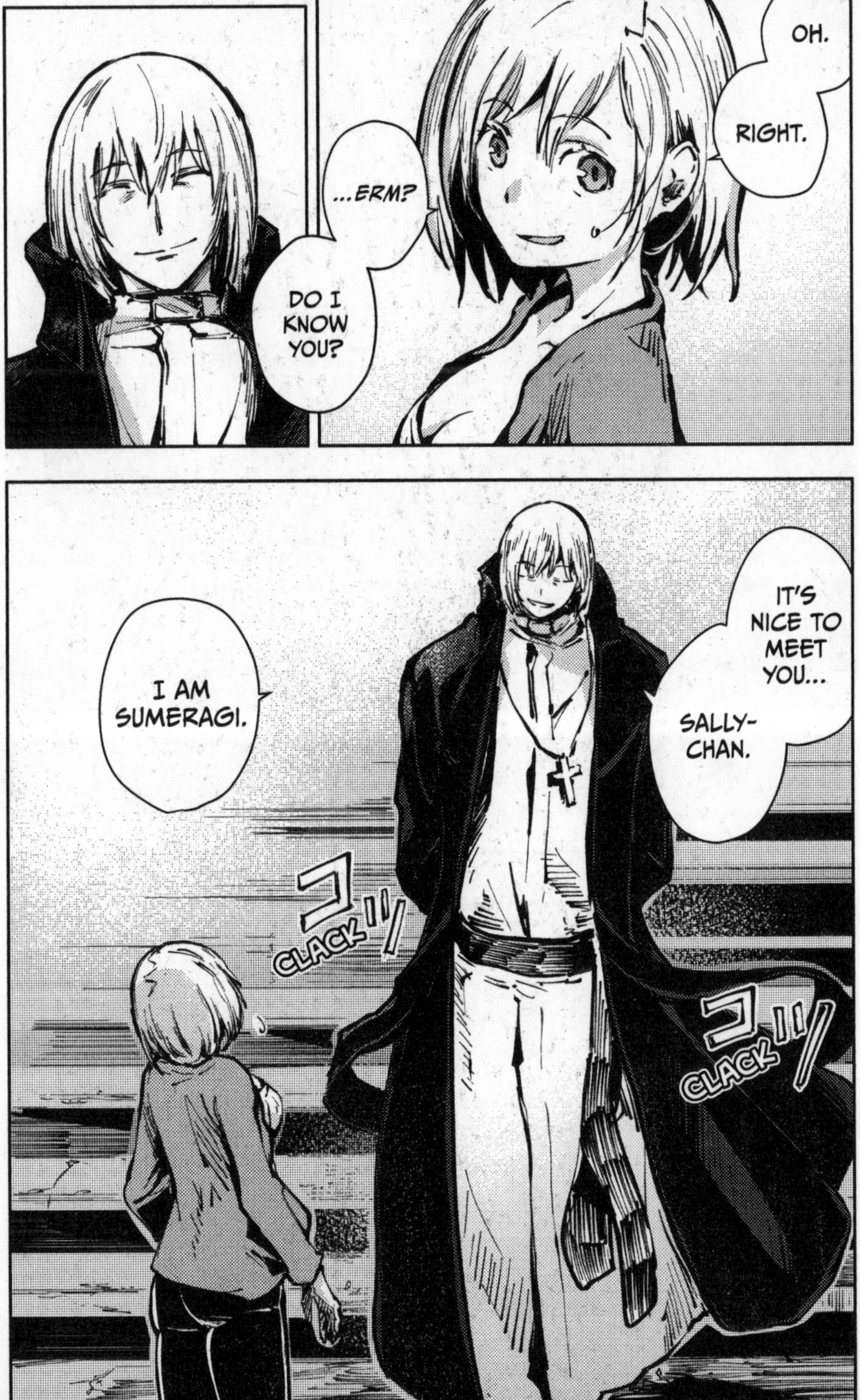
OH.
RIGHT.
...ERM?
DO I KNOW YOU?
IT'S NICE TO MEET YOU...
SALLY-CHAN.
I AM SUMERAGI.
コ CLACK
コ CLACK

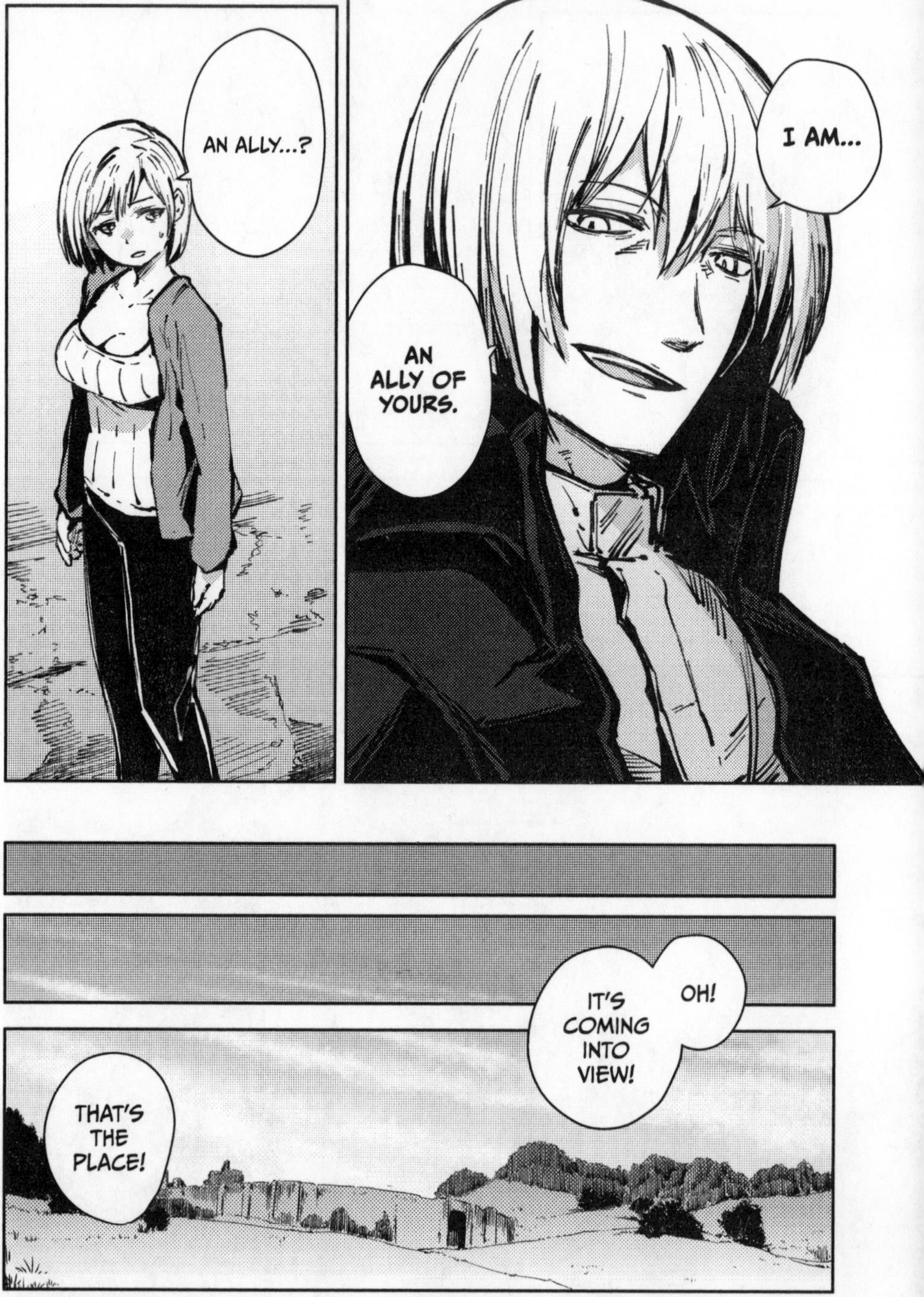
I AM...
AN ALLY OF YOURS.
AN ALLY...?
OH!
IT'S COMING INTO VIEW!
THAT'S THE PLACE!

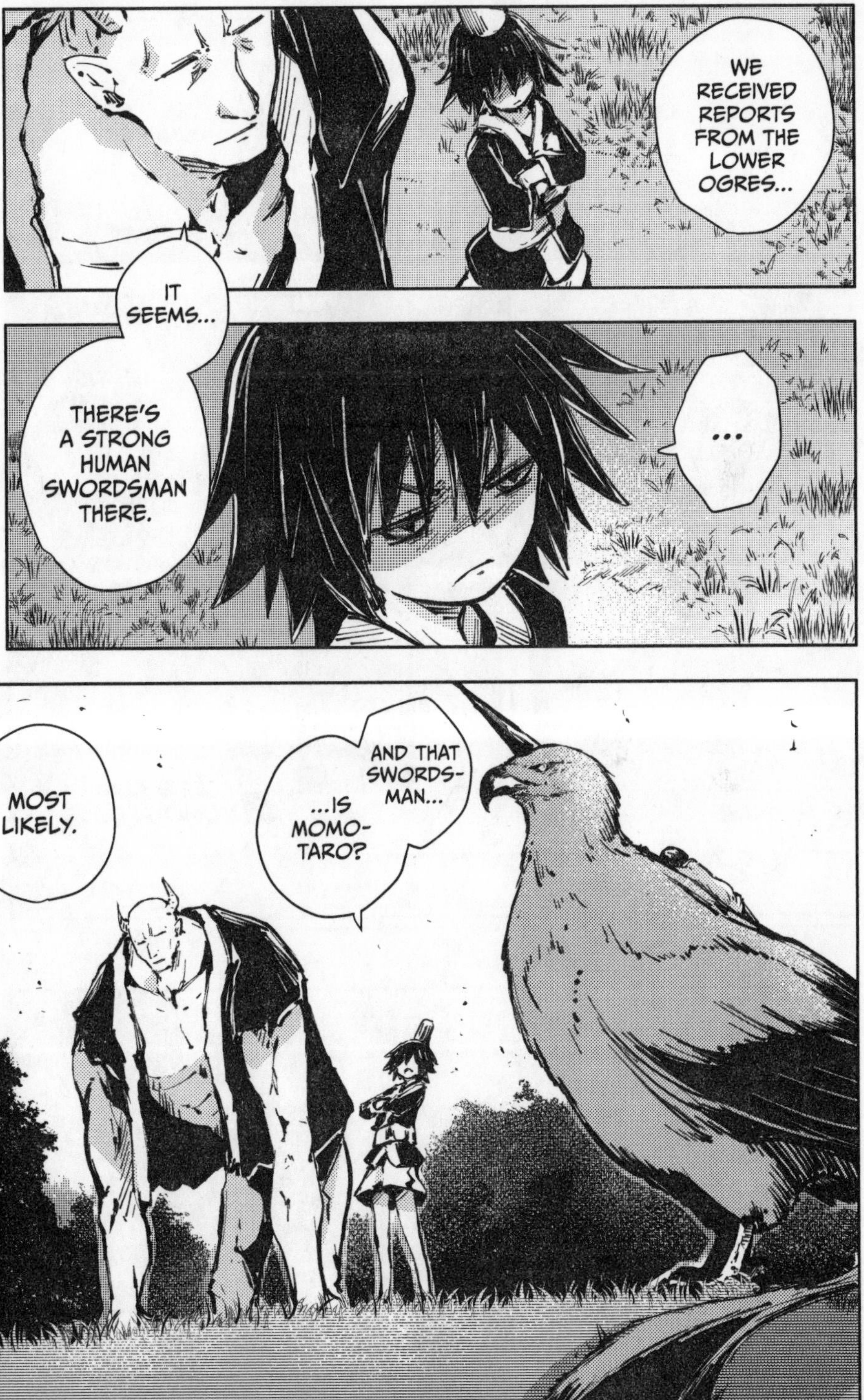
WE RECEIVED REPORTS FROM THE LOWER OGRES...
IT SEEMS...
THERE'S A STRONG HUMAN SWORDSMAN THERE.
...
AND THAT SWORDS-MAN...
...IS MOMO-TARO?
MOST LIKELY.

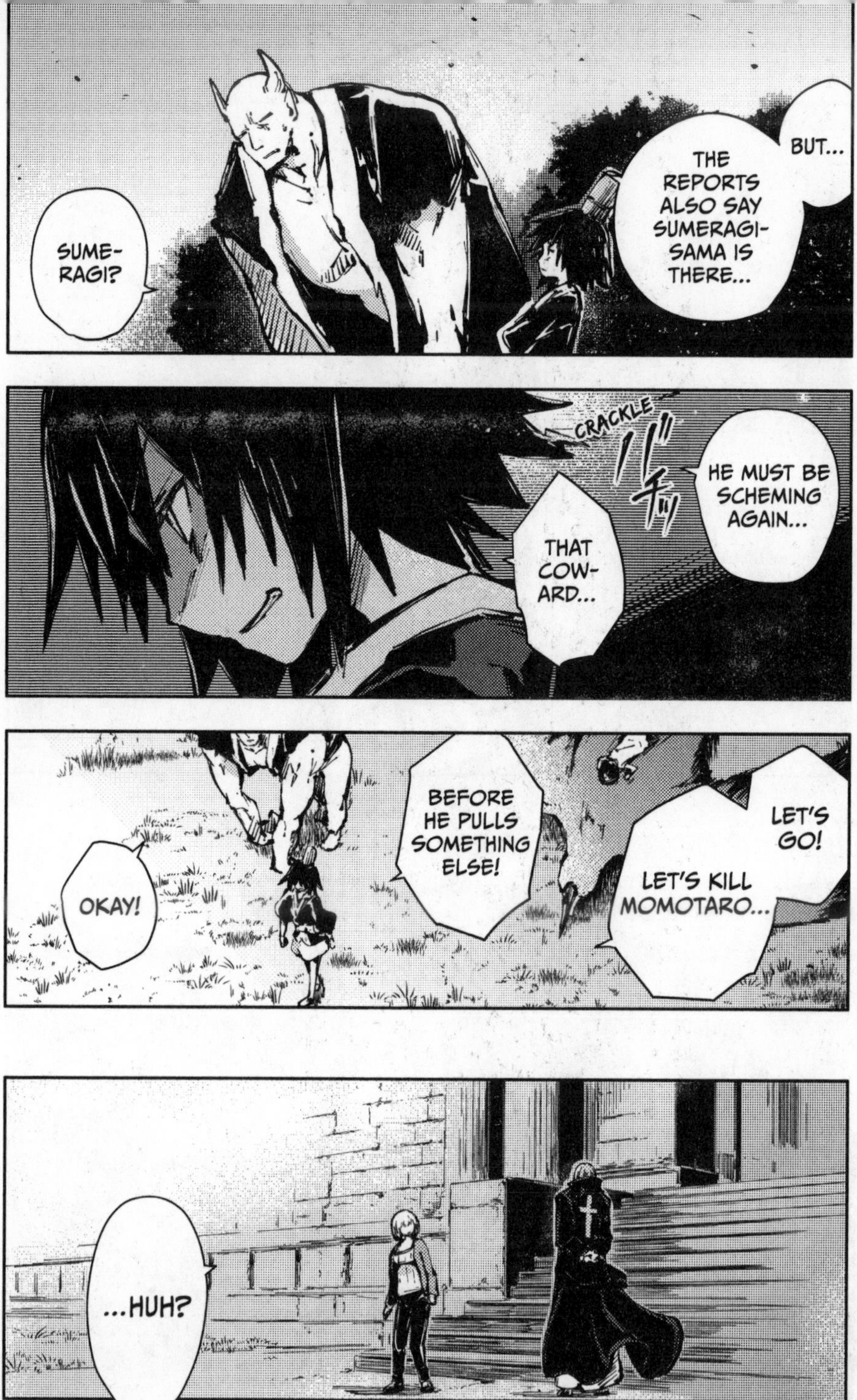
BUT...
THE REPORTS ALSO SAY SUMERAGI-SAMA IS THERE...
SUME-RAGI?
CRACKLE
バヂッ
HE MUST BE SCHEMING AGAIN...
THAT COW-ARD...
LET'S GO!
LET'S KILL MOMOTARO...
BEFORE HE PULLS SOMETHING ELSE!
OKAY!
...HUH?

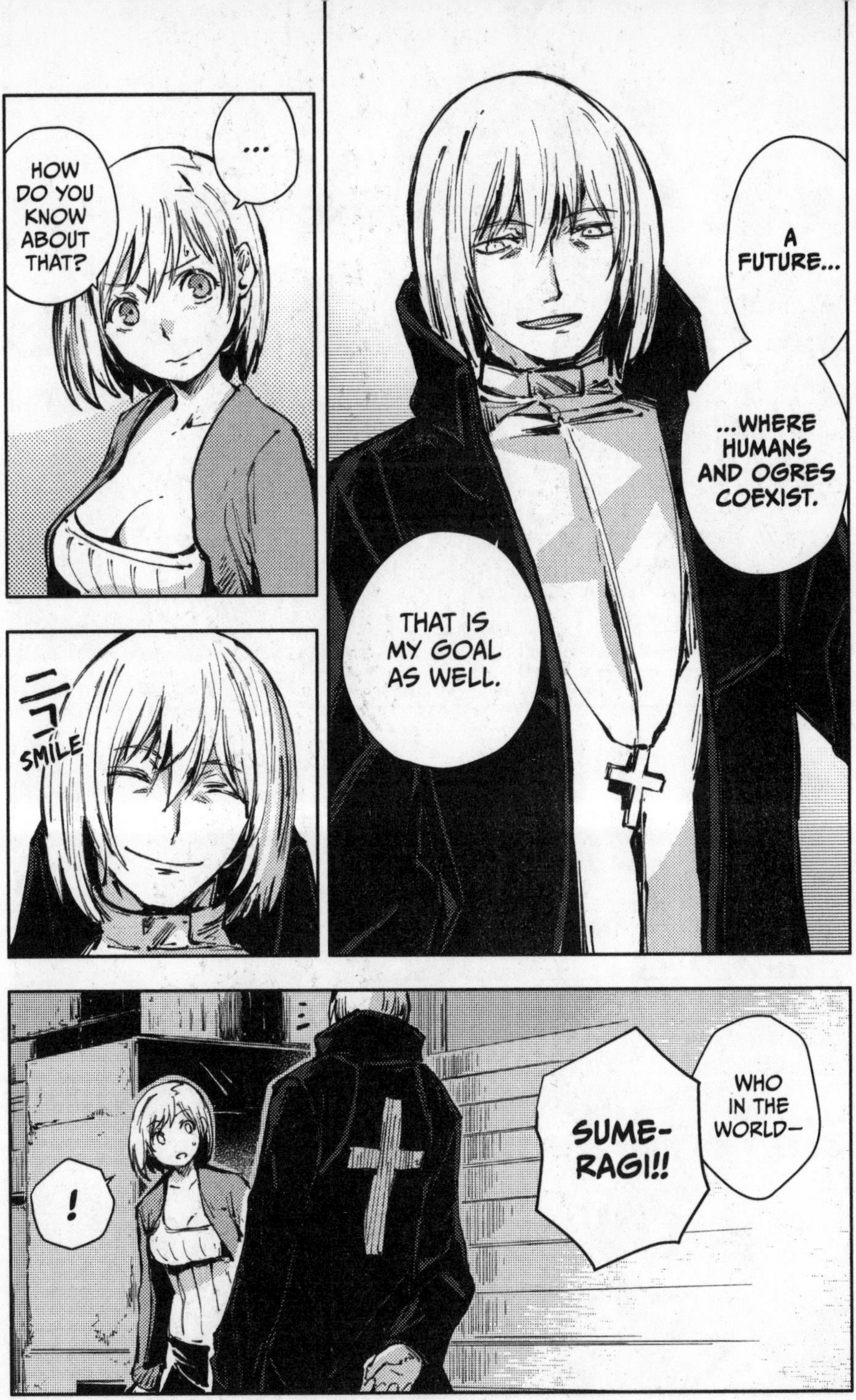
A FUTURE...
...WHERE HUMANS AND OGRES COEXIST.
THAT IS MY GOAL AS WELL.
...
HOW DO YOU KNOW ABOUT THAT?
ニコ
SMILE
WHO IN THE WORLD—
SUME-RAGI!!
!

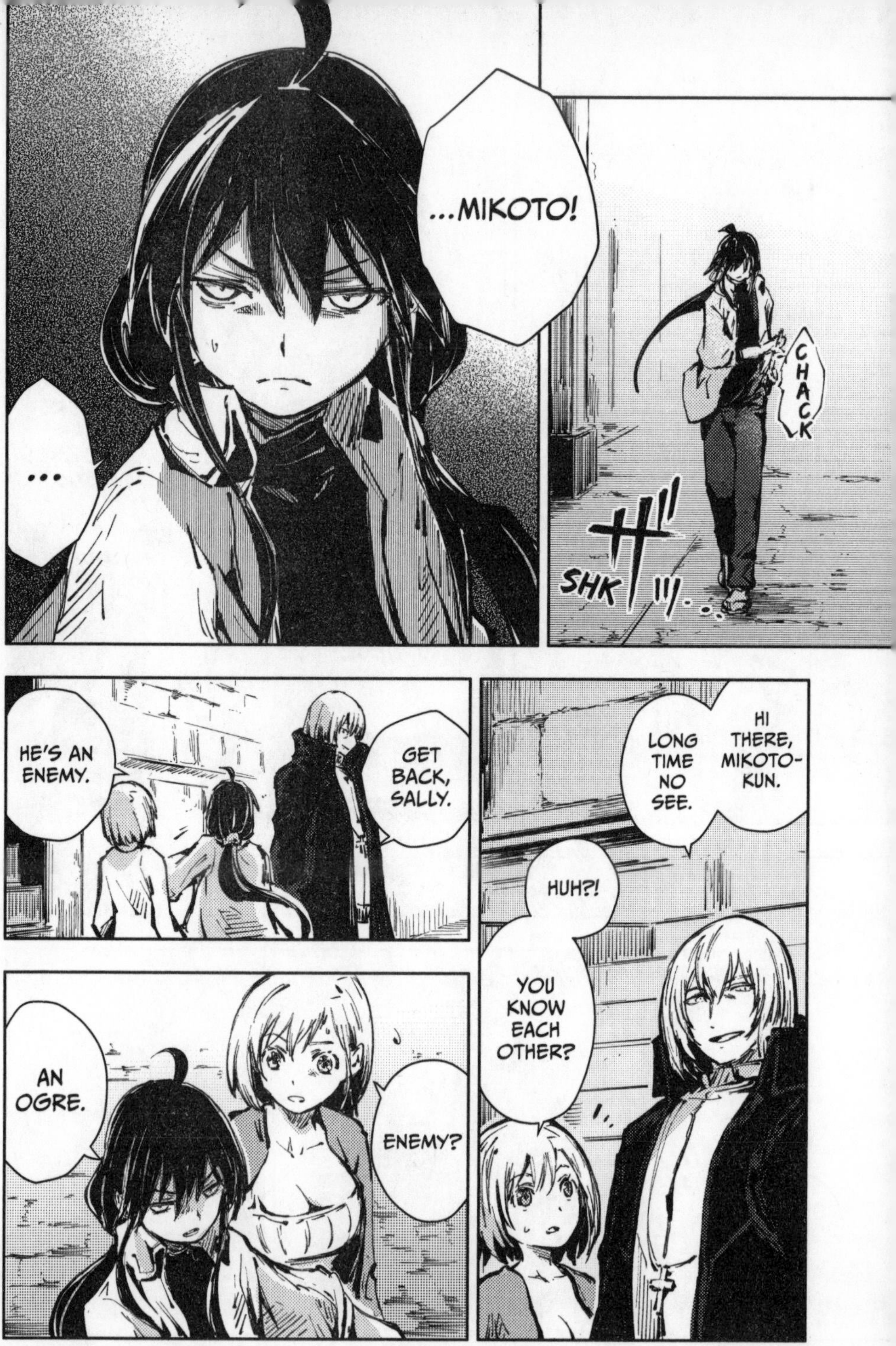
CHACK
SHK
...MIKOTO!
...
HI THERE, MIKOTO-KUN.
LONG TIME NO SEE.
HUH?!
YOU KNOW EACH OTHER?
GET BACK, SALLY.
HE'S AN ENEMY.
ENEMY?
AN OGRE.

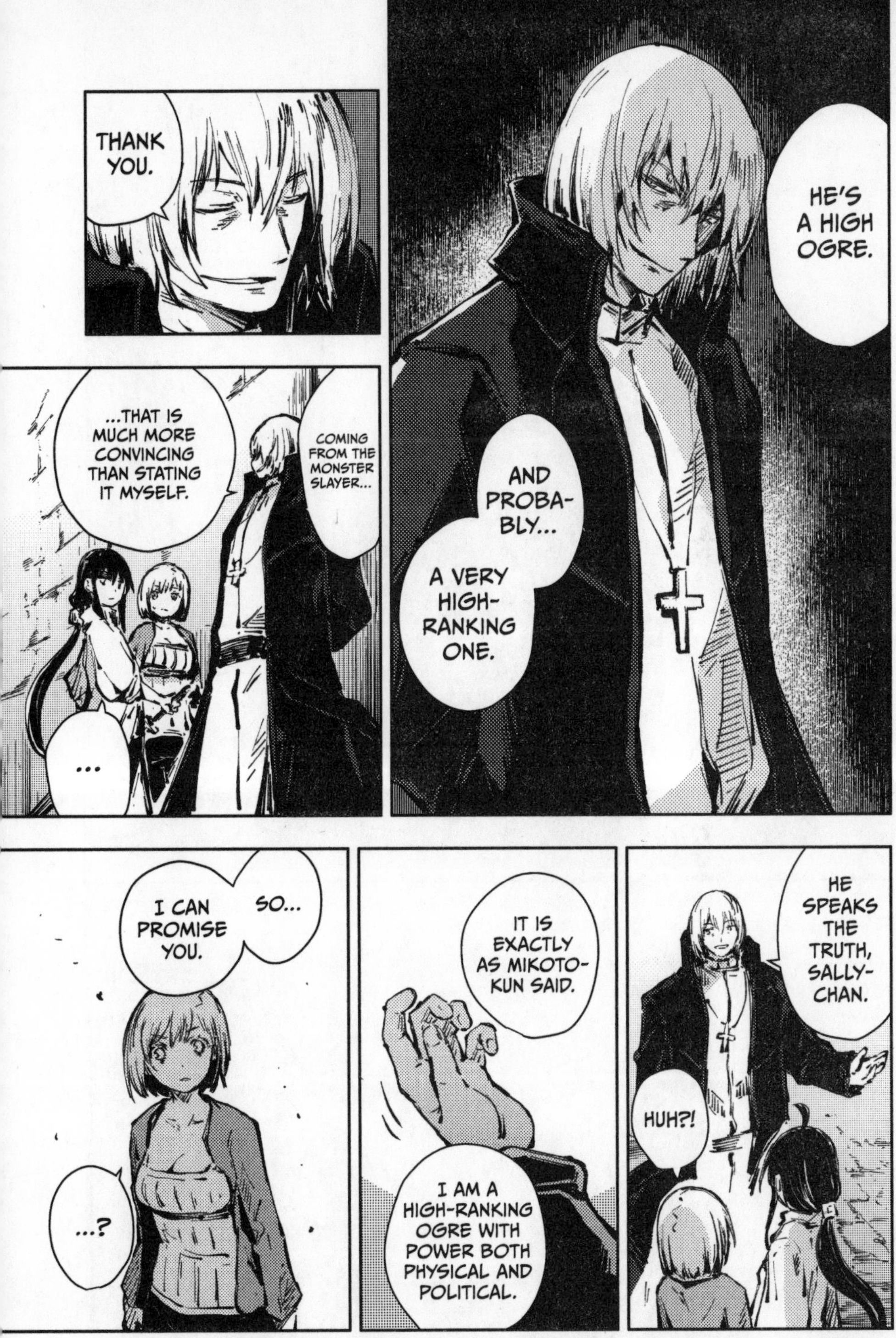
HE'S A HIGH OGRE.
AND PROBABLY...
A VERY HIGH-RANKING ONE.
THANK YOU.
COMING FROM THE MONSTER SLAYER...
...THAT IS MUCH MORE CONVINCING THAN STATING IT MYSELF.
...
HE SPEAKS THE TRUTH, SALLY-CHAN.
HUH?!
IT IS EXACTLY AS MIKOTO-KUN SAID.
I AM A HIGH-RANKING OGRE WITH POWER BOTH PHYSICAL AND POLITICAL.
SO...
I CAN PROMISE YOU.
...?

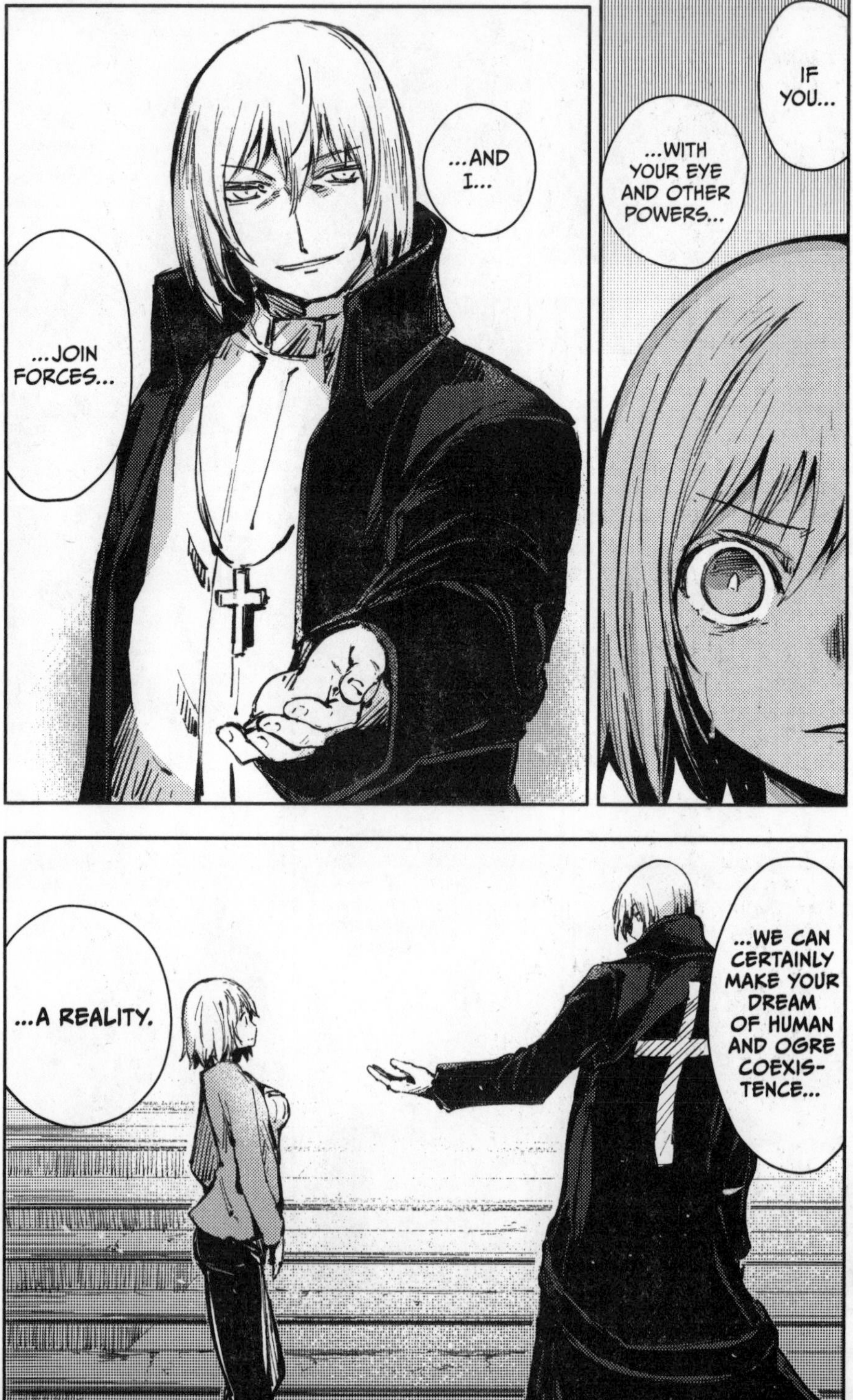
IF YOU...
...WITH YOUR EYE AND OTHER POWERS...
...AND I...
...JOIN FORCES...
...WE CAN CERTAINLY MAKE YOUR DREAM OF HUMAN AND OGRE COEXISTENCE...
...A REALITY.

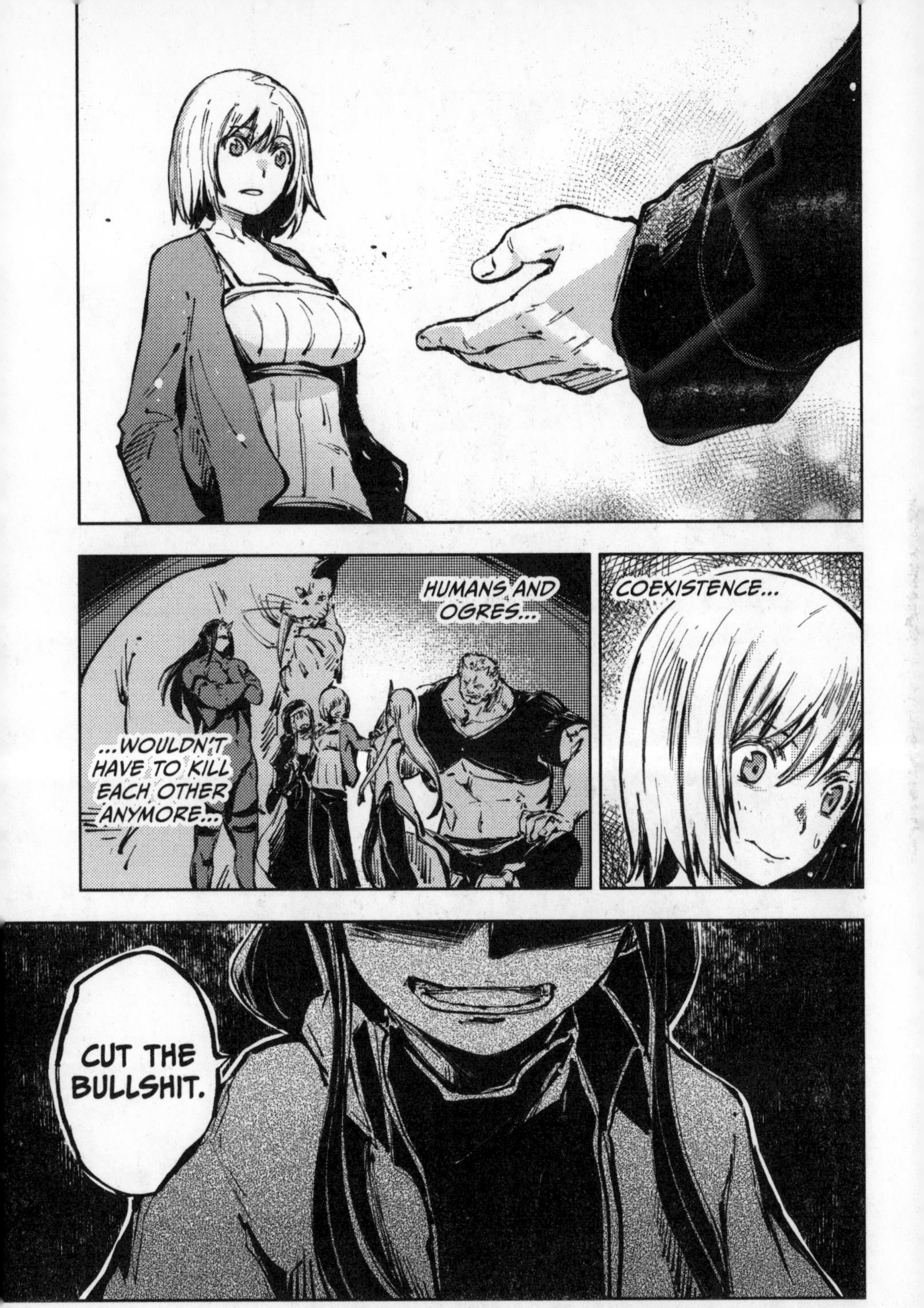
COEXISTENCE...
HUMANS AND OGRES...
...WOULDN'T HAVE TO KILL EACH OTHER ANYMORE...
CUT THE BULLSHIT.

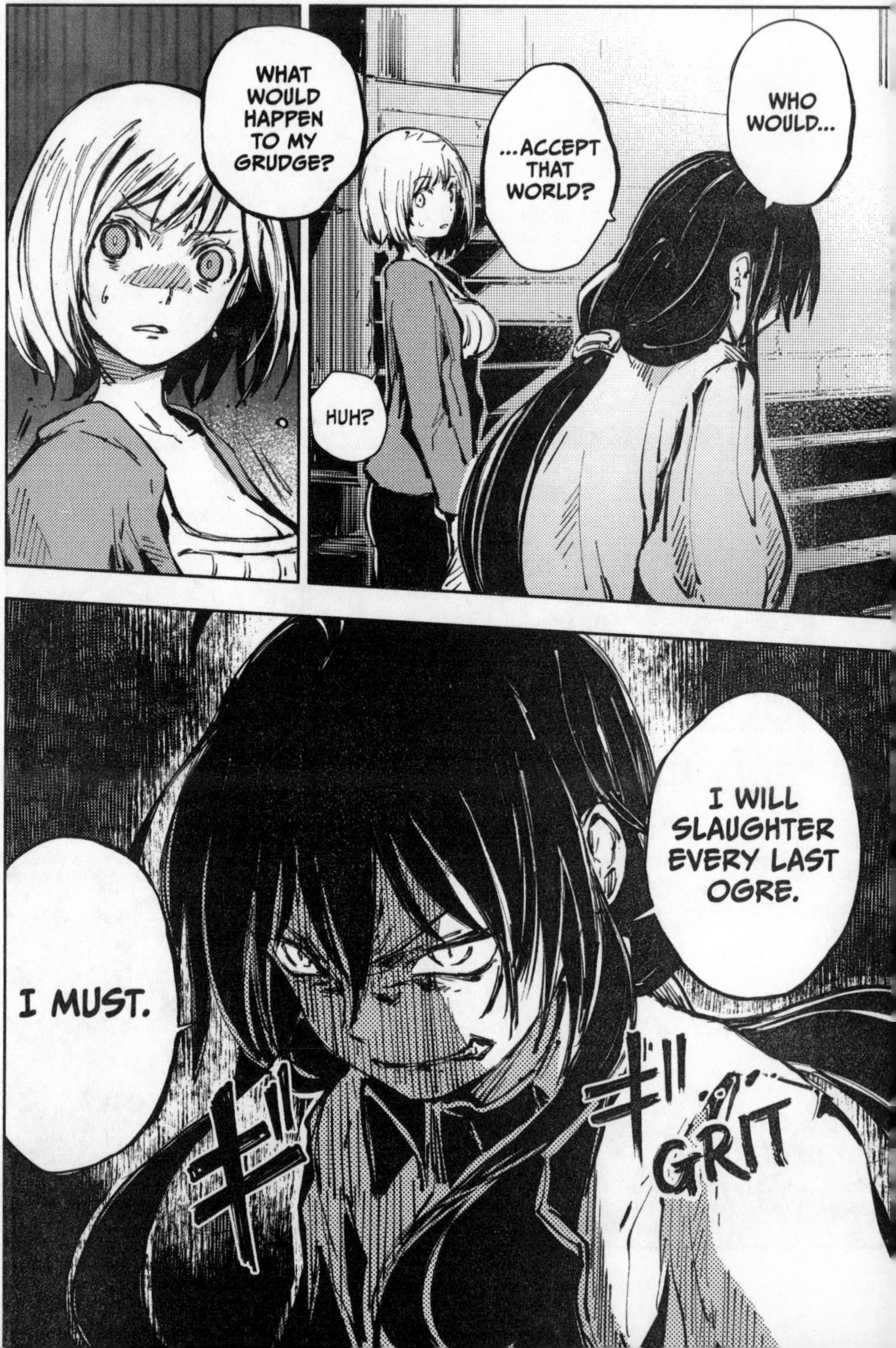
WHO WOULD...
...ACCEPT THAT WORLD?
HUH?
WHAT WOULD HAPPEN TO MY GRUDGE?
I WILL SLAUGHTER EVERY LAST OGRE.
I MUST.
ギリ
ギリ
GRIT

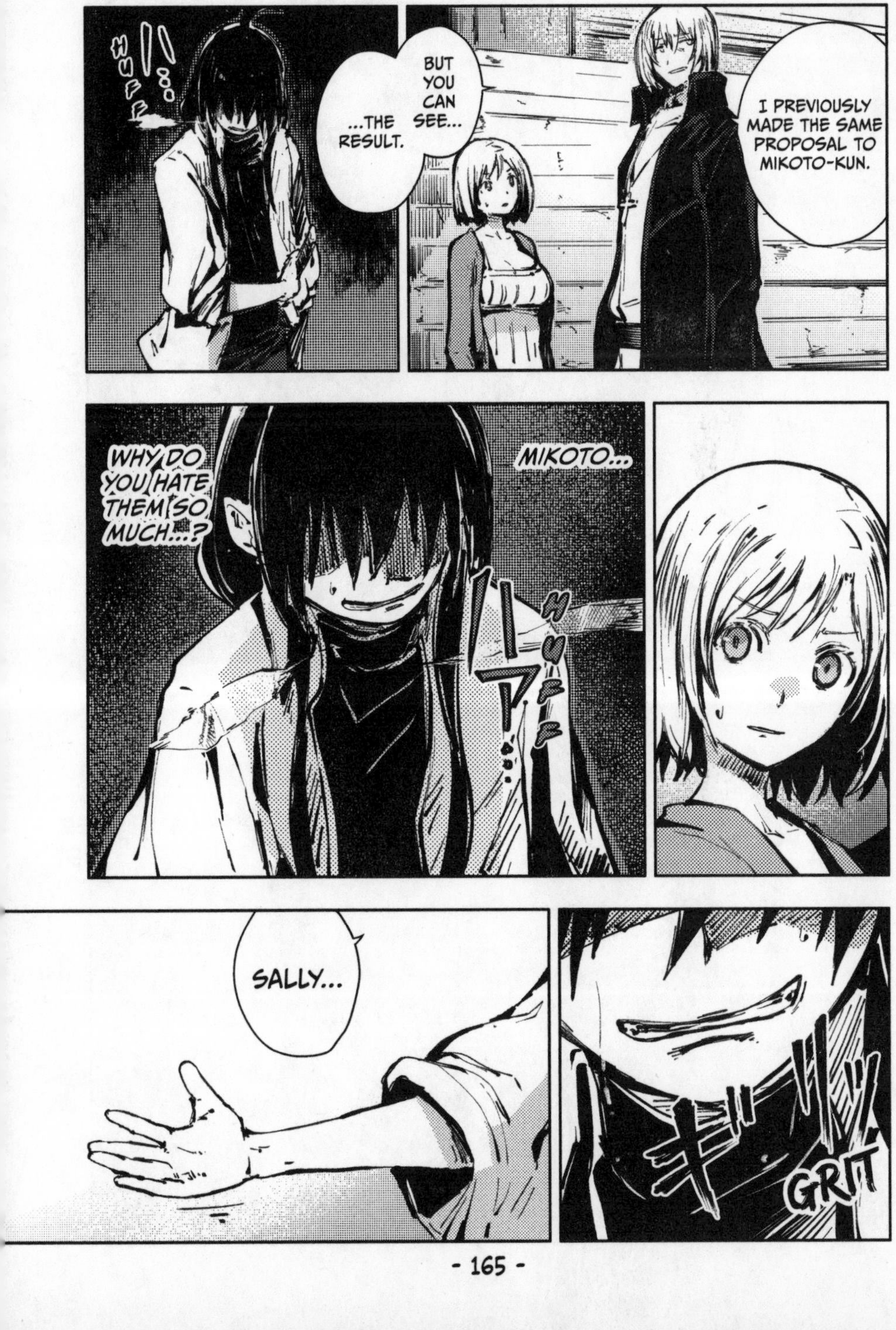
I PREVIOUSLY MADE THE SAME PROPOSAL TO MIKOTO-KUN.
BUT YOU CAN SEE...
...THE RESULT.
HUFF
MIKOTO...
WHY DO YOU HATE THEM SO MUCH...?
HUFF
GRIT
SALLY...

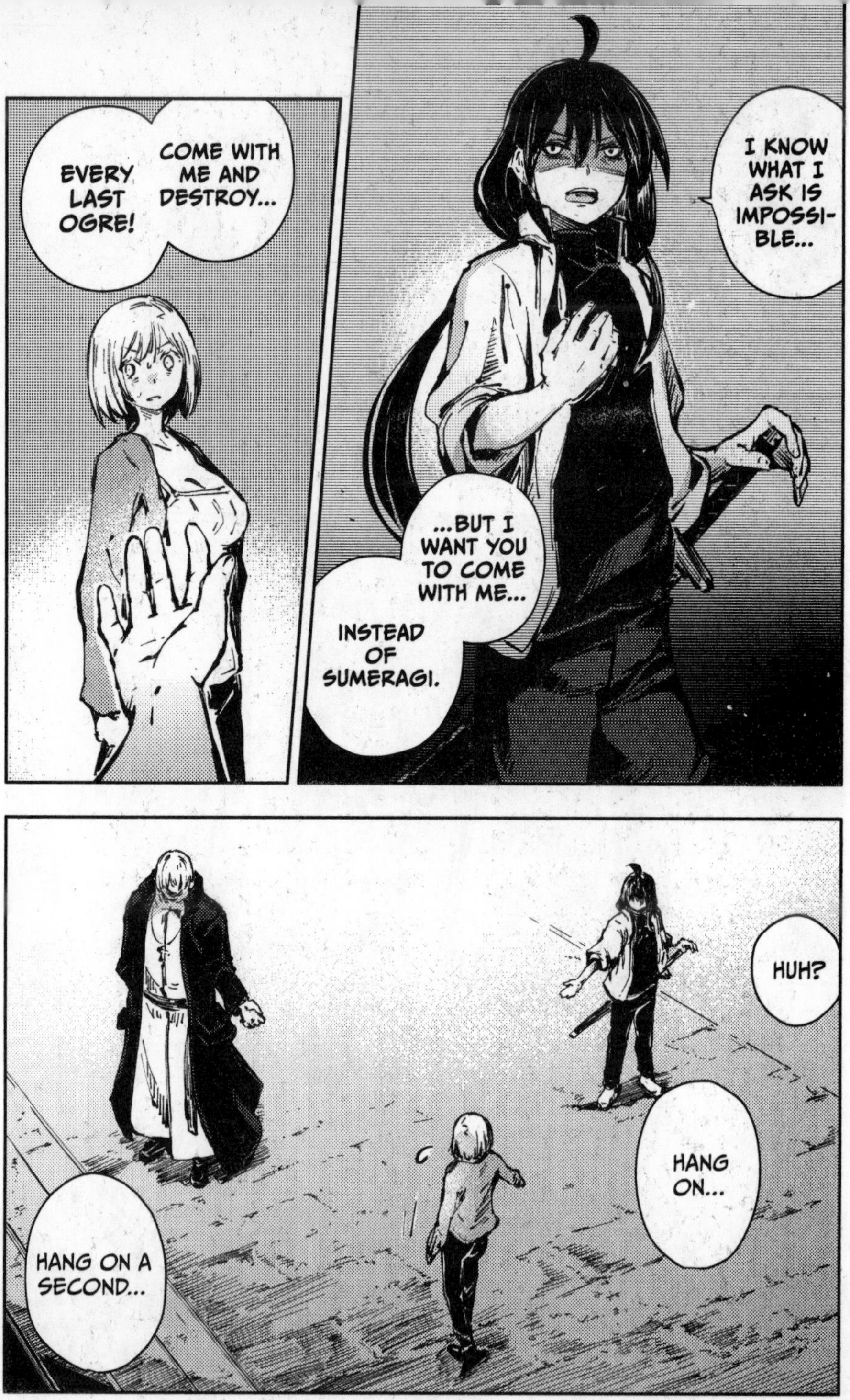
I KNOW WHAT I ASK IS IMPOSSI-BLE...
...BUT I WANT YOU TO COME WITH ME...
INSTEAD OF SUMERAGI.
COME WITH ME AND DESTROY...
EVERY LAST OGRE!
HUH?
HANG ON...
HANG ON A SECOND...

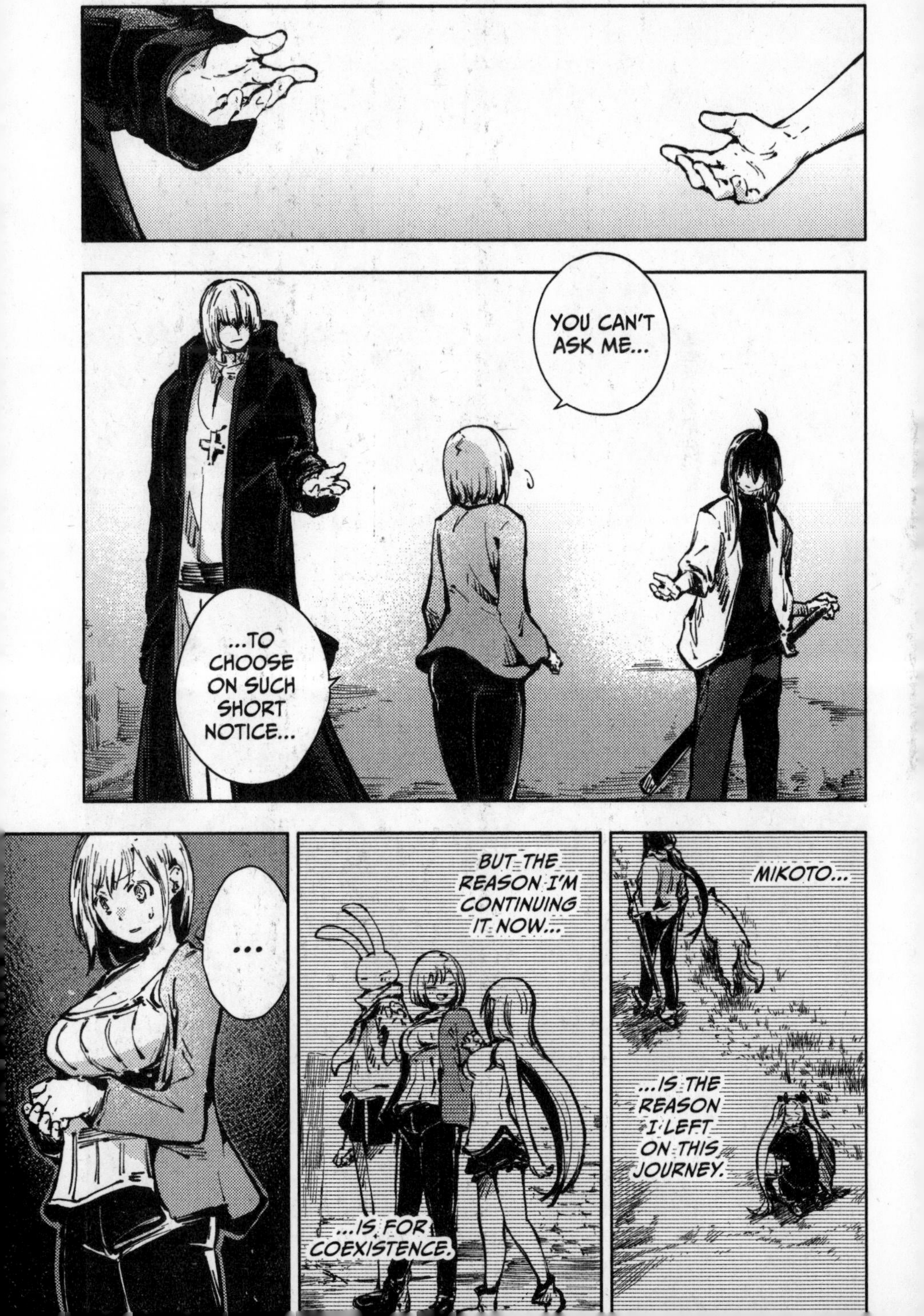
YOU CAN'T ASK ME...
...TO CHOOSE ON SUCH SHORT NOTICE...
MIKOTO...
...IS THE REASON I LEFT ON THIS JOURNEY.
BUT THE REASON I'M CONTINUING IT NOW...
...IS FOR COEXISTENCE.
...

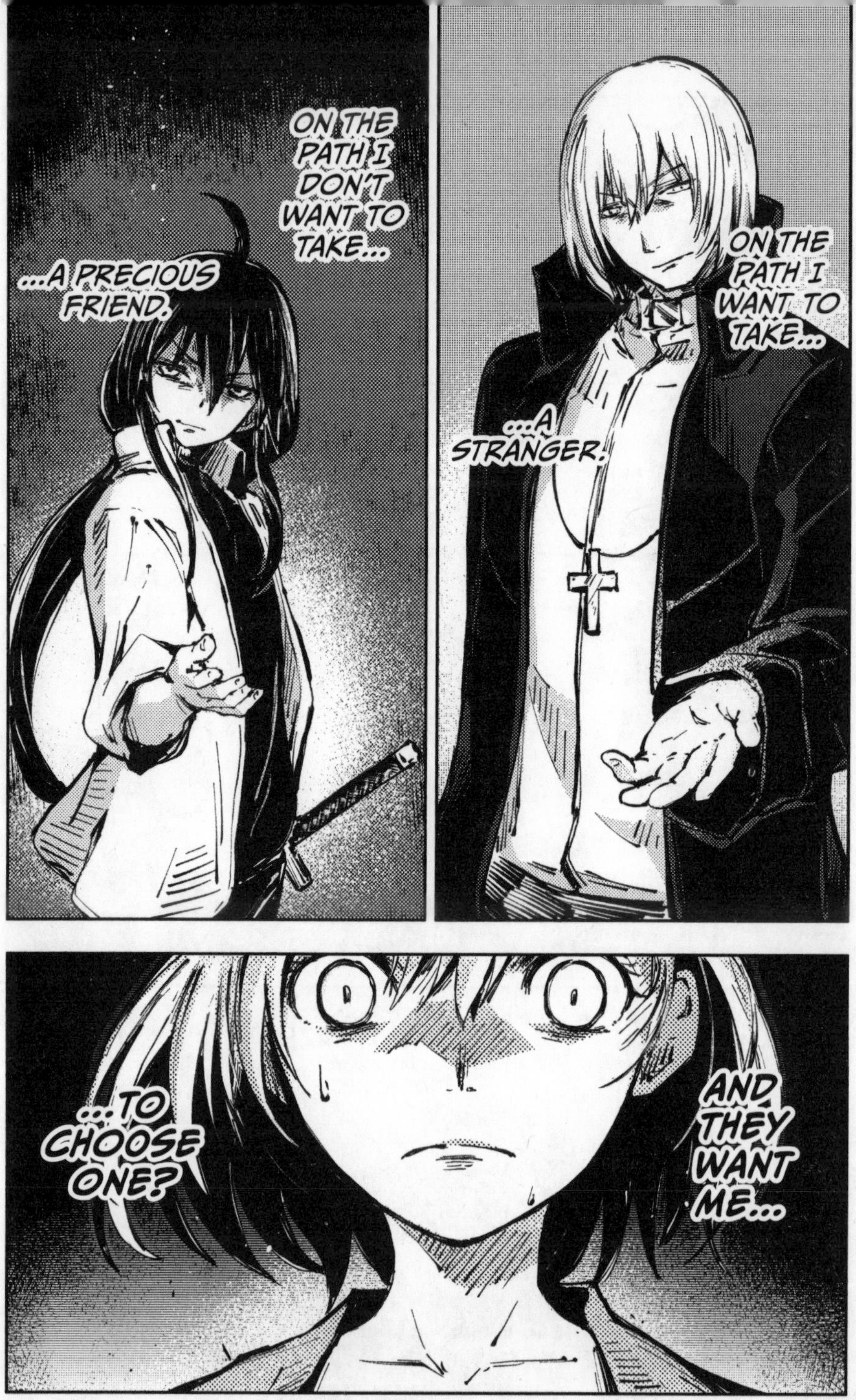
ON THE PATH I WANT TO TAKE...
...A STRANGER.
ON THE PATH I DON'T WANT TO TAKE...
...A PRECIOUS FRIEND.
AND THEY WANT ME...
...TO CHOOSE ONE?

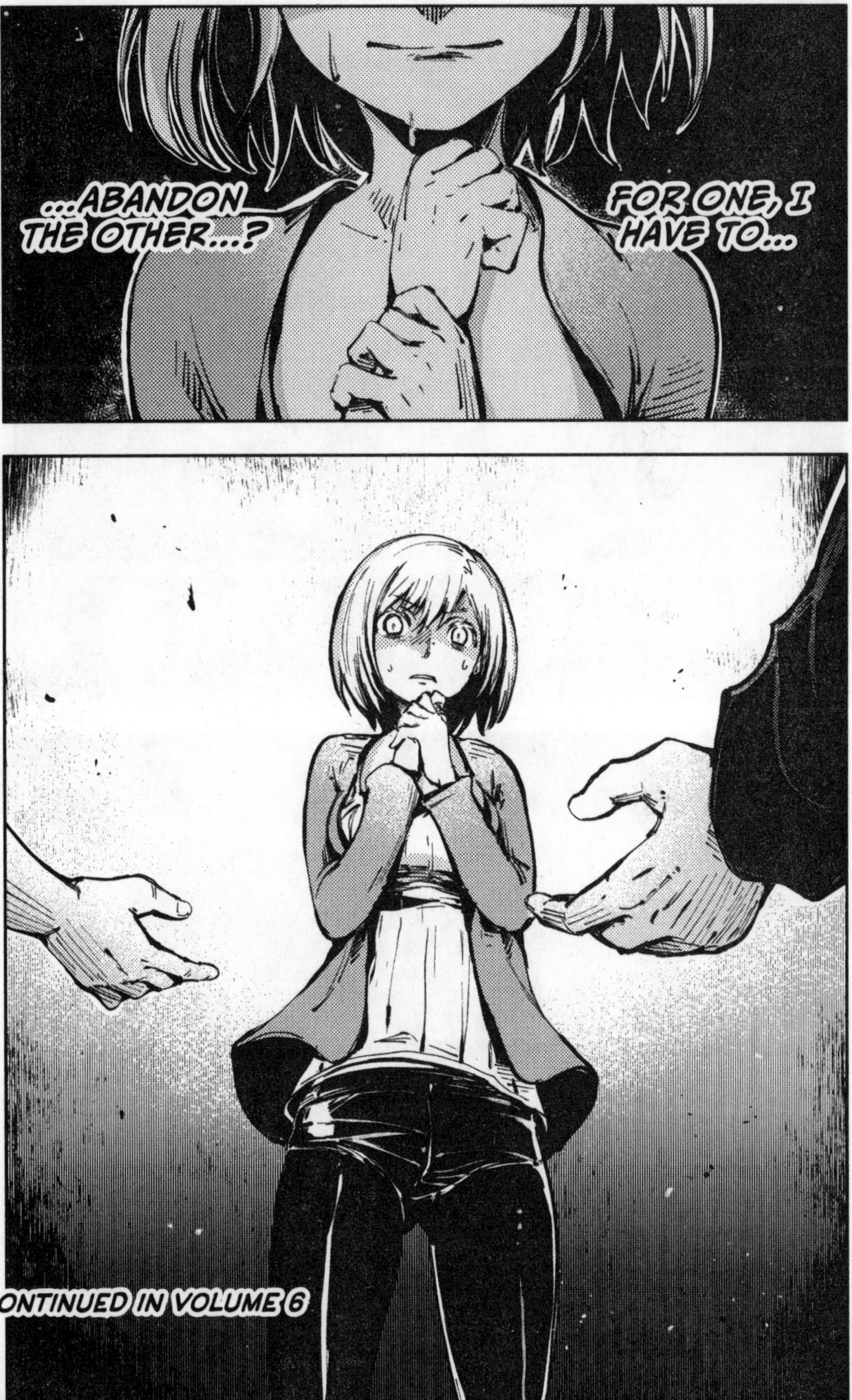
FOR ONE, I HAVE TO...
...ABANDON THE OTHER...?
CONTINUED IN VOLUME 6

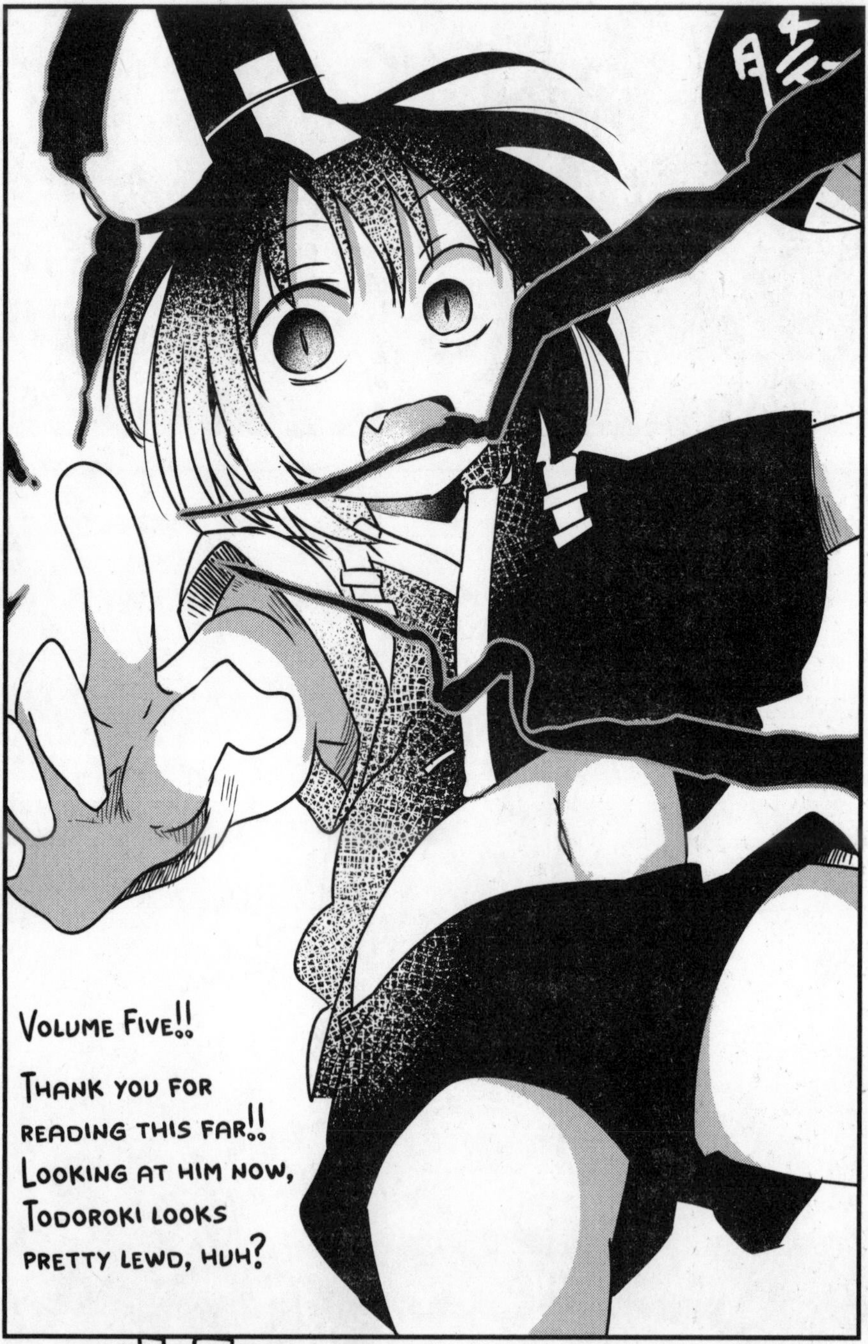
VOLUME FIVE!!
THANK YOU FOR READING THIS FAR!!
LOOKING AT HIM NOW, TODOROKI LOOKS PRETTY LEWD, HUH?

COOLKYOUSINNJYA

Thanks for Reading

The flatty ratio that has skyrocketed thanks to Millia-san and Jucerino-san is going to continue into the next volume. But what can be done about that at this point?

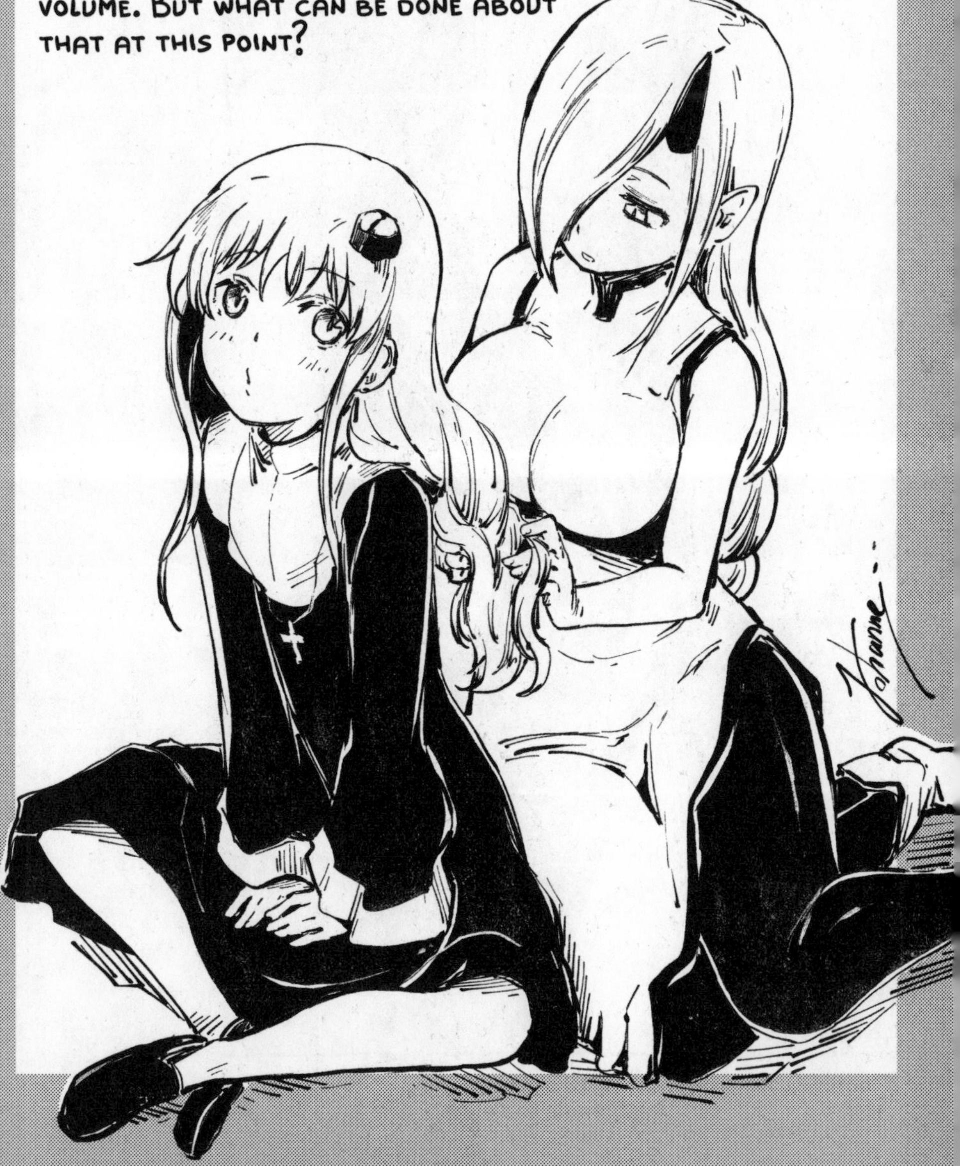

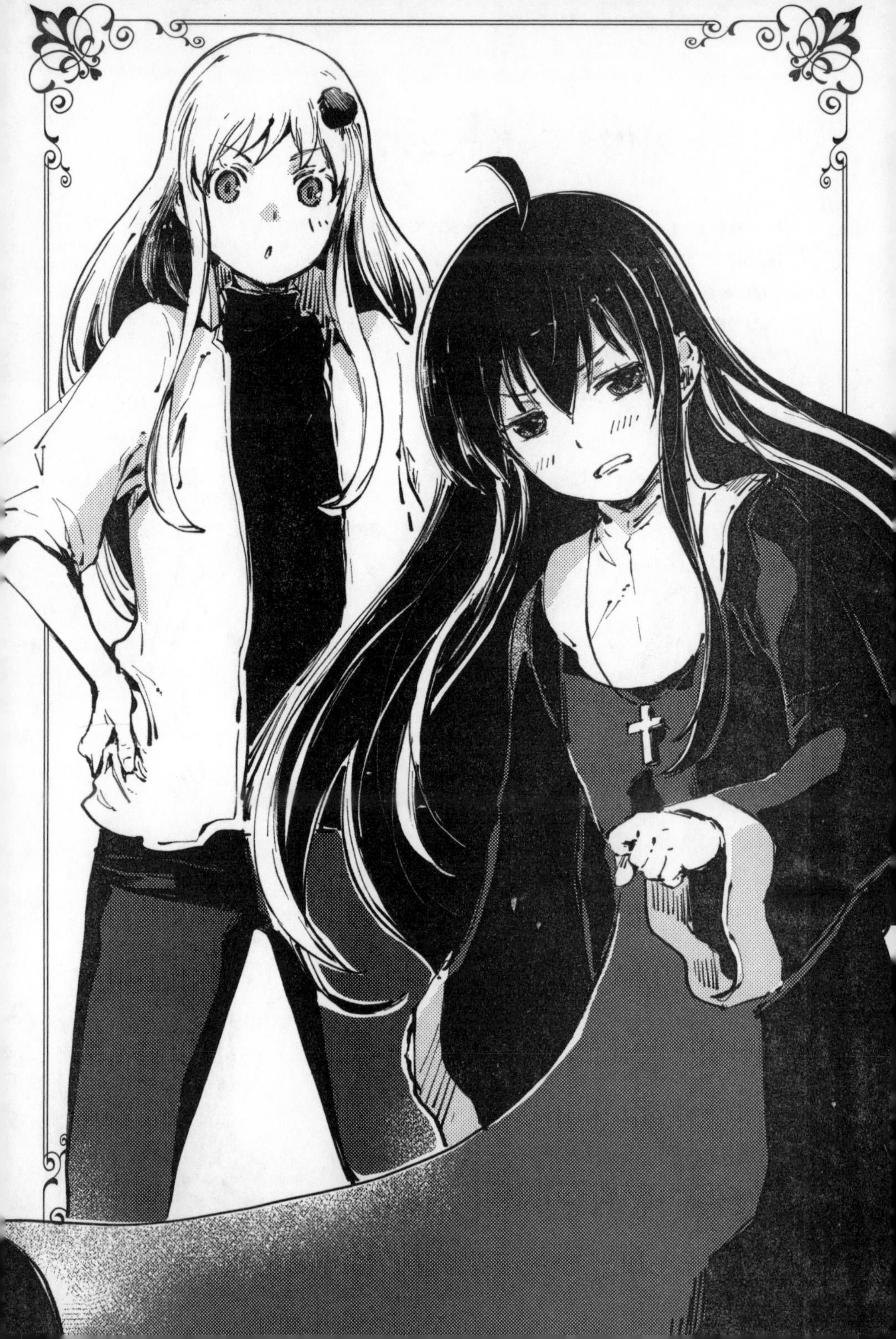

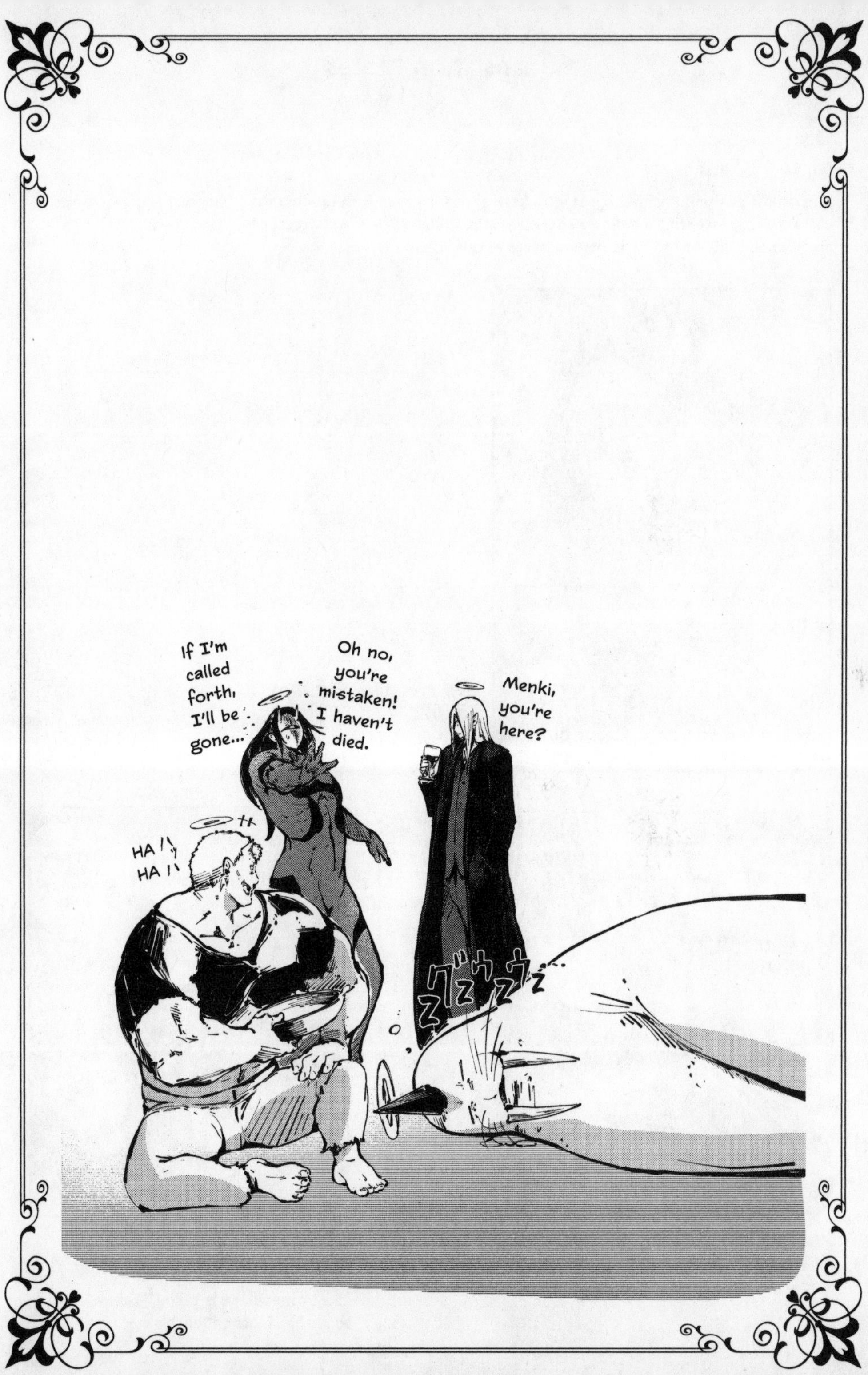
Menki, you're here?
Oh no, you're mistaken! I haven't died.
If I'm called forth, I'll be gone...
HA!! HA!!

Translation Notes

Ogre names, pages 49, 54, 64, 117

The names of the humanoid ogres who have appeared thus far all follow the same formula: a Chinese character representing a defining characteristic, followed by the character for "ogre," which is pronounced "ki" or "gi." The named ogres in this volume were…

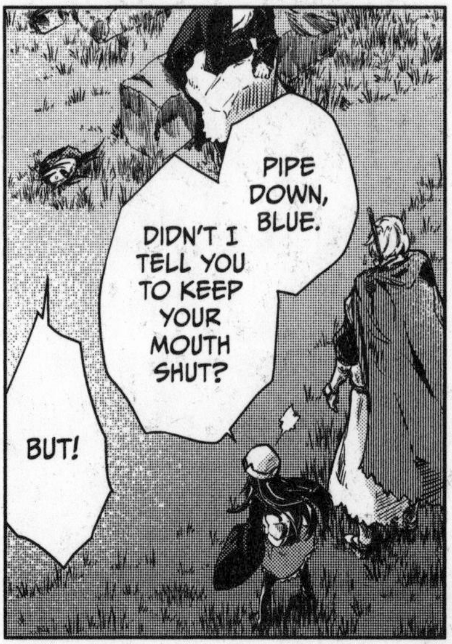
PIPE DOWN, BLUE.
DIDN'T I TELL YOU TO KEEP YOUR MOUTH SHUT?
BUT!

Somenki: "Blue Mask Ogre"
(蒼面鬼)

Menki's full name is "Somenki" and he is called "Blue" for short by his creator, Menshinki.

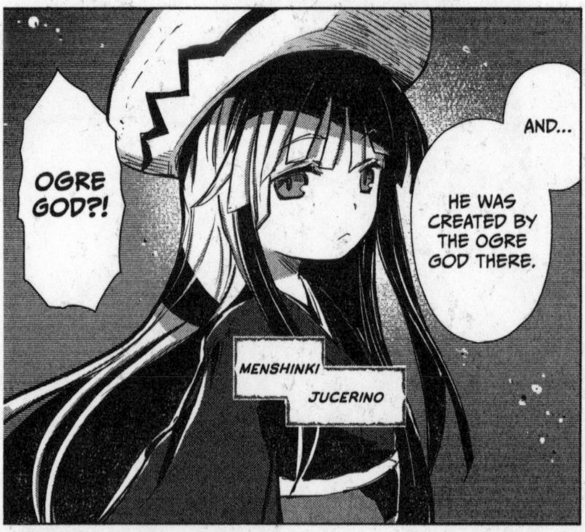
AND...
HE WAS CREATED BY THE OGRE GOD THERE.
OGRE GOD?!
MENSHINKI
JUCERINO

Menshinki: "Mask Ogre God"
(面神鬼)

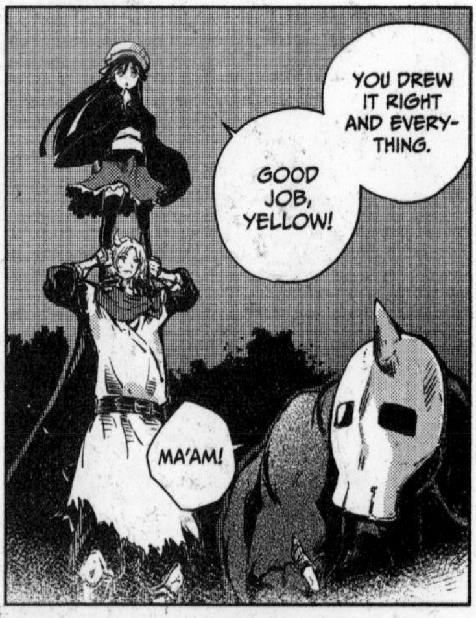
YOU DREW IT RIGHT AND EVERY-THING.
GOOD JOB, YELLOW!
MA'AM!

Kimenki: "Yellow Mask Ogre"
(黄面鬼)

Like Somenki, he is called "Yellow" for short by creator, Menshinki.

Translation Notes

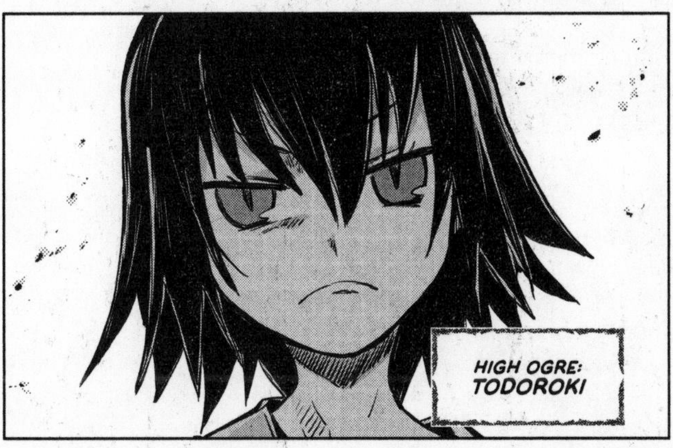
HIGH OGRE:
TODOROKI

Todoroki: “Roaring Ogre”
(轟鬼)

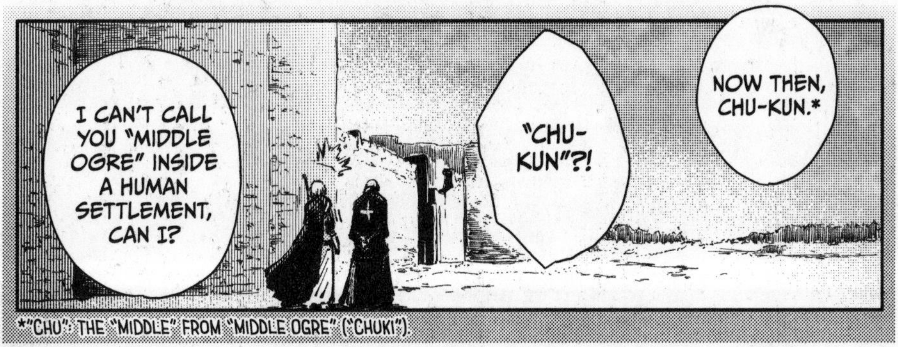
NOW THEN, CHU-KUN.*
"CHU-KUN"?!
I CAN'T CALL YOU "MIDDLE OGRE" INSIDE A HUMAN SETTLEMENT, CAN I?
*"CHU": THE "MIDDLE" FROM "MIDDLE OGRE" ("CHUKI").

Chuki: “Middle Ogre”
(中鬼)

This nameless ogre is called Chuki-kun by Sumeragi in the original Japanese, and around humans as “Chu-kun” removing the “ki” or “ogre.” Adding the suffix -kun is used to address young males, but it can also be used by superiors to inferiors. He also goes by the human name of Swordsman Middle. Unfortunately, ogres might not be known for creating unique names.

A Kodansha Comics Trade Paperback Original
Peach Boy Riverside 5 copyright © 2018 Coolkyousinnjya/Johanne
English translation copyright © 2022 Coolkyousinnjya/Johanne

Published in the United States by Kodansha Comics, an imprint of Kodansha USA Publishing, LLC, New York.

Publication rights for this English edition arranged through Kodansha Ltd., Tokyo.

First published in Japan in 2018 by Kodansha Ltd., Tokyo.

ISBN 978-1-64651-343-7

Original cover design by Tadashi Hisamochi (hive&co.,ltd.)

Printed in the United States of America.

www.kodansha.us

1st Printing
Translation: Steven LeCroy
Lettering: Andrew Copeland
Additional Lettering: Belynda Ungurath
Editing: Thalia Sutton, Maggie Le
YKS Services LLC/SKY Japan, Inc.
Kodansha Comics edition cover design by Adam Del Re

Publisher: Kiichiro Sugawara

Director of publishing services: Ben Applegate
Associate director of publishing operations: Stephen Pakula
Publishing services managing editors: Alanna Ruse, Madison Salters
Production managers: Emi Lotto, Angela Zurlo
Logo and character art ©Kodansha USA Publishing, LLC